Images That Move

Publication of this book and the SAR seminar from which it resulted were made
possible with the generous support of the Wenner-Gren Foundation and
The Brown Foundation, Inc., of Houston, Texas.

School for Advanced Research
Advanced Seminar Series

James F. Brooks
General Editor

Images That Move

Contributors

Ernst van Alphen
Professor of Literary Studies, Leiden University

Christiane Brosius
Professor of Visual and Media Anthropology, Heidelberg University

Steven C. Caton
Professor of Contemporary Arab Studies, Harvard University

Finbarr Barry Flood
William R. Kenan Jr. Professor of the Humanities, New York University

Brian Larkin
Associate Professor of Anthropology, Barnard College

Oliver Moore
Lecturer, Art and Material Culture of China, Leiden University; Curator China, Museum of Ethnology, Leiden

Rosalind C. Morris
Professor of Anthropology, Columbia University

Christopher Pinney
Professor of Anthropology and Visual Culture, University College London

Patricia Spyer
Professor of Anthropology of Contemporary Indonesia, Leiden University

Mary Margaret Steedly
Professor of Anthropology, Harvard University

Images That Move

Edited by Patricia Spyer and Mary Margaret Steedly

SAR
PRESS

School for Advanced Research Press
Santa Fe

School for Advanced Research Press
Post Office Box 2188
Santa Fe, New Mexico 87504-2188
www.sarpress.org

Managing Editor: Lisa Pacheco
Editorial Assistant: Ellen Goldberg
Designer and Production Manager: Cynthia Dyer
Manuscript Editor: Jill Root
Proofreader: Kate Whelan
Indexer: Catherine Fox

Library of Congress Cataloging-in-Publication Data

Images that move / edited by Patricia Spyer and Mary Margaret Steedly. — First edition.
    pages cm. — (School for Advanced Research advanced seminar series)
 Includes bibliographical references and index.
  ISBN 978-1-934691-91-5 (alk. paper)
 1. Image (Philosophy) 2. Visual perception. I. Spyer, Patricia, 1957- II. Steedly, Mary Margaret, 1946-
  B105.I47I477 2013
  121'.34—dc23
                        2012038522

Library of Congress Catalog Card Number 2012038522
International Standard Book Number 978-1-934691-91-5
First edition 2013.

Cover illustration: Streetside Muslim power mural, Tidore, Indonesia, 2008. Artist unknown.
Photograph by P. Spyer.

The School for Advanced Research (SAR) promotes the furthering of scholarship on—and public understanding of —human culture, behavior, and evolution. SAR Press publishes cutting-edge scholarly and general-interest books that encourage critical thinking and present new perspectives on topics of interest to all humans. Contributions by authors reflect their own opinions and viewpoints and do not necessarily express the opinions of SAR Press.

Contents

Figures and Plates

Figures

Plates

follow page 176

Acknowledgments

This book began as a collaboration between Patricia and Mary, inspired by unfolding crises in Indonesia following the 1997 Asian financial crisis and the 1998 fall of the Suharto regime. We were struck at the time by the important role of media—in particular the circulation of images—in these events, which in some ways prefigured the "Arab Spring" of 2011. In 2000 we convened a brainstorming session at Harvard with media anthropologists Faye Ginsburg and Christopher Pinney, sponsored by the Harvard Peabody Museum of Archaeology and Ethnology and by Leiden University. The enthusiastic, creative input of Faye and Chris helped us frame and formulate our original research agenda. From this conversation emerged the Harvard–Leiden research program "Signs of Crisis in Southern Asia," funded by the Harvard Peabody Museum and the Netherlands Organization for Scientific Research (NWO) Humanities Division. Under the auspices of this program, we organized a range of events in Cambridge and Leiden between 2003 and 2007. These included a three-year lecture series, "Signs of Crisis," at Harvard; "After Images," a Radcliffe Institute for Advanced Study Exploratory Seminar in 2004; the workshop "Faces of Crisis" in Leiden in 2005; and, also in 2005, the workshop "Inadvertent Documents: New (and Old) Forms of Political and Historical Mediation in Southern Asia" (with Karen Strassler), sponsored in part by the Harvard University Asia Center.

We were invited participants on a panel at the 2005 International Convention of Asian Scholars meeting in Shanghai, "New Audio-Visual Projects on Asia," including a number of Indonesian filmmakers whose participation we sponsored. In May 2007 we organized and curated the conference "Signs of Crisis: Religious Conflict, Human Rights and the New Documentary Film in Southern Asia" with New York University's Center for Religion and Media (CRM), its Center for Media, Culture and History, and its School of Law. This three-day conference brought together contemporary filmmakers from Indonesia and India with legal scholars, anthropologists, nongovernmental organization workers, and others involved in issues of human rights, religion, and representation. In conjunction with this event, we also organized a documentary film workshop at Harvard entitled "*Transparansi*: New Documentary Films from Indonesia," with additional support from the Harvard Asia Center and Film Study Center.

Increasingly, we realized that the kinds of issues we were grappling with could not be limited to what we called Southern Asia, a gloss we had used to bring scholars working in and on South and Southeast Asia together, nor could they be restricted to the present day. We decided to explore further a set of questions that had evolved over the course of the project but without any regional specifications. Hence, the title we gave to the advanced seminar convened in May 2008 at Santa Fe's School for Advanced Research (SAR): "Images without Borders."

There are a number of persons and institutions we would especially like to thank for their generous support of our collaboration over the years, for their input and suggestions, and for the assistance of many different kinds that we received along the way. We acknowledge with gratitude Harvard University's Peabody Museum and its former director, Rubie Watson, and Leiden University's rector magnificus at the time, Douwe Breimer, for supporting the first phase of this project. The Peabody Museum also sponsored Karen Strassler with a Hrdy Postdoctoral Fellowship at Harvard for two years. Her participation was a most valuable addition to our project. Emma Baulch, a postdoctoral fellow at Leiden, also contributed to the project in significant ways that we would like to acknowledge here. Along the way, we have benefited from support of various kinds provided by the Institute of Cultural Anthropology and Development Sociology at Leiden University; the International Institute for Asian Studies (IIAS) and its former director, Wim Stokhof, also based in Leiden; and Harvard University's Department of Anthropology and Asia Center. In addition to the generous support of SAR, supplemental funds for the advanced seminar were provided by the Wenner-Gren Foundation for Anthropological Research.

This book would not have been possible without the excellent intellectual climate afforded by the School for Advanced Research and the rare opportunity for prolonged discussion and exchange provided by the format of the advanced seminar. The gorgeous surroundings of the SAR complex in Santa Fe, New Mexico, where the seminar took place; the solicitous attention by the staff to the needs of the seminar organizers and participants, from technical facilities to excellent food and drink provided by the lovely kitchen crew; and the guidance and follow-up we have enjoyed since from SAR Press have made this book project a highly pleasurable and productive one from start to finish. We would like to thank Lisa Pacheco and the rest of the SAR Press staff for guiding us with good humor and patience through the intricacies of manuscript submission and production. Two anonymous readers for the Press made this manuscript much better than it would otherwise have been, and we would like to thank them for their careful reading and insightful commentary. We are also grateful for the meticulous attention to detail and efficiency of copyeditor Jill Root.

We would also like to thank Christiane Brosius's research assistant Tina Schilbach for her careful transcription of the seminar discussions, and the IIAS and the German Research Foundation (DGF) Excellence Research Cluster "Asia and Europe in a Global Context" of Heidelberg University for providing subvention costs for the many images in this book.

Much of Patricia Spyer's work on this book was carried out during her appointment as FAS Global Distinguished Professor of Anthropology at the Center for Religion and Media at New York University (NYU). She is indebted to the department and to CRM for hosting her so well and for providing such an exciting intellectual environment. An early version of the book was read and discussed in a graduate student seminar, "Anxieties of Circulation," taught by Fred Myers and Patricia Spyer in NYU's Department of Anthropology in the spring of 2012, and she would like to acknowledge with gratitude their input. Finally, she offers special thanks to Rafael Sánchez for his advice and suggestions throughout.

Mary Steedly would also like to thank her students in several graduate and undergraduate anthropology classes at Harvard, especially "Image/Media/Publics" and "Moving Pictures." Their discussions of this material, as well as their much more sophisticated knowledge of new media production and circulation (not to mention their computer skills), have contributed more than they can imagine to this work.

Last but not least, we are grateful to the contributors of this book for their intellectual stimulation, for their friendship and collegiality, and for their ongoing commitment during the process of bringing this book to publication, which took somewhat longer than we had hoped.

Images That Move

Changes That Heal

1

Introduction

Images That Move

Patricia Spyer and Mary Margaret Steedly

In April 1942, amid the hardships of the 900-day German siege of Leningrad, Pavel Gubchevsky, head of security and longtime tour guide at the Hermitage Museum, led a group of army cadets from Siberia on a

3

tour of the museum. The tour was a token of thanks for their assistance in moving a collection of valuable French furniture, already waterlogged, to a place where it might be protected from the elements and the mischances of war. What made this event remarkable was that the museum's paintings had already been removed from their frames and taken away to safe storage. As the young soldiers walked past the empty frames and labels that remained, the guide described what they would have seen if the paintings had been there. "That was the most curious excursion in my life," Gubchevsky recalled. "And it turned out that even the empty frames left an impression."[1]

This event, one of several Empty Frame tours that Gubchevsky conducted during the war, is the subject of the Dutch artist Melvin Moti's exquisite short film *No Show.* What we see on-screen for the twenty-two minutes of the film's duration is an empty room—not, in fact, the museum's gallery—graced by three tall windows framing some leafy trees. The only visible movement in the room is the lengthening and softening of the light reflected on the floor through the windows; in this gradual darkening of the room, we witness the passage of time, which lends a sense of historical depth and verisimilitude to the narration of the reenacted tour. This still scene has the effect of foregrounding voices and sounds: the tour guide's invitation to the soldier-comrades to gather around as he describes in great detail the pictures that had hung there; his admonitions to attend to the broken glass shattered on the floor of some galleries; the sound of heavy army boots as the men move past and pause before the images; their laughter at the tour guide's jokes. The tour guide makes occasional reference to the pictures' physical absence. At other times he invites his audience to "look closely" while he discloses what was once there.

Viewers of the film are doubly—or indeed triply, in the case of those who must rely on the English subtitles of the Russian narration—removed from the pictures that had previously inhabited the empty frames. The film constructs "an absorbing aesthetic out of a visual void,"[2] an effect that is heightened toward its conclusion, when the screen turns wholly black. Reflected back to us from this increasingly opaque surface is not only the fantasmatic presence of images and the vivid work of the imagination but also the way in which every image evokes an absence and a beyond.

We begin our introduction with this anecdote because it raises a number of themes that run through this book. In the most literal sense it reflects our shared, long-standing interest in the fate of images in situations of crisis, like the vulnerable, contingent materiality of the artifacts composing the Hermitage collection. Crises often put images at risk physically

FIGURE 1.2

Still image from the film No Show, 2004. Reproduced with permission of Melvin Moti.

and may precipitate movement, in the form of being removed to a place of greater safety or confiscated as loot, the fate from which the Hermitage staff hoped to safeguard the collection by shipping off artifacts to more secure surroundings.[3]

In situations of social and political turmoil or profound change, images may be at risk not only physically but also conceptually. What images are, where they may or may not go, what they are expected to do socially, politically, aesthetically, epistemologically, psychologically, ideologically, and so on, may become foci of attention and contribute to their revaluing and refiguration. Images may be abandoned, forgotten, disavowed, or even destroyed, as in the drastic refiguration of iconoclasm, in its literal sense of "idol-breaking"—the physical destruction of images of false gods—or the more widespread and commonplace "metaphorical iconoclasms" of commodification (the image as vessel of exchange value) and philosophical negation (the image as false or outmoded representation), both of which find expression in the protective seclusion of the museum.[4]

Iconoclastic destruction, the collateral damage of incidentally inflicted injury, and even the aesthetics of aging and deterioration can sometimes also be productive and creative. They can initiate a process of literal "re-vision" that opens a space for new ways of looking or in some cases alters the visual field. Thus—to remain within the precincts of the besieged Hermitage Museum—it was only in the absence of the museum's art collection, when the buildings' vulnerability to the forces of war and environment had already been marked on their torn and scarred surfaces, that their architectural beauty came into view. Graphic artist and theatrical designer Vera Miliutina described their exposed, partially ruined grandeur: "The emptied halls were huge and majestic, their walls covered in crystals of frost. They had never before seemed so splendid to me. Before one's attention had usually been fixed on the painting, sculpture or applied art and the art of those remarkable architects and decorators who created the palaces went little noticed. Now, though, all that was left was their astonishing art (and the traces everywhere of the savage, implacable Fascist barbarity)."[5] Such destruction itself can become the subject of image-making. A group of Leningrad artists, including Miliutina, produced a series of drawings documenting "the Hermitage's wounds" the broken windows, the pools of water, the ice-encrusted floors, the damaged façade, and other destruction to the museum buildings resulting from German bombardment and artillery fire. These drawings, now housed in the Russian National Museum, have been the subject of repeated exhibitions, in which they served not only as evidence of "Fascist barbarity" and the indomitable spirit of the Russian people but also as aesthetic objects in their own right.

Beyond the context of endangerment and loss in which Gubchevsky's Empty Frame tours must be seen, *No Show* stages the affective power of images and intimates what viewers themselves bring to them: "even the empty frames left an impression," as Gubchevsky put it. For even if the soldiers on his tour—"country boys" hailing from places like Vologda, Cherepovets, and Ust'-Luga—"came to the Hermitage for the first time and some had never even been to a museum before,"[6] they shared some general reference points and affective resonances with the tour guide who conjured the absent images for them: familiar religious iconography, ideas of natural beauty, perhaps the notion that works of art are—or should be—framed.[7]

Moti's cinematic "reenactment" of the Empty Frame tour also draws attention to *movement*—to those processes of circulation, imagination, and reception in which, as Arjun Appadurai puts it, "moving images meet deterritorialized viewers."[8] The film presumes a movement of objects—antique furniture carried to safety, for which the tour provides a thank-you, as well as the absent paintings themselves—but it equally highlights the *tour's* movement as the guide and soldiers navigate their way, unseen by the film's viewers, through the empty rooms, past the frames and labels that serve as

FIGURE 1.3
Vera Miliutina, Broken Window and Vase, *1942. Image © The State Hermitage Museum. Reproduced with permission of the State Hermitage Museum, St. Petersburg, Russia.*

placeholders for the missing images. Like the tour itself, the film's imaginative appropriation of it highlights the mobility and instability of images as they circulate across genres and forms, taking on new meanings and engaging different audiences in different ways. The multiple, sometimes unexpected publics that may be called up by these moving pictures; the repurposing or "remediation" of visual images that shift from one medium or genre to another;[9] the mutually defining yet contingent relation of image and frame, of object and representation, or of text and image; the significance of the "work of imagination"[10] in the travels and stopping points of images in motion; the material, political, and spiritual conditions of possibility that enable and impede the movement of images—these are among the mobile themes, eloquently evoked by Moti's small film and the tours that inspired it, that play through this collection of essays.

Images That Move is concerned with the ways in which images *take place* in wider worlds and with the role they play in "poetic world-making" projects and political transformations.[11] Our conceptual framework triangulates three key, interrelated terms: circulation, affect, and publics. These concepts, taken together, inform our title in its double sense, both intransitive and transitive, of images that move *around* and images that move *us*.

Looking at images that move may, we believe, illuminate some of the characteristics that apply to images more generally. These include their heterogeneity and inherent instability as forms; the diverse epistemological and aesthetic assumptions that may apply to them; the social, institutional, and historical conditions and ideological formations that inflect their possibilities and limitations; the technologies that delimit and contour their capacities; the media through which images are formed and projected and with which they become identified; the differing status attributed to such media; the translocal circuits along which images move or are restrained from movement; the affective potentiality of images as they encounter, engage, or engender various audiences, or publics, in their travels; and, most crucially, the way in which these myriad elements variously crystallize around, are refracted within, and provide definition to images in motion.[12]

The chapters in this volume were first presented, in some cases in radically different form, at the advanced seminar "Images without Borders" held at the School for Advanced Research on May 4–8, 2008. This original title was intended as a provocation and challenge to consider the implications of the hardly novel yet radically enhanced "borderless" traffic of images often said to be characteristic of our current moment. The proliferating effects of new media technologies, in which certain visualizable events appear increasingly "to be taking place everywhere and nowhere in particular,"[13] are, of course, crucial to any understanding of a globalizing modernity. But we also wished to qualify the "newness" of such media experiences by examining a wider range of modes of image production and reproduction, from such "traditional" media forms as painting to "once new" media like photography and cinema, and, as in our opening anecdote, the mutual imbrication of media forms both old and new.[14]

Attending to images, we believed, could reveal new forms and modes of circulation, from the most narrowly informational to the referentially more open-ended, along with the publicities and publics that these precipitate and from which they emerge, and the wider political, historical, and cultural implications of these circulations and precipitations. As our initial anecdote of frames without images is meant to suggest, such a proposition quickly became both too circumscribed and too expansive. Over the course of our discussions, particularly as these developed among the participants during the seminar, we began to shift our conceptual rubric from the purposefully ironic utopianism of "images without borders" to the richer set of propositions about affect, agency, circulation, and spectatorship implied by the multivalent, troubling notion of "images that move."

Recognizing not only the uniqueness of the present moment in a range of locales but also its historical antecedents and prophetic foreshadowings—the movement of images not only through space but also through time—we convened an interdisciplinary group of participants from the fields of history, art history, anthropology, and literature. We aimed to move beyond disciplinary "turf wars" that would align Western, modern, or elite art with history and art history; non-Western art with anthropology; and contemporary mass art with sociology and cultural studies. Each of us used a particular image or set of images as a jumping-off point to reflect on what images are, what they do, and how they do it. The images under consideration ranged from medieval European representations of Islamic idolatry and iconoclasm (chapter 2) to contemporary art in postapartheid South Africa (chapter 7), from real estate brochures for upscale gated communities in the new "world class" of "India Shining" (chapter 3) to the work of Chinese studio and amateur photographers around the turn of the twentieth century (chapter 5), and from the high art of postmodernity to such "low" forms as Internet pornography and teen horror films (chapters 8 and 10, respectively). Each chapter is at once closely tied to its particular locale(s) and moment(s) and closely attentive to the global and subglobal circuits and vectors along which images travel, to the common pathways and unique detours of images in motion, and to the fragile patterns that emerged as we brought together these disparate, moving pictures.

With varying emphases, all chapters in this collection are concerned with problems of images that move, in both a transitive and an intransitive sense, as well as with the necessary relation between the two. Because of the range of themes that connect and at times divide these chapters, we have not sorted them into topical sections but rather have thought in terms of adjacencies and echoes, clusters and conflicts. There is a rough continuum, from those chapters that are concerned more with the images themselves than with their audiences and publics, to those for which the calling up of publics is the predominant focus.

The first three chapters, by Finbarr Barry Flood, Christiane Brosius, and Patricia Spyer, address images on the border between social and political domains. Taking as a point of departure the controversy surrounding the publication in a Danish newspaper of a series of cartoon depictions of the Prophet Muhammed, Flood (chapter 2) foregrounds the contested image itself as a border phenomenon, a site of confrontation between different visual economies in relations between the Islamic world and the secular/Christian West. This confrontation, he argues, is part of a longer history of Christian (mis)perceptions of Islamic hostility to and overvaluation of representational art reaching back to medieval encounters between the two faiths. Brosius (chapter 3) introduces the term "enclave gaze" to characterize the imagery of upscale real estate development advertising in India, which pictures a cosmopolitan lifestyle of "world-class" enclaves of Greek temples and imperial nostalgia, while simultaneously blocking from view the adjacent "barren arid stretches" that mark the landscape of "a poor country that looked and felt poor." Spyer (chapter 4) also discusses a form of pictorial enclaving, in this case the reclamation of Christian public space in the aftermath of religious conflict in Ambon, Indonesia. In a "dramatic retooling of visual imagination," Ambonese Christians reconfigure public space through the creation of massive murals linking biblical themes to local identities and experiences of suffering, creating a new landscape of trauma and salvation that enframes daily life within a Protestant version of the passion play that is literal rather than allegorical.

The four chapters that follow form a loose cluster addressing connections among the material apparatus of image production, sociopolitical transformations, aesthetic vision, and relations of temporality. The chapters by Oliver Moore, Christopher Pinney, and Rosalind C. Morris are concerned with photography and its "prophetic" potential. Moore (chapter 5) traces the problematic category of "Chinese" photography in the late nineteenth and early twentieth centuries, moving between pictures *of* China and pictures *by* Chinese photographers, pictures intended for Chinese and for other audiences, pictures that measure the "Chineseness" of their subjects and those that index the modernity of the (Chinese) subject. He frames this discussion through the concept of "retrospective aura," in which later audiences read a kind of authenticity or meaning into the picture that may be at odds with its initial status as an image. Pinney (chapter 6), in what could be described (with a nod to Walter Benjamin) as a "little history of

Indian photography," takes up the prophetic capacity of *camerawork* rather than pictures as such.[15] Presenting a series of episodes in Indian photography between 1840 and 2008, he tracks the changing "technical practices" of photography as its gaze shifts from the "physiognomic landscape" of the human face to the "social landscape" of public space and finally to the internal landscape of bodily interiority. Objects of this increasingly prostheticized gaze become, in his account, both less visible to the unaugmented eye and more fully dedicated to the forensic demands of detection and surveillance.

Pinney's opening admonition, borrowed from Walter Benjamin, that the "task of the photographer...is to reveal guilt,"[16] is poignantly realized in Morris's (chapter 7) analysis of images of animal-human hybridity in South African art photography and literature. Here the conjoined themes of the human-animal hybrid, with its implications of bestiality, of rape and miscegenation, and of the disguising mask, provoke a deeply ambivalent approach to the multiple violences of apartheid and to the struggle to "think beyond" it from a subaltern or disenfranchised point of view.

The disturbingly beautiful images of Morris's chapter, with their cryptic or absent titles and captions, point as well to a picture's capacity to "move us" beyond words. For Morris, art works compel attention precisely by eschewing "information," thus, perhaps bypassing the issue of translatability in its literal sense altogether. This possibility connects her chapter to Ernst van Alphen's (chapter 8) analysis of the "release of affect" in contemporary society, as particularly exemplified in certain works of nonrepresentational art. A painting such as Roni Horn's *Gold Field*, van Alphen argues, "neither deals with signification, the meaning of the work, nor articulates the work within a discursive framework." It is thus crucial to develop a way to comprehend the affective force of the image as what "leads to thought" and is "felt" rather than what is "thought" or "recognized or perceived through cognition."[17]

The final three chapters in this volume, by Brian Larkin, Mary Margaret Steedly, and Steven C. Caton, deal with cinematic images and their publics. How do they engage or call up certain "publics" at certain times and places? How do they achieve recognition by—or create—the audiences they, either intentionally or not, address? Larkin (chapter 9), looking at the reception or "uptake" of Indian film in Hausa communities of Nigeria, argues that the capacity of images to reach their publics depends on the "intensities of desire" they incite. This desire in turn involves "complex acts of identification and translation," or what Larkin calls "commensurability," as images move across terrains of cultural difference. Questions of uptake similarly animate Steedly's (chapter 10) examination of contemporary horror films in Indonesia. These films, she argues, play on the ambivalent desire for and fear of visibility that constitutes a novel regime of visuality among urban youth of today's "post-Reformation" generation, who have come of age in the aftermath of the fall of the dictatorial New Order government. Finally, Caton (chapter 11) looks at the "modular image" of the "white sheik" of Western popular media, an ambiguously sexualized figure who is both white and Arab. The avatars of this "ideologically laden" liminal figure are as diverse as Rudolf Valentino's passionate sheik of silent film, General Norman Schwarzkopf emulating the cinematic "Lawrence of Arabia," and the "embedded" anthropologist of military counterinsurgency programs. Caton's chapter demonstrates how an image circulates through time and space, appearing and disappearing, taking on new significance in different social contexts—racial ambiguity here, sexual ambivalence there, warrior self-fashioning or counterinsurgency poster boy.

In each of these chapters, the author goes beyond a simple interrogation of what pictures are or what they mean, to consider how certain images come into being and are taken up affectively; how they spread as if by contagion or "stick" in one particular place or another;[18] how they renegotiate the limits of the visualizable or of vision itself or—far from circulating in a "borderless" medium of free communication—can operate as physical or conceptual borders policing the limits of public space or social identity. Our aim is to begin to appreciate the rather different trajectories and publics that may be available to images through a variety of modes of dissemination and distribution.

In the rest of this introductory chapter, we outline the general framework of the book and stake out some conceptual starting points for the chapters that follow. We begin with a brief discussion of what images are and why they might be worthy of special consideration. Next we take up the issue of movement: how images circulate and problems that circulation raises. We then proceed to questions of enframement and context, the containment of images, and how images might escape such boundaries and embeddings. The next set of issues has to do with *how* images move— through, on the one hand, the enabling and limiting conditions of material, technological, and infrastructural possibility and, on the other, the surges of affect that they provoke in their audiences. Finally, we address the relation between (moving) images and their (contingent) publics. How is it that certain images are taken up (or not) by certain audiences at certain moments? How, in other words, are images apprehended by the multiple publics—diverse, sometimes unexpected, occasionally obtuse—that they encounter? What can we make of these encounters?

WHY IMAGES?

It may be, as W. J. T. Mitchell speculates, that "the problem of the twenty-first century is the problem of the image."[19] At the least, the proliferation of academic studies devoted to the image makes it seem so. This is not because of the emergence of some profound analytical frame reorganizing the field of culture theory, but rather because images have come to be "a point of peculiar friction and discomfort across a broad range of intellectual inquiry."[20]

The "friction and discomfort" that Mitchell identifies come in a variety of forms and approaches, signaling both the long-standing fascination and the iconophobic anxiety of popular and academic critics toward the image.[21] So, to focus on our own discipline only, anthropology has in recent years produced studies of scientific technologies of visibility and representation, including its own historically troubled relationship to them; colonial politics of representation; art worlds and markets; museums and monuments; alternative and indigenous media; the creation (and critique) of ethnographic film; popular photography; art as ideology or media as ideological mode; cultures of viewing or consumption; infrastructures of circulation and distribution; advertising; tourist art; and public art, among others.[22]

Yet, despite all this interest in images and image-making, there is not much clarity about what images are or what they do. "The simplest way to put this," as Mitchell noted in an essay on the "pictorial turn" first published in 1992, "is to say that, in what is often characterized as an age of 'spectacle' (Guy Debord), 'surveillance' (Foucault), and all-pervasive image-making, we still do not know exactly what pictures are, what their relation to language is, how they operate on observers and on the world, how their history is to be understood, and what is to be done with or about them."[23] Mitchell's argument was framed in response to a section of a 1988 National Endowment for the Humanities (NEH) report entitled "Word and Image," which attempted to mark a sharp distinction between the two, with the former symbolically represented by "the book" and the latter by "television." Mitchell quite rightly points out that neither medium can be so neatly categorized, because books have "since time immemorial" been illustrated and television is as dependent on words as it is on images. The distinction, he suggests, has more to do with "deeply contested cultural values" that pit elite against mass culture, academic against public humanities, and "past" against "future" media forms.[24]

More recent works, such as Kajri Jain's study of Indian calendar art, push these points further, with less discomfort and "disillusionment" than Mitchell expresses. For Jain, the internal heterogeneity of the image demands an approach that recognizes its "irreducibility to a visuality mediated exclusively by language."[25] The image, in other words, is always more than what can be said—or written—about it. Indeed, Jain takes this proposition further, arguing in effect that images are ontologically distinct from language and thus cannot be "read" in linguistic terms. She insists on the importance of attending to other aspects of the image—its material existence as an object (as well as a commodity), its circuits of technological reproduction and transmission—and to its audience as "embodied beings" with whom the image engages in more or less significant, more or less lasting, social relationships.[26] This approach opens up new possibilities for "an expansive notion of reception," beginning with an emphasis on both the "corporeal" form and the efficacious presence of the image, in terms of the myriad affective and libidinal engagements on the part of persons and collectivities that it may elicit.[27]

The visual, as Chris Pinney has similarly argued, should not be understood merely as a "kind of language, discursively constituted," an approach that would "disallow any confrontation with the figural and resistant properties of certain visual forms," but neither should it be regarded as entirely antithetical, and inaccessible, to signification. "Perhaps," Pinney suggests, "the visual should be conceived of as a continuum," ranging from the strictly discursive to the "figural" or affective. The image is thus "neither one thing [n]or the other, but encompasses instead a diverse set of forms, differently constituted," which are always open to novel figurations and framings.[28]

Theories of the image and imaging necessarily adjudicate what counts as an image and what does not.[29] According to Bruno Latour's definition, an image is "any [visual] sign, work of art, inscription, or picture that acts as a mediation to access something else."[30] Many of the images dealt with in this book fall easily within the parameters of Latour's definition. Yet, even this loose gloss is perplexing and incomplete. Not all images are material or even mimetic. Must an image represent something else? Must the representation be visual? Or, if it is, must it be primarily experienced as visual? Can we imagine a sonic image, for instance? What about the visual representation of a concept, process, or plan in the form of a Venn diagram, a graph, an organizational chart, or a "strategy map"?[31] One might think of a range of interiorized or immaterial images—dreams, fantasies, drug-induced hallucinations, the visual impressions evoked by a piece of music or a poem, or the verbal description of a landscape (or, as in *No Show*, an absent painting). What of optical illusions, daydreaming imaginings of cloud-pictures, or mirror reflections? What about the visual imagery of written words, as in calligraphic art or even a signature?[32] What of artworks that depict something invisible or even nonexistent, an image perhaps derived from the imagination of the artist; artworks that hover "at the edge of perception"[33] or reject representation altogether? Or objects intended to house or evoke a sacred presence, such as a printed god portrait or a fetish object, or to not be seen by a human audience at all? How would a fingerprint, an MRI, or a genome map be categorized? Must an image be something "made," either through actual labor or through the "work of imagination"? Might it be understood as "found" or revealed, as, for instance, when veined patterns in the carefully placed, marbled paneling of mosque interiors disclose traces of human and animal forms in a space from which all anthropomorphic and zoomorphic images have otherwise been excluded?[34] Should it bear a physical resemblance to the thing represented? Is the image always, necessarily, the sign of an absence, designating the not-there or the not-that of the thing represented?

Most important for our purposes, what is the *place* of the image? Notions of what counts as an image and how it operates depend on disciplinary perspective, each field singling out certain kinds of images as legitimate and worthy of attention while relegating others to a background of "illegitimate," inferior, or second-order images. Academic disciplines "place" the image in another sense as well, by defining the appropriate or relevant context for its examination, study, or appreciation: historical, political, ideological, cultural, aesthetic, and so on—a subject we discuss further in the section "Enframement and Refocalization."[35]

Images are legitimized and delegitimized not only by disciplinary boundaries. Concerns about images often emerge at cultural or political border zones where intolerance is at play and where different stakes and interests are mobilized.[36] In 1994 the runway showing of a strapless bustier-dress decoratively inscribed across the bodice with a Qur'anic passage (mistakenly understood by designer Karl Lagerfeld to be a love poem) led to public protests and death threats against the model, Claudia Schiffer. In an overzealous expression of regret for this religious affront, the dress—nicknamed in the Western press the "Satanic breasts"—was subsequently burned by the fashion house, an iconoclastic move more vehement than the request by Islamic clergy to simply withdraw images of the offending garment from public circulation.[37]

A more recent example of the trouble that may ensue when images move across boundaries of difference is the case of the notorious Danish "Muhammed" cartoons, discussed in Barry Flood's contribution to this volume (chapter 2). In 2005 a small Danish newspaper, the *Jyllands-Posten*, commissioned and published twelve cartoon depictions of the Prophet Muhammed as a protest against restrictions on freedom of expression. The cartoons, repeatedly reproduced in the Euro-American and Muslim press, triggered demonstrations and counterdemonstrations, riots, lawsuits, and diplomatic protests around the world. The cartoons' creation and reception engaged, "rhetorically at least," a notionally European (secular) public that self-identified with tolerance and freedom of expression, in contrast to an imagined (Muslim) counterpublic allegedly "inhibited by the persistence of archaic taboos on image-making."[38] At the same time, the cartoons—whether actually seen or merely heard about—mobilized an Islamic public that perceived their publication as a desecration of faith or, equally important, as a sign of virulently anti-Muslim sentiments given authoritative expression in a legitimate organ of public discourse.

It is, of course, important to recognize that the trouble with images at the border between "Christians" and "Muslims" is a quite different one from the status and problem of images internal to Islam or Christianity and that multiple, contradictory impulses toward image-making and image-breaking have existed in both traditions. It is possible to trace, as Flood does, a history of Christian attributions of both idolatry and iconoclasm to Islam reaching back to the European Middle Ages, one both cited and reactivated in commentaries regarding the cartoon controversy.[39] And despite Western attributions of "primitivism" and "barbarism" to Taliban leaders responsible for the destruction of Afghanistan's Bamiyan Buddhas, iconoclasm, as James Simpson argues in his study of the problematic status of the image in Anglo-American Protestantism, "is not 'somewhere else'...it lies buried deep within Western modernity."[40]

Besides the specificities of any given "border situation," what are at stake in such controversies are also larger questions concerning the "ethics, politics, and polemics of the visual in an era of mass media and transregional information flows."[41] These are questions having to do with the very locus of existential value as articulated, for instance, by the Taliban envoy to the United Nations, who, in the controversy over the destruction of the Bamiyan Buddhas, highlighted the hypocrisy of Western institutions like New York's Metropolitan Museum that appear to treasure artworks over human life: they "will give millions of dollars to save an un-Islamic stone statue but not one cent to save the lives of Afghani men, women, and children."[42] But also at stake are the image's location in public space (whether on the postwar streets of Ambon City or on Claudia Schiffer's breasts on the international fashion runway); the transnational traffic in which it is caught up; and the different image economies through which it moves and is variously taken up, positively and negatively. It is to these topics that we now turn.

IMAGES IN MOTION

Images, Kajri Jain writes, are "bodies that move." Even when they take the form of still pictures, they are always in motion. They travel from their place of origin to where they are sold, consumed, used, displayed, or watched. They change identities, being at different times embodied ideas, commodities, decorations, icons, souvenirs, amusements, gifts, trash. They flicker across the experiences of daily life, dulling or invigorating the routines of the everyday or opening up vistas beyond it. They activate memory, preserve traces of past events; they offer an escape or another way in. They "act on bodies and create relations between bodies."[43]

Today, photographed, digitally produced, globally disseminated images impinge on us from all directions; the intimate zones of everyday life increasingly serve both as subject matter for public display and as screens upon which a multitude of images can be projected. The extraordinary proliferation and rapid circulation of visual images via media both new and old, high- and low-tech, contribute to a feeling of global intimacy on the one hand and to a pervasive sense of danger, instability, and dread on the other. Writing this in the days immediately after the tenth anniversary of the September 11 destruction of the World Trade Center, we cannot help but be struck by the extent to which the experience of watching events unfold, repeatedly, on television was recalled by many as a traumatic, transformative event: "Before 9/11 I didn't know to be afraid," one woman, a schoolteacher from Sikeston, Missouri, remarked on PBS's "Video Quilt" interactive multimedia project, "and because of the footage, it brought to life that there are people out there who want to do damage to me, you know, personally."[44]

Never before has the violent imagery of global crisis and catastrophe been such a fixture of news and entertainment media, nor the boundary of the skin been so permeable to technologies of visual imaging. Nor has it been so easy to purchase, use, and then toss away a camera, so commonsensical to expect the everyday images that crowd one's day to cover the globe, or so unsettling to see the specter of total visibility granted such legitimacy. This enhanced visibility begets ever more visual surveillance, from aerial traffic control and streetside security cameras to nannycams and full-body scan technology. In this climate of enhanced attention to visible signs and mobile images, fear of secrecy and exposure saturates the political imagination.

It is not only the sheer quantitative increase in the circulation of and access to images that demands attention, but also the ways that particular technologies shape certain kinds of images, certain modes of circulation, and certain kinds of audiences, as well as how they affect one another. The fantastic extent and global stretch of such proliferations, the enhanced fetishistic appeal of the spectacle, the heightened sense among social actors of the multiple, overlapping audiences to which they are or wish to be beholden, the ready and repetitive iterations and imitations that images open themselves to, and the growing legitimacy of, and indeed the desire for, total visibility and surveillance are all tele-technical dimensions of this fluid image-environment. Never before, we suspect, has the process of mediation itself been so central to media accounts of global events, as the florid debate about the significance (or not) of social media such as Facebook and Twitter to the rolling demonstrations of the so-called Arab Spring of 2011 demonstrates. In this play of mediation and remediation, it seems that no event is truly "over" if it can be referenced, reenacted, rehashed, or recapitulated in the interests of thickening the media plot.

Unmoored from their sites of production, mobile images may still retain traces of their initial provenances even as they are variously inflected, refracted, reframed, remixed, digitally enhanced, cropped, hijacked, and amplified and their effects intensified or muted. Their presence is reproduced through an array of after-images with lives of their own, moving across different places or emerging rhizomatically in dispersed and disparate sites, perhaps with different senses and agendas. What, to borrow a phrase from W. J. T. Mitchell, do images such as these "want"?[45] What do they demand and desire from us? Or, to put it differently, how might we tell the life histories of such images and their audiences? How do we trace the tangled paths of their travels and returns, unfold their effects and aftereffects, and scan the collectivities—fixed or ephemeral, situated or dispersed—that they invoke or address? What, we might also ask, do we want from them? How are they energized—or materialized—by our desires and demands, and to what ends do we direct them?

Striking in all of this is how the widely acclaimed surplus of images in the contemporary world often, upon closer scrutiny, reduces itself to more modest proportions. Whatever quantitative increase there may have been in image capacity does not necessarily translate into an increase in image variety, as even a facile perusal of Facebook or Flickr will demonstrate. As Pierre Bourdieu points out, the options for what can be considered "photographiable" in any particular context are always extremely limited.[46] The iconic postures of the news photo, the repetitive gestures of "riot porn," and the banality of the snapshot are measures of what counts as a viewable image; so too are the redundant pathos of humanitarian public service announcements and the conventionalized horror of atrocity photographs—which, as Judith Butler notes, are emotionally numbing not because of their sheer surplus accumulation but rather owing to the predictability of their framing, which generates the recurrent sense that one has seen this before.[47]

ENFRAMEMENT AND REFOCALIZATION

"Imagine the damage caused by a theft which robbed you only of your frames, or rather of their joints, and of any possibility of reframing your valuables or your art-objects."[48] Jacques Derrida's provocative suggestion draws attention to the significance of frames, or rather of processes of enframement, in the generation and circulation of images. By "enframement" we mean the various ways the image is foregrounded or separated from its general environmental surround in order to be apprehended *as an image*. Enframement can be the provision of a material enclosure—the wooden frame of a painting, for instance, or the boxed screen of a television or computer—or a marked edge, like the bordering line of a cartoon cell or the application of a "frame template" or "border effect" to a digital image via Photoshop. It can take the form of the segmented interior of multiple "windows" through which information is displayed on a computer desktop screen. Enframement can denote the choice of depth of field or camera angle for a photograph, which compositionally "frames" the image as it is created. It is also at work in the techniques of montage: the relational ordering or juxtaposition of images in a cinematic sequence; the placement and organization of photos in a family album; or the overlay of contrastive or contradictory images in photomontage.

Enframement includes *frames of reference* as well: sets of ideas or assumptions that direct how the image should be evaluated, viewed, or comprehended. Representational genres (the medium of production) and academic disciplines establish and enforce this sort of enframement by determining what counts as a "proper subject" or a "proper style," as well as by setting up proper evaluative mechanisms for these. For instance, Indian calendar art, as Kajri Jain points out, has generally been regarded as "kitsch" and thus of anthropological rather than aesthetic significance, to be treated as a "symptom" of social processes rather than as an expressive object of interest in its own right.[49]

Language, in the form of textual commentary, captions, or talk, frequently serves as an enframing device, even, or perhaps especially, when it is located within the body of the image itself, like the time stamp on a digital photograph or the thought balloon of a cartoon character. In cinema, of course, images and words are inherently intertwined, but such too is the case with photographs or cartoons and their captions. Consider, for instance, the way that captions can serve an "anchoring" function, to the extent that photographs, even those iconic images for which "no caption is needed," may even be perceived as calling out for them.[50] Many actually require some textual explanation in order to function pictorially, not to mention to establish their status as visual icons. The famous "Times Square kiss" photo, Dorothea Lange's Works Projects Administration photograph of the "migrant mother," or the image of Kim Phuc, the Vietnamese "Napalm girl," may be so familiar to us that we provide a mental frame for them, but if we follow Derrida's suggestion rigorously and "un-frame" these images, we may find that they immediately lose their iconic impact.

Enframements may aspire to fix the image in a particular place, to a particular audience, in a particular sociohistorical context, drawn sharply. Morris, in her contribution to this volume (chapter 7), complicates this notion of enframement through what she refers to as "refocalization." Focalization, she writes, "is more than a way of seeing or a point of view; it is...an ideologically inflected perspective that permits one or another object not only to appear but also to cohere as an object of attention." It is through refocalizations of the perceptual field, as in transitional historical moments, that what was previously seen in one way may take on a radically different appearance, stand in a different relation to its general cultural surround, or disappear from view altogether. At such moments the apparatus of prior enframement, formerly rendered transparent or "natural," may also come into view within the refocalized field.

Along with aspirations for "transparent immediacy," images may draw attention to the artifice of genre or medium.[51] Rather than stake claims to the representation of "real life," "actual events," and the like, contemporary image production frequently depends on its self-representation as media object. Self-representation may involve the application of outmoded or already refocalized media practices and technologies—photomontage, for instance, or the application of "handmade" digital overlays on a photograph. Processes such as these serve to remind us of "the inherently delicate, transitory nature of the associations that pertain between any given setting and the image world to which it is provisionally conjoined."[52] The need to attend to the particular constellations and transformative possibilities of such provisional life- and image-world affinities follows from this insight, as does an awareness of how it might be possible to conceive of "a history of images that treats pictures as more than simply a reflection of something else, something more important happening elsewhere."[53]

At one extreme of the visual continuum are highly "enclaved" images, directed toward (and producing) a very specific audience, with very particular intent: advertisements, political cartoons, portraits of public figures, "niche" marketing campaigns. Such images frequently aim to exclude, demonize, or even erase other potential viewers. Even here we increasingly find that reenframements are at work as images move beyond their intended audiences. Reenframement was, of course, the problem with the Danish cartoons, which originally appeared enframed in a discourse of democratic free speech but were taken up elsewhere as expressions of Western hostility toward Islam, moral hypocrisy, and political calculation.

Other images seem to lend themselves to—indeed to relish—reenframement. Take the famous image of the handsome young *guerillero heroico* based on Alberto Korda's 1960 photograph of Che Guevara.[54] Korda's clever cropping, showing Che abstracted from any historical and political context and looking off into an unseen distance, prepared this image for extensive circulation. Changes in artists' technique and technology during the pop art revolution, together with the political circumstances of the late 1960s, enabled versions of the image "to breed like rabbits," in the words of Irish photographer Jim Fitzgerald, who in 1967 produced the stylized Che poster that later became the basis of the notorious fake "Warhol Che," among a multitude of other reproductions. Techniques such as silk-screening and bleach-out methods, which reduced the gray tones in photographs and heightened black-and-white contrast, induced a "flatness" and a simplification of the image, turning it into something like a statement, a brand, or an uncluttered icon more than anything else.

"'The most important thing about the image of Che as seen in mass reproduction is that it is *not* a photograph, its incredible longevity, power, and malleability as an image rests on its rejection of photography'...it remains connected to the original photo in some way so as to retain a reference to the real world in which it arose, but it also blatantly distances itself from any claim to convey that reality...'it is saying this is ink on paper; it is an idea, it is not a representation of the world.'"[55] This (re)enframement is presumably what makes it possible for Che's image, stripped of any reference to Marxist ideology, to figure in a "Muslim Power" mural photographed by Spyer on the island of Tidore, Indonesia, in 2008, alongside depictions of such other historical heavyweights as Indonesia's first president, Sukarno; the local eighteenth-century anticolonial hero Nuku;

FIGURE 1.4

Muslim power streetside portrait gallery, Tidore, Indonesia, 2008. Artist unknown. Photograph by P. Spyer.

Indonesian protest singer Iwan Fals; Muammar Qaddafi; and Osama Bin Laden.[56] Note how the mural not only captures images in motion but also stages the very medium through which they move, the photographic film roll that serves as the portrait gallery's frame.

A similar process of reenframement can be seen in the iconic image of Barack Obama on Shepard Fairey's 2008 poster captioned "HOPE." Like the "Che" image, *HOPE* was a remake of a photograph, in this case a 2006 digital photo of then senator Obama at a press conference on Darfur alongside actor George Clooney (who was the photographer's actual target). Reproduced—and relabeled, the original caption "PROGRESS" being replaced by the campaign-friendlier "HOPE"—in silk-screen format as a poster, a bumper sticker, a refrigerator magnet, or other donor "gimmes," the *HOPE* image, notwithstanding the copyright infringement lawsuits brought against Fairey by the Associated Press and the photographer and despite the fact that it was an "unauthorized" political image, in many ways defined the 2008 Obama presidential campaign. What made the image both striking and effective was its transformation from an ordinary news photograph into a graphic illustration—an "icon"—through the process of retrogressive remediation or, as it is termed by Cartright and Mandiberg, "demaking."[57] Degrading the quality of the image by "reach[ing] back to older media forms, playing up their uses and strictures over those of newer technological platforms," the process of demaking both highlights the technics of image production and loosens the hold of indexicality on our interpretation of the image. Cartwright and Mandiberg argue that rather than engage in a debate over the authorship of the original image and the poster's status as a copy of the photograph, a more fruitful approach is to seek out its other associations. One such referent for the *HOPE* poster, they propose, is Robert Rauschenberg's *Retroactive I* (1964), a silk-screen collage featuring a reworked photograph of John F. Kennedy, whose presidential demeanor is echoed in Obama's lofty gaze, as well as in the "iconic and generic" quality of the image being reproduced. What is being reproduced, they assert, is not so much the image content of a photographic "original" but rather the "remedial act itself." It is, in short, a "stylistic homage to past technologies of political art," constituting a body of resonant images.[58] An even more obvious referent (curiously unmentioned in their account) is the guerillero heroico image of Che and its various remediations as generic political icon, pop art, and global fashion statement, echoed by the international pop-commercial ubiquity of the Obama portrait.

TECHNOLOGIES OF VISUALIZATION

Attending to the complicated operations of enframement means registering the ebbs as much as the frequently naturalized frictionless flow of circulation; it highlights the often less than global yet more than local trajectories along which images travel, along with the foreclosures, inhibitions, or even "stickiness" that may come into play whenever the movement of images is concerned. Technologies of image production and dissemination compose one key aspect of this seemingly natural movement of images through space and time.

In recent years, Brian Larkin (chapter 9) notes, the "transnational movement of images has occupied a simply enormous amount of attention...as scholars try to come to terms with the speed and intensity of image economies brought about by new technologies" of information storage and transmission and by concomitant social and economic transformations on a global scale. Mass-produced images, those technologically reproducible, nonauratic artworks that Walter Benjamin attended to,[59] travel with incredible speed and diversity, and it is this dramatic mobility that has drawn the interest of many subsequent scholars and critics, us included. But it is equally important to note that images do not move just anywhere or in any way they (or their makers) please. Technological reproducibility entails an entire infrastructure of creation, production, and distribution, which enables this flow of images but also channels it in very specific directions and ways.

Global flows are neither frictionless nor ubiquitous; they depend on particular media platforms and their infrastructures, which regulate and restrict the direction and transmission of information; they face interruptive forces, including institutional forms of censorship or the requirements of capitalization or the routine degradation of technological capacities; they generate static as much as signal; they create novel aesthetic experiences and replicate or revamp existing ones. Material infrastructures "create the channels by which media move, and theser are crucial to processes of circulation."[60] These channels, or "vectors," as McKenzie Wark refers to them, constitute the specific but indeterminate trajectories linking points of media transmission and collection with their termini: from satellite to television set, from movie studio to screening room or theater, from pirate DVD-burning operation to home player, from cell-phone camera to Facebook page, from one computer to others.[61] Vectors are inevitably selective: their trajectories and destinations are uneven and unequal. Media infrastructures incorporate weaknesses, limitations, and "breakdowns"; they not only define content and format but also reinforce inequalities in reception and access. Moviegoing depends on the creative and economic vitality of the film industry but also on the presence of movie theaters (or, now, on a VCR or DVD player) and on an audience that wants to enter theaters and can afford to do so. Watching television requires access to a TV set and the creation of programming but also depends on the massive, often state-supported, industrial investment necessary for broadcast networks, satellite access, or the extension of fiber optic cable.

It is easy to imagine media forms as "predestined by the technology,"[62] but as Kristin Roth-Ey points out in *Moscow Prime Time*, her engaging study of media in the mid twentieth-century Soviet Union, they are equally shaped by ideological frames and political choices. The enthusiastic popular response to Soviet TV "was authorized by a centrally planned Soviet industry that produced sets primarily for individual, rather than group, consumption, and by financial incentives (pricing policies, the end to licensing fees) that made owning a TV broadly accessible."[63] The decision of the Soviet state to invest massively in infrastructural development for television broadcast, even at a time of economic austerity, can be understood as a "symbol of Soviet scientific prowess to observers at home and abroad," as well as a potent ideological tool delivering a mass audience for the dissemination of closely controlled information and "cultural uplift" programming. During the same period, television in the United States, as a private industry, flourished largely as a vehicle for advertising, its temporal formatting shaped by the imperative to sell structured bits of time to advertisers and its content determined by the need to deliver an appropriate audience for those commercials.

Visual media technologies not only "select" particular audiences but also "train" those audiences in specific modes of spectatorship and enjoyment. Viewers may also be self-taught, becoming adept at reading the gaps in media delivery, teasing out significance from the static or "noise" in the signal, envisioning the unrepresented, or finding authenticity in technological insufficiency or the naïve immediacy of the untrained operator. Or they may simply "switch channels," like Soviet television viewers in the 1960s and 1970s, who, far from passively accepting the social uplift of state programming of the "model bricklayer" sort, turned to escapist formats such as game shows, sports, and entertainment programming.

If someone like Susan Sontag holds out the fantasy of immediacy in her essays on photography, she can do so only by forgetting not only that certain technologies—for instance, today's high-definition television— produce immediacy's effects but also that these "reality effects" are bolstered by discourses that claim and elaborate upon them.[64] Infrastructures may offer enhanced resolution or build in noise or distortion in the visual signal. These effects then feed back into the image as an aesthetic choice or a value, a mode of exclusivity, or a particular aesthetic. A history of photography's purported technological immediacy can be traced from the initial, grainy depictions of simple inanimate objects, like Niepce's table setting or Atget's unpopulated landscapes and street scenes, to the physiognomy of the human face, the portrait or "type." Studio portraiture, with its slow shutter speeds and extended delays, erased human movement from the surface of the photographic image but also generated mysterious traces that were interpreted as the presence of spirits or mediumistic ectoplasm imperceptible to the naked eye.[65] The formally posed studio portrait gave way, in terms of its perceived authenticity, to the amateur snapshot taken with a cheap Kodak or Polaroid camera, to the extent that the aesthetics of the latter, with its artlessly unposed, "caught on the run" style, came to index immediacy even in the realm of art photography and painting. Digital photography has foregrounded both high-resolution precision and simultaneity—the immediate uploading of pictures to social media sites, for instance—but also falsification, as the seeming ubiquity of the Photoshopped image, whether as comic montage or as manipulated news photo, demonstrates.[66]

It is not merely a matter of the technical verisimilitude or "catchiness" of the image that is at stake here, but also the kind of object that becomes available for observation. One might track, as Pinney does in chapter 6 in this volume, the changing nature of photography's subjects as a succession of different interiorities made public and thus available to a range of political, medical, and sociological surveillances and scrutinies, a trajectory culminating—for the moment anyway—in the utilization of new technologies like retinal scans, magnetic resonance imaging, nanophotography, and full-body X-rays, through which bodily interiorities, the "entrails" composing divination's classic locus, are turned literally inside out in a move that reveals the most intimate private spaces, making them fully exposed to public view.[67] Webcams similarly create new modes of (self-)exposure and new objects of display and observation, from "live sex acts" and the pseudo-reality of "lonelygirl15" to the multitude of owlcam and other "cute baby animal" Internet observation sites and animal livefeeds.[68] New technologies and the objects they bring into focus have not only increased and transformed the nature of surveillance but also exploded the work of detection. As former NYPD detective Edward Conlon wrote in a post-9/11 meditation in the *New Yorker*, "DNA, cell-phone and computer data banks, social media…and, especially, the proliferation of surveillance cameras have provided unimaginable investigative opportunities that require commensurate amounts of labor," resulting in a predictable decline in police morale and creating a general mood of public mistrust verging on paranoia.[69]

THE "RELEASE OF AFFECTS"

The Conlon example above demonstrates the relation between what Ernst van Alphen (chapter 8) identifies as the "explosion of information" and the "release of affects" in contemporary life. Far from reducing insecurity and enhancing confidence in public safety measures, new modes of observation and detection—this proliferation of forensic technologies and objects of visualization—seem to have led to an increase in anxiety about security itself. Each new revelation calls for still more intimate forms of surveillance and exposure, more intense affective responses.

Following Gregory J. Seigworth and Melissa Gregg's definition, we take affect to consist of "those forces…beneath, alongside, or generally *other than* conscious knowing, vital forces insisting beyond emotion—that can serve to drive us toward movement, toward thought and extension, that can likewise suspend us (as if in neutral) across a barely registering accretion of force-relations, or that can even leave us overwhelmed by the world's apparent intractability."[70] Affects are "intensities" or excitations, which are, themselves, without specific content or meaning but which, in Gilles Deleuze's formulation, "lead to thought." Deleuze speaks of the image in its affective sense as an "encountered sign," apprehended via sensuous engagement rather than cognition; it is not something already known, a codification of information, but rather is something that creates "impressions which force us to look, encounters which force us to interpret, expressions which force us to think."[71] Attending to the affective power of images—*other* than conscious knowing yet neither beyond or primordially before it—means tracking the various and variable surges of excitation they provoke and exploring "those resonances that circulate about, between, and sometimes stick to bodies and worlds."[72] This approach takes us beyond questions of what images "want" or what they "say," as well as what their audiences "see in them" in terms of a message or code.

The kind of shock that leads to thought, or that draws and holds attention, is perhaps most evident in the case of images of war and violent death. From Picasso's *Guernica* to the S-21 photographs of victims of Khmer Rouge executions, the eye is drawn to the scene of violence even as the imagination is repelled by it.[73] Whatever the maker's intention may have been, such images have a force that pushes them beyond interpretive closure, into the bodily shock of affective engagement.

The second Gulf War (GW2) has been perhaps the most aggressively mediatized event in history. Whereas Operation Desert Storm was televised via the distancing mechanisms of military briefings, technologically amplified perception, long-focus shots of army convoys moving through the desert, and the barely visible flares of nighttime bombardment, in GW2, visual immediacy was at stake from the start. From the moment we watched the destruction of the World Trade Center on television, first live and then reliving it in the repetitive tape loops of planes hitting towers, crowds fleeing amid dense smoke, the rain of debris, the grief of firefighters, the speeches of politicians—but not the bodies falling from the towers or the thuds they made when they hit the ground, which were deemed too horrific to publicize—we were caught up in the reign of encountered signs. There were the faces of alleged terrorists and enemies staring out from passport photos, mug shots, and terrorist playing cards; the humanizing photos, mystifying in their clarity, of soldiers at work and at rest, taken by embedded news photographers; the taped messages and recruiting videos from al-Qaeda and its offshoots; the recorded and replayed executions of hostages; the injured bodies and the rubble of unidentifiable buildings; the toppling of Saddam Hussein's statue and the cell-phone videos that captured the hanging of the man himself; the multitude of soldiers' blogs, videos, and snapshots, not the least of these being the scandal of Abu Ghraib.

The affective power and, not coincidentally, the possible political power of all these encountered signs are most apparent in what was considered too inflammatory to be shown at all. Like the people who fell or jumped from the twin towers, the severely damaged bodies of soldiers and even their flag-draped coffins were off-limits for public photographic display in the first years of the war. Even the corpse of Osama bin Laden was deemed too provocative to be shown to global audiences, though it was certainly present in the form of incessant talk about it, including the vacillation about whether it should be shown. Bin Laden's death was instead represented for the American public by the "iconic" image of President Obama and his advisors watching a live video feed of the attack on bin Laden's compound by Navy SEALs.[74] Photographs had been taken to prove that the al-Qaeda leader was dead. But it was enough in the end to say that they existed. They were too graphic and disturbing for an American audience, we were told; their display might be offensive to Muslims around the world, thus perhaps inviting retaliatory attacks against US targets.

Despite such efforts of containment or censorship, images like these are capable of escaping the restrictive frames placed on them, whether by governments, journalistic ethics, or reticence or simply by the limits of visual interest and toleration. Pictures alleged to be of bin Laden's corpse circulated widely on the Internet, though it is not clear whether these were actual photographs of his body or doctored ones. (They were soon debunked as a Photoshopped "hoax," at least one of the pictures having been posted on the Internet as early as 2009.) It hardly matters, however, whether the images in circulation were the ostensibly suppressed originals, other "actual" photos taken surreptitiously at the time, faked photographic stand-ins for these, or even imaginative re-creations inspired by the apparent existence of such images. What does matter is the affective potency of the image, which is one among other crucial components that enable it to circulate, spreading virally, bringing into being new and unexpected publics in the process, reinforcing older ones, and indeed contributing to the dissolution of others.

PUBLICS AND UPTAKE

A public, according to Michael Warner's definition, is a social entity or hypothetical group that comes into being in "relation to texts and their circulation" and "by virtue of being addressed" by those texts. In this sense, publics are self-made, created by what he calls "stranger relationality," that is, a form of imagined commensality existing among unfamiliar others. Public discourse, says Warner, is poetic. This means that it is not just "self-organizing, a kind of entity created by its own discourse, or even that this space of circulation is taken to be a social entity, but that in order for this to happen all discourse or performance addressed to a public must characterize the world in which it attempts to circulate and it must attempt to realize that world through address."[75] This is loosely akin to what Louis Althusser means by *interpellation*, the calling-up or "hailing" of subjects by the various ideological arms of the state, whereby one recognizes oneself as if already subjected to state authority.[76] To put it somewhat differently, public discourse creates its subject-audience—"its public"—by acting as if that public already existed and then specifying its dimensions in a compelling manner. Thus, Warner continues, "there is no speech or performance addressed to a public that does not try to specify in advance, in countless highly condensed ways, the lifeworld of its circulation: not just through its discursive claims—of the kind that can be said to be oriented to understanding—but through the pragmatics of its speech genres, idioms, stylistic markers, address, temporality, mise-en-scène, citational field, interlocutory protocols, lexicon, and so on. Its circulatory fate is the realization of that world."[77]

Although Warner recognizes that such "texts" can also be visual or auditory—speech acts, musical works, films, advertisements, and the like—his primary argument focuses on and derives from the circulations of the printed word. But what if we were to theorize publics as formed in relation to images in circulation—that is, not just in terms of a "space of discourse" but also according to the diverse circulatory addresses of images in motion?[78] What difference would it make if analytic emphasis were placed on the viewer of images rather than on the reader of texts?

In focusing attention on images that move, we do not intend to assert a radical separation of images from text or voice. All media are, of course, always and already mixed media.[79] A cartoon's meaning or a news photo's message is located in the interplay between its caption and its pictorial aspect; likewise, much of the artistic work of a film consists in its narrative structure, sound effects, characterization and dialogue, the emotional cues of the musical score, and other nonvisual elements, most of which would be erased if the film were regarded strictly as a series of flickering images. Images themselves frequently have a semantic component. While acknowledging this mutuality of visual, acoustic, and discursive elements in images and in texts, we also recognize an important difference in the modes of linguistic and figural circulation and reception. Figural representations are relatively less bound by the constraints of legibility and translation than are textual ones, less restricted by the limits of language competence in discursive communities, arguably more vulnerable to the unexpected release of affect. The circulation and reception of images may be more promiscu-ous, less containable, and less predictable in their effects than those of verbal texts. It is this greater mobility of the image, its affective capacity and greater potential for resignification and appropriation, that we wish to draw attention to here.

Publics are created by virtue of being "addressed" as such. What we might want to ask, however, is, Why this public, this discourse, this moment, and not some other? Is it the simple coincidence of myriad, more or less random addresses, some of which are able to more effectively capture "their" publics than others? What about the possibility of a "wrong address," through which an utterly unanticipated public is formed? How do we think about the multitude of divergent publics encountered by a single image that moves from one address to another, like the imagined and presumably antithetical audience/s for the unseen photograph of Osama bin Laden? What happens to a public once it has so recognized itself? What kinds of temporalities characterize different publics? Are some publics more prone to dissipate and be re-formed at each separate hailing? Do some retain a residual recognition that is reactivated by further, perhaps even different, forms of address? Where in this model do we make room for belief—or, perhaps, love—which, one imagines, might grip its public in a particularly visceral and lasting manner?

In rethinking publics through images, it is necessary to take into con-sideration the relation between certain technologies of image production and image dissemination on the one hand and the kinds of publics that crystallize around them on the other. This includes, but is not limited to, considerations of the chronotopic dimensions of image circulation, includ-ing scale and scope, interval and duration. The specific nature of plau-sibility and the generation of reality effects are important to examine in any given medium.[80] Material considerations also include the level of capi-talization necessary to produce or consume particular media images and the physical housing that media technologies require for the storage and display of images: in computers or TV sets, on cheaply produced VCDs, painted on public walls, or reproduced xerographically on broadsheets.

Another set of issues involves the social dimensions and location of image reception and transmission. Do audiences come together in the-aters or public meetings or on the streets, or do they inhabit the private or semiprivate zones of home, automobile, or cybercafé? Are audiences "ambushed" by unanticipated images, like graffiti, or must they choose to view them, as in a museum? Do images come with explanatory labels or cap-tions, like the museum tour, or, contrariwise, derive their power precisely from the absence of labeling? To what extent does commercial sponsorship or state censorship shape both the form and the content of the media image, and how does this shaping affect audiences' engagement with those images? To what extent can images "leap" across media to travel beyond their originally imagined audience and, in conjunction with other factors, produce unanticipated publics and counterpublics elsewhere? In what ways does media technology itself transform the "message" of the image?

Some publics, such as the street demonstrations provoked by the Danish cartoons, may be relatively spontaneous, short-lived, and rhizomatic. Some may spread globally, cascading from one site to another, like the 2011 demonstrations of the Arab Spring or Occupy Wall Street and its many offshoots. Such publics may have wide, long-term political implications, both at the level of international relations and quite locally, for the ambitions and profiling of particular groups. Once called up, publics such as these may be provoked or reanimated by new image incidents, in conjunction, inevitably, with other factors; indeed, they may form the basis for relatively stable political action groups or come under the influence of state or other political actors. Other sorts of publics may take the form of momentary "flash mobs," political movements, fan groups, neighborhood associations, charitable donor networks, diasporic "imagined communities," dispersed activity-, faith-, or interest-based groups, or simply spectators whose flickering attention, like that of the strolling flaneur of nineteenth-century Paris, is momentarily drawn by whatever passes before them. Indeed, in a kind of reverse interpellation, publics today frequently constitute themselves as such *in anticipation* of being seen—by others or by themselves—as media images. This act of prefiguration is an increasingly crucial component of politics not only at a broad national and international scale but also within the dynamics of much more local aspirations and designs. What Jodi Dean refers to as "publicity" is predicated on the desire to imagine oneself as a "celebrity subject." This "drive to be known, and the presumption that what matters is what is known, provides a different economy of subjectivization, one in which the technocultural subject is configured as a celebrity.... Much ink has been spilled lamenting the effects of the surveillance society but relatively little on the enjoyments that may accompany the sense *that one is known, that people know who we are, that we are somebody.*"[81] This claim is echoed in Ernst van Alphen's argument that technological innovations such as the webcam have prefigured a shift and a consequent release of affect, from the voyeurism of passive image consumption to a "more active attitude of self-positioning" in the exhibitionistic impulses of self-display.

If for Warner the "mere attention" of an audience is sufficient to consti-tute it as a public,[82] examples such as these suggest that analytical attention should also be paid to the intensity or direction of affective engagement of a public with its constitutive image/text. This is especially true in the context of images' cross-cultural movement. "Images that move are poly-vocal," Larkin (chapter 9) acknowledges, but for images to move across cultural differences, they must be both accessible and legible: "Circulation is not an automatic reflex but something that must be made to happen." As McKenzie Wark puts it, "the trouble starts when one opens a vector between cultures which are not usually in communication with each other and taps the affective responses of peoples one knows only through other images, transmitted along other media vectors. The audience has to decide whether to read the image in terms of 'our' frame of reference, or in the frame of what we know about the other."[83]

This movement depends not only on material and technological infra-structures of visibility and circulation but also on those affective and semi-otic engagements crucial to their relative "stickiness" or slipperiness in a particular context. What Larkin (chapter 9) refers to as the "uptake" or reception of particular media forms is contingent on the intensity of desire they face, which can "range from mere attention to full immersion." But desire is not merely the response to a visceral, affective shock that draws or holds the attention; it also depends on recognition—the discovery of some (imagined, perceived, even utterly mistaken) points of contact or commen-surability between the image and its audience(s). These can be thematic or stylistic; they may be parsed according to the intention of the producer or reframed in terms of local meanings and sentiments. They may be taken up as familiar symbols or reinvested with the currency of foreignness. The central issue here is thus not so much how images move but how they move *us*: in fragile and fitful engagements of desire shaped by the (im)possibili-ties of translatability and equivalence.

We are certainly not the first to look at images that move: from transport art—images that whiz by on buses and trucks or, more slowly, rickshaws—to the metaphorical conceptualization of images as migrants, ill at ease and maladjusted within novel environments; from the elaborate cultural produc-tion involving complicated efforts of translation, curatorial interventions, exhibition catalogs, privileged collectors, museums, and the like, to the appropriation of foreign or outsider images for local purposes. All of these instances of the visual continuum require different ways of highlighting and addressing the problematics of images in motion.[84] We have empha-sized the often considerable work involved in getting images to move and to stay put, the unpredictable passions that images may provoke or address, the multifarious ways that images move and in the process move us, their anticipated and unexpected audiences. We have foregrounded the necessary processes of uptake, enframement, and "stickiness" that abet, hinder, or slow such movement. Throughout, we have endeavored to keep the image in view—even in those instances, from *No Show* to the invoked but unreproduced death photos of Osama bin Laden, when it is absent, obliquely invoked, or merely anticipated. The chapters in this volume represent a range of possible ways to trace the tangled paths of images' travels and returns, to unfold their effects and aftereffects, and to scan the diverse and variable publics—fixed or ephemeral, situated or dispersed—that these moving images call into being.

Notes

1. Pavel Gubchevsky, in Alexander Adramovitch and Daniil Granin, *Leningrad Nine Hundred Days under Siege*, cited in Melvin Moti, *No Show* (Leiden: Mostert Leiden Press, 2004), 34.

2. Mieke Bal, personal communication to P. Spyer (2004).

3. Moti, *No Show*, 44.

4. James Simpson, *Under the Hammer* (Oxford, UK: Oxford University Press, 2010).

5. Vera Miliutina was a graphic artist who was among those Leningrad artists who produced sketches of The Hermitage under Siege. See http://www.hermitagemuseum .org/html_En/05/hm5_3_3_03.html (accessed December 5, 2011). See also S. Varshavsky and B. Rest, *The Hermitage during the War of 1941–1945*, trans. Arthur Shkarovsky-Raffe (St. Petersburg: Slavia, 1995).

6. Moti, *No Show*, 43

7. Mieke Bal, "Invisible Art, Hypervisibility, and the Aesthetics of Everyday Life," in *Nichts/Nothing*, ed. Martina Weinhart and Max Hollein (Frankfurt: Schirn Kunsthalle, 2006), 81–104.

8. Arjun Appadurai, *Modernity at Large: Cultural Dimensions of Globalization* (Minneapolis: University of Minnesota Press, 1996), 4.

9. Jay David Bolter and Richard Grusin, *Remediation: Understanding New Media* (Cambridge, MA: MIT Press, 1999).

10. Appadurai, *Modernity at Large*, 5.

11. Michael Warner, *Publics and Counterpublics* (New York: Zone Books, 2002).

12. On the concept of "refraction," see Karen Strassler, *Refracted Visions: Popular Photography and National Modernity in Java* (Durham, NC: Duke University Press, 2010), 23.

13. Ulf Hannerz, *Transnational Connections, Culture, People, Places* (New York: Routledge, 2002, 11).

14. See Wendy Hui Kyong Chun and Thomas Keenan, eds., *New Media, Old Media* (New York: Routledge, 2006).

15. Walter Benjamin, "A Little History of Photography," *Walter Benjamin: Selected Writings*, vol. 2, *1927–1934*, ed. Michael W. Jennings, Gary Smith, and Howard Eiland (Cambridge, MA: Belknap Press of Harvard University Press, 1999), 507–530.

16. Ibid., 527.

17. Jill Bennett, *Empathic Vision: Affect, Trauma, and Contemporary Art* (Stanford, CA: Stanford University Press, 2005), 7. Here Bennett is paraphrasing Gilles Deleuze, *Proust and Signs* (Minneapolis: University of Minnesota Press, 2004).

18. The notion of the "stickiness" of certain images comes from Alfred Gell, *Art and Agency* (Oxford, UK: Clarendon Press, 1998), 80 and 86; and Wyatt MacGaffey, "Astonishment and Stickiness in Kongo Art," *Res: Anthropology and Aesthetics* 39 (2001): 145–146. Both of these are applications of the influential notion of "catchiness" developed by Dan Sperber. Barry Flood brought the concept to our attention in discussions at the SAR advanced seminar.

19. W. J. T. Mitchell, *Picture Theory* (Chicago: University of Chicago Press, 1994), 2. See also W. J. T. Mitchell, *Cloning Terror: The War of Images, 9/11 to the Present* (Chicago: University of Chicago Press, 2011), especially 69–70.

20. Mitchell, *Picture Theory*, 13.

21. See L. G. Taylor, "Iconophobia: How Anthropology Lost It at the Movies," *Transition* 69 (1996): 64–88.

22. A comprehensive list of anthropological works addressing these various issues would far exceed the space we have here, but a sample of important recent works might include Joseph Dumit, *Picturing Personhood: Brain Scans and Biomedical Identity* (Princeton, NJ: Princeton University Press, 2003); Deborah Poole, "An Excess of Description: Ethnography, Race and Visual Technologies," *Annual Review of Anthropology* 34 (2005): 159–170; Alison Griffiths, *Wondrous Difference: Cinema, Anthropology and Turn-of-the-Century Visual Culture* (New York: Columbia University Press, 2001); Christopher Pinney, *Photography and Anthropology* (London: Reaktion, 2011); Fred R. Myers, *Painting Culture: The Making of an Aboriginal High Art* (Durham, NC: Duke University Press, 2002); George Marcus and Fred Myers, eds., *The Traffic in Culture: Refiguring Art and Anthropology* (Berkeley: University of California Press, 1995); Faye D. Ginsburg, Lila Abu-Lughod, and Brian Larkin, eds., *Media Worlds* (Berkeley: University of California Press, 2002); Raminder Kaur and William Mazzarella, eds., *Censorship in South Asia: Cultural Regulation from Sedition to Seduction* (Bloomington: Indiana University Press, 2009); Andrew Causey, *Hard Bargaining in Sumatra: Western Travelers and Toba Bataks in the Marketplace of Souvenirs* (Honolulu: University of Hawaii Press, 2003); David MacDougall, *The Corporeal Image: Film, Ethnography and the Senses* (Princeton, NJ:

Princeton University Press, 2005); Karen Strassler, *Refracted Visions* (Durham, NC: Duke University Press, 2010); Molly Mullins, *Culture in the Marketplace* (Durham, NC: Duke University Press, 2001). On the use of photographic images to supplement ethnographic texts, see Philippe Bourgois and Jeffrey Schonberg, *Righteous Dopefiend* (Berkeley: University of California Press, 2009); and Kathleen Stewart, *A Space on the Side of the Road: Cultural Poetics in an "Other" America* (Princeton, NJ: Princeton University Press, 1996).

23. Mitchell, *Picture Theory*, 13.

24. Ibid., 1–4. The report referred to here is Lynne V. Cheney, *Humanities in America: A Report to the President, the Congress, and the American People* (Washington, DC: National Endowment for the Humanities, 1988).

25. Kajri Jain, *Gods in the Bazaar: The Economies of Indian Calendar Art* (Durham, NC: Duke University Press, 2007), 27.

26. Ibid., 12.

27. Ibid., 20.

28. Christopher Pinney, "Four Types of Visual Culture," in *Handbook of Material Culture*, ed. Chris Tilley et al. (London: Sage Publications, 2006), 135. See also W. J. T. Mitchell, "There Are No Visual Media," *Journal of Visual Culture* 4, no. 2 (2005): 257–266.

29. For extended reflections on this issue, see Hans Belting, *An Anthropology of Images: Picture, Medium, Body*, trans. Thomas Dunlap (Princeton, NJ: Princeton University Press, 2011); W. J. T. Mitchell, *Iconology* (Chicago: University of Chicago Press, 1986), 7–46.

30. Bruno Latour and Peter Weibel, eds., *Iconoclash: Beyond the Image Wars in Science, Religion and Art* (Cambridge, MA: MIT Press, 2002), 14.

31. See Elizabeth Bumiller, "We Have Met the Enemy and He Is Powerpoint," *New York Times*, April 26, 2010, http://www.nytimes.com/2010/04/27/world/27powerpoint .html?np&_r=0 (accessed December 6, 2011).

32. See Kenneth M. George, *Picturing Islam* (Hoboken, NJ: Wiley-Blackwell, 2010); and "Signature Work: Bandung 1994," *Ethnos* 64, no. 2 (1999): 212–231.

33. MASS MoCA, *Invisible: Art at the Edge of Perception*, exhibition, Massachusetts Museum of Contemporary Art, North Adams, MA, February–June 2010. The text of the exhibition folder notes how "moments of visual quiet can take on unexpected power... amidst a world saturated with a relentless stream of images and stimuli." See also Ralph Rugoff, *A Brief History of Invisible Art*, catalog published in conjunction with the exhibition *A Brief History of InVisible Art* (San Francisco: California College of the Arts, 2005), 7.

34. Flood, personal communication (2008).

35. Mitchell, *Iconology*, 9–14; see also Jain, *Gods in the Bazaar*, 14–16, on postcolonial denigrations of "vernacular" art.

36. See Patricia Spyer, ed., *Border Fetishisms: Material Objects in Unstable Spaces* (London: Routledge, 1998).

37. Kenneth M. George, "Ethics, Iconoclasm and Qur'anic Art in Indonesia," *Cultural Anthropology* 24, no. 4 (2009): 589–621.

38. Flood, chapter 2 in this volume.

39. For a subtle reading of premodern relations between allegedly monolithic, static, and antagonistic "Hindus" and "Muslims" in which forms of circulation and the transactions of material things figure centrally, see Finbarr Barry Flood, *Objects of Translation: Material Culture and Medieval "Hindu-Muslim" Encounter* (Princeton, NJ: Princeton University Press, 2009).

40. Simpson, *Under the Hammer*, 11–12.

41. Flood, chapter 2 in this volume.

42. Sayed Rahmatullah Hashimi, cited in Finbarr Barry Flood, "Between Cult and Culture: Bamiyan, Islamic Iconoclasm and the Museum," *Art Bulletin* 84, no. 4 (2002): 653.

43. Jain, *Gods in the Bazaar*, 218–219.

44. PBS, "America Remembers 911," Jay Ruesler video, 9/11 "Video Quilt" multimedia project, http://www.pbs.org/newshour/multimedia/september-11 -responses/ (accessed September 12, 2011).

45. W. J. T. Mitchell, *What Do Pictures Want? The Lives and Loves of Images* (Chicago: University of Chicago Press, 2006).

46. Pierre Bourdieu et al., *Un Art Moyen: Essai sur les Usages Sociaux de la Photographie*, 2nd ed. (1965; Paris: Les Éditions de Minuit, 2007) (cited by Moore, chapter 5 in this volume).

47. We take the term "riot porn" from Maple Rasza, "'Riot Porn': Protest Video and the Production of Unruly Political Subjects" (unpublished ms.). On atrocity photographs, see Judith Butler, "Torture, Photography, and the Limits of the Secular" (Distinguished Lecture, The Center for Religion and Media, New York University, October 26, 2006); and *Frames of War: When Is Life Grievable?* (London: Verso, 2009), especially "Torture and the Ethics of Photography: Thinking with Sontag," 63–100. See also Barbie Zelizer, *Remembering to Forget: Holocaust Memory through the Camera's Eye* (Chicago: University of Chicago Press, 2000).

48. Jacques Derrida, *The Truth in Painting*, trans. Geoff Bennington and Ian McLeod (Chicago: University of Chicago Press, 1987), 18.

49. Jain, *Gods in the Bazaar*, 16–17.

50. The phrase "no caption needed" is taken from the study of "iconic photographs" by Robert Hariman and John L. Lucaites, *No Caption Needed* (Chicago: University of Chicago Press, 2007). On the "anchorage" achieved by the linguistic

message accompanying an image, see Roland Barthes, "Rhetoric of the Image," in *Image, Music, Text,* ed. and trans. Stephen Heath (1964; New York: Hill and Wang, 1977), 32–51.

51. See Bolter and Grusin, *Remediation,* especially 21–50.

52. Patricia Spyer, "Blind Faith: Painting Christianity in Postconflict Ambon," special issue, *Social Text* 96, vol. 26, no. 3 (2008): 11–37.

53. Christopher Pinney, *"Photos of the Gods": The Printed Image and Political Struggle in India* (London: Reaktion, 2004), 8. See also Christopher Pinney, "Introduction:…'How the Other Half…,'" in *Photography's Other Histories,* ed. Christopher Pinney and Nicholas Peterson (Durham, NC: Duke University Press, 2003), 1–14.

54. Michael Casey, *Che's Afterlife: The Legacy of an Image* (New York: Vintage Books, 2009), 120.

55. Jerry Beegan, cited in Casey, *Che's Afterlife,* 124–125.

56. Patricia Spyer, "Orphaned Landscapes: Religion, Violence, and Visuality in Post-Suharto Indonesia," manuscript in progress.

57. Lisa Cartwright and Stephen Mandiberg, "Obama and Shepherd Fairey: The Copy and Political Iconography in the Age of the Demake," *Journal of Visual Culture* 8 (August 2009): 174. We owe this specific point, as well as the instance of the *HOPE* poster, to Lindsey Lodhie, from an unpublished paper submitted in ANTH 2635, "Image/Media/Publics," at Harvard, Fall 2009.

58. Cartright and Mandiberg, "Obama and Shepherd Fairey," 174. On "resonant images," see Patricia Holland, *Picturing Childhood: The Myth of the Child in Popular Imagery* (London: I. B. Tauris, 2004), 3.

59. Walter Benjamin, "The Work of Art in the Age of Its Technological Reproducibility," 3rd version, *Walter Benjamin: Selected Writings,* vol. 4, *1938–1940,* ed. Howard Eiland and Michael W. Jennings (Cambridge, MA: Belknap Press of Harvard University Press, 2003), 253–283.

60. Larkin, chapter 9 of this volume.

61. On "media vectors," see McKenzie Wark, "The Weird Global Media Event and the Tactical Intellectual," in Chun and Keenan, *New Media, Old Media,* 265–276, esp. 268–269.

62. Raymond Williams, *Television: Technology and Cultural Form,* 3rd ed. (New York: Routledge, 2003), 16. Cited in Kristin Roth-Ey, *Moscow Prime Time* (Ithaca, NY: Cornell University Press, 2011), 178. The complete passage, which Roth-Ey does not quote, continues: "This predestination, however, when closely examined, proves to be no more than a set of particular social decisions, in particular circumstances, which were then so widely if imperfectly ratified that it is now difficult to see them as decisions rather than as (retrospectively) inevitable results."

63. Roth-Ey, *Moscow Prime Time*, 209.

64. Susan Sontag, *On Photography* (New York: Picador, 2001).

65. See Tom Gunning, "Phantom Images and Modern Manifestations," in *Fugitive Images: From Photography to Video*, ed. Patrice Petro (Bloomington: Indiana University Press, 1995), 42–71; Clément Chéroux, *The Perfect Medium* (New Haven, CT: Yale University Press, 2005).

66. A recent exploration of the relation between truth and photography is Errol Morris, *Believing Is Seeing: Observations on the Mysteries of Photography* (New York: Penguin, 2011).

67. On the notion of *plateau*, see Gilles Deleuze and Felix Guattari, *A Thousand Plateaus: Capitalism and Schizophrenia*, trans. Brian Massumi (Minneapolis: University of Minnesota Press, 1987). See also Rafael Sánchez, "Intimate Publicities: Retreating the Politico-Theological in the Chávez Regime in Venezuela," in *Political Theologies: Globalization and Post-Secular Reason*, ed. Lawrence Sullivan and Hent de Vries (New York: Fordham University Press, 2006), 401–426.

68. On the "lonelygirl15" scandal, in which a wildly popular online video "diary" turned out to be a scripted drama, see Joshua Davis, "The Secret World of lonelygirl15," *Wired Magazine* 14, no. 12 (December 2006): 232–239. Perhaps the most famous of the many "owlcam" and wildlife/zoo observation sites is the "owlbox" of barn owls Molly and McGee (http://www.ustream.tv/theowlbox), which, on December 7, 2011, claimed to have had more than twenty-one million live views. In addition to the live streaming site, Molly the Owl has her own Facebook fan page (http://www.facebook.com/mollytheowl), blog (http://mollysbox.wordpress.com/), and Twitter account, in addition to books, a documentary DVD, and a range of other "Molly-endorsed" merchandise.

69. Edward Conlon, "Paying Attention," *New Yorker*, September 12, 2011, http://www.newyorker.com/talk/2011/09/12/110912ta_talk_conlon (accessed February 10, 2012).

70. Melissa Gregg and Gregory J. Seigworth, "An Inventory of Shimmers," in *The Affect Reader*, ed. Melissa Gregg and Gregory J. Seigworth (Durham, NC: Duke University Press, 2010), 1.

71. Deleuze, *Proust and Signs*, 161; on the "encountered sign," see also Bennett, *Empathic Vision*, 7–8.

72. Gregg and Seigworth, "Inventory of Shimmers," 1.

73. On the S-21/Tuol Sleng photographs, see Judy Ledgerwood, "The Cambodian Tuol Sleng Museum of Genocidal Crimes: National Narrative," in *Genocide, Collective Violence, and Popular Memory: The Politics of Remembrance in the Twentieth Century*, ed. David E. Lorey and William H. Beezley (Wilmington, DE: Scholarly Resources, 2002),

103–122; Lindsay French, "Exhibiting Terror," in *Truth Claims: Representation and Human Rights*, ed. Mark Philip Bradley and Patrice Petro (New Brunswick, NJ: Rutgers University Press, 2002), 131–156. Thanks to Sharon Kim for these references.

74. On the "situation room photographs," see Ken Johnson, "Situation: Ambiguous," *New York Times*, May 8, 2011, http://www.nytimes.com/2011/05/08 /weekinreview/08johnson.html?scp=4&sq=situation+room+photo&st=nyt (accessed December 7, 2011); David Brooks and Gail Collins, "The Power in a Photo," *New York Times*, May 4, 2011, http://opinionator.blogs.nytimes.com/2011/05/04/the-power-in-a -photo/?ref=politics (accessed December 7, 2011).

75. Warner, *Publics and Counterpublics*, 65–124.

76. Louis Althusser, "Ideology and Ideological State Apparatuses," in *Lenin and Philosophy and Other Essays* (New York: Monthly Review Press, 1971), 127–186.

77. Warner, *Publics and Counterpublics*, 113–114.

78. A notable recent exception is Hariman and Lucaites's *No Caption Needed*, which accords visual imagery, especially iconic photographs, a central role in the constitution of liberal democratic public culture.

79. Mitchell, "No Visual Media," 257–266.

80. On the realist conventions of cyberporn, see Wendy Chun, *Control and Freedom: Power and Paranoia in the Age of Fiber Optics* (Cambridge, MA: MIT Press, 2006), 77–127; on computer animation and "transparent immediacy," see Bolter and Grusin, *Remediation*; Lev Manovich, *The Language of New Media* (Cambridge, MA: MIT Press, 2002).

81. Jodi Dean, *Publicity's Secret: How Technoculture Capitalizes on Democracy* (Ithaca, NY: Cornell University Press, 2002), 13.

82. Warner, *Publics and Counterpublics*, 87

83. McKenzie Wark, *Virtual Geography: Living with Global Media Events* (Bloomington: Indiana University Press, 1994), 5.

84. A few notable examples include Kuntala Lahiri-Dutt and David J. Williams, *Moving Pictures: Rickshaw Art of Bangladesh* (Ahmedabad, India: Mapin Publishing), 2010; Petra Stegmann and Peter Seel, eds., *Migrating Images. Producing–Reading–Transporting– Translating* (Berlin: House of World Cultures, 2004); Fred R. Myers, *Painting Culture: The Making of an Aboriginal High Art* (Durham, NC: Duke University Press, 2002).

2

Inciting Modernity?

Images, Alterities, and the Contexts of "Cartoon Wars"

Finbarr Barry Flood

Caricature is by its nature an art of exclusion on the one hand and excess on the other.

—Howarth, "Jewish Art and the Fear of the Image"

On September 30, 2005, the conservative Danish newspaper *Jyllands-Posten* (Jutland Post) published an article entitled "The Face of Muhammad" (Muhammeds ansigt) accompanied by twelve specially commissioned cartoons depicting or referring to the Prophet Muhammad (d. 632 CE). Two weeks previously, the Danish daily *Politiken* had run an article linking the difficulties experienced by the Danish author Kåre Bluitgen in trying to find an artist willing to illustrate his book on the life of the Prophet Muhammad with criticism of European self-censorship when it came to the representation of Islam. It was, an editorial in the *Jyllands-Posten* explained, in response to the phenomenon identified by *Politiken* that the cartoons were commissioned.

Attempts by offended Danish Muslims to seek redress against the *Jyllands-Posten* by invoking those sections of Denmark's criminal code dealing with blasphemy and incitement based on ethnicity, color, faith, or race failed. On December 6 a Danish Muslim delegation presented a forty-three-page dossier containing the *Jyllands-Posten* cartoons, along with others faxed to Muslim groups in Denmark, to the Organization of the Islamic Conference (an organization founded in 1969 after an arson attack on the Aqsa Mosque in Jerusalem), leading to a formal condemnation of the "desecration of the image" of the Prophet. By early 2006, demonstrations against the publication of the cartoons had taken place from London to Jakarta. In the following months the global news media reproduced the offending images, provoking more protests and further reproductions throughout Europe, Africa, Asia, America, and Australasia.[1]

By the time the initial fallout from the controversy had subsided, somewhere between fifty and three hundred were dead; demonstrators in London had been jailed for soliciting murder; ministers of the Italian, Libyan, and Lebanese governments had been forced to resign; newspaper editors in Algeria, Belarus, Jordan, and Yemen had been jailed; Scandinavian consulates in Beirut, Damascus, and Tehran had been damaged or destroyed; and the Danish economy had suffered the effects of an international boycott. As of spring 2008 the controversy surrounding the cartoon controversy had still not abated. On February 13, 2008, at least seventeen Danish dailies, along with others in Sweden, the Netherlands, and Spain, reprinted the most controversial of the cartoons—a caricature reminiscent of the antianarchist propaganda of an earlier century, depicting a bearded figure wearing a turban in the form of a lighted grenade inscribed with the *shahāda* (the Muslim profession of faith)—in response to reports of a plot to assassinate its creator, the cartoonist Kurt Westergaard.[2] This reinvestment of Westergaard's image prompted further demonstrations in Africa, the Middle East, and South Asia and the release of an audiotape apparently recorded by Osama bin Laden that threatened the European Union with unspecified retribution for the republication of the insulting drawings (*al-rusūm al-musī'a*), which he attributed to a new crusade led by the pope.[3]

If familiarity has bred a certain cynicism about the power of images, the unlikely vehemence with which the cartoon controversy erupted across the globe poses significant questions about the ethics, politics, and polemics of the visual in an era of mass media and transregional information flows. To quote Ulf Hannerz's characterization of the global controversy provoked by Salman Rushdie's *Satanic Verses* (1988), the cartoon controversy appeared "to be taking place everywhere, and nowhere in particular," a quality enhanced by the advent of cybertechnologies unavailable to protagonists in the earlier drama.[4] In both the Rushdie affair and the cartoon controversy, Muslims were accused of both too leaden and too literal a notion of representation. As a debate concerning images and the visual, however, the recent controversy regarding the Danish caricatures (and their progeny) raised a number of questions irrelevant to Rushdie's textual representations of the Prophet. Although the limits of free speech were identified with the culturally determined boundaries of imaging, the visual is not language, and images are neither speech nor writing, as W. J. T.

FIGURE 2.1

Image problem. *Cox and Forkum Editorial Cartoons, January 31, 2006. Reproduced with permission of Allen Forkum.*

Mitchell reminds us. In this sense the outrage generated by the Danish cartoons bears closer comparison to controversies concerning blasphemy that erupted around images such as Andres Serrano's *Piss Christ* (1989) and Chris Ofili's *Holy Virgin Mary* (1998). However, as Mitchell notes, in the cases of Serrano and Ofili it was the particular specimen rather than the species (crucifixion scenes, depictions of the Virgin) that offended, whereas in the case of the Danish cartoons both were at issue.[5]

This was ostensibly a debate not only about the content or materials of representation but also about the permissibility of depiction and reproduction. The iconography of the caricatures addressed Islam's "image problem," its deficient relationship to the shibboleths of liberal secularism, but their production and dissemination engaged the perceived problem of the image in Islam. One of the original *Jyllands-Posten* cartoons drew (quite literally) a relationship between the visibility of women in Islam and the representability of the Prophet. This relationship was engaged by many subsequent meta-images, among them a cartoon by Cox and Forkum in which the representatives of a public relations (PR) firm confront the

Prophet with his own image (à la Westergaard) alongside a list of Islam's civilizational deficiencies, including "fear of Western culture and pictures of piglet" (figure 2.1).

Through the mapping of differing ontologies of the visual onto apparently incommensurate notions of the cultural, the Danish cartoons and some of the meta-images that they inspired assumed a mythic status (in a Barthesian sense).[6] This mythic status was performative, asserted and constituted by the reproduction and dissemination of the cartoons as an act of resistance to censorious Muslims and their liberal allies. The performative quality ascribed to circulation, its perpetuation of offense as both cause and effect, led to further disputes about (re)mediation and reproduction. The circulation of the cartoons by means of description rather than republication distinguished most of the US media from their European counterparts, some of whom reproduced them at a remove, illustrated by images of readers holding open the offending pages of newspapers that had published the drawings.[7] However, Algerian, Jordanian, and Yemeni print media reproduced the images as they had appeared in *Jyllands-Posten*, and the *Yemen Observer* (an English-language, biweekly publication) reproduced them literally under erasure, marked by a large X. The editors of these publications were prosecuted, fueling debate about differential access to the offending images in the Islamic world and further protests.[8]

Rhetorically at least, creation and consumption of the cartoons generated a public defined by its opposition to limits on the production, circulation, or consumption of images, in difference to those inhibited by the persistence of archaic taboos on image-making. In the text that accompanied the original cartoons, Flemming Rose, the editor of *Jyllands-Posten*, cast the obscure Danish daily as the savior of a secular liberalism indexed by the free circulation of religious caricature, a theme subsequently embraced and enlarged in apocalyptic commentaries on the creeping "Islamicization" of Europe:

> The modern, *secular* society is rejected by some Muslims. They demand a special position, insisting on special consideration of their own religious feelings. It is incompatible with contemporary democracy and freedom of speech, where you must be ready to put up with insults, mockery and ridicule. It is certainly not always attractive and nice to look at, and it does not mean that religious feelings should be made fun of at any price, but that is of minor importance in the present context.... We are on our way to a slippery slope where no-one can tell how the self-censorship will end.

That is why *Morgenavisen Jyllands-Posten* has invited members of the Danish editorial cartoonists union to draw Muhammad as they see him.[9]

Perceived Muslim taboos on figuration were thus yoked to a burgeoning discourse on the threat posed by the "Islamicization" of contemporary European life, pitting, according to one commentator, "the Western democratic assertion of a right to free speech and press freedom" against "the Islamic dictum against the representation of the Prophet Muhammad."[10] In effect the limits of both secularism and modernity were mapped onto the limits of representation so that a reticence about images and imaging functioned as a sign of radical alterity, facilitating contrasts between the "robust importance of taboo in Muslim life" and the rationalism that informed the lives of those who had transcended primitive proscriptions.[11]

Pitting a mystical fetishization of the image against a postmodern cynicism emblematized by the caricature as simulacrum, what *appeared* to be at stake in the controversy was not only the affective potential of caricature but also incommensurate notions of signification.[12] On the one side stood those who, thanks to the Protestant Reformation and the triumph of Enlightenment values, acknowledged the autonomy of the image, the contingent nature of the relationship between signifier and signified. On the other stood those who apparently persisted in eliding the distinction between the two, affording a quasimagical potency to the image in the process. Both propositions are highly suspect and merit much closer attention than they have received to date.[13] My aim here, however, is not to explore theories of signification, despite their evident relevance, but rather the way in which both images and discourses concerning them can be mobilized to deconstruct, define, and reconfigure boundaries of various sorts, constituting publics and counterpublics in the process.

The centrality of images to the cartoon controversy illustrates what Mahmood Mamdani has identified as the culturalization of contemporary debates about commensuration,[14] but the articulation of notions of alterity and assimilation around (apparently) incommensurate theories of the image has a much longer European history. Reified in nineteenth-century Central European scholarship as the *Bilderverbot* (prohibition on images), the "image question" has been historically central to etic representations of both Judaism and Islam instrumentalized in debates about European identity. One way of making sense of the cartoon controversy, therefore, is as a contemporary reinvestment of established discourses concerning the Bilderverbot, a performative assertion of particular epistemologies and

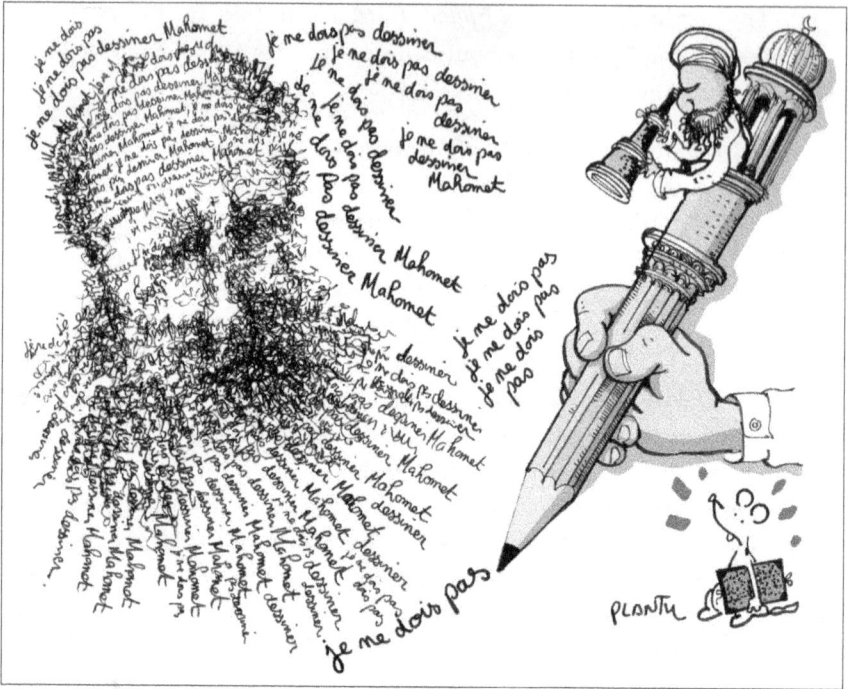

FIGURE 2.2

"Je ne dois pas dessiner Mahomet" by Plantu, Le Monde, *February 3, 2006. Reproduced with permission of the artist.*

ontologies of the visual in the face of a perceived challenge posed by the increasing mobility of both images and individuals.

PROPHETS AND PROFANATION

At the height of the cartoon controversy, an article posted on the website of the BBC explained that "Islamic tradition, or Hadith, the stories of the words and actions of Muhammad and his Companions, explicitly prohibits images of Allah, Muhammad and all the major prophets of the Christian and Jewish traditions."[15] The claim is erroneous, but illustrates a profound confusion as to the source of the anxieties raised by the publication of the Danish cartoons in Euro-American reportage on the episode, even when focused on the *act* rather than on the content or context of representation. The resulting ambiguity was reflected in several meta-commentaries that related the boundaries at stake to the ontological tensions between textual and visual depiction. In February 2006, for example, a Plantu cartoon published on the front page of *Le Monde* showed a bearded face in the process of realization, composed of repetitions of the phrase "Je ne dois

IS THIS DEPICTION OF THE PROPHET MUHAMMAD OFFENSIVE?

FIGURE 2.3
"Is this depiction of the Prophet Muhammad offensive?" by Bruce Beattie, Daytona Beach News-Journal, *February 4, 2006. Reproduced with permission of Bruce Beattie and Creators Syndicate, Inc.*

pas dessiner Mahomet" (I must not draw Muhammad), the cartoonist's work closely observed by a bearded, turbaned figure perched in a minaret emerging from the upper part of his pencil (figure 2.2).

Other cartoonists explored the boundaries as a commonsense question of cognition or degree, recalling a milestone of modern caricature, Philipon's famous 1832 quadripartite image in which King Louis-Philippe metamorphosed into a pear.[16] At the same time as Plantu's cartoon appeared, Bruce Beattie published a tentatively delineated profile of a turbaned, bearded figure with no internal features, accompanied by the rhetorical question "Is this depiction of the Prophet Muhammad offensive?" (figure 2.3)

Contrary to what many commentators assumed, the injunction against prophetic representation is found neither in the Qur'an (which has little to say on the question of representation) nor in the hadith (which have quite a lot to say on the question of images in general but little on the subject of imaging prophets in particular). The hadith evince hostility to the representation of all animate beings (the distinction between animate and non-animate being predicated on the potential to possess *rūḥ*, spirit or breath) in specific contexts.[17] Prophets, as animate beings, are clearly included in the prohibition but are not explicitly mentioned. In addition, accounts of the Muslim conquest of Mecca in 630 CE and the subsequent Islamicization of its shrines indicate an apparent ambivalence toward the representation of prophets, detailing how the Prophet Muhammad ordered images of Ibrahim/Abraham painted in the interior of the Ka'ba to be effaced, but he covered depictions of Jesus and Mary with his hands, guaranteeing their protection.[18] The difference in attitude to the images of the two prophets related to their iconographic content: Ibrahim was depicted with divining arrows, the use of which is forbidden in Islam, whereas Jesus appeared in an innocuous manner, seated as a child on the lap of his mother.

Despite the proscriptions of the Sunna, iconic representations of the Prophet were on occasion produced in the Islamic world. The earliest extant anthropomorphic representation of the Prophet that has been identified with certainty occurs in an illustrated Persian epic produced in Anatolia around 1250 CE, although it is possible that earlier examples once existed.[19] Scattered textual references to earlier portraits of the Prophet Muhammad and his predecessors tend to occur in relation to the Christians of Byzantium.[20] This association of the Prophet's image with Byzantine (*rūmī*) artistry reflects its acknowledged excellence (and perhaps also the existence of Byzantine illustrated prophet books), displacing the act of representation onto Christian artists while asserting Christian witness to the truth of the prophetic mission.

From the fourteenth century onward, depictions of the Prophet produced in the Ilkhanid, Timurid, Safavid, and Ottoman courts of Central Asia, Iran, and Turkey survive, many of them preserved in American and European museum collections. In these images the face of the Prophet is sometimes, but not always, veiled, obscured by light, or, more rarely, inscribed with a type of grid that evokes his variant names, denotations of specific qualities.[21] Complementing the anthropomorphic depictions that it accompanies, this calligraphic evocation of the Prophet and his qualities reminds us that the image need be neither material nor mimetic. The most celebrated representation of Muhammad, the *ḥilya*, was in fact a description of his person and character, transmitted verbally by those who knew him, and was committed to writing following his death.[22] The mental image of the Prophet conjured by the verbal representations textualized in the *ḥilya* is, itself, placed under erasure by their peculiar nature, narrative rather than descriptive, and characterized by dialectical negations (for example, "he was neither too short nor too tall" and "his hair was neither too short nor too curly") rather than direct propositions. The private, mental visualizations promoted by these narrations of the Prophet's person stand in opposition to the public material images proscribed by the Sunna. The textualized traces of these verbal narrations of the Prophet's appearance were, however, sometimes afforded a quasi-iconic status. Starting in the seventeenth century, for example, Ottoman artists produced elaborate spatial arrangements of the calligraphed text composing the ḥilya. In some of these, the script formed iconic representations of objects associated with the Prophet, imbuing the representation with what Valérie Gonzalez (following Husserl) has described as "a double ontology," a Gestalt that oscillates between two modes of depiction, "linguistic/conceptual and visual/corporeal."[23]

In the twentieth century, controversies about the representation of the Prophet in the Islamic world often were related to the deployment and reception of new media, most obviously cinema. As early as 1926 the authorities of Al-Azhar University in Cairo, one of the most important centers of Sunni jurisprudence, issued a *fatwa* emphasizing that the representation of the Prophet was forbidden in Islam, in response to plans for a Turkish film on early Islam. In 1930 this prohibition was enshrined in Egyptian law and extended, in 1986, to all biblical figures and prophets. An ingenious solution to the prohibition was devised in Mustafa Akkad's 1976 film, *Al-Risāla* (The Message), which won the approval of the *'ulamā'* (religious authorities) of Al-Azhar.[24] In Akkad's film the Prophet is never depicted. Rather, as Ella Shohat notes, "the spectator is...placed within the subjective point of view of Muhammad himself," in effect producing the viewer as the Prophet's uncanny double, an eventuality that may have informed the negative reception of the film in some quarters.[25] In its attempt to develop a mode of visual representation that conforms to the spirit of the Sunna, this device is comparable to the depiction of the Prophet under erasure in early modern manuscripts. Similar negotiations can be found in contemporary images produced by and for observant Muslims, among them the cartoon strips produced as pedagogical tools by Islamic organizations in Egypt and Turkey in which the faces of prophets are usually obscured by a carefully orchestrated economy of gesture or by the light of prophecy emanating from their person (plate 1).[26]

The deployment of these devices reminds us that even known iconic representations of the Prophet are hardly lacking in contention. The point is underlined by the defacement of the Prophet's image in several early modern Islamic manuscripts.[27] Although the exact context in which such alterations occurred is unclear, if they were undertaken by pious Muslims concerned about the depiction of the Prophet, this would call into question the widespread assumption that both iconoclasts and iconophiles necessarily elide the distinction between the image and its referent central to modern Euro-American semiotics.

These contentions about prophetic representation were minimized in the anodyne statements about historical precedents for the representation of the Prophet among Muslims that the international news media elicited from museum curators in the United States and Europe during the cartoon controversy. Those seeking historical precedents to illuminate the controversy might, however, have found more germane comparisons not in the artistic production of the Islamic world but in the rich (if largely unexplored) corpus of images of the Prophet found in illustrated English and French encyclopedias and histories of the thirteenth and fourteenth centuries. Unlike Islamic precedents, the relevance of these images lies not in their mere existence but in their iconographic content and the context of their production, both of which highlight the historical centrality of verbal, textual, and visual images of the Prophet to anti-Muslim polemics.[28] Illustrating long-established notions that Islam was a Christian heresy and Muhammad a false prophet whose biography was marked by his deceptive, insincere, and licentious deeds, these medieval images amplify or enhance the vituperative themes of the texts that they accompany. Whereas earlier discussions of Islam were consistent in their depictions of Muslims as inveterate idol haters and iconophobes, in the aftermath of the First Crusade (1096–1099) European representations of Islamic beliefs and practices were marked by the emergence of a contradictory trope: that of Muslims as pathological idolaters offering demonically inspired worship to golden idols of the false prophet Muhammad (plate 2) or to a false Trinity within which he enjoyed preeminence.[29] These foils for the true images of Christianity made use of an established iconography of paganism or inverted the meaning of familiar Christian iconographies. Some explicitly contrasted the sparing use of images by Christians with the idolatrous, image-centered practices of the Muhammad-worshiping Muslims.[30]

In a society in which the illiterate far outnumbered the literate, and that sometimes made use of images in order to communicate the precepts of religion to the uneducated, the didactic value of these images can hardly be doubted. Although it is true that they appear mostly in luxury manuscripts, there are indications that large-scale propaganda images featuring the Prophet and designed to foster crusading zeal also circulated in the crusader states of the Levant and beyond.[31] Like many modern caricatures of Islam, the iconography of these medieval images and the texts that they accompany is marked by a limited number of recurrent themes: demonic inspiration, monstrous deception, and the death and desecration of the Prophet's body through its representation in association with ritually polluting objects, most frequently dogs or pigs.[32] Among the latter is an image of Muhammad in a thirteenth-century copy of the *Chronica majora* of Matthew Paris, which shows the Prophet standing atop a boar (plate 3), illustrating a tale that his death was occasioned by being smothered or devoured postmortem by pigs.[33]

It would be absurd to insist that the genealogy of the Danish cartoons and their progeny lies in the images found in medieval European manuscripts. Nevertheless, the limited iconographies of both attest to the persistence of long-established stereotypes regarding Islam and Muslims and to the dependence of the act of profanation through representation upon a basic knowledge of the tenets of Islam.[34] The interest of Gothic visual polemics lies less in their iconographic details, however, than in their attestation that *both* images and discourses concerning their ontological status and epistemological value in Islam can be and have been mobilized in service of "European" identities defined relationally. From the perspective of the *longue durée*, some of the most striking features of this mobilization have been the inconstancy and instability of Islam's "image problem," despite its historical centrality to etic representations of Muslims. The oscillation of the Prophet between iconoclast and idol underlines the fact that whether as image breakers, image haters, image worshipers, or idolaters, the relationship between Muslims and images in the European imagination has been something of a moveable feast, the ingredients and flavor of which have shifted in accord with the dynamics of contact between Europe and the Islamic world. The only constant is a persistent association between attitudes to images and cultural or religious alterity. There is in fact a demonstrable correlation between historical moments of European angst about either Muslims or images (or both) and the production, modification, or reinvestment of discourses on Islamic aniconism and iconoclasm.[35] Having made this point, in what follows I focus on more recent histories of Islam's "image problem" and on their relevance to the rhetoric of alterity and assimilation that pervaded the cartoon controversy.

PATHOLOGY AND PROTESTANTIZATION

On September 10, 2006, eve of the fifth anniversary of the September 11 atrocities, the *Observer*, a liberal British Sunday newspaper, carried a three-part article by the British novelist Martin Amis. Entitled "The Age of Horrorism," Amis's piece began with a vignette that evoked the proscriptions on images in Islam. In the bazaar outside a mosque in Peshawar, his protagonist finds a stall selling T-shirts bearing the image of Osama bin Laden.

Amis explained, "It is forbidden, in Sunni Islam, to depict the human form, lest it lead to idolatry; but here was Osama's lordly visage, on display and on sale right outside the mosque." The linkage of the proscriptions on images with an iconic sign of Islamist terror highlights the inconsistency and insincerity of belief and believers, providing the prelude to a lengthy, tendentious, and somewhat rambling discussion of the phenomenon of the suicide bomber and contemporary Islamist movements. Toward the end of the same piece, Amis used a simile that linked the sociocultural and psychic threat posed by Islamists to a Euro-American world order with the recent viral epidemics that patterns of global mobility have disseminated throughout the globe: "For quite a time I have felt that Islamism was trying to poison the world. Here was a sign that the poison might take—might mutate like bird flu."[36]

The image question with which Amis began his diatribe and the metaphor of contagion with which he concluded have long been associated in European discourses on Islam. In Islam, as in Judaism, idolatry and idols are sources of pollution and images the vector of potential contamination, associated in the hadith with the unclean dog. In most historical European writings on Islam, however, this trope is inverted so that the rejection of images (manifest as aniconism and/or iconoclasm—the two are often confused) is symptomatic of a contagion with both cultural and religious implications. For Amis, Islamism (an ideology or a movement whose relationship to the religion of Islam is never quite spelled out) has the potential to infect the healthy Euro-American body politic. For earlier observers it was antipathy to images that manifested the infectious potential of Islam most clearly. Hence, the Byzantine historian Theophanes (d. 818 CE) could refer to the emperor Leo III of Byzantium, who initiated the period of Byzantine Iconoclasm in 726, as Saracen-minded (*sarakenophron*), even as a modern scholar of Islam such as Patricia Crone, writing in 1989 of the (much disputed) impact of Islam on the Iconoclast Controversy in Byzantium, could note the ability of the former to make "epidemic what had hitherto been merely endemic in Christianity."[37]

For some modern commentators the question of the image is neither epiphenomenal nor symptomatic. Instead, it forms the core of the infection itself. Perhaps the clearest linkage between proscription and morbidity can be found in Alfred L. Kroeber's "Huxley Memorial Lecture," delivered to the Royal Anthropological Society in London in 1945. Not surprisingly, given the year of its delivery, the "Clash of Civilizations" looms large in Kroeber's text, with Islam springing "Minerva-like full-blown with the life of one man, something as German world-dominance would have sprung with the will of Hitler if it had become realized." Reduction and restriction rather than expansion and enlargement are the cultural hallmarks of Islam, characterized by a catalog of negations that extends to the assumed primary goals of all highly developed civilizations, figuration and mimesis: "Representative art was banned. Purely decorative patterning—the name Arabesque is characteristic—provided only a low-level substitute."[38] As Marshall Hodgson noted in a perceptive article published in 1964, "in effect, Kroeber made the problem of Islâmic iconoclasm a key to the problem of civilization itself. If symbolism was dying in Islâm, the implication of his idea was that the death of symbolism—and doubtless the spread of Islâm itself—meant the death, or contraction, of culture as a whole; and that this might well happen at last universally."[39]

Kroeber's contrast between the rich dynamism of Hellenized civilizations (including those of Europe) and the arid negation characteristic of Islamic cultures reflects the notorious Orient oder Rom controversy that had preoccupied the preceding generation of Germanic scholarship. It was in a similar milieu that the term Bilderverbot was coined in the 1860s to reify a series of proscriptions and taboos believed to characterize Semitic races. Within hierarchical taxonomies of culture, Bilderverbot named both an inability to produce art and a related penchant for aniconism and/or iconoclasm. Whether viewed in positive terms or negative terms, this aniconic tendency served as a sign of alterity within racially inflected discourses concerning the assimilability of European Jewry.[40] Kroeber's text is one the first signs not merely of a postwar unease with the deployment of "Semitic" as a category of cultural analysis, but also of a subtle divorce between its two principal component elements, Arab and Jew.[41] If postwar recognition of Jewish suffering helped mitigate or occlude the historical indictment of the Jews vis-à-vis the Bilderverbot, postcolonial patterns of migration gave rise to a new and singular emphasis upon its persistence among the Arabs and, by (not entirely logical) extension, among Muslims more generally.

Like earlier debates about aniconism and alterity, the cartoon controversy engaged the Bilderverbot in relation to concerns about the nature of European identity, now inflected by teleological narratives of modernity. Analyses of the cartoon controversy (like those of the destruction of the Bamiyan Buddhas in 2001) might mention historical episodes of aniconism or iconoclasm in Europe but were quick to emphasize that although militant Protestant aniconism and revolutionary iconoclasm were necessary stages on the road to European modernity, the advent of its full-blown incarnation rendered such practices obsolete.[42] Since the reordering of both the space and the time of religion is a precondition for the emergence of secular modernity, those who persisted in championing taboos rendered obsolete by the autonomy and secularization of the image were depicted not only as inhabiting a different space from that of modernity but also as denizens of a different time.[43]

However, the allochronicity seen to characterize Islam in relation to the project of modernity is destabilized by the proliferation of information technologies that was central to the cartoon controversy. Refiguring the space and time of dissemination and reception, the advent of cybertechnology imbues moments of seeing and reading with a simultaneity impossible in the era of singular images and material copy. This simultaneity threatens the utility of "circulation" as an analytical category, even as it calls into question the notion of Islam as occupying a space "out there" and a time "back then";[44] as Appadurai notes, global cultural flows "[play] havoc with the hegemony of Euro-chronology."[45] The centrality of new media to reinvestments and rehistoricizations of the transhistorical concept of the *umma*, the metatopical space that defines the imagined community of Muslims, is a case in point, one inseparable from the emergence of a new religious public sphere both in the countries of Asia and the Middle East and among the Muslim diasporas of Europe and the United States.[46]

The centrality of these diaspora communities to the cartoon controversy reminds us that simultaneity of seeing and reading is permitted by the mobility not only of images or imaging technologies but also of human populations. Like the technologies that mediate changing concepts of the umma, the existence of new Muslim diasporas not only reconfigures perceptions of space but also is increasingly seen as threatening to the time of modernity itself. An interesting (and logically contradictory) corollary of this perceived threat is the abandonment of the very teleological narratives within which the persistence of the "image question" functions as an index of recalcitrant medievalism. This was manifest in some of the rhetoric surrounding the publication of the Danish cartoons, which invoked a fear that the allochronic aspect of Islam is sufficiently powerful to arrest or even reverse the forward march of modernity, the "pull to sameness" of what Talal Asad describes as modernity's "moral magnet," prescribing in its stead a "back to the future" model of development for an Islamicized Europe.[47] This rhetoric of reversion cast the controversy as an attempt to hold the fort or reinforce the status quo, ignoring the essentially dynamic quality of secular time, the constant redefinition of boundaries (here, those of religious identity) necessitated by modernity's drive to novelty.[48] While some observers of the cartoon controversy argued the need to extend existing blasphemy laws to include Islam, opponents assailed the same laws as a medieval residue in European public life, remnant vestiges of a presecular past that might be reinvested by the anachronistic, antisecular values of Europe's burgeoning Muslim populations.[49] As with the earlier *Satanic Verses* affair, this charge of retrograde medievalism cut both ways: if European secularists could accuse Muslim critics of asserting a "medieval" mindset (illustrating what Bruce Holsinger identifies as a "discursive compulsion towards the medieval" that marks contemporary Euro-American representations of Islam), the latter could invoke the precedent of the Crusades and the derogatory representations of Islam that they engendered.[50]

If for many secularists the image problem indexed the perpetuation of a medieval mindset, for others the problem lay in a mindset that was insufficiently medieval (a critique of Muslims common to Islamists, if for diametrically opposed reasons). Hence, the insistence upon a distinction between an originary, more liberal Islam and the illiberal attitudes of modern imams with regard to figuration and representation, a historicism at odds with the ubiquitous essentialist characterizations of the relationship between Muslims and images. As mentioned above, this narrative exploited global museum holdings as an archive that could be deployed against protesting Muslims, providing them with object lessons for a more tolerant Islam in the form of Persianate paintings of the Prophet produced up to seven centuries ago.[51] The contemporary geopolitical context against which the global controversy unfolded and that was central to its meaning was largely ignored in favor of a retrospective and reductive emphasis on a past age when images were apparently less contentious.

In a 1990 analysis of the Rushdie affair, recently revised and reissued, the neoconservative commentator Daniel Pipes formulated an analogous variant of this "back to the future" aspiration for Islam, one that offered precedents from Christian rather than Islamic history. Expressing his hopes for the "Protestantization" of Europe's Muslim diasporas, Pipes attributed the controversy engendered by the *Satanic Verses* to those "Muslims opposed to Protestantization."[52] The metaphor of Protestantization was not chosen at random. Writing of Protestantization, proselytization, and modernity in Indonesia, Webb Keane notes that "the project of becoming self-consciously 'modern' can resemble that of religious conversion in certain respects. Both projects often propose to transform the human subject, disabused of earlier errors and abstracted from the constraints of former social entanglements."[53]

As Keane notes, this process is strongly implicated in the promotion of a semiotic ideology oriented toward the production of a subject that recognizes her or his distinction from the world of material objects. It is, therefore, hardly fortuitous that the divorce of signifier from signified that is integral to the emergence of the autonomous image is frequently attributed to the Protestant Reformation and its formative iconoclasm.[54] If the taming of the image, a relegation to its proper place within universalizing epistemologies and ontologies of the visual, is seen as integral to the teleologies of modernity, the apparent recalcitrance of Muslims appears as an evolutionary failure with moral overtones. The temporally interstitial status that follows produces Muslims as ghostlike, "living between erasure of the past and the indelibility of the present" to haunt the triumph once vouchsafed the project of modernity itself.[55] The phenomenon raises significant questions about the discursive production of Euro-American modernity through the invocation of premodern or nonmodern others whose deficiencies are measured in relation to a specific historical experience represented as both sui generis and universally valid.[56]

Given the content and context of publication, there can be little doubt that the Danish cartoons were intended to both promote and provoke a public debate on Islam and the perceived threat that Muslim diasporas pose to the values of liberal secularism, perhaps even a reaction that would fuel that debate. To this end the Danish cartoons (and those that they inspired) suggest themselves as correlates to the hammers of iconoclasts, swinging at the fracture lines of taboo and its objects in order to assert universalizing discourses about imaging as a sign of the modern. The choice of genre is of course relevant, for in the public sphere of post-Enlightenment Europe, caricature has frequently served to test limits and push boundaries, notably those between religion and the secular. If political cartoons can be understood as agentive in their attempts to both reflect and shape public opinion, the subgenre of caricature is "a form of disfigurement and iconoclasm," an active remaking of perception through representation.[57]

The caricatures and the myriad of visual meta-commentaries that they engendered might also be seen as an *incitement to discourse* in a Foucauldian sense, a future-oriented attempt to reinscribe taboo within discourses of the rational.[58] Seen in this light, the *content* of the controversy generated by the circulation and reproduction of the images at its core appears less important than its promotion of universalized epistemologies and ontologies by which both acts and actors are bounded and against which they are measured. As a consequence, the publication of the caricatures necessarily promoted a discourse of assimilation and acculturation rather than one of commensuration and transculturation, a coercive induction into the profane ontologies of secular modernity.[59] The endeavor forms part of more widespread effort to produce the right kind of Muslim, one who inculcates the norms of liberal secularism rather than contests their universal validity.[60] Like the current vogue for imposing democracy at gunpoint, the enterprise is fraught with paradoxes, not least the promotion of profanation as a mode of demystification that performs the universal virtue of tolerance.[61]

If, however, dissemination and viewing of the offending images and their progeny were represented as resistance to censorship within universalizing (and frequently inconsistent) discourses on the virtues of tolerance as a cultural value, the boycotts provoked by the offense (which included the renaming of Danish pastries as "Roses of the Prophet Muhammad") drew upon the economic aspects of consumption in order to stage a rejection of the hegemonic aspects of these discourses. In doing so, they highlighted the increasingly complex ways in which transnational capital can be exploited "to create a global ethics and politics outside the cognizance of states."[62]

CONTAGIOUS REPRESENTATIONS AND CONTINGENT CIRCULATIONS

The global mobility of images and discourses concerning them was a necessary condition for the eruption and sustenance of the cartoon controversy, but it was not sufficient. To illustrate the point, I would like to conclude by considering an interesting counterpart for the Danish cartoons, one that illustrates the generation of alternative publics though the circulation and consumption of quite different images of the Prophet Muhammad. Until very recently, the image in question circulated throughout Iran, reproduced in a number of variants, in poster form and on mundane objects such as car ornaments and key rings. It depicts a slightly androgynous youth, left shoulder bared, head cocked to one side, sporting a turban and wearing flowers above his right ear (figure 2.4).

A caption beneath informs us that this is an image of the adolescent Prophet by the Christian monk Bahira (painted from life or the memory of a living encounter), the original of which is kept in a Byzantine or Christian museum (*muzē-i rūm*). The identification of the photographic image conflates familiar tales of Byzantine portraits of the Prophet with another well-known account of how the monk Bahira recognized the Prophet when the latter traveled to Bosra in Syria as part of a Mekkan caravan before he was initiated into his prophecy around 610 CE.[63] The ground for the reception of the photograph was undoubtedly prepared by the ubiquitous images of the Shi'i martyrs Imam 'Ali, the son-in-law of the Prophet and fourth caliph, and Imam Husayn, the grandson of the Prophet killed at Karbala in 680 CE. Their images are displayed publicly throughout contemporary Iran.[64] The dissemination and reproduction of these kinds of images in Iran, the

FIGURE 2.4
Popular image of Muhammad, contemporary Iran.

government of which was at the forefront of global protests against the Danish cartoons, suggests that, for some Muslims at least, the controversy concerned content and context rather than the *act* of representation.

Recently, it has been demonstrated that the Bahira portrait is in fact one of a number of homoerotic photographs of North African youths produced by the Orientalist photographers Rudolf Franz Lehnert (1878–1948) and Ernst Heinrich Landrock (1878–1966), active in North Africa in the first decade of the twentieth century.[65] This particular photograph dates from 1905 or 1906 and circulated (perhaps as late as the 1920s) in the form of a postcard captioned "Mohamed," even if it was otherwise identified in other publications (figure 2.5).[66]

FIGURE 2.5
An Arab and His Flower, National Geographic Magazine,
January 1914.

The caption evidently informed the selection of this image from among the larger corpus of Lehnert and Landrock's oeuvre, so the generic title came to identify the image as a portrait of the originary holder of the same name. How the image traveled to Iran is not certain, although a recent resurgence of interest in Lehnert and Landrock's work in Europe is reflected in several French exhibitions of their work and at least one in Cairo. Since there is little record of the image in Iran before the 1990s, it has been suggested that the catalogs accompanying these exhibitions provided the prototype of the image.[67] Conversely, the subsequent identification of the source of the image may explain why, as of summer 2009, the image was no longer as ubiquitous in the bazaars of Teheran as it had been just four or five years earlier.[68]

That the Lehnert and Landrock *Mohamed* image was seized upon as an image of the Prophet, rather than any other among the many images of Arab youths produced by Orientalist photographers, underlines the fact that even if images flow freely in a physical sense, circulated by digital and print media, their reception is neither entirely contingent nor informed by an entirely free flow of meaning. Similarly, the emergence of Kurt Westergaard's image of the turban grenade as iconic, even when others of his original cartoons (which made reference to the status of women or the religious status of suicide bombers) were potentially more controversial, recalls Dan Sperber's observation that "human cognitive and communicative abilities might work better on some representations rather than others," so some representations are "more contagious, more 'catching' than others."[69]

However, just as circulation and mobility cannot of themselves explain the translatability of certain images, the invocation of transcultural cognitive factors, even if relevant, offers little insight into why some images are more "contagious," more mobile, and more readily received (both intra- and interculturally) than others. In the case of both the Bahira image and the Westergaard caricature, catchiness was less a quality of the much vaunted power of images alone, or even of generic cognitive factors, than of captions and texts and the mediations of images that these affect. The histories of Iranian icon and Danish anti-icon thus illustrate both the way in which the polyvalence of the image enables transcultural reception and how captions and texts can set the parameters of this process, affecting both translation and transfiguration.[70] The phenomenon was parodied in a Daryl Cagle cartoon from February 2006 that drew upon hackneyed stereotypes of the fanatical Muslim to suggest that what was at stake in the cartoon controversy was not only the content or status of images but also the semiotic potential of naming, which located the abstract or generic within particular histories of images and imagining (figure 2.6).

The relationship between image and caption is, however, by no means determining—images have the capacity to exceed their captions. The Bahira image may ignore geographic and temporal borders in surprising ways, but neither the bare fact of mobility nor the caption is sufficient to explain its production as an image of the Prophet. Rather, its reception was informed by a constellation of its Orientalist caption, ancient hagiographies featuring prophetic portraits, and the canonicity of kinds of religious imagery specific to Iran. The transformation of this piece of kitsch into a

FIGURE 2.6

"Muhammad descending a staircase," *by Daryl Cagle, MSNBC, February 5, 2006.*
Reproduced with permission of the artist.

valorized icon with a historical relationship to its purported subject thus adumbrates more complex relationships between image, text, and technology than those generally suggested by the binaries of tradition/modernity. Similarly, the global impact of the Danish cartoons cannot be attributed to their reproducibility or consequent mobility alone. Their impact is the product of a complex conjunction of contemporary European anti-immigrant politics, coercive attempts to remake Muslim religious subjectivities, resistance to these endeavors, anger and anxieties about globalization, neocolonialism, the violence of both state and nonstate actors, and, ultimately, the increasingly equivocal status of modernity itself.

CONCLUSION

While the mediascapes that Appadurai identifies as a characteristic of modern global information flows may provide the necessary conditions for circulation, neither the emergence of a modern public sphere nor the availability of new technologies of mediation and reproduction is sufficient to explain the ability of certain images to "go global."[71] The transregional reception of the images discussed here illustrates the limits of circulation as an analytical heuristic, suggesting that it may be more useful to think in terms of rhizomatic image flows governed by networks of contingency.[72] The basic fact of mobility is in any case less analytically significant than the semiotic forms and social architectures that facilitate and impede circulation, a theme addressed by Brian Larkin in chapter 9 of this volume. Culturally specific conceptions of the ontological status and epistemological value of images are integral to these architectures. As with the spectacle occasioned by the destruction of the Bamiyan Buddhas, the provocation and global scale of the cartoon controversy would have been unthinkable without the mobilization of preexisting discourses on Islamic aniconism or iconoclasm, discourses that have proved equally instrumental to both Islamists and their secularist opponents.[73] The cartoon controversy thus reminds us that theories of the image and imaging (or at least the rhetoric surrounding them) are part of the conceptual infrastructures that enable or frustrate the circulation of mental and material images and the consequent generation of publics under conditions of commensuration (or their absence).

It is clear that images do not flow freely either within or across borders. The free flow of information and images (as of capital) is seen as central to liberal political formations, but in practice access to both is limited by economic interests and moral norms, enshrined in law as copyright, anti-blasphemy, anti-incitement, anti-libel, or anti-pornography legislation.[74] In addition, pragmatic concerns often mitigate implementation of the Euro-American legislative codes whose absolutist imperatives were said to lie at the heart of the decision (and ability) to publish and reproduce the offending images. Qualifications in the content and implementation of legislation governing freedom of expression are in fact enshrined in the European Convention on Human Rights, which notes that freedom of expression "carries with it duties and responsibilities" and hence that the exercise of the relevant freedoms may be curtailed by law and/or the necessity to protect national security, prevent crime and disorder, and so forth.[75] Whether or not appropriate, these codes are both prescriptive and proscriptive, so free speech (including the dissemination of certain types of images) is circumscribed in European liberal democracies.

The degree of circumscription was highlighted in July 2007, even while the cartoon controversy was raging, when a cartoon depicting Crown Prince Felipe of Spain and his wife, Letizia, having sex was published on the cover of the Spanish satirical weekly *El Jueves*. Judging that the cartoon constituted *lèse majesté*, Judge Juan del Olmo of the national court in Madrid ordered all copies impounded, prompting police raids on newsagents all across Spain. Following a template established a year earlier during the Danish cartoon controversy, the offending image was subsequently posted on the website of *El Jueves* and reproduced on the website of *El Mundo* in solidarity with its sister daily.[76] The convolutions and contradictions intrinsic to both Danish and Spanish cartoon controversies are illustrated by the fate of the *Wikipedia* entry on the Danish caricatures. The original

Wikipedia article was illustrated with depictions of the Prophet drawn from the premodern and early modern Persian manuscripts mentioned above. As of February 2008 the presence of these images led to more than 180,000 requests for their removal. Attempts to remove or delete the images from the site, characterized by its communitarian and self-regulating nature, led its moderators to both block edits and issue a statement against censorship.[77] The proscription and prevention of user edits on a site that built its reputation on being user edited and the representation of such an action as both statement and stance against censorship encapsulate and enact some of the paradoxes exposed by the cartoon controversy.

Perhaps more than any other kind of contention, disputes over the role of religion in modern public life make manifest "democratic deficits" that stem from contradictions in and between the rhetoric and realities of secular modernity.[78] Regardless of the zero-sum rhetoric that they employ, these contentions are rarely about unlimited freedom, but more often about who gets to set the limits and how: in short, about enfranchisement. At issue in the cartoon controversy was the question of Muslims not only as a reservoir of anachronistic and erroneous models of representation (and hence reality) but also as potential stakeholders in contemporary European debates about appropriate modalities of cultural expression. That these debates were emblematized by the image and its incommensurate ontologies is hardly surprising, given the historical utility of the "image question" to European debates about alterity and Islam.

In contrast to the particularist truths attributed to religious belief, the rhetoric of the *Jyllands-Posten* invited European Muslims to subscribe to a series of secular imperatives portrayed as both transcendental and universal.[79] Refusal to acknowledge the autonomy of the image on which this tradition is premised functioned as a sign of alterity vis-à-vis the epistemologies and ontologies of transcendental secularism. The paradoxical depiction of aniconic or iconoclastic Muslims as fetishizers of images thus found its counterpart in the powerful role ascribed to images and imaging by European secularists, confident of their ability to perform and promote the values of secular modernity. Appealing to the universal truth of these values, the paper's editors explained that their publication of the caricatures "was an act of inclusion, not exclusion," integrating Muslims into a modern, secular, satirical tradition directed equally against Christians and Jews. The claim to both inclusion and transcendence was, however, undermined when it came to light that the *Jyllands-Posten* had rejected cartoons satirizing Jesus three years earlier on the grounds that they might have provoked controversy.[80]

FINBARR BARRY FLOOD

Acknowledgments

The author was a Carnegie Scholar in 2007. The research and writing of this chapter were made possible in part by a grant from the Carnegie Corporation of New York. The statements made and the views expressed are solely the responsibility of the author.

Notes

1. The following summary has been synthesized from a variety of reports carried in the print editions and on the websites of American, British, Middle Eastern, and South Asian media between January 2006 and June 2008. For the way in which the affair played out in the Arabic online and print media, see Ana Belen Soage, "The Danish Caricatures Seen from the Arab World," *Totalitarian Movements and Political Religions* 7, no. 3 (2006): 363–369. For a useful survey of the controversy and its local and translocal contexts (although one at odds with the analyses cited in note 12 below), see Jytte Klausen, *The Cartoons That Shook the World* (New Haven, CT: Yale University Press, 2009).

2. Rosalind Ryan and agencies, "Danish Newspapers Reprint Muhammad Cartoon," *Guardian*, February 13, 2008; Michael Kimmelman, "Outrage at Cartoons Still Tests the Danes," *New York Times*, March 20, 2008.

3. Osama bin Laden, "Falatathakilunā ummahātnā ān lam nanaṣara nabīynā ʿalayhu al-salām" (May our mothers be bereaved of us if we fail to help our Prophet, peace be upon him), published by al-Sahab Media. I am grateful to Bernard Haykel for supplying me with a copy of the Arabic transcript. For an English translation, see http://www .nefafoundation.org/miscellaneous/FeaturedDocs/nefabinladen0308.pdf (accessed December 1, 2008).

4. Ulf Hannerz, *Transnational Connections, Culture, People, Places* (New York: Routledge, 2002), 11.

5. W. J. T. Mitchell, *What Do Pictures Want? The Lives and Loves of Images* (Chicago: University of Chicago Press, 2006), 135–136, 140–141. It is, however, worth noting parenthetically Osama bin Laden's discussion of the Danish cartoons as an example of an unrestrained freedom of words (*aqwāl*), not drawings (*rusūm*).

6. Roland Barthes, *Mythologies*, trans. Annette Lavers (New York: Hill and Wang, 1972), 114–117. As of January 2008 the Danish National Royal Library, the Danish National Museum, and the Museum of Danish Cartoon Art in Copenhagen were competing to acquire the originals of the cartoons as primary documents of Danish history: Clemens Bomsdorf, "Danish Museum to Buy Muhammad Cartoons Which Sparked Global Riots," *Art Newspaper*, January 31, 2008.

7. The technique was adopted by at least one Moroccan newspaper: Anver M. Emon, "On the Pope, Cartoons, and Apostates: Shari'a 2006," *Journal of Law and Religion* 22 (2006): 315.

8. Gwladys Fouché, "Cartoons Published in Jordan," *Guardian*, February 2, 2006; Michael Slackman and Hasan M. Fattah, "Furor over Cartoons Pits Muslim against Muslim," *New York Times*, February 22, 2006; Faris Sanabani, "Tolerance on Trial: Why We Reprinted the Danish Cartoons," March 15, 2006, http://jurist.law.pitt.edu/forumy /2006/03/tolerance-on-trial-why-we-reprinted.php (accessed November 28, 2008).

9. http://en.wikipedia.org/wiki/Islam_cartoon#_note-muhammeds_ansigt (accessed December 2, 2008). The Wikipedia entry on the controversy also reproduces the offending cartoons; a full description is provided by Art Spiegelman, "Drawing Blood: Outrageous Cartoons and the Art of Outrage," *Harpers*, June 2006, 48–50.

10. "Fifteen People Killed in Northern Nigeria Muslim Cartoon Protests," *USA Today*, February 18, 2006.

11. Daniel Pipes, *The Rushdie Affair: The Novel, the Ayatollah, and the West* (New York: Carol Publishing Group, 1990), 104, 108.

12. Webb Keane, "Freedom and Blasphemy: On Indonesian Press Bans and Danish Cartoons," *Public Culture* 21, no. 1 (2009): 56–61; Saba Mahmood, "Religious Reason and Secular Affect: An Incommensurable Divide?" *Critical Inquiry* 35 (2009): 841–850; Naveeda Khan, "Images That Come Unbidden: Some Thoughts on the Danish Cartoon Controversy," *Borderlands e-journal* 9, no. 3 (2010): 1–14.

13. Useful starting points are David Freedberg, *The Power of Images: Studies in the History and Theory of Response* (Chicago: University of Chicago Press, 1989); Alfred Gell, *Art and Agency: An Anthropological Theory* (Oxford, UK: Clarendon Press, 1998).

14. Mahmood Mamdani, *Good Muslim, Bad Muslim: America, the Cold War, and the Roots of Terror* (New York: Three Leaves Press, Doubleday, 2004), 17–62.

15. http://news.bbc.co.uk/1/hi/world/middle_east/4674864.stm (accessed December 5, 2008). For an analogous error in an otherwise insightful essay, see Brian Goldstone, "Violence and the Profane: Islamism, Liberal Democracy, and the Limits of Secular Discipline," *Anthropological Quarterly* 80, no. 1 (2007): 216.

16. E. H. Gombrich, *Art and Illusion: A Study in the Psychology of Pictorial Representation* (Princeton, NJ: Princeton University Press, 1984), 344, fig. 282.

17. Daan van Reenen, "The *Bilderverbot*, a New Survey," *Der Islam* 67 (1990): 27–77.

18. G. R. D. King, "The Paintings of the Pre-Islamic Ka'ba," *Muqarnas* 21 (2004): 219–230.

19. For the controversial suggestion that a standing figure depicted on the early Islamic coinage of Syria in the 690s, usually identified as a caliph, is in fact an image of the Prophet Muhammad, see Robert Hoyland, "Writing the Biography of the Prophet Muhammad: Problems and Solutions," *History Compass* 5, no. 2 (2007): 593–596.

20. Oya Pancaroğlu, "Signs in the Horizon: Concepts of Image and Boundary in a Medieval Persian Cosmography," *Res: Anthropology and Aesthetics* 43 (2001): 34, 37; Oleg

Grabar, "Les portraits du prophète Mahomet à Byzance et ailleurs," *Comptes rendus de l'académie des inscriptions et belles-lettres* 146, no. 4 (2002): 1431–1445; Oleg Grabar and Mika Natif, "The Story of Portraits of the Prophet Muhammad," *Studia Islamica* 96 (2003): 19–33.

21. Priscilla P. Soucek, "The Life of the Prophet: Illustrated Versions," in *Content and Context of Visual Arts in the Islamic World,* ed. Priscilla P. Soucek (University Park: Penn State University Press, 1988), 193–218; Christiane Jacqueline Gruber, "The Prophet Muhammad's Ascension (Mi'rāj) in Islamic Painting and Literature: Evidence from Cairo Collections," *Bulletin of the American Research Center in Egypt* 185 (Summer 2004): 24–31; Christiane Jacqueline Gruber, "Between Logos (Kalima) and Light (Nūr): Representations of the Prophet Muhammad in Islamic Painting," *Muqarnas* 26 (2009): 1–34. The aniconic evocation of the Prophet by means of commemorative devices is attested at a much earlier date: Finbarr Barry Flood, "Light in Stone: The Commemoration of the Prophet in Umayyad Architecture," in *Bayt al-Maqdis,* Part II, *Jerusalem and Early Islam,* Oxford Studies in Islamic Art 9, ed. Jeremy Johns (New York: Oxford University Press, 2002), 311–359.

22. Nabil F. Safwat, "The Ḥilyah: The Verbal Image of the Prophet," in *The Art of the Pen: Calligraphy of the 14th to 20th Centuries,* ed. Nabil F. Safwat and Mohammed Zakariya (London: Nour Foundation, in association with Azimuth Editions and Oxford University Press, 1996), 46–50; Grabar and Natif, "The Story of Portraits," 33–34.

23. Valérie Gonzalez, "The Double Ontology of Islamic Calligraphy: A Word-Image on a Folio from the Museum of Raqqada (Tunisia)," *M. Uğur Derman Festschrift* (Istanbul: Anabasım A.Ş., 2002), 313–340.

24. Despite this, concerns that the Prophet was represented in the film were sufficient to inspire threes sieges by a Hanafi African-American Muslim group in Washington, DC, in March 1977 in an attempt to derail the release of the film in the United States: William Greider and Richard Harwood, "Hanafi Muslim Bands Seize Hostages at 3 Sites," *Washington Post,* March 10, 1977.

25. Ella Shohat, "Sacred Word, Profane Image: Theologies of Adaptation," in *A Companion to Literature and Film,* ed. Robert Stam and Alessandra Raengo (Malden, MA: Blackwell, 2004), 33–34; Freek L. Bakker, "The Image of Muhammad in *The Message,* the First and Only Feature Film about the Prophet of Islam," *Islam and Christian-Muslim Encounter* 17, no. 1 (2006): 77–92.

26. Allen Douglas and Fedwa Malti-Douglas, *Arab Comic Strips, Politics of an Emerging Mass Culture* (Bloomington: Indiana University Press, 1994), 83 ff.; Jamal J. Elias, "Visual Images and Religious Pedagogy in Islam: *Du'ā* Girl and the Comic Book" (lecture, Hagop Kevorkian Center for Near Eastern Studies, New York University, October 2005). The distinction between caricatures and cartoons is worth emphasizing here: François

Boespflug, *Caricaturer Dieu: Pouvoirs et dangers de l'image* (Paris: Bayard, 2006), 24–38. A recent judgment by Shaikh Sa'ud al-Funaysan, former dean of Islamic law at Al-Imam University in Riyadh, explains that cartoons are permissible but "should have appropriate content and be used in an appropriate manner": Sa'ud al-Funaysan, "Drawing Pictures and Producing Animated Cartoons," http://www.islamtoday.com/showme2 .cfm?cat_id=2&sub_cat_id=811 (accessed November 28, 2008).

27. Gruber, "Between Logos (Kalima) and Light (Nūr)," pl. 1.

28. Suzanne C. Akbari, "Imagining Islam: The Role of Images in Medieval Depictions of Muslims," *Scripta Mediterranea* 19–20 (1998–1999): 9–27. Largely ignored in the Euro-American media, the broad parallels between the medieval images and modern caricatures were noted in an article by Tarek Kahlaoui published in Arabic in *al-Quds al-Arabi* and *Middle East Online* in February 2006, accompanied by some of the least offensive of the relevant paintings.

29. Jennifer Bray, "The Mohammetan and Idolatry," *Studies in Church History* 21 (1984): 89–98; Jean Flori, "La caricature de l'Islam dans l'Occident medieval: Origine et signification de quelques stereotypes concernant l'Islam," *Aevum* 66, no. 2 (1992): 245–256; Norman Daniel, *Islam and the West: The Making of an Image* (Oxford, UK: Oneworld, 1993); John Tolan, *Saracens: Islam in the Medieval European Imagination* (New York: Columbia University Press, 2002), 105–134.

30. Michael Camille, *The Gothic Idol: Ideology and Image-Making in Medieval Art* (Cambridge, UK: Cambridge University Press, 1989), 129–164, esp. 136–137; Debra Higgs Strickland, *Saracens, Demons, and Jews: Making Monsters in Medieval Art* (Princeton, NJ: Princeton University Press, 2003), 165–192, esp. 167–168.

31. Carole Hillenbrand, *The Crusades, Islamic Perspectives* (Edinburgh: Edinburgh University Press, 1999), 308.

32. John Tolan, "Un cadavre mutilé: Le déchirement polémique de Mahomet," *Le Moyen Âge* 105 (1998): 62; Tolan, *Saracens*, 135–170. See also Walter B. Cahn, "The 'Portrait' of Muhammad in the Toledan Collection," in *Reading Medieval Images: The Art Historian and the Object*, ed. Elizabeth Sears and Thelma K. Thomas (Ann Arbor: University of Michigan Press, 2002), 51–60. The dossier on the *Jyllands-Posten* drawings presented to the Organization of the Islamic Conference in December 2005 reportedly contained three additional caricatures, including those showing the Prophet with the head of a pig and being violated by a dog.

33. Strickland, *Saracens, Demons, and Jews*, 190–192, figs. 97–99.

34. The utility of profanation within polarizing discourses was demonstrated in 2007, when Tatiana Susskind, a twenty-five-year-old Israeli, produced a poster depicting the Prophet (identified by an Arabic caption) as a pig stomping on the Qur'an with one foot while writing the sacred text with the other. The poster was reproduced and

pasted on at least twenty sites in Hebron. In the ensuing violence, at least twenty-four Palestinian demonstrators were shot, and two Israeli soldiers were injured by a pipe bomb: Walter Rodgers, "Pig Insult Sparks West Bank Violence," http://www.cnn.com /WORLD/9707/01/israel.palestinians/ (accessed December 2, 2008). In April 2008 the graves of World War One Muslim servicemen at Arras in northern France were desecrated, and a pig's head was hung on a tombstone: "French Muslim War Graves Defaced," http://news.bbc.co.uk/2/hi/europe/7333344.stm (accessed December 2, 2008).

35. See, for example, Sergiusz Michalski, *The Reformation and the Visual Arts: The Protestant Image Question in Western and Eastern Europe* (London: Taylor and Francis, 1998), appendix. A full discussion of the historiography of the "image problem" in relation to the representation of Islam can be found in chapter 1 of Finbarr Barry Flood, *Islam and Image: Polemics, Theology and Modernity* (London: Reaktion, forthcoming).

36. Martin Amis, "The Age of Horrorism," parts 1 and 3, *Observer*, September 10, 2006.

37. *Theophanis Chronographia* (Hildesheim, Germany: G. Olms, 1963), 402, 404–406, 414; Patricia Crone, "Islam, Judeo-Christianity, and Byzantine Iconoclasm," *Jerusalem Studies in Arabic and Islam* 2 (1980): 59. On the general tendency to view iconoclastic acts as potentially contagious: Dario Gamboni, *The Destruction of Art: Iconoclasm and Vandalism since the French Revolution* (London: Reaktion, 2007), 193.

38. Alfred L. Kroeber, "Ancient *Oikoumenê* as an Historic Culture Aggregate," *Journal of the Royal Anthropological Institute of Great Britain and Ireland* 75 (1945): 10–11.

39. Marshall Hodgson, "Islam and Image," *History of Religion* 2 (1964): 226.

40. Kalman P. Bland, *The Artless Jew: Medieval and Modern Affirmations and Denials of the Visual* (Princeton, NJ: Princeton University Press, 2002).

41. This issue is discussed in detail in Flood, *Islam and Image*, but see Mamdani, *Good Muslim, Bad Muslim*, 35–36; Gil Anidjar, *Semites: Race, Religion, Literature* (Stanford, CA: Stanford University Press, 2007); Matti Bunzl, *Anti-Semitism and Islamophobia: Hatreds Old and New in Europe* (Chicago: Prickly Paradigm Press, 2007).

42. See, for example, Paul Richard, "In Art Museums, Portraits Illuminate a Religious Taboo," *Washington Post*, February 14, 2006.

43. Johannes Fabian, *Time and the Other: How Anthropology Makes Its Object* (New York: Columbia University Press, 1983), 26; Charles Taylor, *Modern Social Imaginaries* (Durham, NC: Duke University Press, 2004), 97–99, 187–188, 193–194; Charles Taylor, *A Secular Age* (Cambridge, MA: Belknap Press of Harvard University Press, 2007).

44. Although the production and publication of the cartoons was presented as an assertion of regional cultural norms in the face of the threat posed by transregional mobility, the controversy was marked by a paradox regarding the differing claims of

the local and global: the Arabic text carried by *Jyllands-Posten* after the controversy had initially broken was, for example, evidently intended for global consumption. The extent of these global information flows was underlined by protests outside the US embassy in Jakarta not only against the Danish cartoons but also against a bas-relief depicting the Prophet in the company of historical lawgivers or lawmakers in the US Supreme Court in Washington, DC: Declan Walsh, "Church Ablaze as Cartoon Protests Continue across Globe," *Guardian*, February 20, 2006, http://www.guardian.co.uk /world/2006/feb/20/pakistan.muhammadcartoons (accessed July 15, 2009). In 1997 the Council on American-Islamic Relations had requested that it be removed, objecting to both the fact that the Prophet had been depicted and the nature of the depiction— his portrayal with a sword. In preceding years the bas-relief had been largely ignored, until the cartoon controversy, when a number of US-based dailies ran stories noting its existence; it was presumably these or similar sources that drew the attention of Indonesian protestors. A recent Saudi fatwa on the permissibility of this depiction of the Prophet provides an interesting example of how understandings of the proscriptions on image-making contained in the hadith are contextually inflected in Islamic jurisprudence: Taha Jaber al-Alwani, "*Fatwa* Concerning the United States Supreme Courtroom Frieze," *Journal of Law and Religion* 15, no. 1/2 (2000–2001): 1–28.

45. Arjun Appadurai, "Disjuncture and Difference in the Global Cultural Economy," *Public Culture* 2, no. 2 (1990): 3.

46. Dale F. Eickelman and Jon W. Anderson, "Redefining Muslim Publics," in *New Media in the Muslim World: The Emerging Public Sphere*, ed. Dale F. Eickelman and Jon W. Anderson (Bloomington: Indiana University Press, 2003), 14.

47. Talal Asad, "Modern Power and the Reconfiguration of Religious Traditions," *Stanford Electronic Humanities Review* 5, no.1 (1996), special issue, *Contested Polities: Religious Disciplines and Structures of Modernity*; Taylor, *Modern Social Imaginaries*, 162. For a novel take on an analogous theme, see Faisal Devji, "Back to the Future: The Cartoons, Liberalism, and Global Islam," http://www.opendemocracy.net/conflict-terrorism /liberalism_3451.jsp (accessed May 15, 2009).

48. Talal Asad, *Formations of the Secular: Christianity, Islam, Modernity* (Stanford, CA: Stanford University Press, 2003), 201.

49. Thus, for example, during the trial of the French satirical magazine *Charlie Hebdo* in February 2007 for inciting racial hatred, its editor, Philippe Val, denounced the "medieval process" to which the weekly was subject. Flemming Rose, editor of the *Jyllands-Posten*, cast the trial of *Charlie Hebdo* not only as a clash of civilizations but also as a contest of temporalities, asserting, "I just cannot imagine the consequences not only for France but for Denmark and Europe if they lose the case.... It would turn back the

clock decades, ages": "French Magazine Sued over Cartoons," February 7, 2007, http://
english.aljazeera.net/news/europe/2007/02/2008525143158419749.html (accessed
November 29, 2008).

50. Bruce Holsinger, *Neomedievalism, Neoconservatism, and the War on Terror* (Chicago:
Prickly Paradigm Press, 2007), 41. In an interview with Michael Kimmelman published
in the *New York Times* on the same day as the Bin Laden tape was released, the editor of
Jyllands-Posten, Flemming Rose, archly pointed out the presence of Danes among the Cru-
saders, posing the rhetorical question "Is this another Crusade now, or what is it?": Michael
Kimmelman, "Outrage at Cartoons Still Tests Danes," *New York Times*, March 20, 2008.

51. Finbarr Barry Flood, "From the Prophet to Postmodernism? New World Orders
and the End of Islamic Art," in *Making Art History: A Changing Discipline and Its Institutions*, ed. Elizabeth Mansfield (New York: Routledge, 2007), 31–53; Jessica Winegar,
"The Humanity Game: Art, Islam, and the War on Terror," *Anthropological Quarterly* 81,
no. 2 (2008): 651–681.

52. Pipes, *Rushdie Affair*, 222. Note that the rhetoric of Protestantization has been
adopted by some Islamic reformists, who explicitly invoke the precedent of the Reformation: Saba Mahmood, "Secularism, Hermeneutics, and Empire: The Politics of
Islamic Reformation," *Public Culture* 18, no. 2 (2006): 324.

53. Webb Keane, "Sincerity, 'Modernity,' and the Protestants," *Cultural Anthropology*
17, no. 1 (2002): 67.

54. Among many others, see Werner Hofmann, "Die Geburt der Moderne aus dem
Geist der Religion," in *Luther und die Folgen für die Kunst*, ed. Werner Hofmann (Munich:
Prestel-Verlag, 1993), 23–71; Keane, "Freedom and Blasphemy," 59–61.

55. S. Sayyid, *A Fundamental Fear: Eurocentrism and the Emergence of Islam* (New York:
Zed Books, 2003), 1.

56. Michel-Rolph Trouillot, "The Otherwise Modern: Caribbean Lessons from
the Savage Slot," in *Critically Modern: Alternatives, Alterities, Anthropologies*, ed. Bruce M.
Knauft (Bloomington: Indiana University Press, 2002), 220–237; Andreas Huyssen,
"Geographies of Modernism in a Globalizing World," *New German Critique* 100 34, no. 1
(2007): 192.

57. Mitchell, *What Do Pictures Want?* 132; Spiegelman, "Drawing Blood," 45. The
genre has been deployed with increasing frequency against both Islam and Muslims in
the postwar period: Christina Michelmore, "Old Pictures in New Frames: Images of Islam
and Muslims in Post–World War II American Political Cartoons," *Journal of American and
Comparative Cultures* 23, no. 4 (2000): 37–50; Peter Gottschalk and Gabriel Greenberg,
Islamophobia: Making Muslims the Enemy (New York: Rowman and Littlefield, 2008).

58. Michel Foucault, *The History of Sexuality*, vol. 1, *An Introduction*, trans. Robert
Hurley (New York: Vintage Books, 1990), 17–35. I am indebted here to Joseph Massad,

"Re-Orienting Desire: The Gay International and the Arab World," *Public Culture* 14, no. 2 (2003): 361–385.

59. On the profane time of modernity, see Taylor, *Modern Social Imaginaries*, 97–99, 187–188, 193–194.

60. See Mahmood, "Secularism, Hermeneutics, and Empire"; Flood, "Prophet to Postmodernism?"

61. William T. Cavanaugh, "Sins of Omission: What 'Religion and Violence' Arguments Ignore," *Hedgehog Review: Critical Reflections on Contemporary Culture* 6, no. 1 (2004): 43; Wendy Brown, *Regulating Aversion: Tolerance in the Age of Identity and Empire* (Princeton, NJ: Princeton University Press, 2006), 149–175.

62. Devji, "Back to the Future"; "Pastry Targeted as the Cartoon Jihad Continues," February 17, 2006, http://www.spiegel.de/international/0,1518,401509,00.html (accessed November 30, 2008).

63. A. Guillaume, *The Life of Muhammad* (Oxford, UK: Oxford University Press, 2003), 79–81; Grabar, "Portraits du prophète," 1442–1444; Grabar and Natif, "Story of Portraits," 35, fig. 4.

64. The iconographic genealogy of these images has yet to be determined, but for an interesting discussion, see Alireza Doostdar, "Religious Commodities, Magical Circulations, and the (Im)moral Economy of Iran," http://www.doostdar.com/articles /magical_circulations.pdf (accessed November 15, 2008). I am grateful to Christiane Gruber for drawing my attention to this article.

65. Pierre Centlivres and Micheline Centlivres-Demont, "Une étrange rencontre: La photographie orientaliste de Lehnert et Landrock et l'image iranienne du prophète Mahomet," *Études photographiques* 17 (2005): 5–15; and "The Story of a Picture: Shiite Depictions of Muhammad," *ISIM Review* 17 (Spring 2006): 18–19.

66. Frank Edward Johnson, "Here and There in North Africa," *National Geographic Magazine* 25 (January–June 1914): 35; Centlivres and Centlivres-Demont, "Une étrange rencontre," 7–9.

67. Centlivres and Centlivres-Demont, "Une étrange rencontre," 10.

68. I am grateful to Talinn Grigor for this information.

69. Dan Sperber, "Anthropology and Psychology: Towards an Epidemiology of Representations," *Man*, n.s., 20, no. 1 (1985): 74, 79; Dan Sperber, "Interpreting and Explaining Cultural Representations," in *Beyond Boundaries: Understanding, Translation, and Anthropological Discourse*, ed. Gísli Pálsson (Oxford, UK: Berg, 1994), 179.

70. Mary Price, *The Photograph: A Strange Confined Space* (Stanford, CA: Stanford University Press, 1994), 55–58; Dilip Parameshwar Gaonkar and Elizabeth A. Povinelli, "Technologies of Public Forms: Circulation, Transfiguration, Recognition," *Public Culture* 15, no. 3 (2003): 387.

71. Arjun Appadurai, *Modernity at Large: Cultural Dimensions of Globalization* (Minneapolis: University of Minnesota Press, 1996), 35–40. The point is made by Warner, *Publics and Counterpublics*, 106; Benjamin Lee and Edward LiPuma, "Cultures of Circulation: The Imaginations of Modernity," *Public Culture* 14, no. 1 (2002): 192; Gaonkar and Povinelli, "Technologies of Public Forms," 387, 392.

72. Christopher Pinney, "Four Types of Visual Culture," in *Handbook of Material Culture*, ed. Christopher Tilley et al. (London: Sage, 2006), 141, drawing upon Deleuze, Guattari, and Latour.

73. Finbarr Barry Flood, "Between Cult and Culture: Bamiyan, Islamic Iconoclasm and the Museum," *Art Bulletin* 84, no. 4 (2002): 641–659.

74. The point has been made frequently: Talal Asad, *Genealogies of Religion: Discipline and Reasons of Power in Christianity and Islam* (Baltimore, MD: Johns Hopkins University Press, 1993), 244–245; Emon, "On the Pope, Cartoons, and Apostates," 310–311.

75. http://www.hri.org/docs/ECHR50.html#C.Art10 (accessed December 5, 2008). These proscriptions extend to new media. It has recently been revealed, for example, that the Internet Watch Foundation, a British watchdog that enjoys government support, prevents British Internet users from accessing approximately ten thousand websites each year, keeping the names and details of these sites secret: Charles Arthur, "Censor Lifts UK Wikipedia Ban," *Guardian*, December 9, 2008.

76. Giles Tremlett, "Police Raid over Sex Cartoons of Spanish Prince," *Guardian*, July 21, 2007.

77. Caroline Davies, "Wikipedia Defies 180,000 Demands to Remove Images of the Prophet," *Observer*, February 17, 2008.

78. Brown, *Regulating Aversion*, 149–175; Emon, "Pope, Cartoons, and Apostates," 316.

79. Goldstone, "Violence and the Profane," 208, 210, 219; Elizabeth A. Povinelli, "Radical Worlds: The Anthropology of Incommensurability and Inconceivability," *Annual Review of Anthropology* 30 (2001): 327. See, however, Edward Said's comments on the reconstitution and reconfiguration of religious forms in the secular frameworks of Enlightenment thought: Edward W. Said, *Orientalism* (New York: Penguin Books, 1978), 121–122.

80. Gwladys Fouché, "Danish Paper Rejected Jesus Cartoons," *Guardian*, February 6, 2006; Fleming Rose, "Why I Published the Muhammad Cartoons," *New York Times*, May 31, 2006.

3

The Enclave Gaze

Images and Imaginaries
of Neoliberal Lifestyle in New Delhi

Christiane Brosius

Every time you go out shopping, remember you are a part of something big that is happening in India. Retail is the mantra of the moment. It's what [is] driving investment. It's generating employment. Most significantly, it is making people like you think and feel a whole lot better about the way you can spend your money and improve your quality of life.... Drive down a highway leading out of any of India's metros. Now look around you. What do you see? A landscape dotted with impressive high rises cased in aesthetically imposing steel and glass. Too much of steel and concrete maybe, but this changed landscape has a story to tell. It is the story of India's growth as a market. Inside those buildings plans are being drawn to bring a million new products and services to tens of millions of middle class Indians who have begun to expect more than the ordinary. Now shut your eyes for a moment. And think back fifteen years.... What did this landscape look like then? Nice and empty for miles on end. What story did those barren arid stretches tell you? That we were a poor country that looked and felt poor. Maybe we are still a poor country. But surely we are less poor today than we were fifteen years back. Our metropolitan cities and their suburbs, however, do not look the type of a third world country.... For better or for worse, Indians (especially middle class urban Indians) have become more nattily dressed, have learnt to exercise specific choices over the brands, and developed enhanced skills in organising their lifestyles.

—*Debra Mookerjee, "It's More Than 'Just Hopping'"*[1]

This quote from *Celebrating Vivaha*, a leading Indian bridal magazine, paints a rather crude picture of India "before" and "after" economic liberalization, before the advent of retail marketing, large real estate companies, and a range of expanding service sectors on the once "barren" landscape of India's urban rims and centers. Most obvious seems the change in urban landscape and consumer worlds. The quote suggests that

FIGURE 3.1

"Drive down a highway leading out of any of India's metros. Now look around you. What do you see?" Faridabad, New Delhi metropolitan area, 2006. Photograph by C. Brosius.

one can clearly *see* the difference; one can *see* the changes taking place and thereby experience the transformation. And this fairy-tale metamorphosis is what seems to matter (more than the slippages in between), setting free urban imaginaries of a prosperous, developed India. Descriptions of postliberalization urban India require the willingness of the beholder to succumb to a very selective look at her landscapes: by no means does the description translate into what one can *really* see while driving down highways or main roads.

Some images chosen from my fieldwork in Delhi should underline what I mean when I write, in this chapter, about such an "enclave gaze" (plates 4–6). Undoubtedly, urban environs in India have undergone massive changes since the early 1990s. Before that, there were manifold reasons for urban reorganization on smaller or grander scales. But the ways in which India's capital, Delhi, has changed her face with economic liberalization have left many puzzled, disoriented, or wondering when the "growth bubble" will finally explode. Delhi has had many spatial ruptures and facelifts since her early days as the center of Mughal emperors, the British Empire, and the new, independent nation-state. Forced and labor migration since India's partition in 1947, ethnic riots, mega-events like the Asian Games of 1982 and the Commonwealth Games of 2010, and the recent fear of terrorist attacks have shaped her fabric too, sometimes traumatically.[2]

The photograph and color plates show you scenes of Noida (Uttar Pradesh) and Faridabad (Haryana), photographed in 2006, one year before the epigraph to this chapter was written. The "boomtowns" located in neighboring states but falling under the National Capital Region (NCR) had predominantly been agricultural plots before, no-go areas for more privileged urban populations, some even abandoned by their owners, who were unaware of the sweeping real estate boom to come. Fields, water buffaloes, and straw huts have now made space for highways and roadway shops selling marble floors, framed pictures, and wooden pillars for living rooms in the residential towers of the new gated colonies. Lines of billboards announcing the construction of a grand themed shopping mall, an "ideal land," or "luxurious villas" (plates 5 and 6) whiz by like a mirage as one drives along National Highway 24. From here, at night, convoys of trucks filled with sand or stones or other construction material move into the city like ghosts, vanishing again before sunrise, leaving no room for silence in the restless, construction-shaken city.

But the images also show that the "perfect" showcase described above is but a mirage itself. In the "real" Indian metropolitan centers, the "highway flaneur" cannot glide along uninterrupted glass facades such as the one in plate 4, where dreams of a "better" or "new" India are built by experts. The epigraph alerts us to a good feeling associated with a drive through this new world. "The feel-good factor" was a key slogan of the Hindu nationalist Bharatiya Janata Party, then still heading the Indian government, for the 2004 general election campaign under the banner of economically liberalized and culturally confident "India Shining/*Bharat Uday*." The idea of a developed India, a global player and a leading nation of the twenty-first century, was linked to economic growth: 8 percent growth in gross domestic product (GDP) and a booming middle class with remarkable surplus income came to serve as evidence of the self-fulfilling prophecy of neoliberalism (until it was shaken with the bank crisis in 2008). But the idea was also connected to a new national confidence groomed particularly by members of the rapidly expanding, new middle classes. The celebratory rhetoric for an election campaign points us toward a particular aesthetic habitus that emerged in the new millennium, which I have termed the "enclave gaze." Generated in the age of globalized neoliberal politics, it is a gaze through which an insular perspective upon a world made up of islands with no particularly relevant, in-between space (from the perspective of the enclave) is created and legitimized. As an "enframing strategy" (see the important discussion on "enframement" in the introduction to this volume), the enclave gaze manifests in and circulates through various visual ecologies, spatial regimes, and moral discourses. These are spread across different spheres, ranging from advertising billboards placed next to highways and shopping malls to lifestyle magazines and real estate brochures. The gaze at stake here is a particularly mobile one that foregrounds a specific mode of visuality and visualization enhanced by a mobility of images, concepts, and people, in particular in urban and highly transnational contexts. The concept of "enclave" addresses concepts of spatial containment and notions of a "right" for exclusive seclusion (from a range of "nuisances"), pleasure linked to conspicuous consumption, and celebration of the Self in a gated yet flexible and highly networked cosmopolitan community. This chapter takes a closer look at these enclaves by studying the ways in which history, culture, and nature are associated with particular visual expressions of high capitalism in urban India, in which the new, affluent middle classes and elites shape a moral community that differs from Nehruvian visions of nationhood.[3] It explores how the circulation of images creates what Michael Herzfeld calls zones of in/efficient space,[4] depending on the quality of pleasure, or nuisance, they provide. What seems particularly interesting is the notion of "public space" as a means of regulating access to gated enclaves in the megacities of the Global South, thus diverging from Jürgen Habermas's Eurocentric concept of respect for an (ideal-typical, bourgeois) public sphere that is marked by inclusivity, disregard for status, and the shaping of civil consensus through debate and participation through institutions such as the forum or arena. The consensual responsibility to shape a moral community by uplifting even the marginalized and underprivileged sections of society, projected in the Socialist vision of the 1960s and 1970s, is replaced by consumer citizenship; this shifts responsibilities from "common will" and the nation as "civil society" to a class-based and hierarchized public sphere. This public space is not shared or shaped alike by all, neither as agora nor arena nor forum. Instead, what emerges is a public sphere that partially looks like a European version (with a growing infrastructure of cafés, bars, neighborhood parks, organic shops, and the like) but is reserved for, and defined by, a few only. It is closely related to the desire of cities like Delhi and their affluent populations to belong to a "world class" and be "world-class."

WHO'S THAT "WORLD CLASS"?

Although accessible to practically everyone, the advertisements enforcing the enclave gaze speak to an affluent and highly ambitious, English-educated middle class that aspires to participate in an elite lifestyle of neoliberal India. This "world-class" lifestyle had previously been unthinkable because access to economic mobility as social mobility was much more restricted, being reserved for the old middle class and Westernized elite (of bureaucrats and wealthy traders, landowners, or industrialists). Today the neoliberal market and state reservation policies for government and education sectors have led to much greater economic mobility and diversity, to the extent that studies refer to 300 million "climbers" and 300 million "aspirants" to the middle class.[5] But the competition is fierce and certainly not based on equal access for equal people. The enclave gaze is part of a strategic placement in the battle for symbolic capital and distinction. Underlining the idea that "world-class" is the great equalizer are distinctions made on grounds other than these: for instance, caste, region, and religious belonging. But it must also be mentioned that Delhi's population has grown from 400,000 inhabitants in 1901 to 19 million in 2011,[6] with another 10 million people living in the NCR, which occupies territory in three neighboring states and turned the NCR into the world's second largest urban conglomerate in 2011.[7]

The images that move the enclave gaze narrate stories of spatial abundance for and upwardly mobile access of "the deserving few," the "crème de la crème." With this exclusive rhetoric they address specifically the "new" middle class, people who have reached that position only after accumulating remarkable amounts of money in a very short span within economic liberalization. My interest is in what role the enclave gaze plays in the projected metamorphosis from "middle classness" to "world classness" and what this transformation has to do with the notion of space as "public" and "private" good. Who "owns" the city in these imaginaries, and what are the visual markers of such ownership? What does this say about the cultural production of Indianness and publicness within this oscillating segment of society, where class allegedly overshadows (but does not replace) birth?

"World-class" habitus and social networks differ from those of the "old" or "established" upper middle class, for example, of bureaucrats in colonial India and in the postindependence period of planned economy. With economic liberalization, new career opportunities opened up, in particular for young, qualified urban people, suggesting new possibilities and more choice, pleasure, and mobility in lifestyles provided by the booming service sector infrastructure, instead of less mobile, "traditional" caste- or kinship-based careers. This change seems to suggest that individual merit, not birth, makes and unmakes careers and lifestyles. The ecology of images related to lifestyle marketing and predominantly accompanied by English text appears, at first glance, universally accessible and standardized. But the images must be seen in the context of a country that wants to demonstrate its transformation from "Third World" to "First World," from caste-based to class-based, from "backward" to "developed." "Progressive" and "new" India is connected to the moral universe of a cosmopolitan upper middle class. The mobile enclave gaze and the visual imaginary of an Indian world class is to a large extent a privatized gaze that sees notions such as public good and public sphere as its property or as a nuisance to be overcome or at least excluded.

Since the early 1990s a globalized corporate aesthetic has emerged in urban India, with thriving residential, travel, beauty and health, leisure, and hospitality sectors. The narrative key figure here is the sophisticated, successful, leisured, cosmopolitan Indian, investing in and profiting from those new ways of life. An urban India, composed of multimedia images and new architectural, islandlike forms and spaces, has become the stage on which Indians discover and display themselves as members of a globalized, cultured, and historically rooted ecumene. The massive construction activity, often also linked to mega-events such as the Commonwealth Games in Delhi in 2010, derives from an upswing in the economy, higher household incomes, and relatively easy availability of housing finance. High disposable income has brought members of the aspiring and affluent middle class into the realty market, along with international and pan-Indian businesses and their employees.[8] Besides ambitious young corporates, the overseas Indians (NRI, nonresident Indians) are another group addressed by the real estate advertisements of "New India."[9] NRIs have increasingly come to invest in India's economy; many have decided to return to India since the 1990s on a temporary or even permanent basis. They bring along expectations of "modern" as a Western lifestyle and seek to adjust these expectations with upper-class living in India (most would not have been able to afford a maid and a chauffeur back in the United States). For these returning NRIs, the images in lifestyle magazines and real estate brochures are a means of creating a familiar home in India without becoming "too Indian." They seek an "authentic" Indian nostalgia, of a world they left behind when going abroad, a world of childhood dreams and innocence, an India without Third World flair yet with (neo)colonial comforts. This nostalgia is placed in a sanitized, hygienic space, without street-kitchen smells, tacky roadside stalls, illegal housing colonies tucked away behind a billboard or a market, and homeless beggars pressing their dirty hands against the windowpanes of chauffeur-driven cars. This nostalgia rests on an enclave gaze. Returning overseas Indians are especially involved in the reshaping of their "home-land" into something that offers the latest facilities for a new international lifestyle without rendering labels like "authentic," "homely," or "heritage" irrelevant. Instead, as I will elaborate, the images help to shape themed environs loaded with nostalgia or with the desire to hold on to something that has never been one's own and seems on the verge of extinction. The salvaging fascination with an idealized past reflects Arjun Appadurai's concept of "nostalgia without memory":

> The effort to inculcate nostalgia is a central feature of modern merchandising, and in particular (gift) catalogues play with many kinds of nostalgia: nostalgia for bygone lifestyles, material assemblages, life stages, landscapes, scenes, and so on.... These forms of mass advertising teach consumers to miss things they have never lost. That is, they create experiences of duration, passage, and loss that rewrite the lived histories of individuals, families, ethnic groups, and classes. In thus creating experiences of losses that never took place, these advertisements create what might be called "imagined nostalgia," nostalgia for things that never were.[10]

Most of these images seem to be soaked with authenticity and origins, rootedness, and spectacle, even though they may well be part of an ongoing process of displacement, de-location, decontextualization, or reproduction. The images discussed here speak of transcultural entanglements of different kinds, of "West" and "India," "elite" and "common," "taste" and "backwardness." They point toward the aspired self-realization of world class as utopia.

This chapter's epigraph suggests that, like a storyline in a road movie, India's success story unfolds when one is driving through its new booming cities and on her highways and flyovers, passing by and gazing at the glass facades of office blocs, shopping malls, or five-star hotels. Relating the idea of moving images to the vision of "New India" also recalls the concept of the flâneur as it was coined in late nineteenth-century Paris, Berlin, or London, to designate members of the social elites and *bohème* who saw the city as a stage for a modern identity and sensory experience (for example, large boulevards, shopping windows, and squares). The ideal of the flâneur as a lonely wanderer, immersed in conspicuous consumption as a marker of modern subjectivity, may not work in India: leisure is very much connected to collective activities, and there are no boulevards and squares that are used for strolling. Public space is not conceived as productive for such an activity. The activity itself is fairly new. What informants often related instead was how their childhood memories were linked to family picnics in parks (such as Lodhi Gardens and Nehru Park) and how this activity has been replaced by mall and hotel visits; picnics were increasingly understood as an unsophisticated activity of people who seek the public because they have no other, "better" place to go. Crudely put, streets are for the poor to live on. Those who "have" stay inside or drive through. Today's flâneurs rather flip through magazines and advertising brochures that bridge the gap between imaginary and physical spheres. Such virtual and actual *flânérie* is an important component of the enclave gaze because it alerts us to the dynamics of images on the move within a network of enclaves. It speaks of the relevance of joyful and ambitious mobility of "New Indians" aspiring to the enclaves. The enclave gaze is part of a selective perception of reality that shapes and legitimizes the lifestyle aspirations and identification of the new, affluent middle classes. The search for smooth gliding through space begins to see "gaps" and "hurdles" as "nuisance." For instance, several people I met in Delhi told me that they switch on the air conditioning to avoid hearing the sound of the street; they close the curtains because they do not like to look out. Balconies are usually not used "publicly," unless for washing, smoking, or waiting for the vegetable seller to arrive with his cart.

Individual and national success stories have triggered narratives of an Indian American Dream, a Cinderella narrative of a formerly colonized, backward, poor "Third World country," finally dancing along with the rest of the world's celebrities. The narrative is one of the new Indian middle classes marking India's much awaited departure from international stigmatization as backward, spearheading and celebrating capitalist progress and the management, as well as mobility, of personal and new lifestyles. The concept of the enclave gaze enables us to consider this new subjectivity and its related notions of public and private.[11]

PLANET INDIA'S IMAGE CIRCUITS AND NOMADISM

"World class" is based on an enclaved visuality, which imports images and perspectives from various ecologies of circulation, isolated yet globally connected enclaves and images, generating imagined colonies that nest, or piggyback like spaceships, on the "foreign planet India." The images evoke an Indian cosmopolitan competence that diverges from "liberal" cosmopolitanism, or "world-citizenship," coined by authors such as Ulrich Beck. World-citizenship, ideally, goes hand in glove with civic solidarity, participation, and responsibility (albeit "only" that of paying taxes).[12] It is rather related to Aihwa Ong's concept of global nomads and flexible citizens (1999), in which citizenship of the new transnational class is difficult to identify with linear emplacement and solidarity. Certain images that circulate through the domains of mainstream mass media such as lifestyle magazines anchor in and enframe a globalized yet local imaginary of "world class" and cosmopolitan, urban lifestyle. Most of them, signifying change and progress, have not been created anew but already existed in a global imaginary, from which they have been appropriated and altered. My fieldwork on Delhi's imaginaries as world class was conducted between 2004 and 2009. When I started, the real estate imagery was hardly older than five years and beginning to spread "virally." Many open spaces emerge to imagine new life concepts and practices of a new, growing class of affluent Indians. To me, the images can even be understood as "didactic guides" for the new wealthy, who enter the New India like a *Wunderkammer*, like Alice in Wonderland.

In my discussion of the images-on-the-move that shape the rather cynical, privatized public spheres and imaginaries of the "world city" New Delhi, I want to draw upon W. J. T. Mitchell's talk at a conference at Berlin's Haus der Kulturen der Welt in 2003.[13] There he referred to images as migrants, imbued by various disciplinary formations through which they gain speed, quality, value. The migration of images also draws our attention to concepts from diaspora theory, such as "emplacement" or "homing strategies"—that is, the ways in which migrants develop ways to make themselves feel at home away from home (integration, assimilation); the concept of "deterritorialization" as a new approach toward the production of locality and neighborhood; and "creolization," for which I propose another relevant concept taken from history, that of transculturally entangled histories.[14] Images move as "nomadic objects" with seasonal or illegal itineraries and biographies, transgressing borders of various kinds (for example, geographical, cultural, historical, and media based) or rendering them open in order to challenge our notions of cultural identity as nested in one territory. For my research it was important to acknowledge cross-referentiality as a substantial method for exploring itineraries. Besides newspaper, magazine, and billboard advertising, I visited construction sites and spoke to real estate developers, urban planners, architects, and inhabitants of gated communities to better understand the relationship between image, gaze, and spatialization.

Images of metropolitan cities are dominant signifiers of "India Shining," because new models of flexible, and leisure, time and space are exposed and shaped here. They respond to a new infrastructure of "world-class" visibility, where new lifestyle and leisure experiences can be availed, for instance, in wellness spas, fitness centers, or yet another "buzzing" shopping mall. Class—more than caste or religious alliances—becomes a key force and indicator of social alliances and practices. It is the driving force behind the structuring of urban space, sometimes in interesting entanglements with caste, region, or kinship.[15] I agree with Patricia Spyer, who argues in chapter 4 of this volume that the city "provides an especially pregnant site for thinking the place and diversified manifestations of the 'visual' today," in terms of both architecture and image, of marking frontiers and transla-tions. Spyer notes how billboards in Ambon, Indonesia, mark and trace the element of religious difference in urban space. In contrast, the billboards of real estate developers in New Delhi mark hardly anything but "world-class" space. The billboards are put up along national highways, near construc-tion sites, and in dense zones of urban planning, real estate development, and speculation (for example, South Delhi, Gurgaon, and Noida). Some of the real estate developers have been in the business since the 1940s and 1950s, when they bought up large patches of often agricultural or uncul-tivated land, for example, from farmers. Most have sprung up during the past fifteen years or so, with the rapid spread of real estate development.[16]

Much urban planning is connected with the preparations for mega-events such as the Commonwealth Games in Delhi in 2010 or the Asian Games in 1982. These are moments when a globalizing city seeks to present a clear aesthetic and spatial statement in terms of its branding, not so much to its inhabitants but rather to potential investors, creative classes (media persons), tourists, corporate business people, or the "First World." Global cities depend increasingly on private investment, and possibly even more so in the Global South. Besides creating new spaces for consumption, busi-ness, and leisure, developers brand spaces by "theming" them, by situating them to specific narrations of history, culture, and nature.[17]

Obviously, a lot of themed space has to be created by altering previous spaces: converting agricultural land or redefining already occupied land for development by means of demolition. The envisaged enclave demands major adjustments, something that becomes evident when we compare the slum clearances and demolition in nineteenth-century Paris and in today's New Delhi. In the 1930s Walter Benjamin not only drew attention to the world exhibitions and arcades as sites of experiencing urbanization and modern-ism by means of flânérie. He also argued that the urban reconstruction of Paris by Baron Haussmann was based on imperial state politics, privileging "investment capital" and speculation. Haussmann even went so far as to put Paris under a state of emergency and legitimized the spatial removal of the poor so that the gaze of the bourgeois beholder could remain undisturbed and notions of civil security could be upheld.[18] Today such "strategic embellishment" is referred to as the "beautification" and "gentrification" of urban segments.[19] Herzfeld has observed similar processes in Bangkok and refers to them as "spatial cleansing," arguing that this process was also enabled by a different notion of public space in the Global South and Southern Europe and a different concept of "civilized living" in the respective countries.[20] In our case I make the comparison between Paris and New Delhi here to highlight the idea of Delhi as a world-class city. Union cabinet minister for Tourism and Culture Jagmohan (2001–2004) himself underlined the connection between the imagined city beautiful and the neoliberal pragmatics of urban planning in Delhi:

> I'll give you an example of Paris. Paris was a slimy area before 1870 and all the slums were resettled or removed by a person called Baron Hoffman [sic]. He was very much accused of sending the people away and so on, but he organized Paris, created huge boulevards, parks, beautiful places and created an organized way of life, and now Paris has become a hub of tourists, who came from all over the world. Today, as a tourist spot, Paris alone is earning much more than all our cities combined. Why? It is called vision and problems of poverty are solved like this.[21]

Jagmohan intended to transform the embankment at the city's center around Red Fort into a wide boulevard cum leisure and business sites by removing all the illegal structures that had been there since the 1980s.[22] His statement exemplifies India's, and particularly New Delhi's, attempt to move from Third World to First World, or "world class," involving a subtext of someone's having to make sacrifices on behalf of the citizenry. This vision also highlights what Amita Baviskar termed "bourgeois environmentalism," in which alleged sources of threat to the enclave are rendered invisible, unwanted, and illegitimate—thus enforcing a hierarchy of citizens.[23] The term aligns the concept of the new civic "duty" to protect and preserve nature with a bourgeois perception of its pollution, destruction, and diminishment as a class statement. The awareness of the problematic of climate change has entered this debate only recently.

To some extent New Delhi and her capital region look like landscapes with one sprawling housing project after another. They remind us of other global sites of construction, like the Spanish Gold Coast, where hardly an inch of space is free from real estate development, making one wonder who actually occupies these residential blocks. The enclave gaze of the advertisements I discuss here ignores the fact that this saturation of the real estate market has become a problem for Indian global cities. Frenzied construction activity, marking the real estate boom, surfaces everywhere, turning shopping malls and private towns into environmental disasters exceeding those allegedly produced by their slum counterparts.

INDIA AND THE WORLD

The growing association of Indian cities with cosmopolitan lifestyles accessible and legitimate for large segments of society is a recent development connected with the infrastructural emergence of new media technologies, advertisement, leisure culture, and urban planning since the 1990s. The images tied to "India Shining" that I have chosen to focus on here must not be explored in isolation but should be understood as part of a multisited, multimedia orchestration—sometimes in juxtaposition or complementary to other visual narratives (for example, of the idyllic rural village and its ethnic, simple lifestyle). New places emerge and with them new ways of behaving and modes of *savoir vivre*. They are not in fact exactly new: 1960s and 1970s romantic travelogues such as *An Evening in Paris*, directed by Shakti Samanta (1967), already displayed new sites and practices of pleasure and leisure and a remarkable fascination with world metropolitan centers such as Tokyo, Paris, London, and New York. But then, it seems, the booming global cities of the Global South did not exist, only ideas of Indian cities lagging behind. The "world" and "world class" were beyond India's borders, out of reach for most. It was not even desirable to associate nationhood with conspicuous consumption, or with what William Mazzarella describes as the pleasure of consumption as national duty. During the period of Socialist planned economy in the young postcolonial nation, leisure life and cosmopolitan lifestyles necessitated "escapes" to cities and places in the "developed" world. Urban settings were important for anonymity of romantic encounters, beyond the gaze of the family or caste, for the staging of leisure activities such as holidaying or shopping. Heroes and villains of this era of the Indian film industry move through magnificent hotel lounges and suites, watch go-go girls at dance clubs, drink cocktails by the swimming pool, water-ski, walk through airports and parks, and take their lovers for a ride along the coast or to a picnic in the hills, but they only rarely do this in India. Until the 1990s such places were not available outside the frame of the cinema hall or a five-star hotel in a major world city. The idea of the "global Indian," the flexible businessman, was neither fashionable nor particularly appreciated in public discourses related to civic national responsibility; instead, it was seen as morally dubious. With economic liberalization, however, an idea of a public sphere has paradoxically become more visible and seemingly more accessible and varied in urban environs, through the circulation and ubiquity of images of malls, fun parks, and other leisure sites. But it has also become more restricted because most of these "public spaces" are guarded by gates, entrance fees, and membership or dress codes. On planet India, one finds private islands in public spaces.

New spaces and new social types enforce each other. Meanwhile, the abbreviation *NRI* has undergone retranslation and been filled with new meaning. The former "traitor" or "Non-Reliable Indian," who left India in search of prosperity, has been transformed into a driving motor of "new India" and is now even referred to as a "National Resource of India." Many real estate brochures appeal to NRIs, assuming that they want to invest in residential or commercial property in India's booming economy. This, and the growing segment of young professionals educated in India, has consequences for the language used, which is predominantly English, and also with respect to the images and metaphors: "Global living for global Indians" is a slogan by real estate developer Assotech, offering "a historic address for those shaping India's future." "For the next generation of winners" is another, by an Emaar MGF brochure promoting a luxury condominium on the (protected) bank of the river Yamuna in New Delhi.[24] Images and texts in the advertisements appeal to "world-class" Indians who want to make a living in India only so long as they are being offered "international standards." But the language used is also one that assumes the perspective of the "outsider Indian" who is persuaded by the language of colonial history, ethnic chic, and cultural heritage and who cares for a "clean," safe, and green environment.[25] The enclave gaze reveals an interesting tension between the visual ubiquity and availability of images of all kinds of places by means of panoramic options and holistic microcosms, on the one hand, and their increased practical restriction and elaboration of lifestyle rules, on the other hand. The advertisements reproduced for this chapter also come from Eros Group and Emaar MGF. There are a number of other large real estate developers, such as Assotech, DLF Group, Omaxe Limited, Parsvnath Developers Ltd, and Vatika Group, to name a few. They are active not only in residential housing but also in commercial, retail, and entertainment complexes. Most of them promote their philanthropic activities and agenda, thus linking investment to morality.[26]

The little kingdoms of the "modern maharaja" investors are impressive in their security measurements (the more important an inhabitant, the more security upon entering his compound). Breathtaking success stories of global Indians and multimillionaires such as steel tycoon Lakshmi Mittal or industrialists Anil and Mukesh Ambani are the new mythologies of Arabian-Nights-cum-Cinderella, reminding us of the fabulous stories by diplomats, travellers, and missionaries of an enchanted, exotic, fairy-tale India. The names of these kingdoms reflect this royal colonial heritage of the new club culture of world class: Grand Mansions, Windsor Park, Victoria Gardens. With Europe and the United States marketed as oversaturated economies allegedly suffering from a loss of values and social instability, and now even economic crisis, India is painted as a "promised land," next to China, stable for both investors and "cultured" persons. India has been turned into a mirror image of colonial Orientalism, only this time the new Indian elites are orientalizing themselves.[27]

In the rest of this chapter, I discuss three "repositories" of images that are drawn upon frequently: history, culture, and nature.

REPOSITORY I: MAKING AND HAVING "EMPIRE" HISTORY

The tension between a panoramic view and the regulatory practice of exclusion also surfaces in these images in terms of the construction of certain stereotypes imbued in the enclave gaze: "Europe" is the place referred to when calling upon the dramatic and pompous histories of empires such as those of Roman and Greek antiquity or even the British Raj, upon cultural heritage and cultured lifestyle, and upon quality architecture and interior design. Against this "rich historical" symbolic capital from "old worlds" and "ancient histories," the Arabian Emirates serve as points of reference for globalized business and flexible lifestyle in a corporate world. India's past is squeezed into a miniature world of Vedic civilization, tradition, and values and, seemingly paradoxically, a cradle of modernity. Images of history—Indian or Western history—are recurring motifs through which real estate advertising is theming space and lifestyle as part and parcel of cultural capital. Text and image reflect the production of entangled, transcultural connections, of a "world-class" history, where the Indian/Hindu culture and Golden Age emerge as topographically intertwined with Greek antiquity, the Roman Empire, and the Egyptian pharaohs. The desire to improve one's status and power by means of quoting from other cultures and lifestyles, as well as to oppose the values and lifestyles of socially, culturally, and financially weaker groups from one's own society, can be understood as a form of neocolonial distinction.

Let me give an example: the Greek emperor Alexander the Great is a red thread for one of India's largest and oldest corporate firms and real estate developers, Eros Group from New Delhi.[28] In the A3-format color brochure for its luxurious villa project Grand Mansions in Gurgaon, the boom town bordering the south of Delhi, we learn that Alexander was "the world conqueror from the ancient Mediterranean." "Yes! The ancient Greeks were a perfect people and inspired builders." We are then encouraged to imagine the following: "Stand on the Parthenon-like balconies and look out unto the world. Defy constraints of space with great sized living rooms...that can accommodate whole legions of guests.... Walk in, into the league of kings and conquerors"[29] (plates 7a, 7b). Another brochure of the same real estate developer, for Eros Grand Mansions II, promises that "[f]inally, couches can be placed far apart. The door can invite more than one person at the same time. You can look for a bed that is bigger than kingsize. You can give that big and exquisite Persian carpet its due place!... This is the magic of classic Greek architecture.... It stretches the mind."

To some extent, this is certainly also a reference to the ongoing lack and high cost of space in a city like Delhi and to the fact that simple middle-class families may not have more than one or two bedrooms, a living-room, one kitchen, and a bathroom at their disposal. This way, overcoming the alleged "constraints of space" means having a royal attitude and thus a sense of space needed for the display of wealth and (leisure) time.[30] The option (to own a large Persian carpet and more than a king-size bed) turns into an imperative for a particular life conduct that accompanies the luxury goods, and vice versa. Attributes of Alexander and the lifestyle associated with him include "all-conquering power...great Mediterranean spirit with its stately elegance and generous spaces." And "his architecture is conquering the modern world of lifestyle yet once again."[31]

Clearly, there are elements of both auto-Orientalism and Occidentalism in the statements. The front page of the Eros Group brochure sports (but does not cite) a famous quote from Plutarch, "Seek out a kingdom worthy of thyself" (plates 7a, 7b), when Alexander's father, King Philip II, ruler of the highly militarized kingdom of Macedonia, tells him to establish his own kingdom larger than Macedonia. Alexander conquered Egypt and Persia and came to India with no motive beyond lust for war and curiosity about India as enchanted fairyland.[32] The portrait heading the quote with this appeal shows an engraving from 1800. How did this image of the Mediterranean move in, and why Alexander the Great? Why is this narrative thought to appeal to urban upper-middle-class Indians? Below the surface of the city's new topography lies the desire to "have history"—and not just

FIGURE 3.2

"Rejuvenating the royal lifestyle in contemporary world in Jodhpur," Parsvnath City.
Advertisement by Parsvnath Developers, 2006.

any history, but that of an empire. In the real estate advertisements I have explored, constant references are made to reviving the glory of Alexander the Great, the Egyptian Pharaohs, and Roman antiquity but also of the British Raj and the "royal lifestyles" of Rajasthani Maharajas—for the contemporary, modern world.

For many, Alexander the Great is the stereotypical heroic and noble Greek, known for somewhat megalomaniac attitudes, having invaded the eastern Punjab after taking over Egypt and Persia (he died at the young age of thirty-three). Such a figure may serve as a projection screen for the desires of many businessmen to "be free" and adventurous and to secure access to new markets. But Alexander's prominence could also derive from the fact that his was possibly the first encounter between India and "the West," and one without annexation, thus not reckoned as part of a history of humiliation and conversion such as that of the later, much more consequential and traumatic invasions by the Mughals or the British.

Having—that is, owning—history and appropriating European or Egyptian empires into the rhetoric of world class in the real estate narratives are also consequences of lifestyle theming (compartmentalization) and of a strategy that must be seen as a counter to the British Raj's and European Enlightenment's allegation that India lacked history and could not represent itself but had to be represented.[33] Thus, Europe is exoticized much as colonizing countries in Europe once exoticized foreign cultures, rendering them as fascinating yet timeless "ancient" civilizations, based on an imagined nostalgia. Yet, the same is done with India as well, turning it into a brand and a sounding board for self-orientalization.[34] It seems as if "culture" is with Europe but "civilization" is with India; thus, heritage is embedded in an asymmetrical relationship. Images of both world history and Indian history contribute to the notion of a "world class" or "cosmopolitan lifestyle" and gain their value by circulating along national and transnational flows.

REPOSITORY II: INDIAN FOLKLORE AND CULTURAL HERITAGE

Part and parcel of the enclave gaze and the creation of nostalgia without memory are the sites and goods of consumption in the shopping malls located next to the residential areas. These are very informative sources of information with respect to the landscape of taste among the upper middle classes, meant to furnish the lifestyles of those living in enclaves. Often they are items bought for interior decoration and spiritual activities. While there may well be objects appropriated from other geographical regions, such as busts of pharaohs and figures of baroque flute players or scantily clad dancers à la art nouveau (plate 8), a strong tendency of marketing "Indian folk traditions" and "ancient Vedic civilization" can be found in plates 9 and 10. They are examples of the commoditization and fetishization of history, like the paintings of "Indian beauties" with origins in Raja Ravi Varma's works of art, which set the pace for a "national realism" of Indian life and people or Hindu deities.[35] Today these circulating images and objects shape what I would call a "transnational realism." Varma's portraits of ladies and goddesses of the late nineteenth century have been translated for today's ethnic wedding fashion, for beauty standards, and for notions of simple rural life and of noble, cultured, and aristocratic life, both imbued with and generating "Indianness." Plate 9 shows reproductions of these for sale just as one enters India's most rapidly and drastically expanded real estate hub, Gurgaon, on Mahatma Gandhi Road coming from South Delhi, along with plaster or terracotta figurines for the balcony, garden, or living room and marble "made in Italy" for bathroom floors or entrance signboards. Raja Ravi Varma's works circulate through the world from the bazaar and sidewalk stall to international auction houses, shaping for the new middle classes what an Indian past might mean for the present and future, bringing it close to the beholder, suggesting to him or her that cosmopolitan lifestyle is intimately and instantly within reach of one's own four walls.

Plate 10 demonstrates the museumification of religion and spirituality as logos of India's cultural heritage. Also, as a response to Delhi's alleged "dominance" by Muslim monuments, the Akshardham Cultural Complex (ACC) is a massive religio-spiritual leisure site cum Hindu temple on the banks of the Yamuna River. It opened in 2005 almost directly across from the embankment Jagmohan had envisaged for his "Paris of the East."[36] Indeed, it is one of the rare "public" spaces in the heart of Delhi, open to all, for free, who succumb to the sect's rules and regulations (such as not wearing a burqa). While the ACC has already been appropriated by the tourist industry and marketed as the "largest Hindu temple in the world" by the Guinness Book of Records, urban planning also profits from this huge real estate monument: in close proximity to Akshardham, the transnational real estate joint venture Emaar MGF developed the Commonwealth Games Village 2010 as a "landmark address" and "lifestyle statement" and part of the world-class city branding.[37] With the Commonwealth Games Village, Emaar is promoting "a new standard in good living for the next generation of winners" and has set itself next to the ACC as a spiritual and glorious heritage landmark for Delhi and India. Both the Akshardham complex and the Commonwealth Games Village are enclaves of exclusive wealth and cleanliness, visual spectacles by the Yamuna River, and brand sites of a New Delhi, circulated and repeated endlessly through various circuits of media representation. Each site nurtures the other's legitimacy and attraction and generates images that evoke a high capitalist attitude. Respectively, they celebrate spirituality-as-charity and capitalism-as-national-progress, quite different from the Socialist visions of preliberalization India. In short, the enclave gaze and rhetoric also open up a space of legitimization in which the pleasure of consumption and affluence shapes the imaginary of new middle classes and elites as moral communities giving a new face and a new voice to "New India."

The image narratives and performances played out by real estate developers and other lifestyle advertisements suggest rapid progress ("India Shining," "feel-good") and fade out or integrate for the purpose of juxtaposing images of a dark time "before" or images of current danger. However, these images appeal by means of written text: surveillance technology for the sake of security, cleanliness and nature for the sake of physical and mental health, and stress-free life are prerequisites of an image's efficacy in the circuits of neoliberal lifestyle management.

Despite the new enclaves that emerge all over Delhi, the city still promotes itself as public, suggesting free access for all, as part of a rhetoric of "automatic" neoliberal progress. What is interesting here is that the public sphere is highly ambivalent; while suggesting equal access to all, it sidelines all those who do not belong to club culture/world class. This can be equated with the slogan of "India Shining" and its critique: India was a shining experience for a few only, while the "rest," more than 50 percent, would remain, at best, spectators. Moreover, the economic meltdown that also affected India in 2008–2009 has reduced the previous enthusiasm for and "trust" in the bubble of national growth for all and for long. Yet, the neoliberal idea of economic growth and prosperity also implies a drastic change in the notion of common good and civic participation. Under neoliberal guidelines the "poor" and workers are expected to sacrifice themselves for the ideal of progress, whereas under the Nehruvian planned economy, national progress was directed more toward the interests of workers and farmers, demanding sacrifices from the social and economic elites of the country instead.

Leisure and pleasure are center stage in how urban experience is marketed. Cities become "event zones" placed next to images and topographies of taste and spectacle. The city is transformed into a living museum or a theme park, as Michael Sorkin has suggested in the context of urbanization in America.[38] The transformation takes place in an incomplete, patchwork fashion: some places are privatized and restricted to particular social groups; others remain or become publicly accessible. Sharon Zukin's challenging question about who owns the city and its culture/s, and for what reasons, becomes crucial in this context and tells us much about the production, circulation, and consumption of the images discussed here.[39] It underlines the relevance of aesthetics and urban imaginaries in the creation of difference and, as Zukin argues, the creation of fear. The concept of the "themed" environment refers to the design of a public or private space or site according to a particular theme that evokes pleasure and aspirations and to a heightened desire for controlled and safe spaces. For instance, a restored part of an old city can be a "themed" environment, as in the case of Old Delhi or colonial Delhi, as much as an ethnic urban village like Hauz Khas that specializes in marketing traditional folklore, ethnic consumer goods, and cuisine.[40] Museumification and monumentalization, plus accessibility through the newly built metro, have also decreased the notion of danger so often associated with unplanned and dense neighborhoods.

REPOSITORY III: NURTURING NATURE

There is a strong concern to enrich the aesthetics of technological perfection and safety or architectural historicism and exclusiveness with a surplus of nature. The corporate aesthetic of the enclave gaze also affects the visualization and definition of "nature" in urban planning. Nature, in the context of the global city, has become an exclusive good, available to those who know how to appreciate and defend it against threats such as illegal occupants. In the past few years private parks and nature reserves have led to the demolition of squatter settlements, the first carried out by so-called residential welfare associations that have discovered the use of small parks for the recreational enjoyment of citizen-neighbors.[41] Many real estate advertisements promote biodiversity, an abundance of green within the residential complex, stretching toward almost endless horizons, wide enough for each tenant to find a silent spot for meditation, long stretches for jogging, and plentiful meadows for the family to play in and enjoy a picnic—this time, within their own vicinity. There are pools, tennis courts, and, increasingly, even golf courses incorporated in private cities. Several developers have advertised the preservation of natural diversity for nature lovers versus the purportedly careless pollution, if not extinction, of nature outside the gates. This is an interesting move through which the new "world class" proposes to take innovative steps toward a more responsible climate and environmental policy, alleging that this has been neglected by reluctant politicians and the media thus far. In fact, it might be argued that the new middle classes have played a major role in forcing changes in government policies, introducing new solutions to new concerns (such as organic food) and more civic participation by founding residential welfare associations in the gated complexes and other neighborhoods. And it might be the conviction that, once successful at this elite level, these interests might "trickle down," reaching the "rest" of India one day. But there are also worries that this concern with environmental protection is only an alibi to reserve yet another leisure and luxury niche for the few. One often hears it said that the noneducated have no respect for nature. But I remember that when I arrived in India for the first time, in 1989, one was unlikely to find Indians who appreciated a holiday trek or a swim or even a leisurely walk. Today, since the new millennium, more and more people, mainly youth, see the recreational value of nature for their own well-being and prestige, and the tourist industry has been slowly picking up on this trend.

In cities like New Delhi, direct access to nature, solitude, and fresh and clean air is a sign of status distinction, a luxury good. And so is the appreciation of solitude and peace within the enclave world. The advertisement showing a man in his thirties, dressed in a business suit, meditating with eyes closed on the lawns of a park, underlines the association of nature with winners and world class, as the title "The way the world lives" indicates (plate 11). But it has not always been like this: the notion that nature is like a resort, nurturing and thus good for body, soul, and family, is new, as is the notion of having to preserve (rather than just exploit) nature. Yet, what is "preserved" is highly artificial in that the environs are made up of golf courses, palm trees, exotic plants—all in need of much water. In Delhi, water is a scarcity. Some neighborhoods have water only for a few hours a day, if at all!

In fact, several real estate advertisements and brochures claim that in light of nature's erosion and scarcity in megacities like Delhi, the condominium comes to replace "real" nature and even preserves natural diversity for generations to follow, turning New Delhi into a "Green City." The upper middle class and the real estate industry define themselves as environmentalists, caring and taking responsibility for what is destroyed elsewhere in India, for instance, by slum dwellers, who are often referred to as polluters of nature.[42] While exclusiveness is manifest in the advertisements for "world-class" lifestyle by joining the global Indian with the nostalgia of a grand past, the "enclave gaze" is thus also shaped and legitimized by references to idyllic nature and paradisiacal solitude, a concept relatively new to an Indian majority and previously associated with (unreal) asceticism rather than an inner-worldly orientation and lifestyle, had to be exported to the West and turned into a trend before it could be reimported to India.

These perfect natural havens come with hi-tech security systems and CCTV. The fear that unwanted elements might enter this paradisiacal garden is enhanced by associating a rhetoric of wilderness, dirt, danger, and unruliness with the "outside world" and its inhabitants. Where "good" nature can be tamed and salvaged by means of these condominiums, "bad" nature needs to be disciplined, controlled, or excluded if necessary, much as in Jagmohan's quote about "slimy Paris" earlier in this chapter. The desire for nature and security feeds into a growing aspiration among upwardly mobile, urban middle classes to have access to artificially created, privatized spaces. In this way and in these spaces, they hope, withdrawal from stressful work and public urban environs is enabled. Such sites might be gated communities, fun parks, malls, golf courses, or clubhouses, as in "a city full of concrete, a living garden resort to live and breathe. In Delhi. Victoria Gardens. Your Living Garden Resort" (Victoria Gardens, Model Town, North Delhi, developed by M2K). One almost cynical result of this hope is the argument that everyone is responsible for his own environment and if people cannot keep their place tidy, they themselves are to be blamed and must bear the consequences. This attitude becomes particularly evident in the context of open spaces that, until recently, formed part of a gray zone, unwanted, neglected, occasionally surrounding ancient monuments. Often these sites were occupied by migrant workers from rural areas, a parallel economy of places outside the state's topography, quite like the "urban villages." In the 1990s and even more so in the new millennium, these ancient monuments have been increasingly turned into items of a themed heritage environment. The "illegal encroachers" are removed, fences erected, and parks established, protecting the buildings from certain populations on the one hand and making them available on the other, embellished by NGOs such as the Aga Khan Foundation for "cultured" consumption. Paralleling this development, the project of creating undisturbed nature for leisure purposes is also a means of legitimizing the removal of "unwanted elements" from "public spaces." Next to the branding of the ecofriendly city, the aesthetic of tamed nature responds to an aesthetic of security manifest in large wide roads, high walls, marble floors, and spotless cleanliness.[43]

CONCLUDING THOUGHTS

This chapter explores the mobile, print-produced "enclave gaze" of the new, affluent middle class in urban India. I argue that this gaze is closely related to urban planning, to the creation of a corporate aesthetic that celebrates "world class" as moral citizenship over those Indian populations who dwell in the spaces in between the enclaves, spaces that become increasingly associated with threatening, polluting, and disorderly forces. I also scrutinize images of real estate and lifestyle advertising for their ambiguous purposes: serving the needs of high capitalist enchantment and providing a didactic guide to "world-class" membership and habitus. The new spatialities, architectures, and visual regimes enable consumers/ beholders to imagine nostalgic hybrid, modern, extraordinary concoctions. These are ways of seeing, creating, and inhabiting a fantasy world or "planet" called India, having not much in common with the "India" outside the gates of these privatized islands. One is tempted to think of "parallel worlds." But the seemingly hermetically enclosed worlds of privatized India and the "other, public side" of India, less efficient and glamorous, enforce each other and sometimes even spill into each other. The alleged openness of concepts such as "world-class" and "cosmopolitan," in the context of these moving images and their structuring of an urban and globalized imaginary, are often a strategy of exclusion and distinction. But it is too early to say whether this is a one-way street that ultimately leads to the closing down of the public sphere as an openly accessibly space defined by participation and solidarity across social borders—we witness similar conflict-laden contestations of public responsibility and participation all over Europe while this final note is written in the summer of 2011.

The importance of imagination, the pleasure and agency of consumption, and the shaping of alternative modernities in the wider frame of these transcultural visual regimes help us to shift attention away from modernity as an imported Western Enlightenment product and disenchantment, toward a multicentered modernity as a new subjectivity, the cultivation and care of the modern persona, based on an enclave gaze and the notion of "world class." Conspicuous consumption becomes part of economic progress, individual enchantment, charity, and nature preservation. The images and their appearance on imagined and geophysical topographies discussed here show this ambivalent if not cynical public sphere—the emplacement of one group by means of displacement of others—as an appearance of commensuration.

How this belief in progress will be challenged by the current global financial meltdown coupled with domestic economic slowdown remains to be seen. In October 2008, property sales dropped by 30 to 50 percent, in parallel with an oversupply of property and an absence of investors. The great hope, the NRI, has left many disappointed because loyalty toward the homeland seems to be dominated by investment priorities: NRIs have started investing in plummeting US and European markets.[44] Some malls and residential enclaves already show signs of withdrawal of their consumer-tenants; they have become Indian neoliberalism's first set of ruins, empty sites of speculation. What may be left of this upper crust of "India Shining" in that case are perhaps only the images, as sites for archaeological excavation by future anthropologists. The opening quote of this chapter begins with the appeal to "shut your eyes for a moment." Maybe the enclave gaze can be practiced only with eyes shut.

Acknowledgments

I want to thank Patsy Spyer and Mary Steedly for having given a crucial number of critical comments and suggestions for this chapter. I must also express gratitude to the German Research Council (DFG), which funded the research for this larger study on the urban middle classes in India in the context of the Collaborative Research Centre "Ritual Dynamics" (2005–2008) and the Research Cluster "Asia and Europe in a Global Context," both at Heidelberg University. See Christiane Brosius, *India's Middle Class: New Forms of Urban Leisure, Consumption and Prosperity* (New Delhi: Routledge, 2010).

Notes

1. Debraj Mookerjee, "It's More Than 'Just Hopping,'" *Celebrating Vivaha* 6, no. 3 (2007): 48–49.

2. See Veronique Dupont, Emma Tarlo, and Denis Vidal, eds., *Delhi: Urban Space and Human Destinies* (Delhi: Manohar, 1996).

3. See Sunil Khilnani, *The Idea of India* (Delhi: Oxford University Press, 1997).

4. Michael Herzfeld, "Spatial Cleansing: Monumental Vacuity and the Idea of the West," *Journal of Material Culture* 11 (2006): 132.

5. Numbers about the Indian middle classes vary to such an extent that scholars have begun to define categories such as aspiring and established affluent middle classes, "seekers," and "climbers." See Pavan Varma, *The Great Indian Middle Class* (Delhi: Penguin, 1998). Statistics as to how many people (can actually afford to) live in the gated communities of the upper real estate market do not exist.

6. See http://www.indiaonlinepages.com/population/delhi-population.html (accessed August 19, 2011). Since 2001 the city has expanded by seven million people. Approximately 50 percent live in illegal housing colonies.

7. In this list of the *World Urbanization Prospects* report (2009 revision) by the United Nations, Tokyo ranges on the first place. See http://esa.un.org/wup2009/unup/index.asp?panel=2 (accessed August 10, 2011).

8. Attractive tax deductions with interest paid on housing loans plus better conditions for long-term loans and a drop in interest rates from 14 percent in 1996 to 7.5 percent in 2005 contributed to the boom. Earlier, people bought their first homes mostly toward the end of their careers, before retirement. Now they invest when they are in their twenties. See Shampa Dhar-Kamath, "Will the Boom Last?" *India Today* 30, no. 5 (February 2005): 40–47.

9. Until the global economic meltdown in 2008, NRIs had been dominant buyers of high-end properties. See *Reality Plus* 5, no. 3 (November 2008).

10. Arjun Appadurai, *Modernity at Large: Cultural Dimensions of Globalization* (New Delhi: Oxford University Press, 1997), 76–77.

11. See Georg Glasze, Chris Webster, and Klaus Frantz, eds., *Private Cities: Global and Local Perspectives* (London: Routledge, 2006), 9–30.

12. Ulrich Beck, *World at Risk* (Cambridge, UK: Polity Press, 2008).

13. See W. J. T. Mitchell, "Migrating Images: Totemism, Fetishism, Idolatry," in *Migrating Images: Producing–Reading–Transporting–Translating*, ed. Petra Stegmann and Peter Seel (Berlin: House of World Cultures, 2004), 14–24; and http://netzspannung .org/tele-lectures/series/migrating-images/ (accessed December 23, 2008).

14. Avtar Brah, *Cartographies of Diaspora: Contesting Identities* (London: Routledge, 1996); Appadurai, *Modernity at Large*, 1997; Aihwa Ong, *Flexible Citizenship: The Cultural Logics of Transnationality* (Durham, NC: Duke University Press, 1999); Wolf Lepenies, *Entangled Histories and Negotiated Universals: Centers and Peripheries in a Changing World* (Frankfurt: Campus, 2003).

15. See also Manfred Fassler, *Urban Fictions: Die Zukunft des Städtischen* (Munich: Fink, 2006), 11.

16. Some of the land under speculation borders Delhi but lies in the National Capital Region (NCR), where neighboring states Haryana and Uttar Pradesh attract investors by means of low taxes and other investment privileges. Much development happens in South Delhi, east across the river Yamuna and toward the international airport southwest of Delhi.

17. See Stephanie Donald, Eleonore Kofman, and Catherine Kevin, eds., *Branding the Cities: Cosmopolitanism, Parochialism and Social Change* (London: Routledge, 2008).

18. Walter Benjamin, "Paris, Capital of the Nineteenth Century," *The Arcades Project*, ed. Howard Eiland and Kevin McLaughlin, trans. R. Tiedemann (1939; Cambridge, MA: Belknap Press of Harvard University Press, 1999), 23; for the case of New Delhi, see Lalit Batra and Diya Mehra, "Das neoliberale Delhi: Der Blick vom Trümmerfeld eines planierten Slums," in *Mumbai Delhi Kolkata: Annäherungen an die Megastädte Indiens*, ed. Ravi Ajuha and Christiane Brosius (Heidelberg: Draupadi, 2006), 157–172.

19. Benjamin, "Paris, Capital of the Nineteenth Century"; for the case of New Delhi, see Batra and Mehra, "Das neoliberale Delhi."

20. Herzfeld, "Spatial Cleansing," 137–146.

21. Ruzbeh Bharucha, *Yamuna Gently Weeps: A Journey into the Yamuna Pushta Slum Demolitions* (New Delhi: Sainathann Communications, 2006), 167. Such comparisons with non-Indian "global cities" are shared by many officials, for example, chief minister of West Bengal Mamta Banerjee, who heralded the idea of Kolkata as "another" Hong Kong in 2011.

22. Batra and Mehra, "Das neoliberale Delhi."

23. Amita Baviskar, "Between Violence and Desire: Space, Power and Identity in the Making of Metropolitan Delhi," *International Social Science Journal* 55 (2003): 89–98.

24. Emaar MGF Land Limited, *Commonwealth Games Village 2010*. For the online brochure, see http://emaarmgf.com/CGV/index.html (accessed December 29, 2008).

25. See Emma Tarlo, *Clothing Matters: Dress and Identity in India* (Chicago: University of Chicago Press, 1996).

26. For general and brief information about these developers, see http://www .iloveindia.com/real-estate/builders/ (accessed December 26, 2008). Emaar MGF is a rather recent joint venture with major building activities and its origin in Dubai.

27. See also William Mazzarella, *Shoveling Smoke: Advertising and Globalization in Contemporary India* (Durham, NC: Duke University Press, 2003).

28. Eros Group started operations in 1940 in Lahore, Pakistan, and then moved to India. Its core business activities are real estate development, five-star hotels, residential buildings, cinemas, commercial complexes, and shopping plazas.

29. Eros luxury apartments cost around India rupee (INR) 1.5 crore plus (about Euros [€]30,000), independent houses cost a minimum of INR 2.25 crore (about 40,000). Some villas have a private pool, and the plot size is 800–1,000 square meters. In the upcoming and well-planned township of Noida, residential condominium projects range from INR 30 to 85 lakhs per unit (1,200–3,000 square feet, about €55,000–1.5 million) in so-called "Grade A" residential buildings. See Jayant Varma, "Property Watch," *India Today Buyer's Guide*, July–September 2006, 8–14. Prices in New Delhi and Bombay can be compared to those in New York.

30. See Appadurai, *Modernity at Large*.

31. Eros Group brochure, 2005.

32. Sabine Müller, "Alexander's India: Terra Incognita as Propaganda," *atopia* 8 (October 2005). See http://www.atopia.tk/index.php/terra8/ (accessed December 26, 2008).

33. This is in reference to Said's book *Orientalism*, in which he quotes from Marx, *Notes on the Eighteenth Brumaire of Louis Bonaparte* (1852): Marx argued that some people

have to be represented because they cannot represent themselves.

34. See Christiane Brosius, *India's Middle Class: New Forms of Urban Leisure, Consumption and Prosperity* (New Delhi: Routledge, 2010); Veronique Dupont, "The Idea of a New Chic Delhi through Publicity Hype," in *The Idea of Delhi*, ed. Romi Khosla (Mumbai: Marg Publications, 2005), 78–93.

35. See Erwin Neumeyer and Christine Schelberger, *Popular Indian Art: Raja Ravi Varma and the Printed Gods of India* (New Delhi: Oxford University Press, 2003).

36. See Brosius, *India's Middle Class.*

37. See www.akshardham.com (accessed December 22, 2008); and www.emaarmgf. com (accessed December 27, 2008). Emaar, better known as the company that built the Burj Dubai, so far the world's tallest tower, has a global presence with operations in sixteen countries. MGF is a ten-year-old real estate developer from North India with developments such as City Square Mall and MGF Metropolitan in Delhi to its credit. In 2009 the Delhi Development Authority had to intervene and financially support the cash-strapped giant Emaar to finalize the project in time.

38. Michael Sorkin, ed., *Variations on a Theme Park: The New American City and the End of Public Space* (New York: Hill and Wang, 1992), xv.

39. Sharon Zukin, *The Cultures of Cities* (Boston: Blackwell, 1995).

40. See Tarlo, *Clothing Matters.*

41. See also Partha Chatterjee, "Are Indian Cities Becoming Bourgeois at Last?" in *Body.City: Siting Contemporary Culture in India*, ed. Indira Chandrasekhar and Peter Seel (New Delhi: Tulika Books, 2003), 170–185.

42. Batra and Mehra, "Das neoliberale Delhi."

43. Teresa Caldeira, *City of Walls: Crime, Segregation, and Citizenship in São Paolo* (Berkeley: University of California Press, 2001); Lalit Batra, "Out of Sight, Out of Mind: Slum-Dwellers in 'World-Class' Delhi" in *Finding Delhi: Loss and Renewal in the Megacity*, ed. Bharati Chaturvedi (New Delhi: Penguin Books Delhi, 2010), 16–36.

44. *Reality Plus* 5, no. 3 (November 2008).

4

Images without Borders

Violence, Visuality, and Landscape in Postwar Ambon, Indonesia

Patricia Spyer

The city is in crisis, its great walls crumble, rocks and debris pile up below. Smoke shrouds large swaths of the country, tongues of flame leap out of churches. A populace in ancient garb is on the move; they raise trumpets and shake tambourines in defiance. Above, the angry face of God etched red and grimacing against dark clouds, behind him a crowd of angels borne on the storm. This is a scene of dramatic devastation.

> *—Description of a painting housed in a warehouse on the outskirts of Ambon City*

It's as if we are praying in his hands...one feels as if one is praying in his hands...Gethsemane in miniature.

> *—Interview with a Protestant minister about the prayer room in his home in Ambon City*

A Christ with a heavy beard and a busily patterned shirt gazes down lovingly at the five children held in his embrace. The boys and girls wear necklaces; bands with flowers and feathers catch their hair; one wears a cloth draped over her shoulder. Noteworthy is the warm intensity of Christ's look and the crisscross of gazes among the children. It is Good Friday, March 31, 2002.

> *—Description of a charcoal drawing by a Protestant minister in Ambon City*

Christ looks down in sorrow, bloody tears on pale cheeks, upon a globe turned to Ambon Island.

A serene Christ portrait with frayed edges stands out against the unfolding of canonical scenes from his life—birth in Bethlehem's manger, a boat carrying Christ and apostles tossed at sea, his body bent under the great weight of the cross, crucifixion, resurrection.

—Description of a billboard and an adjacent mural facing a motorbike-taxi stand in Ambon City.

Scenes from a wreckage, these fragments from an Indonesian postwar urban landscape—bits of citation snatched from conversation or more formal interviews and my own thumbnail sketches—foreground the provisional, incomplete, and exploratory nature of the images that are the focus of this chapter. My interest is in the diversity of the scenes these images conjure, ranging from God's-eye views and apocalyptic visions to intimate physical exchanges between God and humans, from the Christian sacred geography of Gethsemane to God in situ or in close proximity to Ambon. Christ blends as an Ambonese intimately with local children, dark complexioned, in native dress, with wavy hair and beard, or overlooks from a distance the Moluccan Islands below—although then, too, he is clearly moved by what he sees. I am struck by the way these pictures seem to pull in different directions. Foreground and background easily trade places or slide into each other; scale is up for grabs, shifting from one picture to the next or even within a given picture, as, for instance, in the superimposition of Christ's gigantic cameo portrait onto a narrative unfolding of his life. Perspective and views on the city and its inhabitants are mobile and varied as the landscapes envisioned in the pictures migrate seemingly without effort among this-worldly and other-worldly scapes and novel topographical formations, including those that sacralize Ambon's conventional cityscape, as when Christ overlooks Ambon Bay rather than Jerusalem or his head hovers over the attack on one of Ambon's landmark churches. Striking in all of this is the strong sense of movement.

Elsewhere, I have written of my initial encounter with these pictures.[1] How, during a brief visit in 2003, under emergency conditions, my curiosity had been piqued by the few pictures that whizzed by me as I navigated the city by car with colleagues from a local university. How, subsequently, as I came to know Ambon in its new postwar circumstances, I encountered a city crowded with such pictures. Since then, I have not ceased to be amazed by the surprising facility with which the oversize Christian images emerged in the streets, rose up behind church altars, and infiltrated the more intimate spaces of some of the city's more well-to-do Christian homes. I have discussed their scale, their abundance, their repetition, and the interocular field in which they flourish, where visual print media, artisanal takeoffs of print examples, dreams, prophetic visions, designs on T-shirts, and images from murals and billboards cycle seamlessly into one another.[2] I have suggested how the pictures refract different scales and modes of visuality, from the evidentiary and the bureaucratic eye of state-seeing, to the hypervisibility of media "spotlights" that single out "hot spots" around the globe,[3] and, importantly, how the turn to picturing constitutes a more spectacular part of the larger play of visibility and invisibility that is one important legacy of the city's recent war.

Here I explore the diversity of the pictures and in particular the visual presence they give to what I call landscape and figures of territory. Relatedly, I attend to the exploratory frameworks of visuality, power, and perspective that the pictures and related picturing practices call up and put into place and through which they are made efficacious. By calling these works "landscapes," I want to underscore how, much as in traditional landscape painting, they are animated, broadly speaking, by the effort to secure a perspective or vantage onto things, "to set meaning in place or fix a moral frame of reference through the composition of relatively static visual scenes."[4] In this case, too, they would still a world in restless and, at times, terrifying motion and reestablish and secure the familiar terms of quotidian existence, along with the timeworn outlines of previously taken-for-granted lifeworlds. Doing so, however, while at war and in the deeply changed circumstances thereafter, has meant a dramatic retooling of visual imagination that involves drawing upon the range of media and models already at hand and on those salient or introduced during the conflict.

Prominent among the former are the traditional print media of the Christian canon on which the bulk of the city's new pictures generally rely. To be sure, prior to the war, calendars and, to a lesser extent, posters were conventional props of religious identity in Christian homes and stores; together with Sunday school manuals, they are a familiar component of the transnational Christian print repertoire that has long been available in Ambon. Yet, if the Christian sacred was never invisible or faceless in the city, prior to the war it was—visually at least—not a privileged focus of attention, public or otherwise. To assess, therefore, the creativity of the drive to picture, as well as that of the pictures themselves, it is worth considering the discontinuities that mark this newly invented practice. Let us listen first, however, to some explanations provided by Ambonese themselves concerning the turn to pictures. The context is the war that in religion's name ravaged Indonesia's provincial capital, Ambon, from 1999 to 2002, spilled over into the surrounding islands, and, notwithstanding a peace treaty signed in early 2002, saw occasional outbreaks thereafter.[5] I begin with a street painter, one of Ambon's most prolific, a man named John:

> The moment was actually during the violence, when the faith of us believers, us Christians, was shaking—many people fled from Ambon…so we thought even if it is only a picture, a painting, we were always convinced that he was here.… Back then, the situation was really hot, so we imagined this spontaneously. We wanted to ensure that God would really and truly be present in the conflict, we wanted to do this even though the city was burning on all sides, but we were convinced God was here. So I painted while Ambon was in flames, God on clouds.[6]

Another account comes from a council member of the traditional, colonial-derived Protestant Church of the Moluccas, or GPM. Here he explains why his church commissioned a Christ reaching with extended arms from behind the altar in 1999—the war's first year:

> There was a general atmosphere of panic and fear, so this was done to strengthen the faith so that people would know that God was always here. People had the feeling that God was not here. Violence was all around. Fires were everywhere. The picture was [intended] to provide the assurance that God is with us, that he lifts us up. Faith was still shaky.[7]

Lastly, the remarks of a motorbike-taxi driver about the picture of Jesus looking down on a map of Ambon, which is painted on a hijacked billboard over a former Sempurna cigarette advertisement:

> During the conflict in Ambon, Christians were slaughtered by Muslims. We took the decision to do this picture even as the Muslims were attacking us. We took the decision with John, who is a youth from here. John said, "Why don't we paint Jesus blessing Ambon here?" The guys liked that idea because Jesus blesses Ambon so that we feel close to God. Lord Jesus cries as he looks

down on Ambon City. He cries to see the suffering of the community of Ambon City. Long ago we lived happily, but now we kill each other.[8]

Echoing similar observations and commentary that I often heard in the city, these citations all beg the following question, even as they answer it: when did the Christian God begin to appear inaccessible via the ordinary means available to his followers? When did he become so painfully distant that a picture of him—albeit "just a picture"—needed to be put in place to offer the assurance that he really and truly was here, always here? To paint pictures and to turn to them in the calamitous, edgy environment of the war was to experiment in certain desperation, to launch a new medium in the hope that it might engage and moor the Christian God, who appeared to be drifting or at least too far away to provide the necessary solace. Alternating paintbrush with prayer, the paintings that proliferated during and after the conflict bear poignant testimony to a vast effort to anchor God in the world, to visually pinpoint and circumscribe his location here in the midst of violence and in the face of a severely taxed religious faith.

Yet, to paint in these exacerbated circumstances was not to illustrate something already in place in the sense of re-presenting that of which the existence can be safely assumed. At stake, on the contrary, is the articulation of a desire and a force that is daring, experimental, and aggressive; hence, not just the urgency that drove the pictures' production but also the undeniable energy with which they sprung up and spread across the city. Sites of experimentation in more than a few respects, the paintings break with the past and, specifically, with the aniconic tradition of Ambon's Dutch-derived Calvinist church, the GPM, and they are assertive in the new publicness they accord to religion—although certainly not alone in this in Indonesia after Suharto. So, too, are they radical in seizing upon the traveling images of a globalized Christian print capitalism and in the inspiration the new artisanal practice finds in the range of other "materials" around. Daring, also, are the city's Christian images in their envisioning of myriad mise-en-scènes as the possible loci of new understandings of community and in their visualization of heterotopias that potentially transport those who engage and negotiate their effects beyond the discursive frames of the Indonesian state and its codified forms of citizenship. They are radical as a new medium of expression and communication. Last but not least, they are novel in their self-organizing capacity—no church or other institution or authority has rallied around or pushed the production of the images.

Yet, while radical in so many ways, not the least in the banal fact of their physical presence at prominent crossroads and along the city's main thoroughfares, in other respects these picturing projects are quite conservative, especially in their positing of a visual public that excludes anything considered incompatible with a wholly Christian universe. Constituting what might be called a postwar *poetics of world-making*, in Michael Warner's formulation, what these pictures *want* is to repair and restore the everyday lifeworlds of a previolent moment when Ambonese Christians still, by and large, enjoyed relative power and privilege.[9] They are *world-making* too, in their dramatic sense of arrival and in the novelty with which the pictures and the Christian scenes these portray stand out aggressively from the ruins of the recent war and force themselves into public view. Given that this public performance unfolds on the ragged edges of a recent war, the poetics of Ambon's pictures are as much shot through with the doubts and desires, the violence and the force, of that restricted, perilous environment as they are by the need to describe the horizons of possible future Ambonese Christian habitation, as well as its general conditions and place. It is to some examples of these new horizons and poetic landscapes that I now turn.

LANDSCAPE I: CHRISTIAN ENCLAVE

Tucked away in a Christian neighborhood in the hills overlooking the city, the miniscule prayer room in a Protestant minister's home is painted entirely from floor to ceiling. Forming a single unbroken surface, it envelops those who enter the room to pray within a miniature Gethsemane Garden. On the far wall that is the room's immediate focus when one enters, Jesus Christ prays in profile against a shiny green background. Although lavishly sprinkled with flowers and boasting luxuriant vegetation, incongruous rock formations, an occasional palm or olive tree, and a few stiff, glossy sheep, the remaining three walls in the room are predominantly green (plate 12). Not a single spot has been overlooked—even the door to the room has been painted over to resemble a cave. Bent on ensuring its Gethsemane effect, the minister took care to plant leafy green trees in his garden immediately outside the room's only window. Since the room's décor is also minimal, there is little to distract one from the painted surroundings, so one's eyes tend to gravitate toward the quiet, silhouetted Jesus bent in prayer. This directionality, along with the shiny seamlessness of the space, may be why the sense of closeness and of being physically held in Christ's hands is one of the room's celebrated effects—and something that the minister, his family, and, reportedly, those congregation members who come for counseling and enter the room to pray remarked upon continually.

The moment we enter the special room—the minister explained
—it's as if we are in his hands. There are olive trees painted there.
And there is a painting of Jesus praying. And if we open the window, I planted some green trees outside, so if we pray with the
windows open, one feels as if one is praying in his hands. And
my desire was like that, Ma'am. I created an atmosphere in the
prayer room like that of the Garden of Gethsemane.... It happened that in the magazine *Gloria* there is a photo of the Garden
of Gethsemane with those olive trees. I said, "Please paint like
this. I want a picture with the atmosphere of Gethsemane."[10]

Yet, while some congregationalists may be invited into the prayer room,
the majority of those who consult the minister do so in the reception room
that one enters upon coming into the house. On the wall opposite the
door, an immense Jesus rises behind some chairs, his arms extending to
the viewer. When I had first visited the minister in his office at the GPM's
head Maranatha Church, he mentioned the painting, emphasizing how it
is *truly full of love and care*. As we sat before it in his home some weeks later,
he elaborated on this dimension:

After John finished painting [the Christ picture], this room
began to be used for counseling, and everyone who came here
felt really pleased. Before a person would even be involved in the
counseling, as soon as he sat down with whatever troubles he had,
he would feel very relieved [*Bahasa Indonesia*]. "Pak Minister, the
atmosphere is delicioussssss...." It was as if the painting...helped
him so that he felt there was assistance in an indirect fashion.

Although the painting in the foyer has a soothing atmosphere, it pales
by comparison with the effects of the room set aside for prayer. To enter
this "special room" is to leave one world behind and be enclosed in another,
a Christian "elsewhere" that bears only an oblique, tenuous connection to
the first. The existence and circulation of such Christian elsewheres and
sacred sites or, differently, those of other religious traditions, like Islam,
are, in themselves, not remarkable. Adam Becker observes, for instance,
how "Scripture as well as Jewish and Christian traditions carry with them a
certain geography and it is natural for Jews and Christians to employ this
geography when they reside in those regions it describes (as some of the
contemporary American evangelical Christian support for the invasion of
Iraq shows for Christians" even outside the land.[11] Along with this inbuilt,
portable geography, the religious universality of Christian holy places like

Rome or Jerusalem and affect-laden sites such as Gethsemane is one that "pushes them beyond any linguistic or geographical particularity," making it "difficult for them to be circumscribed within entirely regional, not to mention national, geographies."[12]

Notwithstanding such mobility, what strikes one here is the careful hedging of such circulation, the carving out of a cavelike enclosure, and the creation of a miniature Christian enclave cut off from the world outside. In my use of the phrase "Christian enclave," I draw on Christiane Brosius's understanding of a visually induced space or "enclave gaze" that "imports images and perspectives from various ecologies of circulation...generating imagined colonies that nest, or piggyback like spaceships, on [in her example] the 'foreign planet India'" (Brosius, chapter 3 in this volume). Notable in this definition is not only the enclaving gesture but also the complete incongruity with the larger world outside—like spaceships arriving to wholly distinct surroundings. Like spaceships, too, at least in their common portrayal in popular media, such enclaves often signal an attack against or, at the very least, a defensive stance toward the "foreign" environment around them. The Christian prayer room or otherworldly enclave that lovingly encloses and physically extracts those who pray within from the world beyond resonates with the widespread, historically infused, postwar desire to turn time back, to reclaim Ambon as a city with a "Christian impression about it," which it was until the 1980s—one, also, dominated politically, economically, and culturally well into the 1990s by Protestant Ambonese.[13]

To a large extent the defensive attitude exemplified by the miniature Christian enclave has to do with the changing nature and physical transformation of public space in Indonesia and, in particular, the enhanced public visibility and publicity of the nation's religious composition since approximately the 1980s. Ambon's pictures rise in the midst of what scholars describe as a burgeoning "public Islam"—including its salient visible, audible, and physical presence in Indonesia, as in other parts of the world since the 1979 Iranian revolution, along with more recent factors.[14] In the streets of Ambon and across Indonesia, Islam's indisputable public presence registers visibly and audibly in the many new mosques being built, the popularity of Qu'ranic reading sessions and typical Muslim fashions, the rise in the number of Indonesian Muslims performing the hajj, the resurgence of Islamic print media, the development of new forms of *da'wa* (proselytizing) like cyber-da'wa and cellular-da'wa,[15] and the spread of Islamic economic institutions. Or, as the GPM minister with the home prayer room volunteered, characterizing the city's new street paintings as a direct parallel to this public Islam, "it's the same. They don't make pictures much, but they wear headscarves as their own kind of special characteristic. To show that 'we are Muslims.' Yes, that's what stands out."

That which stands out and figures as an "invisible backdrop" to the Christian pictures in Ambon's streets, churches, and homes is the very fact, then, of Muslim presence, in the form of the overwhelming numerical dominance of Muslims in Indonesia—some 90 percent of the total population—in the public prominence of Islam throughout the large majority of the country, and in the conviction prevalent during the war among Ambon's Christians that they were the target of a Muslim-driven genocide.[16] Claiming and proclaiming the city as Christian, the pictures perform God's partisan presence in Ambon; at the same time, they pictorially efface the Muslim who hovers at the edge of the frame and charges these public pictures affectively. In an article on the "colonial backdrops" of photographs, Arjun Appadurai writes about how the backdrop relevant to understanding a given photograph is twofold: the first is the visible backdrop and the second an invisible one, a secondary order that shapes the interpretation of the "intended viewers" or photograph's addressees.[17] In Ambon, against the "backdrop" of an encroaching public Islam, a religiously inflected war, an urban environment where "societal spaces as well as individual bodies" continue to be "*marked* by the signs of the [recent] brutality" and where violence remains visible,[18] it takes little imagination on the part of those who engage these images to see, as it were, the larger "invisible" backdrop looming behind.

Another way of thinking about this is as the *ground of the image,* as the philosopher Jean-Luc Nancy calls it, or as that which gives the image its force. In his understanding, the image is both detached from a ground and cut out within a ground, a double movement that pulls the image away from and brings it forward out of this ground so that "the ground disappears because the cut-out image is what appears."[19] The image attracts attention precisely because it is both a gathering and a withdrawal and thus always maintains this distinct or "cut-out" character.[20] From this perspective the ground of the image does not serve as its support but figures as the image's underside, as that from which the image withdraws, draws together, and focuses its energy, becoming an intense presence that exerts a powerful force. Because the image does not cease to be distinct, the nature of engagement with it is inevitably one of shock, confrontation, tête-à-tête, or embrace. Generally speaking, this force animates all the new Christian images in Ambon.

To pray in the miniature Gethsemane Garden is, in Nancy's terms, to enter into a kind of tête-à-tête that realizes itself through the embodied mimicry of the painted God's gestures on the part of the person praying and can lead to that person's being swept up in this physical exchange by the incredible sensation that he or she is caught protectively in God's hands. Together with the unbroken seamlessness of the space, this sensation seems to be an effect of being momentarily suspended and hermetically sealed, spaceshiplike, from any outside surroundings; with leafy trees planted immediately outside the prayer room's windows, even the city's "invisible backdrop" can briefly be held at bay. In its place, a delicate and moving closeness comes to the fore that the minister's wife was at a loss for words to describe—one in which the room's painted backdrop forecloses the invisible one pressing in from the outside, thereby allowing those praying in the foreground to merge tenderly with the affectively powerful Christian scene.

Although highly condensed here, this is a landscape that has spread more diffusely throughout the city, carried by the pictures that have arisen in its streets. It is one in which Ambonese Christians aim to gather a visual world around themselves, hence the frequent emphasis on the public pictures' "comforting" nature, on the need for their multiple, large-scale presence and continual reiteration. Itself an image, this landscape is mediated by a Christian canon that was formerly identified with intimacy and interiority and, as such, a long-standing conventional feature of the city's more domesticated Christian spaces. This has recently been stood on its head. It is worth considering how the pictures' prior exclusive association with the more intimate spaces of the Christian everyday may contribute to their current appeal. As the images moved out of houses and stores and grew in size, they did not displace the earlier calendars, posters, or embroidered Last Supper scenes but merely supplemented them. Given this local trajectory, the pictures may still somewhat retain the promise and buttress the performance of a Christian Ambonese subject as visually construed in familiar, comfortable, and essentially interiorized surroundings—even as these surroundings have been stretched in new directions.[21] At issue, then, in some basic sense would be a new acute awareness of the subject's emplacement within a field of vision.[22] Such a thematization of the visual, together with the larger field around it, provides, as we will see, a connecting thread that runs through all of the city's new pictures.

LANDSCAPE II: *PANCASILA* JESUS

If the previous landscape was faithful to Christian print culture, the following on our truncated tour of the postwar city departs explicitly from the canon that, by and large, figures as the reference for Ambon's new images. This landscape is deceiving in its simplicity—a sketch on an A4-size sheet

Chr. I. Tamaela NJACM   Jumat Agung 31.03.2002

Tete Manis polo sayang anak-anak
di tana Maluku

FIGURE 4.1

Chris Tamaela, "Tete Manis" (Our Sweet Father), Ambon, 2006. Reproduced with permission of the artist. Photograph by P. Spyer.

of paper made at the height of the war by another GPM minister, on Good Friday, 2002. "It was 2002, Ma'am, Good Friday," Chris began. "The war was going on and I made this. I drew this at the time." Rendered in charcoal, the drawing shows a cluster of six figures at its center, strongly outlined against the white page—a swarthy Christ bends over protectively, enclosing five children in his arms, clothed in traditional Malukan dress. Several are easily identified with specific regions; others evoke a more generic custom.

It is captioned in Maluku Malay: "Our Sweet Father lovingly embraces the children of Maluku."[23] As in an earlier conversation when the drawing first came up, Chris highlighted the Malukan appearance of Christ.

Why did I depict Jesus as a Malukan? Because I thought that Jesus would be closer, we would feel his presence more in our lives, more in us…. There is no problem even if Jesus has a European face. I can see this is my God, my Jesus. But I thought, well, maybe, maybe ALSO…I can feel the presence of Jesus with the face of an Ambonese…. It's the same, no? So I drew him as an Ambonese, Jesus as an Ambonese. I feel that Jesus is really concerned with the lives of us Malukans. Jesus knows exactly what Malukans are like—their attitude, their lives, the way they live. So I believe that Jesus can know our Malukan language, he can speak Ambonese Malay. If we say to embrace [A.M. *polo*], he understands [that we mean] "to embrace" [I. *memeluk*]. I know that Jesus can know all our languages. Jesus also knows how to eat cassava, Jesus knows how to eat sago, we eat sago porridge together. Jesus knows how to eat the pickled vegetables like the ones Ma'am eats. So Jesus can feel the hunger of Malukan children. When we cry, we call out to Jesus in our own language. We suffered from the violence. Jesus embraces us, he cares for us. So this is what I think…. I already did this with music. [*He broke into a song about the Holy Ghost with refrains in Ambonese Malay.*]

As Chris spoke, visibly moved, he wove song, drumming, myriad voices and local expressions, costume pieces, and other custom-marked paraphernalia through his multiply mediated performance, creating a deeply embodied, sensually vivid, vernacular Malukan world. Set off and reiterated by the drawing, this world unfolded and expanded narratively as Jesus's name became sutured to predicates that in rapid succession mapped this world by drawing the divine subject increasingly near and folding him into the lives of Malukans. With extreme tenderness the performance developed a far-reaching physiognomic and physical identification with a Malukan Christ, the image of whom looked up at us from the floor. In Chris's rendition, this Christ is one who not only resembles you physically but also, with a breathtaking intimacy, knows and tastes the food in your mouth, has your language on his lips, feels the weight and texture of your clothing on his skin. He is someone who moves, breathes, and lives alongside and within you.

Different from though echoing the physical tête-à-tête of the prayer room, this poetic world-making issues not in any enclave but in a densely knit landscape conjoining God and humans, accomplished by riveting Christ as an *inner presence, present during the violence, quite internal* at its core.

Yet, Chris's ambition, articulated the same evening, to disseminate the drawing widely, to blow up and display it in Indonesia's national library, belies or at least complicates this inward-looking, small-scale vision, as does his understanding of the children caught in Christ's embrace. While Malukan in appearance, the drawing also folds the state ideology of the Five Points (Pancasila) within this image of tradition and paternal shepherding. Pointing to the drawing, Chris indicated how the children number five and invoke thereby not only the Pancasila but also its first point especially, the belief in one Supreme Being and, through it, the obligatory allegiance for Indonesian citizens to one of the five allegedly monotheistic religions recognized by the state: Islam, Protestantism, Catholicism, Hinduism, and Buddhism.[24] From this perspective, the picture with the little group boldly outlined as a unitary form presents an unambiguous image of a state-endorsed Pancasila Christ.

But for Chris, not only the portrayal of state-endorsed religion or the richness of Malukan tradition had motivated him, but also, especially, the *quality* of the relationships between Christ and the children and among the children themselves.

> Ma'am, see how they face each other, the one looks at the other, not all are looking ahead. They are asking each other, their faces—one smiles, another looks a bit wary—"Why? Why must I suffer? Why must I become a refugee? I have done nothing wrong. My father is wrong, the government is wrong, or the church is wrong. Or our congregation." Don't blame them, Chris went on, gesturing to the drawing. But then there is one who smiles, another who is, like, "Well, we have to be patient." Yet another says, "Quiet!" To give hope, still another is, like, "OK, then I will have to be patient." And another looks ahead, full of hope.... And this is characteristic.... I intended to blow this picture up to remind [people], I wanted to put [this drawing] everywhere to show that this Jesus is a universal Jesus. How can we divide Jesus's good will—yes, his good intentions towards everyone?

Although there is more I could say, I highlight here only the multiplicity of perspectives—indeed, of opinion and experience—the diversity of directions, and the movement among widely divergent scales envisioned in Chris's interpretation of his drawing. In classic Barthesian fashion, the picture's Ambonese Malay caption would anchor the circuit of visual exchange, mutual gazes, and dispersed looks and tie these to a tradition-bound local world.[25] Yet, even at this tightly "contextualized" level, Christ contracts and expands simultaneously as he inhabits the Malukan subject's image and invokes the objects that progressively populate a Malukan world that, in principle at least, appears limitless, even universal.

If, in part, this Pancasila Jesus stands in for the Indonesian state—underscoring therewith the political theology on which this state, especially under the authoritarian Suharto regime, was based—the binaries of state and citizen, unity and diversity, and Godhead and religious subject neither neatly subsume nor summarize the relationships or visual field at issue here. Christ's gaze may be steady and close, but those of his children are more dispersed—they look at one another but also away; one appears wary, another hopeful, still another waits patiently, eyes on the future. If the recognition by authority—albeit a caring and loving one—remains visualized here, there also appears to be room for horizontal exchange that not only acknowledges a diversity of experience and subject position but also is neither exclusively dependent on nor mediated by authority. In this respect Chris's drawing may be described as both "foundational" and quietly revolutionary in its novel vision of a Pancasila-informed Indonesia. This is so because the visuality that figures centrally in this landscape is multidirectional and open-ended: folded into some elastic version of the Malukan local, it stretches the national toward the universal, spilling over the mobile boundaries of this loosely centered visual field with an indeterminate excess.[26] Nor is this excess all that different from the future that the children, following Chris, embody or from the multiple scales and directions and therefore, too, signifying capacities that are mediated by the Pancasila Christ. Put otherwise, if Chris's Good Friday picture has anything to do with the Indonesian state ideology of Pancasila, then it is one that is being submitted to a radical re-vision.

LANDSCAPE III: SIDEWALK CITIZENSHIP

In this last section devoted to analyzing Ambon's new landscapes, we turn to the streets, where the large majority of the city's Christian pictures stand. The two landscapes considered thus far—the prayer room and the Pancasila Jesus sketch, both initiatives of GPM ministers—are interiorized and less public than those in the streets, albeit differently so. The hijacked billboards and the public walls tagged along Ambon's highways and at Christian neighborhood gateways decidedly win in spectacularity. In Indonesia this is owing not only to the startling publicity that the pictures accord to religion but also to their enormous scale and direct, in-your-face mode of address (plate 13).[27] Placed not only at crossroads and streets leading into the city's Christian neighborhoods but also commonly across from or adjacent to motorbike-taxi stands that flourished during the war and thereafter, they stand directly in the shadow of the city's recent conflict. Then such neighborhood gateways served as command posts (I. *pos komando*) where prayers were spoken, trumpets sounded, and Christian songs sung to embolden the men of the neighborhood as they set off for battle. Apparently, once the painted billboards and murals emerged as part of these sites' décor, they occasionally functioned as impromptu open-air photo studios where young men would be photographed, battle-ready with arms in hand. In more everyday circumstances, as elsewhere in Indonesia, the male cohorts who hang out here, smoking, chatting, and awaiting the odd motorbike-taxi customer, act as an informal neighborhood guard.

There are many such groups of young men in the city, and the creative dynamism of the street art is, in part, owing to the considerable competition among them, for instance, in the context of putting on the most splendid display in the weeks preceding major Christian holidays. Indeed, beyond the drive to visually publicize Christianity, these pictures are sustained by other forces, specifically a Malukan masculine youth culture that recognizes no religious boundaries. Motorbike-taxi stands tend to have platforms on which men sit, framed against backdrops painted with the emblems of loud musical groups like Guns & Roses or—depending on the season—those of soccer teams or the faces of Indonesian electoral candidates. Faces like those of Che Guevara or the Indonesian protest singer Iwan Fals also move indiscriminately across Indonesia's many regions and religions and, along with the other images, settle into the rich stratigraphy of these sites.[28] This is another example of how Ambon's turn to the visual, although novel, was prefigured in different ways.

Another remarkable feature of the motorbike-taxi stand is its acute combination of territoriality and mobility, but not just in its location straddling the "gated Christian community" and the world beyond or via the figure of the motorbike-taxi driver, who stands in for the neighborhood but also leaves it behind as he traverses the city, navigating its postwar boundaries and more implicit social divides. The image that comes to mind is not the spaceship sealed off from alien surroundings, but one offered by a motorbike-taxi driver when imagining the décor of the coming Christmas celebration: not only were the mural and the adjacent Christ billboard due for an annual "refreshening," but also cords of lanterns would be strung along the road leading up into the hills, "like the lights on either side of an airport runway."[29] In fact, this vision of the taxi stand as a point of departure for an expansive, spectacular mobility belies its more common-place status, both prior to the war in Ambon and across the archipelago, where, taken for granted, the descendants of the Javanese guardhouse (*gardu*) blend into their immediate surroundings and remain, by and large, even for scholars, "tiny constructions located at the margin of the [architec-turally] monumental."[30] As signposts of sorts and neighborhood brands, the motorbike-taxi stands are highly topo-sensitive in their attachment to the physical and social context around them.[31] Given this topo-sensitivity, their wartime defensive function, and the youthful bravado of the motorbikers, it is not surprising that at these sites the paintings are the most daringly experimental in their explorations of different constellations of perspec-tive, power, and visuality in relation to figures of territory and landscape.

I turn now to one especially complex example that, owing to its com-plexity, helps to highlight some of the tendencies of the other street paint-ings. The cluster that I call a triptych—three adjacent paintings composing a mural: canonical scenes summarizing Christ's life, a huge cameo portrait of Jesus as a young man, and a billboard showing him looking down on a globe turned to Maluku—faces the opposite motorbike-taxi stand at the crossroads of a road leading into a Christian neighborhood and a busy highway that skirts the city's coast (plates 14–15). Reflective in this respect of the motorbike-taxi stand's general environment and the urban cross-roads at which they stand is the strong sense of movement that animates these images (plates 16–17). The hijacked billboard conjoins the movement of the rotating globe with that of God's eye honing in on an acute situa-tion. It recalls the establishing shot of many a news feature, in which the image of a globe turns to zoom in on a particular location or "hot spot" where something newsworthy is taking place. The wider sense among many Indonesians that, following Suharto's step-down, the eye of the interna-tional community was upon them (*di mata internasional*) appears to inform this image,[32] as, too, does Ambon's own intense wartime mediation by national and international media representatives, humanitarian aid work-ers, NGOs, and the like. Seen in this light, it is perhaps telling that the pic-ture that captures the precise moment in which Maluku visually enters the world stage (albeit a Christian-inflected one) should be cast by the motor-bikers as the city's first one.

By the time I arrived in Ambon in 2003, this billboard had been removed from its scaffolding and propped up at the end of a private drive-way. Two reasons were given for its removal: the scaffolding had rusted but the time had also come for more "comforting" public scenes, ones that did not, in other words, directly reference the war. The narrative of Jesus's life counts as such a "comforting" scene because of its contrast with the pictures preceding it, whether those showing Christian Ambon under siege or incendiary wartime graffiti sprayed on city walls (plate 18). But this narrative is also comforting because, as I said before, its canonical scenes speak to the Christian interiors that they relinquished for the streets, and the visual unfolding of Christ's life along familiar lines is similarly "comforting" in its normative predictability. It is for this reason, one suspects, that the scenes out of which the narrative is composed do not change their general outlines but are simply retouched or undergo a change of color preceding the Christmas holidays. What *does* change and is a privileged object of attention is the Jesus portrait, which is either inserted into or superimposed onto the visual narrative of his life. Thus, I have photographs of different portraits dating from 2003 and 2005, respectively. While both emphasize their distinct or "cut-out" character in relation to the canonical mural backdrop, the first, from 2003, achieves this effect through the portrait's carefully painted serrated frame, whereas the second appears frayed at the edges. The painter, John Yesayas, invoked the worn edges of old parchment to explain this distinctive feature. Specifically, he spoke of how Romans in films present their official proclamations on unfurled pieces of parchment that are read out in public. Indeed, John showed me walls in the city where early in the war he had painted Christ surrounded by Roman soldiers. But whether visually explicit or implicit, the Romans—or state power and authority—remain part of the picture. The parchment model is a fitting one for Ambon's monumental Jesus portraits, which proclaim to all passersby, "This is HE—and, by the same token, this is [the Ambonese Christian] ME." What these cameos codify, in other words, is "the moment of recognition, the dramatic 'That's him!'" of identification.[33]

Elsewhere, I have discussed these cameo portraits and, in particular, John's long exegesis on Christ's face—specifically, how, though variable, this face is inevitably European. John explained, "[The Christ face may not be] like mine, but the important thing is that it is alike and in our image. That is the essence for me. This in itself is what makes me paint. So sometimes people say, 'Hey, here Jesus has a different face, this Jesus face is different,' [but I answer], 'No, that's not true. That face is also like your face, right? It also has a nose, it also has a mouth, it also has eyes. The point being, the face of Jesus is like your face." Suffice it to say here that the identificatory circuit that John aims to establish—in the face of possible objections—between the Ambonese Christian man-in-the-street and a transcendent authority via his Christ portraits evokes the Indonesian Citizen's Identity Card, or KTP (I. *Kartu Tanda Penduduk*). A critical material

FIGURE 4.2

John Yesayas, Christian mural with Jesus cameo, Ambon, 2005. Reproduced with permission of the artist. Photograph by P. Spyer.

token of proper belonging, the KTP lists not only the requisite religious affiliation but also things like *ex tapol*, which, under Suharto, branded former political prisoners for life as officially designated "former political prisoners" (I. *ex tahanan tapol*). The KTP comes with an identity photograph, the *pasfoto*, which "became an idiomatic shorthand for the state's assertion of its power to authenticate who was a citizen and who fell outside the fold of state recognition and protection."[34]

It may, indeed, be possible to see the Romans as stand-ins for a state authority that gestures beyond Christian sacred geography to Suharto's authoritarian rule, with the painted Christ pasfoto doubling as the crucial token of visible placement and proper belonging. But it is also possible to see these images in motion, by noticing how, over time, the Romans recede into the background, disappearing altogether from view as Christ's cameo comes to the fore. In this latter perspective, the emphasis is less on authority and Indonesian forms of governmentality than on the possibilities conjured by the KTP identity card in post-Suharto times. It intimates a move through which the visible token of the traffic between state and citizen, the Christ pasfoto, is pried loose from the state forms in which it was previously moored and opened up to circulation. Admittedly, this may not seem a momentous shift in focus, but it opens the way to seeing the Christ face as a landscape in its own right, a heterotopia that, potentially at least, makes all the difference.[35] While framed in familiar terms, this landscape is mobile and relatively open-ended, pushing beyond the familiar terrain of the nation-state to venture into new territory that may not be straightforwardly Indonesian or perhaps even Christian. What this landscape seems to put in place is a call for recognition; those voicing the call await, as it were, the arrival of some authority *here* who would acknowledge the Christian Ambonese as *alike and in his image*. But it also potentially opens a space for a horizontality that moves away from authority into the kind of loose camaraderie characteristic of the motorbike-taxi groups that support the street images.

CONCLUSION

"Scenes from a wreckage" is what I call Ambon's new pictures at the opening of this chapter. I keep the provisional, incomplete nature of these images in view together with the "ground"—in Jean-Luc Nancy's sense— from which they have emerged. But I also emphasize their urgent exploratory character as world-making projects and how the pictures are driven by the desire to install one or another landscape that not only offers solace but also constitutes an imaginary terrain of Christian habitation. From the Christian enclave and the Pancasila Jesus to the motorbikers' triptych, these landscapes are diverse and experimental. Even though the triptych may be understood as conjoined, it comprises three landscapes that orient the viewer in different directions. The first dramatically visualizes the theme of mediation by an empathetic authority. The second offers the canon's comforting, enlarged public contours. And the poignant dilemma of recognition for a community that felt itself abandoned to possible genocide by the Indonesian state and by its potential stand-ins—from the European Union, the International Monetary Fund, and the United Nations to the former Dutch colonizer—is condensed in the identificatory gesture of the third.

To be sure, there is always more to any view than that which it reveals, just as there are more landscapes that I might have considered. Notwithstanding the occasional protestations by the painters, the GPM ministers, or ordinary Ambonese that the city's new images are "just pictures," it is clear that these landscapes cannot be reduced to simple views sustaining conventional Protestant distance. One part of my argument is, indeed, that the pictures can be seen as landscapes, as deep gatherings and "cut-outs" offer-ing precision and location, as a way of slowing a world in motion and gain-ing perspective within terrifying uncertainty. But the image also emerges as an efficacious and at times overtly aggressive force, or a presence in both the physical and the ontological sense. It is an efficacy that has to do with the very fact of visibility, one shaped and sustained by a poetics that is all about the making visible or the act of bringing into vision.

In this light, it is possible to see these images as patches of visibility within a postwar situation that I have characterized elsewhere as emerging out of a situation of blindness. Killing, maiming, and uprooting its popula-tions, Ambon's war left not only a physically and psychically damaged urban environment but also novel forms of figuring the nexus of community, local-ity, authority, and recognition. Across the city's painted landscapes, this fig-uring or, put otherwise, the poetics of these postwar world-making projects consists of a thematization—indeed, a visualization—of the very fact and value of visibility or the "visual" itself and the forms this takes with respect to power and perspective. More obliquely, Ambon's Christ pictures offer an impression of the impact of a range of processes that have unfolded across Indonesia following Suharto's May 1998 step-down after some thirty-two years of hard-handed, uncompromising rule. With varying consequences across this vast archipelago, these are processes that have inflected the figuring of community, locality, and religion and, more broadly, the rela-tions between citizens and the state. In Ambon specifically, they include the deterritorializing forces of war, the religious and ethnic purification of neighborhoods, and the development of new spatial practices and new mobilities that have increasingly redrawn the shape of the city.

But beyond Indonesia, this Malukan city also provides an especially pregnant site for thinking the place and diversified manifestations of the "visual" today. In ways that are often poignant, as well as urgent, the city's postwar situation and, specifically, the Christian pictures' emergence and spread appear to underscore those critical forces and developments of our times that elsewhere perhaps remain more implicit. Relevant are the varied ways in which images move and are made to move in our contemporary world, the perspectival fragmentation that more widely than in Ambon or Indonesia characterizes our current moment, and the multiplication of visual modalities and discourses that in part attend to these. It is no coincidence that the impact in Ambon of the communications revolution, the liberalization of media during the late Suharto years, and the spread nationally of VCD, cell phone, and video technologies really registered only when the circumstances of war provided this impact with an undeniable impulse. Along with the mobilization of media technologies in and with respect to the conflict, there was the brief if critical identification of the city as a media "hot spot" with all the complicated implications thereof. These include the influx of national and international media practitioners and the bolstering locally of the national TV station, along with the expansion of Jakarta-based stations into the area. There was also the novel commodified value attached to audiovisual testimony of the war and to the documentation of human suffering and urban destruction, along with such new experiences as seeing one's own locality relayed back in the form of national and international news or via the more locally produced VCDs that spun off the conflict.[36] These conditions, along with other factors, contributed to and buttressed a wider thematization of the visual in Ambon City and its surroundings.

Earlier I described Ambon's new pictures as the most spectacular dimension of a city undergoing profound change. But spectacular as these certainly are, this does not mean that the pictures will not fade from view with the same surprising ease with which they sprung out of the war's ruins. And dramatic as they may be, they are both symptoms and transitional solutions to crisis and, as such, may soon exhaust the part they play in Ambon's postwar world-making.[37] Change often registers in less spectacular and quieter ways, such as in the unfolding dynamics and the institutional rearrangements within and among Ambon's churches during the war and in its wake and in the considerable realignments in the religious affiliation and practice of Christian Ambonese—not to mention all the postwar shifts in the larger social landscape of the city's ethnically and religiously mixed population. But if and when these pictures vanish into the texture of city walls and the usurped billboards are, once again, covered with cigarette and cell phone ads, they still count as the initial signposts that not only marked and proclaimed significant change in the city but also dramatically contributed to it by contouring the shape of the postwar world to come that is currently in the making.

Acknowledgments

The research on which this chapter is based was begun within the context of the Indonesian Mediations project of the Indonesia in Transition program funded by the Royal Netherlands Academy of Sciences. I would like to thank this institution for its support of this research and Leiden University's Institute of Cultural Anthropology for supporting subsequent fieldwork. I am grateful for the excellent feedback on an early version of this chapter from the participants in the SAR advanced seminar and to Mary Steedly for her constructive input throughout. I have also benefited from questions and comments on versions of the chapter presented at Aarhus University, University of California at Berkeley, University of Colorado at Boulder, University of Rochester, New York University, and the Center for Contemporary Art and Politics at the University of New South Wales. Rafael Sánchez accompanied me on multiple trips to Indonesia and offered sound advice and excellent suggestions throughout, as well as on this chapter. I owe an immense debt to the painters with whom I worked in Ambon, to the city's religious and community leaders, and to the many journalists, NGO activists, and ordinary Ambonese and Indonesians who shared generously of their accounts and insights into Ambon's wartime and postwar conditions.

Notes

1. Patricia Spyer, "Blind Faith: Painting Christianity in Postconflict Ambon," special issue, *Social Text* 96, vol. 26, no. 3 (2008): 11–37.

2. Drawing on the term *interocular*, coined by Arjun Appadurai and Carol Breckenridge, Christopher Pinney uses it to situate photographic images against the wider background of popular film and calendar art. See Christopher Pinney, "Photographic Portraiture in Central India in the 1980s and 1990s," in *Portraiture: Facing the Subject*, ed. Joanne Woodall (Manchester, UK: Manchester University Press, 1997), 137.

3. See James C. Scott, *Seeing like a State: How Certain Schemes to Improve Human Conditions Have Failed* (New Haven, CT: Yale University Press, 1998).

4. Kirsch in Stuart C. Aitken and Deborah P. Dixon, "Imagining Geographies of Film," *Erdkunde: Archiv für Wissenschaftliche Geographie* 60 (2006): 330.

5. For an overview, see International Crisis Group, *Indonesia: The Search for Peace in Maluku*, Asia Report no. 31 (Jakarta: ICG, February 8, 2002).

6. Recorded interview by author, Ambon, June 22, 2005.

7. Notes from an interview by author, Ambon, July 15, 2006.

8. Notes from an interview by author, Ambon, July 26, 2006.

9. W. J. T. Mitchell, *What Do Pictures Want? The Lives and Loves of Images* (Chicago: University of Chicago Press, 2005). See also Christopher Pinney, who writes regarding Mitchell: "Addressing the 'wants' of pictures is a strategy advanced by W. J. T. Mitchell as part of an attempt to refine and complicate our estimate of their power. Mitchell advocates that we invite pictures to speak to us, and in so doing discover that they present 'not just a surface, but a *face* that faces the beholder." Christopher Pinney, *"Photos of the Gods": The Printed Image and Political Struggle in India* (London: Reaktion, 2004), 8.

10. Recorded interview by author, Ambon, July 25, 2006.

11. Adam H. Becker, "The Ancient Near East in the Late Antique Near East: Syriac Christian Appropriation of the Biblical East," in *Antiquity in Antiquity: Jewish and Christian Pasts in the Greco-Roman World*, ed. Gregg Gardner and Kevin Osterloh (Tübingen:

Mohr Siebeck, 2008), 410. On military evangelicals and the Iraq and Afghanistan wars, see Jeff Sharlet, "Jesus Killed Mohammed: The Crusade for a Christian Military," *Harper's* 318, no. 1908 (May 2009): 31–43.

12. Faisal Devji, *Landscapes of the Jihad: Militancy, Morality, Modernity* (London: Hurst and Co., 2005), 66.

13. Richard Chauvel, "Ambon's Other Half: Some Preliminary Observations on Ambonese Moslem Society and History," *Review of Indonesian and Malaysian Affairs* 14 (1980): 40–80.

14. The term "public Islam" was coined by Armando Salvatore and Dale Eickelman. See Armando Salvatore and Dale F. Eickelman, eds., *Public Islam and the Common Good* (Leiden: Brill, 2004). For an analysis of the development of public Islam in Indonesia, see Noorhaidi Hasan, "The Making of Public Islam: Piety, Middle Class and Youth in Indonesia's Democratising Politics" (unpublished book ms. presented at the In Search of Middle Indonesia program seminar, Royal Netherlands Institute for Southeast Asian and Caribbean Studies, Leiden, June 2010).

15. Bart A. Barendregt, "Mobile Religiosity in Indonesia: Mobilized Islam, Islamized Mobility, and the Potential of Islamic Techno-Nationalism," in *Living the Information Society in Asia*, ed. Erwin Alampay (Singapore: Institute of Southeast Asian Studies, 2009), 73–92.

16. On the other side of the world, Moluccans in the Netherlands codified their own fears along similar lines in an appropriately romanticized fashion—given the nostalgia and fetishization of tradition that tends to describe the relation of many Dutch Moluccans to their traumatically estranged place of origin. A poster in black and white showing a strikingly handsome young man in profile wearing a headdress with a palm-frond feather and captioned dramatically in red "The Last Moluccan" circulated among the Moluccan community during the war. Featuring one of several early twentieth-century photographs of teenage dandies from the southeast Moluccan island of Tanimbar taken by the Dutch missionary Petrus Drabbe, the poster not only depicts a bona fide Moluccan in the prime of youth but also evokes James Fennimore Cooper's novel *The Last of the Mohicans* (1862), with its theme of doomed Indians and the genocidal extermination of Native American life. See Nico de Jonge and Toos van Dijk, eds., *Tanimbar—De Unieke Molukken: Fotos van Petrus Drabbe* (Leiden: Periplus Editions / C. Zwartenkot, 1995).

17. Arjun Appadurai, "The Colonial Backdrop—Photography," *Afterimage* 24, no. 5 (March–April 1997): 1–7.

18. Veena Das and Arthur Kleinman, introduction to *Remaking a World: Violence, Social Suffering, and Recovery*, ed. Veena Das and Arthur Kleinman (Berkeley: University of California Press, 2001), 8.

19. Jean-Luc Nancy, "The Image—The Distinct," *The Ground of the Image*, trans. Jeff Fort (New York: Fordham University Press, 2005), 7.

20. Nancy, "The Image—The Distinct," 7.

21. See Kajri Jain, *Gods in the Bazaar: The Economies of Indian Calendar Art* (Durham, NC: Duke University Press, 2007), 138, on the "personalizing, affective, libidinal aspect" that makes the divine accessible to devotees "as an empathetic presence."

22. See Kaja Silverman, *The Threshold of the Visible World* (New York: Routledge, 1996), 195–227.

23. In Ambonese Malay, the local dialect of Malay spoken on Ambon and on the surrounding Lease Islands of Saparua, Nusalaut, and Haruku, the caption reads: *Tete Manis polo sayang anak-anak di tana Maluku.* In this chapter I distinguish between Ambonese Malay (A.M.) and the national language of Indonesia, Bahasa Indonesia (I.).

24. In 2006, Confucianism was again officially recognized as a religion in a Ministry of Religion circular stating that there were six official religions in Indonesia, including Confucianism.

25. See Barthes's "Rhetoric of the Image" on how the first message of the advertising photograph is linguistic, so captions, labels, and the like, fulfill a function of anchorage that serves to limit signification. Roland Barthes, "Rhetoric of the Image," in *Image, Music, Text*, ed. and trans. Stephen Heath (1964; New York: Hill and Wang, 1977).

26. Abidin Kusno, the Indonesian historian of architecture and urbanism, identifies what he calls a "looseness at the center" for post-1998 Indonesia. It has to do with how, in a country with a long tradition of political suppression and authoritarianism, "the sense among the population that the center is no longer there, fixing, watching, and ordering their conduct" has given rise to a feeling of disorientation and vulnerability but also enabled the creation of "small centers that coexist uneasily with each other. The state is still there, but it has been perceived as merely one center among many others." Similarly, albeit in an aesthetic register, Chris Tamaela's drawing of the Pancasila Christ appears to document a loosening at the center. See Abidin Kusno, "Whither Nationalist Urbanism? Public Life in Governor Sutiyoso's Jakarta," in *The Appearances of Memory: Mnemonic Practices of Architecture and Urban Form in Indonesia* (Durham, NC: Duke University Press, 2010), 36.

27. In Jain's work on the economies of Indian calendar art, she underscores how "the contemporaneity and publicness of the sacred is the real scandal of calendar art" and "an index of its 'alternative' modernity"—an alternative, generally speaking, to national space as defined by secular modernity. In Indonesia the scandal is somewhat different and can be glossed with reference to the term *SARA*, an acronym comprising the first letters of the Indonesian words for "tribe," "religion," "race," and "class" (I. *suku-agama-ras-antar-golongan*), designating those forms of societal difference that were

banned under Suharto as either topics of discussion or sources of conflict. With the fall of the regime, *SARA* has been lifted and we find, along with violence carried out in the name of religion, a new openness toward and about the subject. Until 1998 the Suharto state was the arbiter that allotted religious identity and guaranteed that religion remained in its proper place; with the reconfiguration of the state post-Suharto and its retreat on some fronts, religion appears to be obeying a logic of its own—albeit one that was enabled and energized by the regime's particular mode of governmentality. Kept, in other words, under tight wrap during the long Suharto era, religion is out in the open in Indonesia today, with religions bursting from their allotted places in public search of audiences, bodies, and spaces. Given the novelty of all highly public expressions of religion in light of this recent history, such expressions still often exude a sense of scandal.

28. On the branding and rampant circulation of Che, see Michael Casey, *Che's Afterlife: The Legacy of an Image* (New York: Vintage Books, 2009). For these other images, see the cover photograph and figure 1.4 in chapter 1, this volume.

29. *Kiri kanan seperti jalur pesewat terbang.* Notes from an interview by author, Ambon, July 17, 2006.

30. See Abidin Kusno's "Guardian of Memories: Gardu in Urban Java," for an excellent history of these guardhouses, in *Indonesia* 81 (2006): 95–149.

31. On the topo-sensitive, see Umberto Eco's *A Theory of Semiotics* (Bloomington: Indiana University Press, 1979), 3.

32. Karen Strassler, "Gendered Visibilities and the Dream of Transparency: The Chinese-Indonesia Rape Debate in Post-Suharto Indonesia," *Gender and History* 16, no. 3 (2004): 705.

33. Valentin Groebner, *Who Are You? Identification, Deception, and Surveillance in Early Modern Europe* (Boston: MIT Press, 2007), 22.

34. Karen Strassler, *Refracted Visions: Popular Photography and National Modernity in Java* (Durham, NC: Duke University Press, 2010), 138.

35. In the Deleuzian sense of the face as not just a corollary of the landscape in the sense of a milieu but rather as "a deterritorialized world." Deleuze in Ronald Bogue, *Deleuze on Music, Painting, and the Arts* (London: Routledge, 2003), 93.

36. See Alan Klima's reading of images from Bangkok's Black May massacre of 1992 in his discussion of the "dialectic of local and global imagery." Images were "spirited over the surface of the globe by the BBC" only to be returned and recycled in cassettes sold locally by Thai traders in the exact same location where the violence first took place. Alan Klima, *The Funeral Casino: Mediation, Massacre, and Exchange with the Dead in Thailand* (Princeton, NJ: Princeton University Press, 2002), 2, 3. See also Nicholas Mirzoeff's *Watching Babylon: The War in Iraq and Global Visual Culture* (New York: Routledge, 2005). Mirzoeff's specific concern is how images from Iraq are watched

and how this relates to the exercise of power from specific localities. The implications of his argument for thinking about how "visual subjects"—people defined as agents of sight and objects of certain discourses of visuality—relate to globalized images, including images of themselves, are more generally relevant here.

37. On this understanding of crisis, see Michel de Certeau, *The Possession at Loudun*, trans. Michael B. Smith (Chicago: University of Chicago Press, 2000).

5

Narrow Predictions and Retrospective Aura

Photographic Images and Experiences from China

Oliver Moore

If we were to imagine a history of early "Chinese photography," what would the subject of such a history be? Answers must confront the perilous task of assigning images to particular categories and historical conditions, across whose borders they will inevitably and obstinately stray. The multiple ways in which photographic images work in different social conditions and the possibility for their meanings to fluctuate according to the media through which they are presented are daunting obstacles in the way of writing a single history of Chinese photography. Anyway, apart from the extremely general and colloquial sense of photography connected in any way to China, I suspect that the notion of "Chinese photography" is not entirely viable. Many histories of photography concerning China are possible, and I will not attempt to argue that one history is better validated than another. Instead, I select from a mass of visual evidence and documentation—whose entirety I will never fully grasp—in order to explore the unstable ground on which different subjects stated what photography equaled in their various claims and how and when it did so. This chapter accepts that these claims vary enormously, according to the status and engagements of those making them. They vary too through analysis of photographic images, since these bear a shifting array of "meanings inscribed in forms, uses, trajectories."[1] The same shifts support the arguments with which Mary Price rightly claims that the meanings of photographs depend overwhelmingly on their uses.[2]

China itself is a variable factor. Diverse histories emerge in the light of the uneven political experiences and the separate developments of photographic media and technics in two Chinas—the mainland People's Republic and the island Republic of Taiwan (formerly Formosa)—which have been military antagonists now for well over half a century. Space precludes saying more about this division and its effects on two histories of photography, but it will surely surprise no one that mainland Chinese accounts of photography's history prioritize matters quite differently from those published in Taiwan. Other histories of photography could be predicated upon photographic projects undertaken by the individuals mentioned in this chapter, figures whose interests diverged sharply. They include the celebrated Lang Jingshan, a professional photographer who during a long career spanning most of the twentieth century in China, Taiwan, and abroad eventually achieved the status of an artist. They also include the entirely forgotten Zhang Dingfang, a Chinese diplomat and amateur photographer whose work, no longer extant, is documented during his residence in London around 1900, and Peng Ruilin, a professional active in Taiwan during the 1920–1930s, whose best work is known and discussed only by art and photography historians in Taiwan.

This chapter considers categories of photographic engagement that are likewise instances of either professional or amateur effort, as well as examples of whatever is a Chinese image from either mainland China or Taiwan, or indeed by agents from somewhere else. The material discussed in this chapter comprises the work and claims of a tenuously linked assembly that encompasses Isaac Baker, probably the most famous photographer of the California gold rush; Fu Bingchang, a senior political figure in 1930s Republican China, whose amateur output—including published and exhibited work—was prolific; a French individual named Prat, who resided in Guangzhou during the 1880s; the adventurous figure of James Ricalton, voyager and photographer in China during 1900 on behalf of the major image distributors Underwood and Underwood; Xun Ling, the junior courtier appointed to photograph the empress dowager Cixi, China's last effective imperial ruler; and an unnamed Chinese diarist who recorded his vexatious encounter with the immigration authorities of Boston in 1905. This is a disparate group, yet purposely so because its very heterogeneity announces how many histories of photography are possible.

In the first section of this chapter, I discuss the unreliable notion of Chinese photography. Instead of looking solely at China as a site for the practice of photography, I consider Chinese cultural environments as transit points among many others in various cosmopolitan circularities. In the complex temporality that arises with the first introduction of new media into a given social environment—in this case, China—powerful circuits are activated through the transnational worlds of education and training, club and society membership, exhibition, publication, and technological exchange. This raises only a few of the many conditions that have not yet attracted sufficient attention for the history of photography in China. The problem deepens, especially when considering that equally little analysis has been directed at China as one cluster among many in the galaxy of photography's developments, themselves subject to temporalities that varied between different parts of the globe. Across these temporalities material images appear and reappear in diverse cosmopolitan circularities, within which patterns of membership and exchange are not always parochial but often precociously global.

In the following three sections, I discuss the aforementioned individuals, who were responsible variously for photographs taken in China, photographs of Chinese subjects abroad, and records of making photographs. I adopt these things and texts, which date to the first century of photography's history, in order to pursue a historical discussion of photography that explores how images are defined at the moment of their creation and then again following the onset of historical distance. Clearly, between the two moments, the accretions of unfamiliarity, indifference, and forgetting build up thickly. But the aim is not to execute an archaeological stripping away of layers until the content and form of any visual object are as historically true as possible to some original moment. The game is not worth the candle. Rather, it is to work within the confines of a retrospective analysis that stresses how shifts in meaning occur in the later viewing of photographs. This task foregrounds how retrospective interpretation redefines both the historical and aesthetic status of images.

My aim is to redefine, not to distort. Either a material artifact or an imagined object of discussion, a photograph generates much of its visual and imaginary power in the interesting space between its index of an appearance or an event and the viewer's desire to control what it stands for in the sense that the photograph advocates a new order of things, what Chris Pinney in chapter 6 in this volume calls the photograph's prophetic quality and elsewhere identifies as the photographic image's "creative, transformational space."[3] The indexed can be a portrait, a scene, or a document of what went on. On the one hand, this indexical reference to people and things often reflects a social prediction of only the narrowest range of options for this or that category of content. The same documentary significance, on the other hand, is never entirely isolated from the viewer's more complex and numerous desires, manifest in various ways in the examples below. Sometimes at stake is a blend of cultural and commercial expectations, perhaps even an obstinate insistence on what China should look like. Expectations vary, however, in the face of photography's different technical options. One of the texts cited in this chapter provides the basis for my argument that photography's various technics can also contribute to enhancing the expectations of an image, especially when the viewer—and the subject of a portrait—perceives that a casual snapshot advocates none of the order contracted and arrested in a formally posed studio portrait. Since its primary content is human, the vast category of the portrait is the best exemplification of photography's prophetic quality of performance. Such images announce emphatically what their subjects aspire to be, and they owe their indexical and metaphorical inception to a performed moment. Finally, the voices of some informants, the earliest of which dates to the 1880s, persuade me that, apart from the real or imagined responses of those whom any image circulation targeted, images and the events of making images also gained meaning according to the media that circulated them. I also suggest, then, that the history of photography, especially concerning China and inasmuch as it may be a history of images that move, must be a history of images *and* their media of circulation.

Specifically, the last three sections of this chapter link three aspects of photography's history, namely, social predictions of the image, the enhancement of technics, and retrospective aura. Showing first that the social prediction of image content permits only a narrow range of options, I then suggest that a widespread strategy for deepening the significance of an image was the employment and overt enhancement of one set of technics as opposed to another. In this process, outcomes that overstressed photography's mechanical performance were often not esteemed. Finally, I argue that a retrospective teleology controls how modern viewers often choose to emphasize a particular set of technical origins in order to reinvest an image of multiple reproduction with the aura of a sacred object. That the image is index to a unique visual performance invariably makes this retrospective choice all the more convincing. Although their existence is easy to overlook, the technics underlying an image form one of its most defining characteristics. So too does the medium of its circulation. Any opportunity to look at how technics and media feed a retrospective act of imagining an image's early life shows just how crucial these categories are in defining also its historical significance and aesthetic status. And that the same categories can only retrospectively assert the historical validity of an image demonstrates how strongly such a retrospective mode affects insights into the early history of photography in China.

THE NOTION OF CHINESE PHOTOGRAPHY

Despite the regional focus of this discussion, it is necessary to express some distrust of the notion of "Chinese" photography. We may imagine China as one of many areas in as many histories of the reception and localization of what was realized as a global practice and medium at virtually the moment of China's first formal announcement in 1839. Yet, since this globalism was intended from the outset, it thoroughly disrupts attempts to speak of French photography as much as it does Chinese.

Instead, images that are often claimed as items of Chinese visual culture can be more usefully released from terms of cultural reference and seen as elements that constitute primarily a visual economy. The "visual economy" is a term I borrow from its recent and most successful exploitation in Deborah Poole's study of image-making in Peru.[4] Poole justifies the use of "economy" and her avoidance of "visual culture" by suggesting that for an image-world constituted by societies as widely separated as those of the Andes and Europe, it makes better sense to think of a shared visual economy. The residents of Paris and Lima may well have understood similar economics within the complexity of transactions that underpinned business and social life around photographic studios in both places. But the extent to which members of each group in their own setting used, circulated, stored, and replaced images differed according to cultural priorities that were much less easily rendered equivalent. Also, even if some photographs taken in conditions far away from Europe attest to how taste and fashion in a European metropolitan center dominated these images' content and style in an Andean setting, others show an obvious turning away toward local preferences. Likewise, between Europe and China, strongly differentiating fissures opened up in the preferences for subject positioning, proximity, lighting, and backdrop that are manifest in studio productions, which Laikwan Pang and Roberta Wue have recently analyzed in a study of Chinese and Western visual priorities during the same period.[5]

Thinking about a global economy is helpful because it usefully provincializes the role of Western metropolitan centers and it enhances possibilities to understand the lives of images that move across national and cultural borders. Nationally bound narratives of photography tend to distort what are, in fact, interflows—even riptides—of historical development across cultural and linguistic dividing lines. Equally, they ignore cosmopolitan circularities that are thoroughly enmeshed. Nor is any history of photography well served by categorizing photographers on the basis of national affiliation or ethnic membership. To be sure, some indigenous Chinese photographers did attempt to cultivate a hallmark Chinese identity in their social profile, as well as to invest most strongly in Chinese categories of visual content and style. Lang Jingshan (1892–1995), for example, persisted with a cultural performance of "the Chinese photographer" that spanned his careers in both mainland China and Taiwan and that lasted almost an entire century.

But Lang is an exceptional figure whose early success privileged his ability to adopt a role more akin to the world of traditional painting (*guohua*, "national painting") and to make photographs that, once graphically manipulated at the printing stage, insistently project artistic imagination rather than directly reference physical surroundings. Lang was no less susceptible than some of his Western contemporaries to charges that his work was not true photography but instead only the ghost of any one of a number of painting categories, such as impressionism, pictorialism, and forms of visual allegory that had been long under critical attack. This is not to denigrate his achievements, but it remains true that not even his best work won him uncontested recognition as a Chinese photographer. Following the spate of obituaries dedicated to him in 1995, one Chinese journalist in Taiwan was prompted to question, "In what way Chinese?"[6]

A more globally scrutinized social history of photography in, from, and concerning China has to conclude that the topic cannot be simply set behind established borders. Consider a case from one generation earlier. The amateur photographer Zhang Dingfang (formerly spelled Chang Tingfang) was a diplomat stationed in London at the Chinese Legation and later at the Chinese viceroy's residence in Wuhan (the major Yangzi port in central China). According to the British Royal Photographic Society's membership lists, Zhang is one of seventeen Chinese members who joined the society between 1859 and 1940—an incomplete total since it is restricted to Chinese members formerly or currently resident in mainland China. (Chong Lee Chit, for example, a member in 1939, gives an address in Jamaica.) Zhang exhibited photographs at the society's annual exhibition in Pall Mall, London, in 1890 and 1891. Probably none of this work is extant (and the society's journals do not illustrate entries before 1895), but an exhibition guide at least lists the following captions: *Conway Castle; Cottage and Rustic Bridge; Ye Olde Red Lamp of the Holborn Camera Club; Fishing Boats off Strood Pier, Rochester; On the Beach-Brighton.* These captions—once attached to exhibition objects judged by the photographers Henry Peach Robinson

FIGURE 5.1

Peng Ruilin, self-portrait, probably 1932 in the Apollo Studio, Taipei. Reproduced with permission of Dr. Peng Liangmin. After Taiwan sheying 3 (1994): 12.

(1830–1901) and Valentine Blanchard (1831–1901)—prove the inadequacy of talking about photographs either "of China" or "from China."

Photography's circularities within East Asia are no less complex. Peng Ruilin (1904–1984) was born in Taiwan, then a Japanese colonial possession.

In his late teens he started training at the new art college in Taipei, so his syllabus, indeed the whole educational system in Taiwan at this moment, was developed primarily in Tokyo and adapted for local conditions. One of his teachers and his chief mentor was the celebrated painter and theorist Ishikawa Kinichiro, who is today adopted by many Taiwan-based historians of modern art as a pioneer of Western watercolor painting (on behalf of the Western genre of landscape). A forceful internationalist in both cultural outlook and practical engagements, Ishikawa traveled frequently, following courses at the Royal Academy in London and visiting Paris, Venice, and Rome, cities that had become hot tourist destinations in an East Asian update of the Grand Tour. One of his paintings from this period is a view of Hampstead Heath. Ishikawa successfully recommended Peng to study at the Tokyo Art School. Following this training, Peng founded a studio in Taipei and named it Yapoluo—a Chinese transliteration of Apollo. He photographed portraits and landscapes that have gained increasing recognition recently, even dividing the show windows of his studio premises—which occupied a street corner—into "commerce" (portraits) and "art" (landscapes and other subjects). Later, in response to nationalist pressures to make Chinese cultural values ascendant over the recent colonial past, he abandoned the name Apollo. Not long after World War Two he abandoned photography.

Where do we begin to qualify in particular this second career as Chinese? Even if the island of Taiwan is taken as culturally integral to something sometimes called "greater China" (and many dissent from this view), Peng's own ethnic and cultural background belongs in Taiwan's large Hakka (Kejia) community. His several children still live in a number of villages that bear Hakka names and where Hakka is normally spoken. And what about Peng's training, supervised by Japanese instructors, with several of whom he maintained affectionate relations? Throughout his career he submitted work to photography shows organized in Osaka and other Japanese centers. Particularly awkward and little noticed is the fact that when he signed his photographs, he used a Japanese transliteration of his name. Was he, then, a Japanese photographer?

Even these brief career paths reveal the pitfalls beneath any simple assumption that photography's past circularities can be reduced to a transparent notion of "Chinese photography" or indeed that what circulated was invariably an uncomplicated "Chinese photograph." The presence of Western residents in China further complicates the issue. These temporary residents often compiled albums of views of the country, but they were not necessarily the agents of those visualizations. Although some individuals may have dictated their visual preferences toward a final result, they still often contracted local practitioners to photograph and print the images. Hence, there is good reason to see the mass of all surviving photographs in China and Taiwan as evidence of how indigenous and allochtonous agents shared the work—if cooperated is not quite the word—in creating the productions of a shared visual economy, a term that is especially apt considering that the practitioners of photography mentioned above and below have more in common in their economic operations than in their cultural preferences. Seen in this way, China has attracted relatively little engagement from historians of photography. Through understanding the visual medium in an economic framework, then, the history that I propose encompasses a broader—by no means exhaustive—conception of photography's activities, and it tries to imagine China more fully included within the larger global space that permitted far-flung circulation of the categories of photographic images, considered next.

SOCIAL PREDICTIONS OF THE IMAGE

Whatever the category of image and however extensive the range of its potential circularity, one persuasive sociological argument has long held that the options for selecting photographic content are invariably limited. In Pierre Bourdieu's contributions to *Un Art Moyen*, the famous report that a group of French sociologists compiled on uses of photography, he insisted that the medium of photography is perpetually ensnared between the ideals of an academy art (like painting or music) and the reality of an extremely limited number of options—always according to different social classes' varying usages—for selecting whatever is *photographiable*.[7] For instance, it is perhaps unusual that a place is worth photographing. A reaction that Bourdieu documents time and again is his many informants' distrust of the photographic image, including even the content of possible images. For example, why photograph a street that its inhabitants see every day? What Bourdieu and his colleagues' informants reveal as distrust of the image and its universal technology helps us understand the disdain that the photographic image (long before the advent of digital photography) often attracts, frequently because of its high degree of mimetic reality, its *immediate* referentiality to observable life.[8] At a complete disadvantage beside the manugraphic traces of brush strokes or the engraver's burin in other visual media, the photographic image's realistic and "invisible" techniques of reproduction render its content all the more banal to those for whom the depicted locus is their everyday surroundings.

To some extent, possibilities of a deeper aesthetic experience of content—a place or a human subject—may be repaid only through the effort to photograph mundane reality when it is someone else's reality. This is the highly persuasive power that images apparently assume in travel magazines, popular scientific journals, and other media that reproduce views of pristine nature, other people's unknown lives, and gradually modernizing worlds. But this power is deceptive, for what makes the image of a location iconic—in a colloquial sense—is only how the image reconfirms viewers' expectations of what they hope to see. Such iconicity also depends on conditions of the image's publication, distribution, and eventual paratextual annotations. However, Bourdieu's informants despised photographs of the village street because they were asked to comment on a visual possibility that they had never entertained. In the cases of images showing what the spectator does hope to see, photography is a functional tool that justifies its usefulness with practical and symbolic meaning far in excess of the images themselves. A photograph of a farmhouse where a grandparent was born, lived, and worked means something entirely different from an image of a visually analogous building in unknown surroundings. Similar reactions motivate individuals and communities to undertake a quite limited range of requests for certain photographic images, if not to grasp again familiar referents, then at least to satisfy desires concerning tourism, wealth, physical comfort (or forbearance), and self-fulfillment. Without the constant effort to capture larger physical surroundings and to represent certain topographical prioritizations, the postcard industry would never have been what it eventually became.

Bourdieu's various remarks on photography, photographs, and photography worlds are also useful because he was acutely aware of isolated patterns of circularity. He recognized a relationship that the new medium—new in 1839—and its mechanical technics compacted with the European academy arts and never entirely extricated itself from. Awareness of such a compact is obviously visible in the few aforementioned facts of Peng Ruilin's career. Bourdieu's analysis of the tension spanning photography's technics and its imitation of academy visions will be worth recalling in later discussion of retrospective attempts to turn studio-produced images of China's empress dowager Cixi (1835–1908) into art.

Quite a different photographic project, however, one that demonstrates that the content of images can be predicted through the confirmation of past experience, is the document of a French resident's ambitions to expand the contents of an album of photographs recording his residence in Guangzhou about 1890. This picturing ambition will be compared also with the recollections of an intrepid traveler-photographer who earned a living at this stage of his career by taking photographs for the gigantic, stereoscopic photograph distributors Underwood and Underwood. These cases of foreign presence in China emphasize the manner in which images from China—or images of China—were strongly determined by the narrow range of local conditions and social contexts that documented the country ever more familiarly, whether as imaginary place or reality. Photographers trod carefully in a landscape whose contours and inhabitants the Western popular imagination had largely dictated in an age before mass tourism.

The residential album was a visual document of where someone lived and perhaps also worked. The example considered here is an album recovered in France and now located in the Getty Research Institute, Los Angeles. The agents of this album's production may have been several, but the one whose voice is still clearly audible is an individual named Prat, who filled several pages of the album with comments and instructions on how best to obtain a number of views of Guangzhou (Canton). These frank remarks make the album a most unusual document.[9] It would seem that its optimistic owner, Prat, collected or commissioned photographs of Guangzhou during his residence there until 1884, then relocated to France and decided at a later date to create an updated revision. Prat transcribed these intentions into a "list of photographic views to request in Canton," containing eighteen subjects—seventeen plus one afterthought at 8a:

1. view of the main avenue of the French concession;
2. panoramic view of the buildings of the French concession on Shamian island;
3. view of the main avenue of the English concession, taken from the address of Jardine Matheson et Co. so that the view shows the avenue as it enters the French concession;
4. the area of the Fati [botanical gardens];
5. the Fati gardens, including a miniature tree distorted into an animal shape;
6. Chinese cemetery along the road to Baiyun shan [hills north of the city];
7. the waterclock;
8. the "chamber of horrors" (hell) in a Daoist temple;
8a. the entrance to the viceroy's yamen [Chinese government offices];
9. statues representing the "Five Rams" in the temple of the Five Worthies [associated with the mythical foundation of Guangzhou];
10. panorama of the forts at Humen [on the Pearl River estuary];
11. the prison yard with detainees in *cangues* [wooden collars];
12. opium den;
13. a game of *fantan* [gambling with dice], taken in Macao or Canton;

14. beggars, especially blind ones;
15. carrying chairs of four kinds (for dignitaries; for women; the common chair; mountain chair);
16. a view of the dragon boat festival.

Prat's list encompasses the usual reductions of China to the commonalities of Western experience, in terms of both the fabric of foreign residence in the country (1–3) and some destinations of work, commerce, religion, and leisure. Expressions of China's political and military power (10, 11) will be documented and, only as an afterthought, one of Guangzhou's most elevated arenas of Chinese commercial decisions (8a). The list fulfils widespread Western preconceptions of China as a land of quaint productions (waterclocks and distorted trees) and social decadence, in its various expressions of punishment, drug dependency, gambling addiction, and indigence. At least the several grades of carrying chairs (15) present some extra nuance, since they hint that hierarchical forms patterned society in China with greater complexity than is otherwise suggested. (Yet, even this brief quest to understand Guangzhou through its artifacts reflects not so much the realities of the place as Western society's reflections on its rising use of mechanized forms of transport in the 1890s.) All the content described in Prat's seventeen preferences can be matched easily with images from surviving albums, collections, studio-ordered images, and the contemporary postcard industry.

Particularly fascinating is the author's desire to see China from France, beginning in the *allée centrale* of the French concession (1–2), and then, rather than see France from China, to take stock of the situation from England (3). As Prat's remarks demonstrate, photography potentially enabled visual consumption over great distances—some 120 degrees around the planet's surface—but it is remarkable how parochial that consumption often remained.

Prat also tried to predict the future of the new images: "All of these photographs could be adopted, I think, for sale via the press [*vente journalière*] for the benefit of Canton [foreign] residents or else glob-trotters [*sic*] who hope to preserve a memory of the curiosities of Canton. An intelligent Chinese photographer could not fail to make a profit."

Several interesting points emerge. Prat is aware that pictures sell and that there is a newspaper industry available to facilitate sales. The author does not explain—or is not aware of—whether these images will enter a wider circulation as photographs or as lithographic reproductions or even as woodcuts (least likely by this date). In other words, will these images' entry into a particular strand of the media preserve them as photographs or turn them into some other form of image? And, in whatever form they assumed, who could guarantee that Prat's totalizing vision of a locality, reduced to eighteen images, would be marketed as just that? The proposed collection imparted a meaning that would soon be distorted if consumers only acquired no. 12, "opium den." This is a question of images' targets and trajectories, to which discussion of Empress Cixi's photographs will return. Prat's desire is that, once made, the images will be commodified in a market for Westerners in Guangzhou and farther afield. The photographer will be "intelligent" enough to take up a position in that market and no other. More precisely, Prat perceives a division of the collective images' function for local and global consumers. In Prat's imagination, "globe-trotters," whose travels take them hypothetically everywhere, as well as Guangzhou, nevertheless must come to Guangzhou to secure images of the place. If not, they will be in no position to "preserve a memory." It is almost as if the photograph can fulfill all its ontological expectations only if its content addresses directly the owner's biographical past. This demand on the image's consumption is so particular that it is questionable whether the image could ever be determined as an item entirely suited to global exchange. The rise of Western tourism would have the effect of setting still more limitations upon what is photographable (via brochures and the postcard industry, for example, accompanied also by the popular imagination of what to see), yet tourism would also enhance even more strongly the links between each biographical past and a particular image. Robert Gordon's study of imaging practices in Namibia documents how colonial travelers eventually brought back their own photographs as new possessions to replace what had been hitherto only the photographs of others or even loans from a stock of more broadly available images.[10] Beyond these biographical considerations, however, Prat's understanding of global media was probably not profound, but his expectation of what it meant to make images of a location had no doubt kept pace with the possibilities for photographs' translation into half-tone images and their diffusion via a growing number of media and economic opportunities.[11] Answering successfully to a range of limited options, the images on Prat's list were predictable, precisely because their significance would ultimately be determined by the experiential past and memory that all viewers shared.

Not only does Prat voice what the concrete objects of a particular local visualization ideally should be, but also surviving photographs of the relevant period—photographs whose archival existence is still quite chaotic —reveal that their consumers desired and responded to a narrow range of visual objects. This phenomenon is not necessarily a disappointing one,

FIGURE 5.2

James Ricalton, Paddy fields, farm houses and patches of tea, at Matin, Kiangsi [Jiangxi] province. *Stereograph Cards collection, Prints and Photographs Division, Library of Congress, LC-USZ62-49133.*

because the limits it suggests are hardly to be attributed to photography but rather to the restricted social imagination that attempts to create order through geography, tourism, and travel. At the same time, a Barthesian priority for "reference" as ontologically key to the photographic image explains why the image options with which a European ex-resident of Guangzhou engaged were quite circumscribed.[12] Finally, Prat's efforts confirm once more the findings of Bourdieu and others that most material and social phenomena are not "photographiable." Indeed, what can be meaningfully photographed belongs to an extremely narrow range.

Evidence from a slightly later moment shows the massive industrial scale by which the execution of images of locations and people was activated according to minutely determined agendas. Western and Japanese photographers—pioneers about whom much more is recorded than their Chinese assistants—set off into the interiors of China and Taiwan as executors of a broad assemblage of interests in these areas as the objects of proselytizing, ethnography, archaeology, botany, zoology, navigation, surveying, and military intelligence. These external and sometimes overlapping interests could dictate richly informative images of variously large- and small-scale subject matter. An example combining both is the view of a Chinese man overlooking a landscape, an incongruous positioning that soon entered the gigantic circulation of early twentieth-century stereoscope cards (stereographs) and eventually featured—now monoscopically, we should say—in a famous exhibition of photographs of China that toured Philadelphia and other American cities during 1978.[13]

James Ricalton (1844–1929) took this image in 1900. Its copyright belonged to Underwood and Underwood, for some time the leading international commissioners and distributors of stereograph images, who titled and misdated it: *Rice paddies and tea shrubs in the hills on Kiangsi, Southeast China, 1902.*

Matching Western preconceptions of China, Underwood and Underwood commissioned images—purportedly taken only weeks earlier—that would fulfill market expectations of barely accessible places. Ricalton's published diary reveals that his task was to locate a number of scenes and to capture their image for resale as stereoscopic views. As James L. Hevia reminds us in his penetrating analysis of photography's role in promoting the "seeming truth" of China both during and since the Boxer Rebellion of 1900–1901, Ricalton's diary was the indispensable transport for its accompanying images on their journey into turn-of-the-century public consciousness.[14] Ricalton observed a preconceived checklist of categories, which the image fulfilled admirably in that it reports a particular landscape (farmland), social inhabitants (a farmer), economic purposes (tea bushes), life and work (dwelling houses), and farming methods (irrigation). What is remarkable is the length to which Ricalton would go in order to create a tranquil rural scene. The "farmer" was almost certainly a town dweller or a member of a boat crew from one of the nearby great watercourses, and he posed patiently while Ricalton apparently wrested this image from the teeth of a small riot going on several yards away. Ricalton usually retold his difficulties with buoyant exaggeration, but many country areas in China during the summer of 1900 were indeed simmering ahead of the violent Boxer Rebellion, which exploded later that year. Having been pursued by angry peasants into the uplands of Jiangxi, Ricalton recalls the following:

One bold fellow advanced, and with a pole uplifted threatened to smash my camera. Childs [Ricalton's travel companion] stood near with a heavy stone in each hand and held them in check until this stereograph was hurriedly taken. During this time a heavy clod from some one in the rear of the crowd landed on the camera, but did no serious damage. They were emboldened by the fact that we had no weapons of defense, not even sticks. We had expected the mandarin to accompany us, and so left our guns at the palace.

We need not, however, let the rabble disturb our enjoyment of the landscape. Our faithful servant is before us and looks off into space, as though he were unconscious of the cowardly demonstration taking place behind him, and that by his own countrymen.[15]

Here, once more, is an instance of how the image was not a collection of geographical facts and social events that inspired the photographer in a manner he had never predicted. Rather, it was an emergence of preconditions, both serendipitous and induced, that fitted a commercial contract and its accurate interpretation in the field.

THE ENHANCEMENT OF TECHNICS

So far, discussion has centered on social conditions of circulation in order to support Bourdieu's contention that the content of photographs is inevitably made in the face of limited options. However, content can be limited also by photography's technics, which dictate content and form irrespective of picture-making decisions informed by the human eye. The history of photography's technics flows through numerous courses. One practical method does not stop where another starts; they may race each other over long distances, propelled by technological advance and commerce and cultural preference.

An early example of content shaped by technics is the famous view of the Beijing city walls and guard towers photographed by Felice Beato in the autumn of 1860. The scene is eerily unpopulated, and with this seeming absence of movement the city's most massive brick structures have attained a sort of lyrical life of their own. The required exposure time was sufficiently long that all passersby moved literally out of the picture, and even the pale chasm in the foreground refutes any notion of imprint, only disclosing where the moat water has shimmered beyond documentary arrest.

Studio portraiting also contended with long exposure times, the elusive

FIGURE 5.3

Isaac W Baker, Chinese man, *ca. 1850. Reproduced with permission of the Oakland Museum in California. After* Lao Zhaopian *14 (2000): 19.*

perfection of lighting requirements, and complications added by a photographic subject who was also an autonomous agent with ideas on how to determine the content of the image. As a result, the studio portrait presents a pose that was variously imposed upon and accepted by the subject, yet it may offer too a positioning that usually assimilates successfully its immediate visual context (for example, background and lighting), its presentation in a frame, or its inclusion in an album. Historically, many portraits belong to the period when few options existed to maneuver outside the technical limits imposed by slow light absorption and long exposure, not to mention the laborious chemical operations needed to prepare and finish the photographic plate. Of course, the same limits might force a photographer's efforts toward results of visual genius, as was certainly the case in the portrait of a Chinese man—perhaps a gold seeker—posed in his new tunic (plausibly, at Chinese New Year) for the daguerreotype portrait made in California probably by Isaac Baker (1818–ca. 1862), the most famous visual recorder of the gold rush.

With the passage of decades, photography's technics would undergo several shifts, some of which were so radical that it makes more sense to write the histories of successive developments of photographic media rather than reduce these various trajectories to a single narrative. One outstanding development was the reduction of exposure times, which led eventually to the marketing of hand cameras designed to make snapshots. The snapshot represented a departure so unprecedented that it is no exaggeration to call it revolutionary. The term "snapshot" existed probably as early as the mid nineteenth century, but the earliest true snapshots date to 1888, when the Eastman company in New York started manufacturing the Kodak camera. Later, in 1900, Eastman launched the Brownie Kodak, marketing it energetically both toward and around children. The operation of the Brownie was described as childishly simple and no less because children were advertised as the most photogenic visual commodity of the new technology's growing market.

The snapshot is a crucial instance of new technics dictating a shift in imaging practice. The shift was further driven by the growth of photography's mass market and the fall in photography's costs, phenomena that were constantly encouraged through the rise of manufacturer's literature, including eventually a Chinese edition of *Kodak Magazine*, which, published in Shanghai, ran for eighty-seven issues between 1930 and 1937. The ascendancy of snapshot photography was soon internationally widespread, but never absolute. Not a few photographers in China and Taiwan consciously sought creative strategies to define their productions as isolated from—even resistant to—both the technics of the global photographic industry and its most common media of reproduction. In the early 1930s Peng Ruilin, for instance, probably during his studies in Japan, developed a laborious method of printing with gold solutions on convex surfaces of wood. In the same period, even though soon trapped within the restrictions imposed by painterly imitation, Lang Jingshan led photographic practice away from the constant search to capture new instants toward a composite method of assembling images from a preexisting and limited range of morphological elements, for example, clouds, peaks, tree branches, animals, and birds.

Nevertheless, the possibilities of fast exposure times—already growing in the increased sensitization of dry plates throughout the 1880s—facilitated the use of hand cameras and the abandonment of tripods, all factors that provided the photographer with unprecedented mobility. The snapshot's widespread use and consumption fuelled the expectation, exactly as it was voiced by Prat, that images gained their meaning through the biographical fact of having visited the actual location of a visual reference. That the snapshot image influenced expectations for images created with more senior, photographic technologies is also palpably obvious in thousands of picture albums whose pages present images of each category side by side.[16] Snapped images are often characterized as informal, instantaneous, candid, and somehow less ponderous than studio productions. The effect of these visual characteristics was also that it "deepened the association between informality and truth,"[17] even in images that were not technically definable as snapshots. Whether professional or amateur, even those photographers whose relationship to the photographic industry was determined entirely by their use of complex equipment and techniques aimed for a snapshot style of the casual and unposed image.

The promiscuous reach of the snapshot, then, did not always dictate that the aesthetics and commerce of other categories of photography decline, but it did affect them. Two classes of data from China—one textual and the other visual—document the snapshot as an object to be successively rejected and accepted, thereby mapping not so much a trajectory of the medium's ascent but showing rather how snapshots might fit one set of social conditions better than another. The established visual forms of portraiture endured tenaciously, and expectations of how a portrait should appear in contrast to a casual snap comprise the thick emotional layer of a rare Chinese recollection of an immigration crisis in America. The writer of this short travel diary in 1905 is male but not otherwise identifiable. He describes how in that year he and a group of fellow students had finished their studies at the Royal Academy in London and prepared to start home for China, planning to cross the United States en route. They secured passports from the Chinese embassy in London because Chinese citizens' possession of a passport was obligatory for entry to the United States following the Exclusion Act of 1882. The standard Chinese passport of this period did not require a photograph, and the diarist was clearly aware of this, for he remarks that only laborers were required to submit their *xiaozhao* (literally, "portrait") in preparation for overseas travel. (The writer's sense of what counted as racial/national humiliation was entirely relative.) Officials, merchants, tourists, students, and preachers constituted five privileged categories of the unphotographed, those permitted to travel with a document that stated a few personal details without visual proof of identity.

The travelers' transatlantic landfall brings a rude shock: Boston customs officials refuse the students entry into the United States because their passports do not contain photographs. Following protracted wrangling (and an extra night on board), they are allowed ashore with strict instructions to visit a nearby photographic studio for the purpose of taking their pictures. Things get worse: "Once ashore, along the ships' wharves and in the streets there were numerous local people who wanted to take our photographs with their portable cameras. It was utterly embarrassing. Only after several flights and dodges did we finally manage to escape."

Not only proof that Orientalism can be flipped through the looking glass to meet the Other as an infuriating crowd of barging and importuning Western metropolitans, this document records a traumatic confrontation with the swirling image economy of early twentieth-century America as the irruption of one temporality of photography's technics into another. The Chinese visitors have to summon as much forbearance as they can in order to endure a conflict between differing cosmopolitan expectations and to survive until calm is restored in the safety of a Boston photographic business: "When we had reached the Portrait Studio everyone commissioned a photograph in three prints. The prints were over two inches long and cost in total sixteen American dollars, which is equivalent to more than thirty Chinese dollars."[18]

The diary documents an attitude to snapping pictures that reveals it as a practice fundamentally distinct from studio photography. Histories of photography seldom plumb these variations to their full extent, and a history devoted purely to snapshots, for instance, is no more unlikely a proposition than a history of watercolors, a distinct category within the larger description of painting.

The writing of this diary in 1905 fits historically with larger narratives in time and space. Since 1903 at least, Chinese public opinion around the Pacific had been agitating for equitable treatment at US ports of entry. On May 10, 1905, the Shanghai chamber of commerce announced a boycott of American goods, which gained little effective momentum but certainly promoted greater awareness of a growing issue only one year before Gandhi's satyagraha movement targeted similar institutions of control imposed by British colonial rule in South Africa.[19] The Chinese traveler in Boston records the vexations of exclusion experienced by millions of subjects of global migration history, fittingly recounted in this instance through attention to a passport, the primary symbolic institution of migration control, and to photography, one of global immigration's leading technologies of supervision. The interest of this diarist's story extracts from a global history of border-crossing the fundamental procedure of photographic identification. What turns his account into a significant success story, however, is how he recounts his submission to the rituals of a studio visit in order to (1) transcend above the humiliations dealt out at a site of immigration control; (2) outwit the local canaille of snapshotters; (3) traverse the divisions between snapshot and studio photography; and (4) feel emotionally reintegrated following commercial investment in a photographic portrait.

The diarist is no keen observer of details, but his reflexes in the face of mundane surroundings are fascinating. What he says about his eventual arrival at a studio and the transaction there provides the sense that he has returned safely to a familiar performance—he has been in the city for barely an hour or two—and that the transaction itself is an exchange that restores self-respect and status. It is significant that many biographical inscriptions on studio portraits in China bear exact statements of what the subject paid. The Boston visitor is especially satisfied that he can repeat this popular gesture of financial commitment outside China, perhaps because he is also aware that the American studio he visits is but one of thousands of stopping places in a global visual economy. He invokes a rhetorical code closely bound up with Chinese photographic practices in new transnational conditions.

Snapshots did not invariably provoke trauma. Provided that consent was granted by all those involved in the performance, the medium—and its style—flourished. Indeed, the practice created a new visual trope of the natural, the real, and the individual, an alluring combination that would be hugely dominant in portrait conventions throughout the 1930s–1940s. One arresting photograph that is a self-reflexive address to these issues is the image of Min Chin by Fu Bingchang.

Fu was a Republican politician, diplomat, and thoroughly engaged amateur photographer who developed and printed his own photographs. Eventually, he acted on numerous occasions as official photographer for Jiang Jieshi (Chiang Kai-shek). He was also a member of Britain's Royal Photographic Society during 1928–1931 but was evidently much more active in submitting his photographs to the growing number of photography magazines burgeoning in Shanghai during the same period. Min Chin crouches slightly as she adjusts the controls of a Voigtländer Superb camera. No Brownie this, but the best camera on the market after 1933 for professional and amateur work and, ironically, the machine designed primarily for expert manipulation rather than quick and casual snapping.

FIGURE 5.4

Fu Bingchang, Min Chin, 1940. © C. H. Foo and Y. W. Foo. Courtesy of Historical Photographs of China project, University of Bristol.

Fu's image is a portrait of Min Chin *and* a leading product of the precision optics industry. The image of Min Chin looks snapped, but, of course, it is arranged, not least in the manner of her pose before a pattern of ascending tree branches. Photographed with Fu's second camera, the image is a photograph of taking a certain kind of photograph, and it documents a portrait aesthetic that had become increasingly ingrained at the expense of studio work. (It is interesting to consider how this trend was reversed in mainland China after 1949, when personal possession of a camera was disdained as a symptom of bourgeois individualism.)

The woman smiles and aims the camera downward, perhaps to suggest photographing a child. The marketing of the snapshot had targeted children for several decades by now. Hundreds of pages of Kodak literature, for example, published in Chinese and distributed from Shanghai throughout the 1930s give ample space to children and how to photograph them. The easy intimacy that Fu Bingchang and Min Chin created together in this image of her recalls similar images of women in the popular illustrated press, as well as commercial advertising imagery that used feminine content in its attempts to establish affinity between potential consumers and the mechanical equipment necessary for snapping photographs.

Some of the examples in this and the preceding section concern trajectories of the image over long distances. Beato, before the walls of Beijing and elsewhere, enabled the consumption of visual objects from far away, and three decades later Prat, touring the sites of Guangzhou, stated his mission to continue this ideal, albeit in a more explicit symbiosis between travel and residence in China. Even with missiles apparently flying near his head, Ricalton never hesitated to capture the scene that his employers, Underwood and Underwood, had demanded. Historical distance has proved that his achievement ranks with Beato's in that the image he made lasted until the post–World War Two thaw in Chinese-US relations enabled the organizers of an exhibition to co-opt it as one among many others for an exhibition entitled *The Face of China*.[20] The trajectories of portraits were usually more circumscribed, although in terms of sheer mass it should not be forgotten that the Chinese constituency with which Isaac Baker in California was in contact posted thousands upon thousands of portraits back to China. Amid all this traffic, attitudes to snapshot informality changed, making it eventually possible for practitioners and consumers— sometimes subjects who were both—to deploy two systems of visual aesthetics in the categories of portrait that they demanded.

These examples are defined also by their various trajectories into an album, into a stereoscope, or simply deeper into the unpredictable chaos of the Boston foreshore. Past and modern trajectories have changed, and this change affects the retrospective values that photographs gain. One remarkable example from China is the trajectory that began with the

FIGURE 5.5
Xun Ling, Cixi, Empress Dowager. *Courtesy of Palace Museum, Beijing.*

performance of imaging the features and body of the empress dowager, once taboo and now ever more publicly visible.

RETROSPECTIVE AURA

Modern retrospection on images of the empress dowager reinvests them with an auratic power that depends upon a deep revision of these images' circulation history. Such viewing displaces objects from the medium of commercial publishing and emplaces them within a—perhaps invented—

space of sacral restriction. At stake in both displacement and emplacement is a question of control. If, as visual objects of historical research, photographs command the esteem that they do, it is because, once more, their fascination is located somewhere in the tension between their indexical moment and their viewer's control, whether that concerns subjecthood, history, or the sacred. Not the history of technics alone, then, but acts of retrospection that also take into account temporality and the narrow range of content options are the means through which this retrospective engagement with photographs is possible.

The empress dowager's appearance has today become widely recognized worldwide. Among royal contemporaries, perhaps only Queen Victoria and Tsar Nicholas II rival her for visibility. Rosalind C. Morris's sensitive reading of even earlier images of King Mongkut of Siam, however, provides a salutary reminder that during the early history of photography, transnational exchanges of royal portraits tracked circuits far beyond those of European rulers' mutual exchanges of the visions of power that they incarnated.[21] The empress dowager and her entourage had themselves photographed almost invariably in highly elaborate circumstances: amid dense floral props and heavy furnishings, in many layers of clothes—a good few of these images were later tinted with painstaking accuracy—and even drifting over palace lakes in lavishly decorated barges. She is recognizable as the ruler who went to exaggerated lengths to be pictured. This exaggeration is often used inside and outside China to mock her as both a villain of history and a paradigm of female vanity, but it ignores that she more than likely grasped strategically how the photographic image could serve as a nation-forming symbol. Morris points out that King Mongkut based his earlier venture into the burgeoning royal image economy on similarly astute deductions. According to court archives, Cixi's interest in making photographic portraits dates from 1902, when the Russian ambassador presented her with a photograph of Nicholas II and his family on a crystal mount bearing the emblem of the Eastern Orthodox Church.[22]

Aside from showing an example of royal photographic performance, the image juxtaposes photography with a Chinese category of "academy art." Bourdieu's reflections stand for more than simply a polarization between photography as low-brow and art as its opposite, for such absolute categories would obscure the rich flows that have long operated between photography and painting, not to mention other manugraphical techniques. (It would also ignore Bourdieu's lifelong fascination with art history.) Also, any discussion of aura and sacrality recalls the earlier ideas of Walter Benjamin, who, although he commented very little on painting, should not be invoked to authorize a similar division: art possesses auratic uniqueness, whereas any photograph lacks this quality simply because it is ontologically bounded within an extensive category of reprographics, that is, the technics of reproducible—mechanical—representation. Even long after it has been sentenced to a passage of notionally infinite reproduction, the content of a photograph can express aura of a kind that is separate from its mediated ubiquity. For, although the technics of infinitely generating the image—including the category of snapshot—via reprographical processes destabilizes notions of uniqueness, photographic content presents something in excess of the mere capture of a visual moment; it is also the record of a performance, a major part of which is the aura of a unique performance, not to mention the aura of royal sacrality whose visual presence or record—as Louis Marin's study of regal representation reveals most particularly in Morris's allusion to it—is constantly exceeded by even larger notions of narrative, ceremonial, and architectural framing.[23]

Most remarkable in the recent interest in images of Cixi is a retrospective process in which the subject's visuality and the history of her portraits are retold in the guise of court painting; thus, both are displaced into a story of photography as art. The story is not pure invention. It is a partial account that suppresses the trajectories that the Chinese court ambitioned and implemented for images of the empress, yet it emphasizes certain kinds of practice that recall the performance of the court painter.

The key figure in this account is the so-called "court photographer" Xun Ling. He was the son of a senior diplomat and accompanied his father during several years' service in France, eventually returning to China with an enviable acquaintance of European metropolitan life and an expert knowledge of photography. In 1903 the empress dowager recruited Xun Ling to the palace service, and during the next two years he took many of the famous surviving images of her and her courtiers. The acceptance of his status as a court photographer has taken deep root, and it is certainly not gainsaid by some of the surviving documents that attest to detailed theatrical planning ahead of some of the portrait sessions that he organized. The photographs that Xun Ling made of the empress were handled with the same special reverence reserved for portraits in the imperial cult. Other kinds of observance generated new rituals. When in 1904 Cixi decided to donate a photograph of herself to the future German empress Augusta Viktoria, then staying in Tianjin, the object was transported from Beijing in a state carriage before it was handed over to the German consulate and later transported to Berlin.

Today the notion of a palace collection of photographs offers strong—

and historically renewed—imaginative appeal. Recent publishing in China has discovered at home and abroad an avid audience for the Qing palace culture of one century ago, and it excites the thrill that these images reside in an exclusive and rarely accessible treasury of visual truth, one whose access also recalls a poignant realization of the past as an intimation of what is on the verge of disappearing. In short, the guardians of the palace's photograph collection control the presentation of this material—by no means all of it authored by Xun Ling—in the same way that they expose paintings, porcelain, carvings, and mechanical devices, effectively all samples from a mass of symbolic capital that defines their surroundings as both palace and national archive. In the new relationships that viewers form with these photographs, the images acquire the status of art in a royal collection; Xun Ling's services are then retrospectively reengaged as court photographer in a position that is emphatically reminiscent of court painter.

By contrast, little if anything is published at present concerning the commercial origins of printing photographs and mounting them. Historians in China have trawled assiduously through official documents to reveal how palace agents dispatched the empress's portrait to visiting German royalty, but no one has surveyed which studios in Beijing were commissioned to print what images or how they were mounted and embossed with studio names and addresses on the mounting card verso and recto. Research of this kind would no doubt lend welcome support to the recent drive to imagine sections of Chinese society one hundred years ago swept up in—or unshaken by—the rampant ambitions of retrieving national salvation in the unleashed energy of a "commodity nation."[24] Details of a photograph's production can usually be read on its mount (but this is rarely reported); the identity of the photographer can be discovered (was he Chinese or foreign? And was he indeed the photographer?). Even the first viewer(s) of the image can be tentatively categorized. Questions like these shift interest closer to the circulation of these images. Remarkably, the same questions emerge and find answers, albeit vague, in the visual record itself. For instance, is the photograph of the royal entourage that a female palace servant is holding qualitatively different from other reproductions of that image then?

Is it a common sort of mounting? Is it usual that it is not framed? Is it a standard size or an enlargement of uncommon dimensions? Was its production expensive? Why is the servant holding it? Why is she photographed holding it? Who took that photograph? What studio printed it?

Of course, obscuring the commercial, high-street origins of photographs allows for a deeper sacralization of these images. Yet, the sacral in this instance is residually quotidian and mundane. One of the leading

FIGURE 5.6

Palace servant with photograph, *by unknown photographer, ca. 1912. After Beisi Liu and Qixian Xu, eds.,* Gugong zhencang renwu zhaopian huicui *(Beijing: Zijincheng chubanshe, 1994), 199.*

insights in Morris's aforementioned discussion of early Thai royal portraits centers on her linkage of photography's functions to the "transition from absolute monarchies to populist forms of governmentality." Cixi had not arrived at the brink of instituting constitutional monarchy, but, in a sign of the times, several leading Chinese reformists advocated it as a new way forward (and had to flee the country as soon as they said so). Still, paradoxically, the category of visual populism in which the empress dowager did store her own political hopes led—as the Thai case already convincingly suggests—to a deeper sacralization of the monarchy. This tension between popular dissemination of the image and its sacral constraint has withstood a remarkably long test of time. Museum curators and editors in a sense reengage the services of Xun Ling to authenticate photographic images as objects that the palace once generated and still can. Their tacit claim that a royal portrait was done for restricted, exclusive usage by royalty—and circulated to no one but other royalty—fetishizes the image entirely as a "terminal" commodity.[25] Unless challenged, this restriction, of course, impedes any historical recourse for understanding other possible trajectories of the photographic image. In the case of Cixi's

FIGURE 5.7

R. F. C. Hedgeland, Residence of Senior Customs' Assistant, Macao, *1906.* © *SOAS, University of London. From R. F. C. Hedgeland papers, SOAS Library, PP MS 82/16.*

portrait, it is well known that, aside from donating her likeness to the German empire, the palace silently approved when the Japanese publishing entrepreneur Takano Bunjiro in Shanghai prepared a number of the empress dowager's portraits for commercial distribution.[26] Two years later, according to a report in the Shanghai newspaper *Shibao* (November 12, 1906), the publisher's recommendation to potential buyers of these images encouraged them "to gaze on the venerable face, in the same way as Westerners who hang an image of their ruler in their homes."

The trajectories of these royal images carried much farther than previously expected, and at least one British resident in China hung an edition of the dowager's image at home. A recent rearchiving of British collections of photographs has revealed her framed in the drawing room of the Chinese Maritime Customs senior assistant's residence at Macao, placed there perhaps as soon as a few months after the Shanghai press advertised the sale of Cixi's images in 1904.[27]

This is a small discovery—only a magnifying glass will confirm it—but nonetheless an enthralling visual rejoinder to the story of the empress dowager's earliest attempts to put her image into public circulation. Exhibited in this particular residence, the presence of the dowager also highlights the unique political relations between the Customs Service, an internationally staffed institution (1854–1949), and the de facto ruler of the Qing empire. Regardless of how the Macao assistant, Reginald Hedgeland, acquired these portraits, his ownership suggests strongly that Cixi's efforts to have herself photographed in a number of costumes and surrounded by a changing repertoire of elegant objects was not impelled by palace boredom and vanity. Instead, it was consonant with a Qing government strategy that subjected the photographic image to its full potential in hitherto untested functions of foreign and internal diplomacy. Worth recalling too is the same government's awareness that until 1905 the Customs Service was also responsible for China's representation at international exhibitions.[28] One hundred years later, only because telltale signs of the image's technics have been suppressed—and the wider mediation into transnational circularities has been forgotten—can these representations instance a common retrospective tendency to enhance their visual enchantment as unique objects.

The projection of Cixi's image into the drawing rooms of China's Western residents notwithstanding, it is easy to see why accounts of her several images so often suggest that over a longer duration of time the photographic image of a royal subject has emplaced itself more, not less, within the sacral aura of palace performance. These photographs are weighted not only with their indexicality of the moment but also with the indexicality of rehearsed performance. One photograph of the dowager shows her surrounded by female family and courtiers in the process of adjusting her hair ornaments. This is no chance snapshot, but a decidedly theatrical pose that subject and image-maker exploited for a posteriority of performance quite distinct from that of the frontal and symmetrical arrangement of a portrait. It is not so much the moment that has been captured but a before-and-after, that is, rehearsal, performance, and representation. Beyond the opposition between auratic uniqueness and the technics of infinite reproduction, this last reference to images of the dowager empress does subtle work within the totality of her images. It indexes a stage-managed moment; it recalls that every gesture can be repeated, just as every image can be reproduced. As such, it extracts from an infinite series of repetitions. No other image proposes so strongly the arrest of this indexed moment. Yet, like all photographs, its eerie stasis is the same measure of its prophetic overflow.

CONCLUSION

Nowhere in this chapter do I claim priority for anything called "Chinese photography." Instead, I emphasize conditions at the crossing points of separate communities and transnational circulations. Photography is interesting precisely because of its ability to move far beyond what seem like impenetrable frontiers. Looking at communities and patterns of circulation shows how drawing boundaries of cultural and national division is a self-defeating task in almost any set of historical conditions. Instead, more discreet acts of cultural definition occur when it is possible for those in control of images to mediate them in new patterns of circulation, both real and imagined. The price of a studio transaction in Boston can be rated beside a monetary value in China, and even this humdrum record of spending recalls a specifically Chinese practice of circulating the image and its text by subjects participating in a visual and commercial economy of studios located somewhere other than a Western metropolis. To understand in retrospect this resistant enhancement of studio practices is to grasp historically the preference for particular technics that enjoyed favor at the expense of the snapshot, another combination of technics that was at worst an offense to biographical ambitions. The final instance of how certain technics invoke particular affinities is apparent in the history of photographs of Empress Dowager Cixi, when the imaginative emplacement of her image squarely within the boundaries of the sacred again diminishes one set of technics by recalling another. Both instances indicate a larger tendency to look back at photographs and retrieve them between their index of an event and their users' prophecy of what each image means. Much of that effort to recall meaning, however, is borrowed from the image's technical history and its mediation and is steered toward a reimagination of where the image is placed and to whom it circulates. If this helps to discern the priorities of photography's history in China, then that may be because these images are instances not of how or why photographs are Chinese but of when.

Acknowledgments

I would like to acknowledge The Hulsewé-Wazniewski Foundation for the advancement of teaching and research in the archaeology, art, and material culture of China at Leiden University for financial support of my travel and research on this project in Taiwan and China.

Notes

1. Arjun Appadurai, ed., *The Social Life of Things: Commodities in Cultural Perspective* (Cambridge, UK: Cambridge University Press, 1988), 5.

2. Mary Price, *The Photograph: A Strange, Confined Space* (Stanford, CA: Stanford University Press, 1994).

3. Christopher Pinney and Nicolas Peterson, eds., *Photography's Other Histories* (Durham, NC: Duke University Press, 2003), 13, 214–215.

4. Deborah Poole, *Vision, Race, and Modernity: A Visual Economy of the Andean Image World* (Princeton, NJ: Princeton University Press, 1997).

5. Laikwan Pang, "Photography, Performance, and the Making of Female Images in Modern China," *Journal of Women's History* 17, no. 4 (2005): 56–85; Roberta Wue, "Essentially Chinese—The Chinese Portrait Subject in Nineteenth-Century Photography," in *Body and Face in Chinese Visual Culture*, ed. Katherine R. Tsiang and Wu Hung (Cambridge, MA: Harvard University Press, 2005), 257–280.

6. Guo Lixin, obituary for Lang Jingshan, *Zhongguo shibao*, October 30, 1995.

7. Pierre Bourdieu et al., *Un Art Moyen: Essai sur les Usages Sociaux de la Photographie*, 2nd ed. (1965; Paris: Les Éditions de Minuit, 2007), 24.

8. Ibid., 56–57.

9. I am grateful to Fran Terpak of the Getty Research Institute, Los Angeles, for permission to cite and translate passages from this source.

10. Robert Gordon, "Backdrops and Bushmen: An Expeditious Comment," in *The Colonizing Camera: Photographs in the Making of Namibian History*, ed. Wolfram Hartman, Patricia Hayes, and Jeremey Silvester (Cape Town: University of Cape Town Press, 1998), 111–117.

11. Quentin Bajac, *L'image Révélée: L'invention de la Photographie* (Paris: Gallimard / Réunion des Musées, 2001), 111–127.

12. Liz Wells, ed., *Photography: A Critical Introduction*, 3rd ed. (London: Routledge, 2004), 30–31.

13. Nigel Cameron and L. Carrington Goodrich, *The Face of China as Seen by Photographers and Travelers, 1860–1912*, catalog of an exhibition first shown at the Philadelphia Museum of Art, April 15–June 25, 1978 (Millertown, NY: Aperture, 1978), 73.

14. James L. Hevia, "The Photography Complex: Exposing Boxer-Era China (1900–1901), Making Civilization," in *Photographies East: The Camera and Its Histories in East and Southeast Asia*, ed. Rosalind C. Morris (Durham, NC: Duke University Press, 2009), 99–103.

15. James Ricalton, *James Ricalton's Photographs of China during the Boxer Rebellion: His Illustrated Travelogue of 1900*, ed. Christopher J. Lucas (Lewiston, NY: Edwin Mellen Press, 1990), 146.

16. Alison Nordström, "Making a Journey: The Tupper Scrapbooks and the Travel

They Describe," in *Photographs Objects Histories*, ed. Elizabeth Edwards and Janice Hart (London: Routledge, 2004), 86.

17. Mary Warner Marien, *Photography: A Cultural History* (London: Laurence King Publishing, 2002), 170.

18. *You Mei shounüe riji* [Diary of disdainments endured during a journey through America], comp. unknown, reproduced in *Lidai riji congchao* [Diachronic compendium of diaries], vol. 155, ed. Delong Li and Bing Yu (Beijing: Xueyuan Chubanshe, 2006), 609–613.

19. Adam McKeown, *Melancholy Order: Asian Migration and the Globalization of Borders* (New York: Columbia University Press, 2008), 295–308.

20. Goodrich and Goodrich, *The Face of China*.

21. Rosalind C. Morris, "Photography and the Power of Images in the History of Power: Notes from Thailand," in *Photographies East: The Camera and Its Histories in East and Southeast Asia*, ed. Rosalind C. Morris (Durham, NC: Duke University Press, 2009), 121–160.

22. Jing Lin, "E huang Nigula ershi quanjia zhao" [A portrait of the Russian Tsar Nicholas II and his family], *Zijincheng* [The Forbidden City] 76 (1993): 27.

23. Morris, "Photography and the Power of Images," 135.

24. Karl Gerth, *China Made: Consumer Culture and the Creation of the Nation* (Cambridge, MA: Harvard University Press, 2003), esp. 203–281.

25. Appadurai, *The Social Life of Things*, 23; Igor Kopytoff, "The Cultural Biography of Things: Commoditization as Process," in Appadurai, *The Social Life of Things*, 73–77.

26. Ge Tao, *Juxiang di lishi—Zhaoxiang yu Qingmo Minchu Shanghai shehui (1844–1920)* [A material history—Photography in late Qing and early Republican Shanghai society (1844–1920)] (MA thesis, Shanghai Academy of Social Sciences, 2003), 37.

27. Robert Bickers et al., *Picturing China, 1870–1950: Photographs from British Collections*, Chinese Maritime Customs Project Occasional Papers no. 1 (Bristol, UK: University of Bristol, 2007).

28. Ibid., 1.

6

"Augurs and Haruspices"

Photographic Practices and Publics in India, 1840–2008

Christopher Pinney

It is no accident that Atget's photographs have been likened to those of a
crime scene. But isn't every square inch of our cities a crime scene? Every
passer-by a culprit? Isn't it the task of the photographer—descendant of the
augurs and haruspices—to reveal guilt and point out the guilty in his pictures?

—*Walter Benjamin, "A Little History of Photography"*

Every passerby a culprit?[1] The proliferation of CCTV and the introduction of retinal scans and "millimeter wave" scans currently being unrolled
on a test basis in various airport terminals are certainly predicated upon
such suspicion.[2] They also testify to the reconfiguration of photography's
subjects, not as *surfaces* but as *interiorities* made public. The *inside*, made
public through being made visible and subject to surveillance, makes possible a convulsed interiority that becomes the ground on which a new kind
of public is constituted.

In engaging the question of "images that move," this chapter is concerned more with the apparatus of imaging than with images sui generis.
My concern is with photography as a "technical practice," an ever-changing
set of possibilities that has profound consequence for the construction
of publics. Following Walter Benjamin and more recently Bruno Latour,
my concern will be with *camerawork* rather than *photographs* as secondary
screens onto which a primary "ideology" is projected.

There is a curious formal reanimation of much earlier imaging technologies: the most recent innovations in photography (for example, backscatter X-ray) produce images that formally are almost indistinguishable
from the first photographs (uncannily echoing the look of John Herschel's
cyanotypes), and the latest Transportation Security Administration (TSA)

screening devices resemble the "dark room" of the *camera obscura*. But this should not blind us to the profound repositionings—the new *prophetic* triangulations—of "physiognomy" that an evolving practice of photography demands and through which the physiology of the public is constituted.

Our understanding of photography's prophetic quality derives from Jacques Attali's proposal concerning music. He argues that music, in certain circumstances, acts in advance of social reality—its code is "quicker" than that of society as a whole, its prophecy operating on a semiological frontier. Photography, likewise, seems to often act as prophecy, as a tactic of inquiry and imagination, precipitating behavior that otherwise remains latent, encouraging a faster exploration of possibilities, as with Attali's music, "which makes audible what will gradually become visible."[3]

PHYSIOGNOMIC ASPECTS OF IMAGE WORLDS

The bulk of this chapter is concerned with photographic imaging in India, but I do not intend India to be the anthropological end point of my analysis. I am not interested in showing how a globally circulating technics is "localized" or "appropriated." Rather, India provides a complex empirical terrain from which I hope illumination can be thrown on the broader question of *camerawork* in general. Before we examine practices in India, we can learn much from a brief consideration of key figures in a global history of photographic and cinematic experimentation, such as Eugène Atget, Karl Blossfeldt, and Dziga Vertov, whose camerawork practice has experimented with and clarified the issues of concern here.

The precise question that interests me is photography's role in the transition from a facial physiognomy to a public physiognomy, through what Gilles Deleuze and Felix Guattari describe as "facialization." In Deleuze's account, in *Cinema 1: The Movement-Image*, facialization—a form of landscaped physiognomy—is approached through filmic close-ups that present the face as if it were a landscape from which "the viewer seeks to fathom meaning from its darker or hidden regions."[4]

The first part of this movement, from the facial to the public, is much easier to establish, and grasp analytically, than the second part. Early photography deposited aura in its "ultimate point of retrenchment"—the face. The technology for the production of the face created a new time-space: "The procedure itself caused the subject to focus his life in the moment rather than hurrying on past it; during the considerable period of the exposure, the subject...grew in to the picture, in the sharpest contrast with appearances in a snapshot."[5] In consequence, daguerreotypes transcribed peculiarly powerful, individualized physiognomies. Benjamin cites Karl

Dauthendey's anxiety about the facial presence in these early images: "We were abashed by the distinctness of these human images, and believed that the tiny little faces in the picture could see *us*."

But for Benjamin the concern with what he calls "the soulful portrait" (and also "atmospheric landscapes") is a derailment of what is "more native to the camera." Just as psychoanalysis permits us access to the instinctual unconscious,[6] so photography—when it follows what is truly "native" to it—allows us to discover the optical unconscious around which swirl practices of prophecy and divination. Benjamin describes Blossfeldt's close-up plant photography, in which are revealed "the forms of ancient columns in horse willow, a bishop's crosier in the ostrich fern, totem poles in tenfold enlargements of chestnut and maple shoots, and gothic tracery in the fuller's thistle."

Here technology reveals itself as a magical process, a mode of diagnosis. Photography, as Benjamin continues in a crucial and justly oft cited phrase, "reveals in this material physiognomic aspects, image-worlds, which dwell in the smallest things—meaningful yet covert enough to find a hiding place in waking dreams, but which, enlarged and capable of formulation, make the difference between technology and magic visible as a thoroughly historical variable."[7]

Benjamin is here concerned with the "smallest things": cellular tissue, a foot frozen in motion. But the rest of his "A Little History of Photography" connects these insights to larger plateaus, such as Atget's photography of architectural detail and August Sander's documentation of the "social face" of Weimar Germany. Atget's work is important for Benjamin because of the way it fragments landscape into symptoms: his pictures "work against the exotic, romantically sonorous names of the cities: they suck the aura out of reality like water from a sinking ship."[8] In this respect, his images were the forerunners of Surrealist photography (and would indeed be claimed by *Documents* as such). In both "A Little History" and the later "Work of Art" essay, Benjamin describes Atget's images as being like "crime scenes": evacuated of people, they relocate physiognomy from the face onto buildings, walls, stairs, and shop fronts: participants in a new symptomology of the city. "With Atget," Benjamin wrote in the "Work of Art" essay, "photographs become standard evidence for historical occurrences, and acquire a hidden political significance."[9]

The physiognomy at work in Sander's project is best understood through a detour via Soviet cinema: "The Russian feature film was the first opportunity in decades to put before the camera people who had no use for their photographs. And immediately the human face appeared on film with new and immeasurable significance. But it was no longer a portrait. What was it?"[10] Although Benjamin only mentions Eisenstein and Pudovkin in this essay, this quote makes sense only in relation to Vertov's *Man with a Movie Camera*.[11] In the last few minutes of that remarkable film, several giant cameras on tripods hover above a surging crowd that is intercut with other "faces" of the city: tramlines, street scenes, and a shadowy kinesthetics of bodies entering and leaving buildings.

"No longer a portrait." Here Benjamin directs our attention not to the disappearance of the face but to its mutation into new distributed incarnations in the form (in Atget) of the city and (in Sander) of a "tremendous physiognomic gallery." With Sander we see the fully articulated physiognomy of social worlds, but not one informed by ethnographic or sociological imperatives. Instead, Sander was driven by the desire for "direct observation," and here Benjamin invokes Goethe's description of that "delicate empiricism which so intimately involves itself with the object that it becomes true theory." Photography maps a new physiognomy through a new kind of observation, one with the capacity to constitute new kinds of publics. As we will see, there is much in the archive of Indians' encounters with photography in the nineteenth and twentieth centuries that affirms Hariman and Lucaites's claim that "public life is a way of seeing."[12]

TECHNOLOGY AND MAGIC AS HISTORIC VARIABLES

Perhaps photography's most obvious magic lay in its prosthesis. Norman Chevers's remarkable text *A Manual of Medical Jurisprudence for India*, first published in 1856, noted that "there could scarcely be a doubt that PHOTOGRAPHY would, before many years elapsed, be employed throughout India as a means of identifying bodies, anticipating the disfigurement of rapid decay, and enabling the magistrate and the civil surgeon to examine, in their offices, every detail of a scene of bloodshed, as it appeared when first disclosed to the police, in a place perhaps sixty miles from the sudder station, which no activity on the part of the police or themselves could enable them to visit in time."[13]

Chevers here granted photography powers over time and space: decay could be arrested through the frozen image of the corpse; the location of a murder could be studied sixty miles away in the police station. The photograph's value resided in its ability not simply to freeze time and to translocate space but also to serve as a simulacral body. Chevers's *Manual* is a massively extended eulogy to (in his words) "that silent witness who never lies—the Corpse." Chevers engages with photography as a duplicate body, a matrix of forensic marks of a past event. The truth of the photographic corpse aside, Chevers still presents a vision of photography as a technology whose true potential remains opaque. Looking back at his earlier prognostications, he notes that "*we have yet to judge* the effect which would be produced upon [a] conscience...obstinate in the denial of guilt, by placing before him, in the stereoscope, the actual scene of his atrocity—the familiar walls, the charpoy, the ghastly faces—as they last appeared to his reeling vision—the sight which haunted his brain every hour since the act was done—while he believed to certainty, that its reality could never come before his eyes again."

The most striking example of this prosthetic ambition is actually imported into the 1863 *Journal of the Bengal Photographic Society* (*JBPS*) from the *British Journal of Photography* but reported with such glee by the *JBPS* that we are left with a clear sense of how this resonated with ambitions for photography in India. The news item was headed "Photography and Murder" and reproduced a letter from W. H. Warner, the Metropolitan Police photographer at Scotland Yard, who had written to a detective investigating the murder of one Emma Jackson. The letter alerted the detective to the fact that "if the eyes of a murdered person [are] photographed, upon the retina will be found the last thing that appeared before them, and that in the present case the features of the murderer would probably be found thereon." Warner also noted that four years earlier he had taken "a negative of the eye of a calf a few hours after death, and upon microscopic examination of the same [he had] found depicted thereon the lines of the pavement of the slaughterhouse."[14]

"ALWAYS ORIENTED TOWARDS A PUBLIC"

The year in which the first edition of Chevers's text appeared was also the year in which Johnson and Henderson's *The Indian Amateur's Photographic Album* commenced publication. (It would run, under the patronage of the Bombay Photographic Society, for another two years, ceasing publication in 1858.) Each issue contained three pasted-in, albumen photographic prints and offered amateurs the prospect of a national audience in the company of images produced by the publishers, Johnson and Henderson. Image no. 11, titled *Brahmani Ladies*, depicted two young Brahman girls, one seated and one standing, on a flight of steps upon which are arranged fragments of carved stone, signifiers of an antique culture from which their bodies seem to propose an escape.

The letterpress pasted on the back of that image positions the faces of these girls within an emergent public physiognomy and allows us to see the precise mechanism through which the private is made public:

> We have great pleasure in submitting to our friends a Photograph
> of two very interesting female representatives of the Brahman

tribe. They are at present in Bombay, under the care of their venerable grandmother, enjoying instruction…at the missionhouse, Ambrolie, under the direct guidance of Dr Wilson's family. The attention shown by their father,—who is much distinguished in the judicial service of the Government,—to their training and culture, is highly exemplary, and much to be commended.

In the public display of Arala Bai and Lakshmi Bai in Johnson and Henderson's image, we can see "that new conception of personhood where the private and intimate are…always oriented towards a public."[15] In the case of Arala and Lakshmi, the care of their "venerable grandmother" and the "attention shown by their father" cease to be purely private domestic matters and are redirected to a new public that is constituted through the complex semaphore of the text, signalling them as "representative," invoking a unitary moral world in which they are "exemplary" and mirroring back the commendations of this imaginary public.

PHOTOGRAPHY'S "DYNAMITE OF THE TENTH OF A SECOND" PREFIGURED

Photography's "That-has-been" (as Barthes terms its preservation of an earlier time in the present) was always a key element of its *magical* power— the "lacerating emphasis of the *noeme*." Intrinsic to all photography, it is usually melancholically embraced: "Daguerreotype presumed to be a portrait of Major Edmund C. Vibart who was killed at Cawnpore" declares the text on a small card enclosed in the brown case of a Bakers' daguerreotype in the British Library. An additional note bestows finer points of time: "Edmund Charles Vibart 1825–1857, 11th Regiment Light Cavalry, 1842. Captain 1855. Killed at Cawnpore during Mutiny 27 June 1857." Barthes notes of Alexander Gardner's 1865 *Portrait of Lewis Payne*, a thwarted assassin depicted in his cell, his wrists shackled, prior to his execution, "*He is dead* and *he is going to die*." Vibart's photograph also positions us in this double time of "*this will be* and *this has been*."[16]

Willoughby Wallace Hooper, perhaps more than any other photographer in India during the nineteenth century, was preoccupied with the magical double-time of photography. In 1886 his experiments with the *eidos* of death during the Third Burma War would provoke extreme opposition and concern. Hooper was provost marshal of the Burma Expeditionary Force from November 1885, charged with the maintenance of civil order in occupied territories. In his battle with a Burmese civil insurgency, Hooper used executions as a routinized response and on January 15, 1886, took two

FIGURE 6.1

Burmese insurgents being executed "for the benefit of" W. W. Hooper's camera. British Library, Photo 447/8.

photographs of three hooded Burmese being executed by a party of nine sepoys under the command of Lieutenant Oswald.[17]

This event, together with the protestations of the Reverend Colbeck of the Society for the Propagation of the Gospel, formed the basis for a lurid account by a disgruntled journalist—Edward Kyran Moylan—published in the *Times* on January 21. Moylan reported Colbeck's condemnation at a public meeting of "the grave public scandals" of Hooper's love of "ghastly" executions:

> The Provost Marshall, who is an ardent amateur photographer, is desirous of securing views of the persons executed at the precise moment when they are struck by the bullet. To secure this result, after the orders "ready" and "present" have been given to the firing party, the Provost Marshal fixed his camera on the prisoners, who at times are kept waiting several minutes in that position. The officer commanding the firing party is then directed by the Provost Marshal to give the order to fire at the moment when he exposes his plates. So far no satisfactory negative has been obtained, and the experiments are likely to be continued.[18]

As John Falconer has shown, Moylan's account was "riddled with distortions, exaggerations and downright lies."[19] The subsequent controversy in Parliament and the court of inquiry in Burma into Hooper's activities revealed a slightly less sensational (the prisoners were blindfolded, and no delay occurred on account of Hooper's activities) but equally disturbing version of events.

Hooper engaged this quality of the image, perhaps hoping to stall time through his investigation of the astonishing and unimaginable space between *he is dead* and *he is going to die.* In doing so, he succumbed to a logic of photography's mortiferous eidos: the camera as trigger and a ballistic photographic image, hitting the spectator "like a bullet," as Walter Benjamin would later write. Hooper's *camera macabre* projects us into a future practice in which photography's "dynamite of the tenth of a second...reveals entirely new structural formations of the subject."[20]

"PHOTOGRAPHS BECOME STANDARD EVIDENCE FOR HISTORICAL OCCURRENCES AND ACQUIRE A HIDDEN POLITICAL SIGNIFICANCE"

As photographic technology became increasingly miniaturized and increasingly mobile, especially in the early twentieth century, its habitus changed. It was no longer dependent on the kinds of official support or financial investment that were so central to photographers such as Samuel Bourne (active in India 1863–1870). If nineteenth-century Indian photography's paradigmatic location was the Himalayan foothills, in the twentieth century, photography's preferred location became the street. One of the key moments of transition was Curzon's decision that the 1903 Delhi Durbar should be covered by as many photographers and journalists as possible. Curzon had announced his hope, in a speech in September 1902, that "a good many eyes in a good many parts of the globe" would be "directed upon Delhi,"[21] and he encouraged the international press and freelance photographers to document the event. This was a key moment in the history of facialization that I am attempting to describe here.

A mobile photographic technology was increasingly able to document more easily the chaotic public spaces in which colonial hegemony appeared increasingly fragile. The Jallianwallabagh (Amritsar) massacre on April 13, 1919—in which 379 peaceful protesters were shot by troops under the command of General Dyer—was to kick-start a resurgence in anticolonial struggle. Soon after this event a committed young photographer, Narayan Vinayak Virkar, arrived to photograph the evidence of this atrocity. Virkar's images document the bullet-pocked wall against which so many hundreds

FIGURE 6.2

A survivor of the 1919 Jallianwallabagh massacre in Amritsar directs the viewer's gaze to evidence of Dyer's atrocity. Photograph by N. V. Virkar, Nehru Memorial Library 1054.

of villagers died and which is now covered in anti-Dyer graffiti. Bullet holes are ringed with white chalk, and various crouching figures point to these.

In 1922 Amritsar was once again a flash point. In this year, however, cameras were there to record events as they unfolded. One of the cameras belonged to an American cinematographer named A. L. Varges.[22] An official report described how Varges had photographed an Akali protest procession en route to the Guru-ka-Bagh. Four waves of protestors attempted to access a disputed piece of land and were beaten back by lathi-wielding police, all of this being filmed and photographed by Varges.

"Eventually 23 of the Akalis were taken off on stretchers, the remaining two, who were more obstinate, were treated more roughly by the Police... meanwhile the cinematograph operator and other photographers and Press representatives were all busy," an official report noted.[23]

The governor in council proclaimed that he did "not feel happy about the activities of the cinema operator and the possible ill-effect of these films in fostering anti-British feeling in the United States" and then instructed the Home Department to ascertain whether there was any way of stopping

FIGURE 6.3
Police brutality at the Guru-ka-Bagh, Punjab, 1922. Photograph by A. L. Varges, Nehru Memorial Library 23088.

Varges from shooting more film, of identifying his whereabouts, and of making clear to him the necessity of "exercis[ing] caution that none [be] exhibited which [would be] likely to cause misunderstanding."[24]

In Varges's images—these scratched, panicked slices of reality— we see evidence of photography's indiscriminate capture, which (as the media theorist Friedrich Kittler noted) "shifted the boundaries that distinguished...random visual data from meaningful picture sequences, unconscious and unintentional inscriptions from their conscious and intentional counterparts."[25]

Official response to Varges initiated a notion of the "embedded" photojournalist, whose resonance in the early twenty-first century will be obvious. The Guru-ka-Bagh episode precipitated an official discussion about whether unsanctioned filming of public places could be controlled. In December 1922 the secretary of state for India concluded that section 144 of the criminal procedures code could be used to "prevent the photography or filming of objectionable subjects" and asked for further clarification of this possibility by the Legislative Department. The reply was that section 144 probably did not apply but even if it did, "it would be quite useless. In practice a film would be taken long before an order preventing it had been received."

It is clear that at this moment a profound anxiety was at large, an anxiety that marked the deep and destabilizing realization that the control of photography as a technical practice had now slipped from the hand of the state. Photography's "penetrating certainty," which earlier colonial figures had extolled, had been desirable to the extent that it was a certainty that the state could own. Colonial surveillance and proscription, like photography itself, was now caught in a vortex of its own making. Perhaps nothing sums up—and prefigures—this paradox better than the official anxiety about Sher Ali, a convict who murdered Lord Mayo during a visit to the Andamans in 1872. This was the same Mayo—Richard Southwell Bourke—who, three years earlier, had awarded the viceroy's medal to Samuel Bourne in the Bengal Photographic Society annual exhibition. Sher Ali was first photographed as an object lesson in colonial punishment, but his love of the camera and sense of himself as a celebrity started to unhinge a colonial system of discipline structured around visibility. Clare Anderson notes W. W. Hunter's description of how Sher Ali was "childishly vain of being photographed as the murderer of a Viceroy" and Hunter's subsequent refusal to publish details of his identity. Anderson also notes that although there are three images of Sher Ali in the British Library, in only one of these is he named: in the other two he is an anonymous murderer and assassin.[26]

Photography, Barthes noted, belonged to that class of "laminated" objects "whose two leaves" of Good and Evil "cannot be separated without destroying them both."[27] In the logic of the *pharmakon*, precisely the same qualities that make photography a cure are also conditions by which it becomes a poison. *Pharmakon* is a term used by Plato in *Phaedrus*, and it catches Jacques Derrida's attention because of its fluidity and reversibility—its potential for "leading astray." In a resonant passage, Derrida points out that "in the most striking manner the regular, ordered polysemy...has, through skewing, indetermination, or overdetermination, *but without mistranslation*, permitted the rendering of the same word by 'remedy,' 'recipe,' 'poison,' 'drug,' 'philtre,' etc."[28] This doubleness, Derrida continues, "*is a difficulty inherent in its very principle*, situated less in the passage from one language to another, from one philosophical language to another, than already...in the tradition between Greek and Greek."[29]

During the heyday of mid-1850s enthusiasm, one of the most enthusiastic proselytisers on behalf of the wondrous new technology was the

Reverend Joseph Mullens. In his celebrated lecture "On the Applications of Photography in India," delivered to the Photographic Society of Bengal in October 1856, he noted the following:

> There are some applications of Photography, less peculiar but equally professional and of great importance to the Government. *The scene and circumstances of a riot, the damage inflicted by rioters*; the mode in which a robbery was committed; the scene of a murder and all its attendant circumstances.... *A very active Photographer, in whom the ruling passion was very strong, might be able to sketch a riot during its actual progress, and by successive pictures to show who was most active, to identify the ringleaders, and show the murderous hand in the very act of inflicting a fatal blow. The purpose of justice would in this manner be served to the most material degree.*[30]

Mullens assumed that photography's indexicality would serve the interest of the British colonial presence. We have seen how that same indexicality, photography's nondiscriminating trace, did come to serve the purpose of justice (and ultimately of an emergent democracy), but not in the way Mullens anticipated.

As with the Derridean pharmakon (the untranslatable zone of the remedy, drug, philter, cure, and poison), this transformation reflected not a distortion of photography but a set of effects potential to photography itself. A technology dependent on a colonial habitus found itself reproducing that habitus's "structuring determinations."[31] As this protean technical practice found itself freely roaming the streets—capturing fleeting and secret images—it located new subjects through which to construct new publics.

ENTRAILS: "NO LONGER A PORTRAIT: WHAT WAS IT?"

In 1921 a strange episode unfolded in Bengal in which the evidential role of photographs would once again come to the fore. In this episode we can perhaps see further evidence of the dispersal of physiognomy away from the face and toward, on the one hand, the fingerprint as an inscription of individuals "within the law" and, on the other, the social physiognomy of the public that interests me here.

In 1909 the dissolute twenty-four-year-old second kumar of Bhowal died of a fever in Darjeeling. He was then cremated, a process that was interrupted by an exceptionally heavy rainstorm. Shortly afterward his widow and her brother took over the wealthy Bhowal estates. In 1921 a naked holy man appeared in Dacca (Dhaka), and rumors began to circulate that he was the second kumar, returned. The second kumar's sister met with him and then convinced most of the family that it was indeed the prince returned. The second kumar's widow and brother, however, now enjoying the benefits of the Bhowal estate were unconvinced and found themselves facing this Bengali Martin Guerre in the courtroom in 1937.

The plaintiff's case was that he had been poisoned with arsenic and that the rainstorm halfway through the cremation (during which all the onlookers took shelter at some distance) awakened him and that a band of *sadhus*, hearing his strange sounds, took him to be one of their own. It was in their company that he spent the next twelve years until his rediscovery in Dacca. The putative second kumar spent sixteen years in litigation in three major cases, during which "976 witnesses swore that he was unquestionably the second Kumar and 374 called by his wife" testified otherwise.[32] Finally, on July 30, 1946, the Privy Council in London sustained his claim; he died three days later, after which he was cremated, never to return again.

In the various court outings, the identity of the second kumar and the identity of the plaintiff were phantasms to be collapsed or separated. In this contest a whole repertoire of identity effects were called into play, many of which have been addressed by Partha Chatterjee in his recent account of this case.[33] Photographs—which Chatterjee does not consider—were central to this contest of identities, and the defense (the kumar's wife) made much play of these, hoping to illustrate by "mathematical certainty" the divergence of the plaintiff's physical marks from those of the second kumar as deposited in the eight images exposed prior to 1909.

In the process of comparison, ears were juxtaposed; noses, eyes, and the tilt or curl of the lip were extracted and analyzed, many of these being traced from photographs and tabulated in comparative visual columns for display within the courtroom.

This was a venatic quest fully worthy of Sherlock Holmes or Giovanni Morelli.[34] As Barry Flood has noted, Brown's comparative symptomological tables reproduced a visual method that he had perfected in his earlier publications on Hindu and "Mahommedan" architecture.[35]

Justice Biswas in his 1937 judgement in Calcutta drew attention to the inadequacy of photographic evidence. Photographs, he concluded, "throw *no light* on points such as age, height, figure, complexion, colour of hair, moustache and eye-brows, and colour of eyes." Percy Brown, the principal of the Calcutta School of Art, had given evidence in the case that a photograph is not a map and that "measuring photographs is useless for comparison, and worse than useless, if they are different in scales

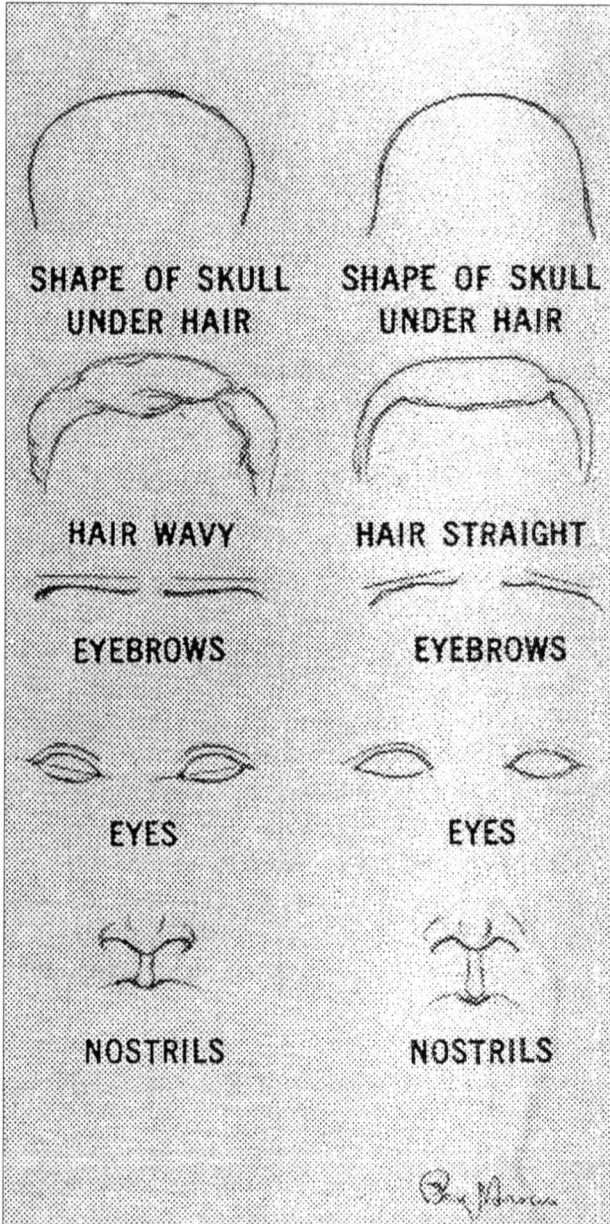

FIGURE 6.4

Image showing features of the kumar and of the claimant, presented by the defense in the Bhowal case, Life, September 2, 1946. Drawn by Percy Brown.

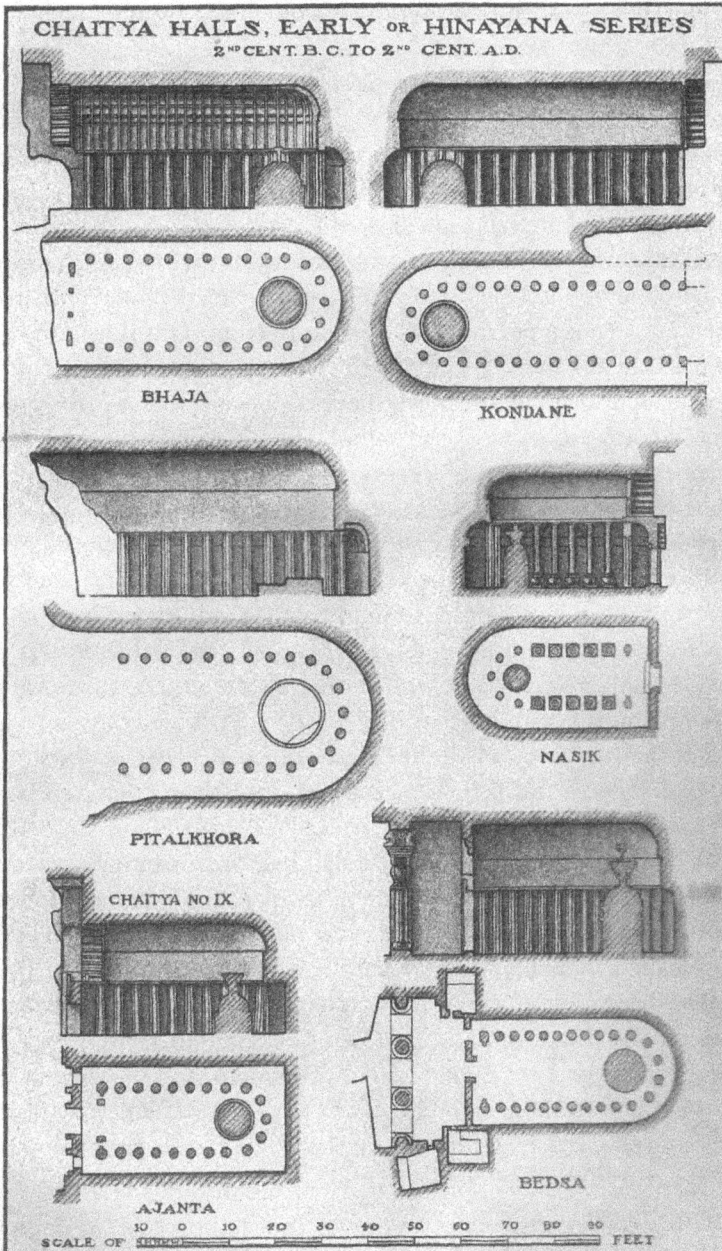

Figure 6.5
Drawing by Percy Brown showing Chaitya Halls, from Brown's Indian
Architecture (Buddhist and Hindu), *2nd ed. (Bombay: Taraporevala, n.d.).*

or at different angles; you must go by the eye, meaning thereby no doubt the eye of the trained artist."[36]

Elsewhere in the judgment, the photographs' potential indexical claim is undermined by an emphasis on the conventionalized context of their appearance. Justice Biswas pours scorn on one witness's introduction of photographs: "[It] seems to me to have been invented by someone who had seen too many sentimental pictures from Hollywood."[37]

Here, an earlier form of photographic portraiture—what Allan Sekula has called "sentimental realism"—collapsed under the weight of its own sentimentality: "not a portrait," as Benjamin wrote. This unwillingness to render the face as a map is undoubtedly partly a product of the relocation of juridical identity in *dactylography*, that is, fingerprinting, which appropriately enough was pioneered by William J. Herschel (in Bengal), the son of John Herschel, the inventor of the cyanotype process.[38] But this relocation of authority also reflects the seepage of a facial physiognomy onto a social physiognomy, where photography's venatic eye searches for entrails.

Photography as divination appears in a highly marked form in 1956 in the report of the Netaji Inquiry Committee. Netaji is the popular appellation for Subhas Chandra Bose, a former Indian National Congress president who, following conflict with Gandhi, decided that alliance with the Axis powers was the most efficient way to rid India of her colonizers. Japan supported the formation of the Indian National Army (INA), with whom Bose fought against the British in Burma. He died in contested circumstances in a plane crash in Taiwan.

Bose might be described as the Indian Elvis: many Indians are unwilling to believe that he died as claimed, or died at all, and a number of committees of inquiry have attempted to put matters to rest.[39] The 1956 inquiry headed by Shah Nawaz Khan, a former major in the INA, was charged with investigating the "circumstances concerning the departure of Netaji Subhas Chandra Bose from Bangkok about the 16th August 1945, his alleged death as a result of an aircraft accident, and subsequent developments connected therewith."[40] On that day—the day after the Japanese surrender—two planes, organized by the chief of the Japanese Liaison Mission, were due to take Bose and a small party of key personnel to Saigon for onward transport to a place of safety. In Saigon Bose was offered only two seats on a plane (a twin-engine heavy bomber from the Third Air Force stationed at Singapore), although Bose insisted that the whole party travel to the aerodrome in an attempt to get aboard. The plane left with Bose and Captain Habibur Rehman, leaving the rest of the party behind in Saigon. The plane refuelled at Tourane, where all surplus baggage and twelve

PLATE 2

Inspired by the devil, Muslims worship a golden idol of Muhammad, from Vincent de Beauvais,
Miroir historiale (Speculum historiale, *French translation by Jean de Vignay), Paris,*
fourteenth century. Bibliothèque nationale de France, Manuscrit Français 52, folio 97, detail.
Reproduced with permission of the Bibliothèque nationale de France.

PLATE 3

The Prophet Muhammad, from Matthew Paris, Chronica majora, *St. Albans, thirteenth*
century. Parker Library, MS16, fol. 44r, detail. Reproduced with permission of the Master
and Fellows of Corpus Christi College, Cambridge.

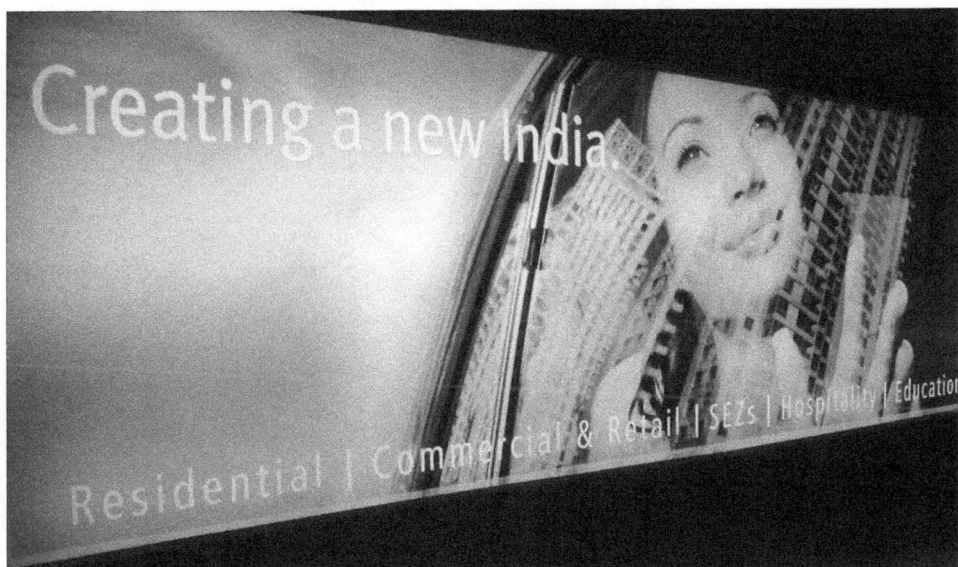

PLATE 4

"Creating a new India," billboard at South Delhi's Khan Market, 2006. Photograph by C. Brosius.

PLATE 5

The gated community as a parallel world, real estate billboard, Noida, 2006. Photograph by C. Brosius.

PLATE 6

"Unveiling the Art of Timeless Living," Florence Villas, Gurgaon, 2006. Photograph by C. Brosius.

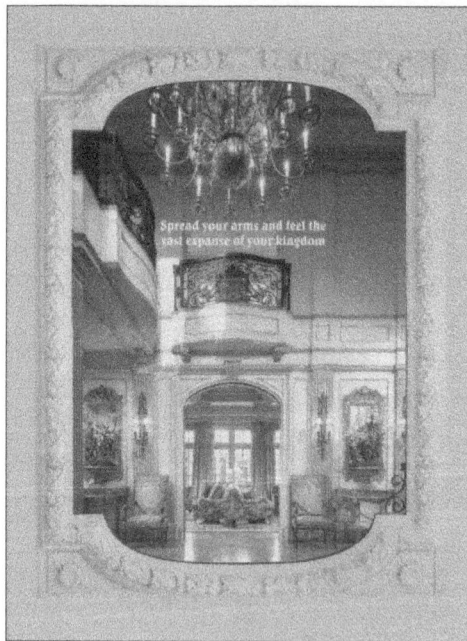

PLATES 7A AND 7B

"Seek out a kingdom," Eros Grand Mansions II. Stills from an Eros Group brochure, 2006.

PLATE 8

Figurines in a Feng Shui shop at a Gurgaon mall, 2006. Photograph by C. Brosius.

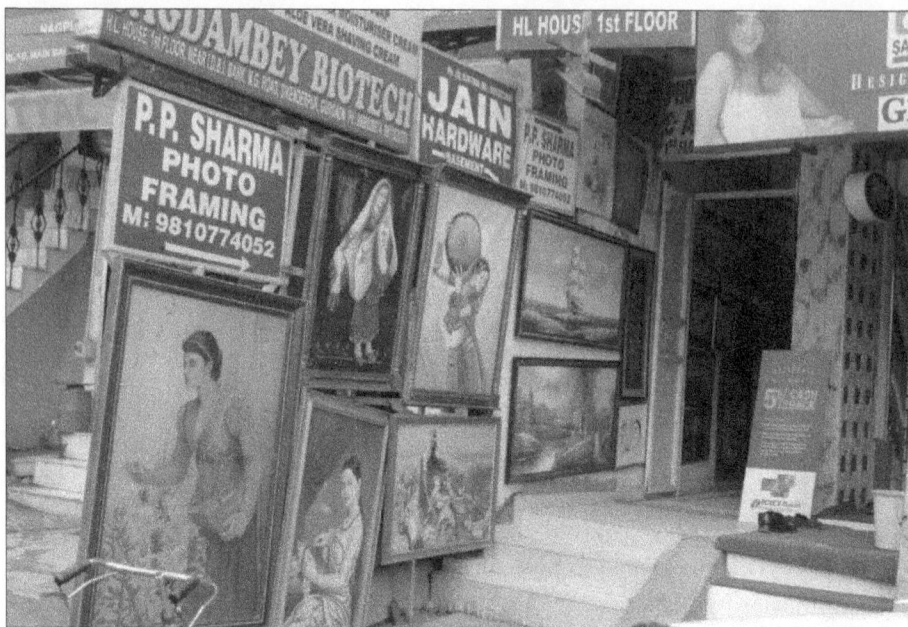

PLATE 9

Paintings of traditional Indian women, for sale en route to Gurgaon, 2006. Photograph by R. S. Iyer.

View of Akshardham Cultural Complex with Commonwealth Games Village construction site in the background, 2010. Photograph by C. Brosius.

PLATE 11

Meditating in Windsor Park: a "win-win situation," advertisement by Assotech Realty, Indirapuram, New Delhi, 2006. Reproduced with permission of Assotech Realty.

PLATE 12

Christian prayer room, Ambon, 2006. Reproduced with permission of John Yesayas and A. K. Pattinaya. Photograph by P. Spyer.

PLATE 14

John Yesayas, Christian mural with Jesus cameo, Ambon, 2003. Reproduced with permission of the artist. Photograph by P. Spyer.

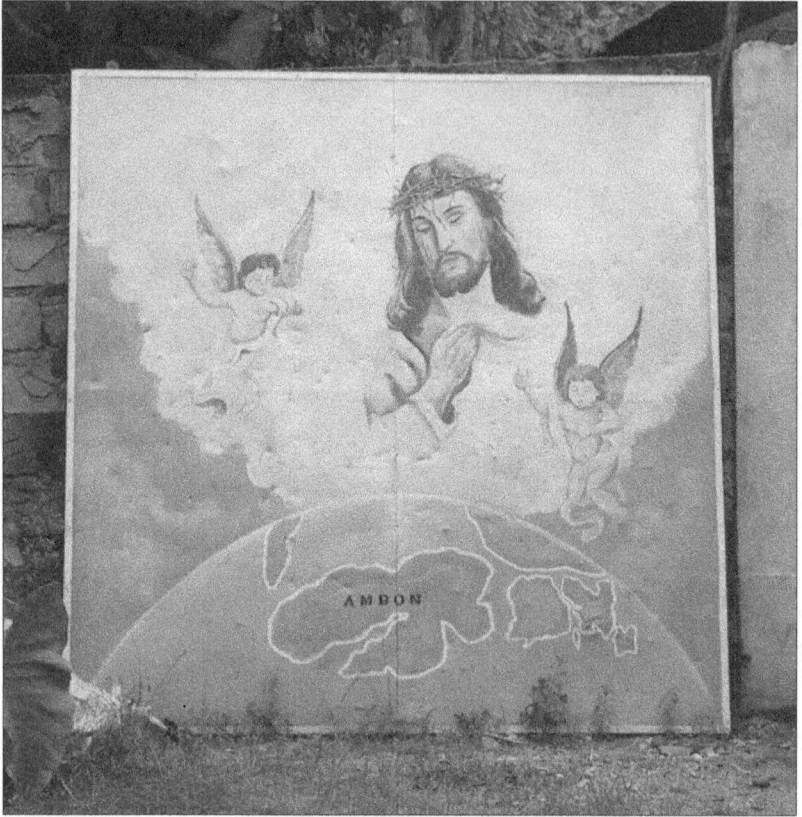

PLATE 15

John Yesayas, Jesus Christ overlooks Ambon, billboard in Ambon, 2003. Reproduced with permission of the artist. Photograph by P. Spyer.

PLATE 17

Motorbiker with Christian mural, Ambon, 2006. Artwork by John Yesayas. Reproduced with permission of the artist. Photograph by P. Spyer.

PLATE 18

John Yesayas, Jesus overlooks the destruction of the Silo Church, *painting after a mural, 2005. (Painting in author's collection.) Reproduced with permission of the artist. Photograph by P. Spyer.*

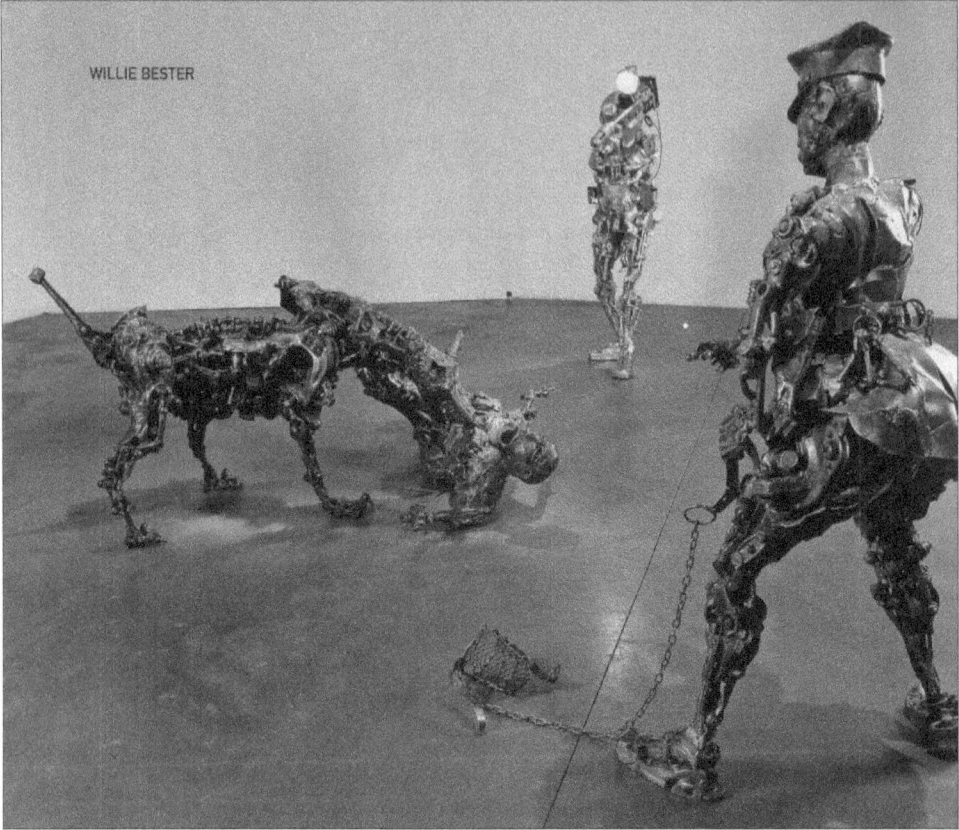

PLATE 19

Willie Bester, Who Let the Dogs Out, *2001. Courtesy of the artist.*

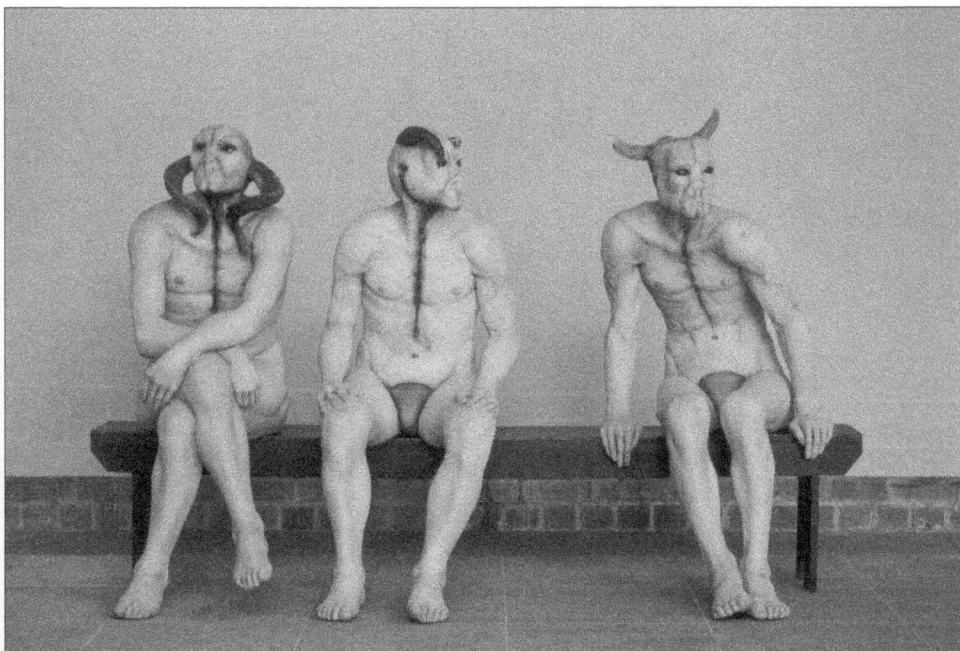

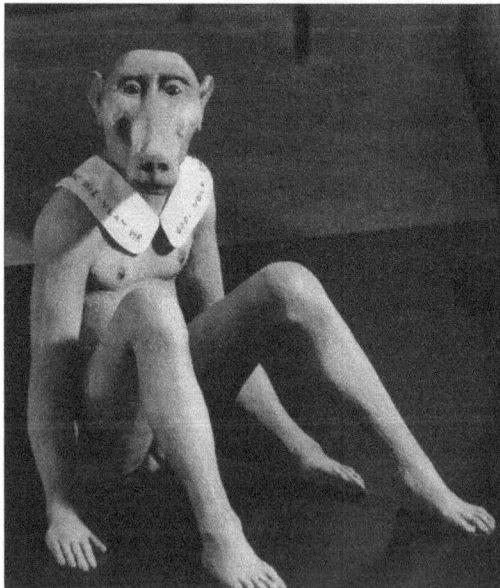

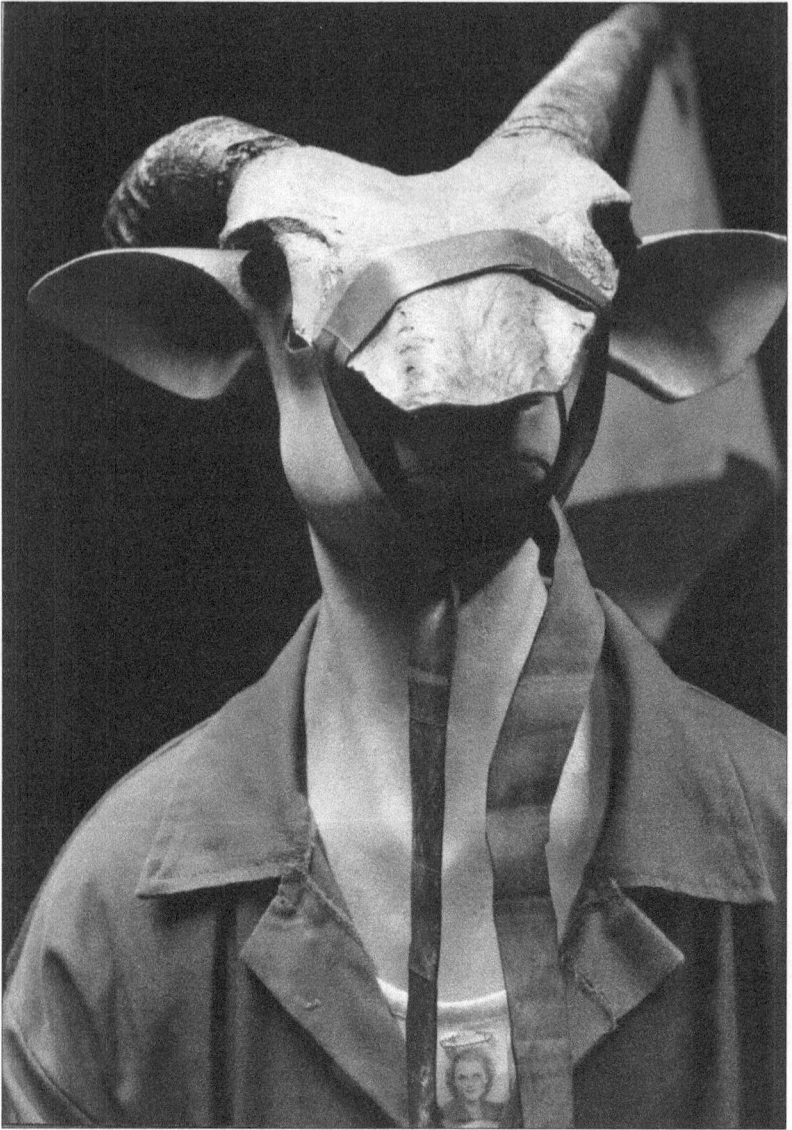

PLATE 25

Jane Alexander, "Harbinger in correctional uniform" (detail from Courtroom 21 in the absence of Judge Woo Bih Li/Courtroom 21 Title withdrawn/Verity, Faith and Justice, *2006. 100 smooth black thread sewn guilt edge 100gram 1000 blank wood page free books; 1000 new red industrial strength gloves; 1 Singaporean judicial ceremonial robe commissioned from a Cape Town judicial seamstress; 1 set of South African pre-democracy prisoner's clothing issue; 1 set of shackles loaned from Pollsmoor Maximum Security Prison, Cape Town; 2 Dutch East India Company flags; 10 sculptures, including Harbinger, pictured here. Art © Jane Alexander/DALRO, Johannesburg/VAGA, New York. Photograph by Luke Tan.*

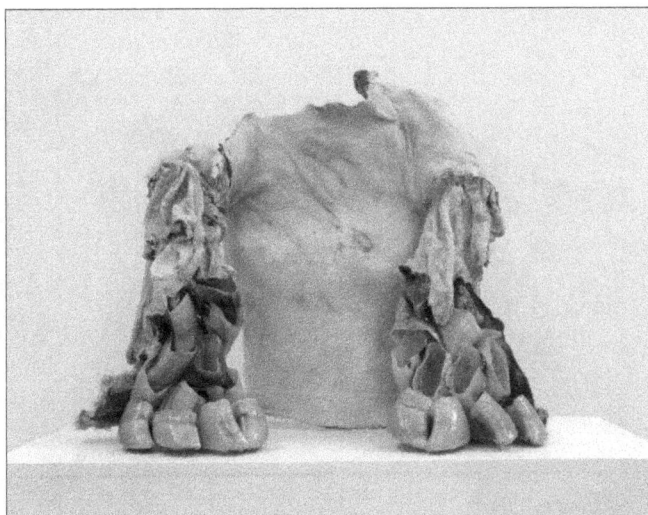

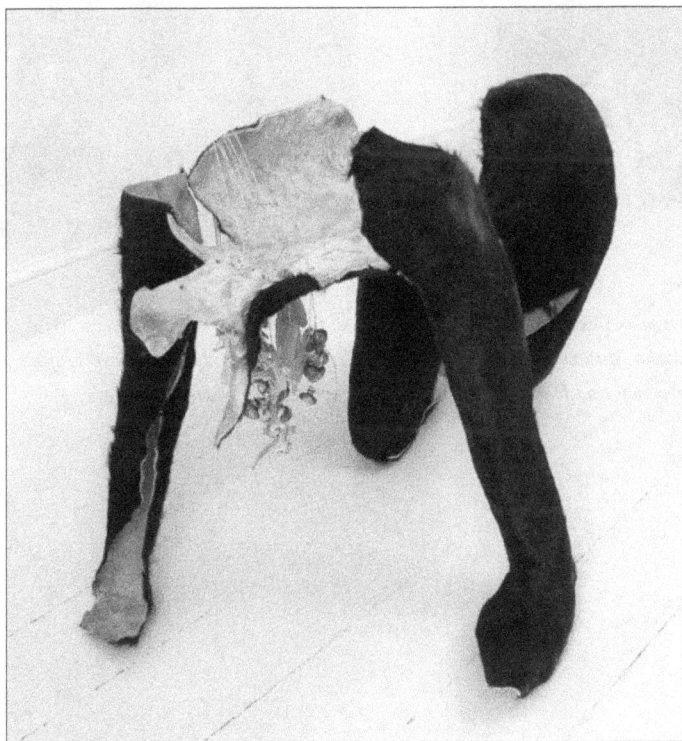

PLATE 26c

Nandipha Mntambo, Silent Embrace,
*2007. © Nandipha Mntambo. Courtesy of
Stevenson, Capetown and Johannesburg.*

PLATE 26d

Nandipha Mntambo, Indlovukati, *2007.
© Nandipha Mntambo. Courtesy of Stevenson,
Capetown and Johannesburg.*

PLATE 27

The semiotics of rain and the metaphorics of grilled duck," mise-en-scène, Kuntilanak 2, *MVP Pictures, 2007.*

PLATE 28

Rayyan Pratama, contemporary Indonesian moviegoers as occult celebrity subjects, street mural, Jakarta, 2012. Reproduced with permission of the artist. Photograph by Aryo Danusiri.

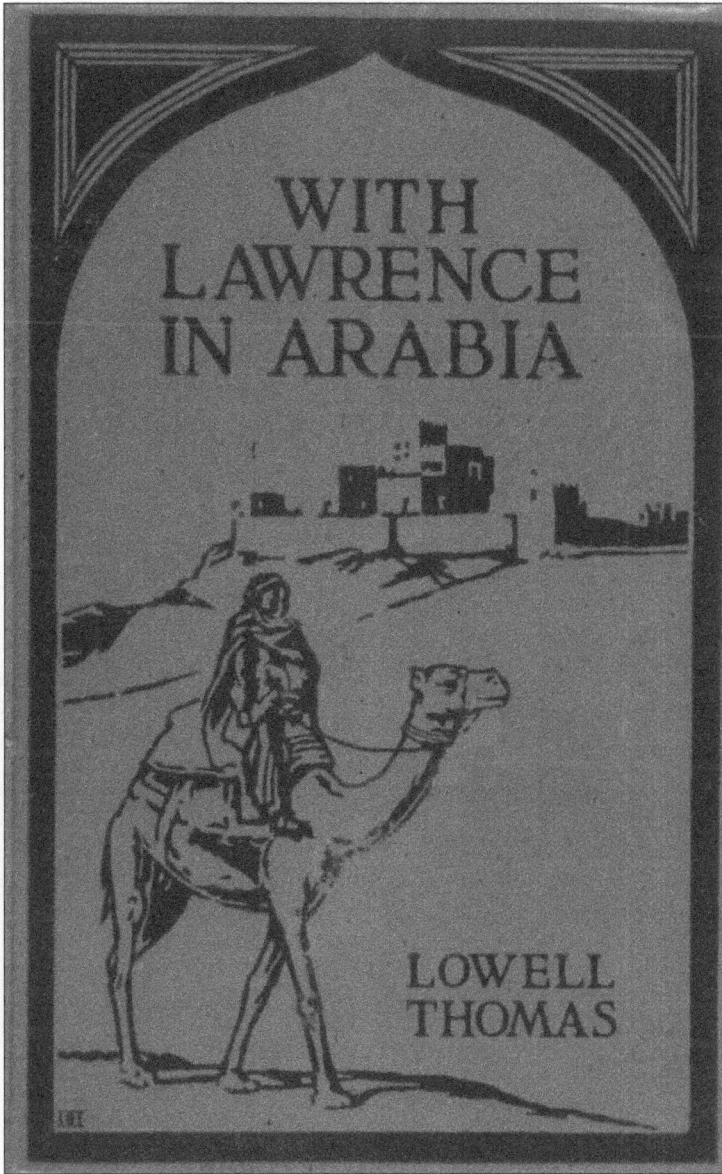

WITH
LAWRENCE
IN ARABIA

LOWELL
THOMAS

PLATE 29

Book cover, With Lawrence in Arabia *by Lowell Thomas, 1926.*

PLATE 30

Cover illustration, theater brochure for Lawrence of Arabia, *Columbia Pictures, 1962.*

PLATE 31

Lawrence de Arabia, *Argentinean movie poster, 1962.*

PLATE 32
Lawrence of Arabia, *movie poster, 1989.*

antiaircraft guns were stripped out. The next day, it transited to Taihoku [Tapei] in Taiwan, where it then headed to Tokyo on the final leg of its journey. According to the 1956 inquiry, it was here that things ended. Shortly after takeoff there was an explosion and the propeller and port engine fell off; "the plane nose-dived, making a wailing noise."[41] Remarkably, seven of the occupants survived, but not Netaji.

The committee's report exhibits unqualified faith in the power of photography to uphold its narrative. In establishing the destructive force of the fire after the crash, for instance, Major Kono's burns are described: the burnt appearance of his face eleven years after the event are commented upon, and his four misshapen fingers enumerated: "Both his hands were deformed. A picture of Major Kono's hands was taken. They tell their own story."[42]

My own copy of the Netaji committee report was purchased from a street market in Old Delhi and was originally bought by one "Anand" in 1968 from the Publications Division. It is this Anand who has heavily underlined key passages of the report and inserted numerous arrows and question marks on the photographic plates that form a key part of the committee's sifting of evidence. Anand's lines, arrows, and question marks subject the divinatory space of the inquiry's images to his own, competing venatic system. The very first plate in the report is adorned with two arrows and another questioning line—"visual marks of invisible analogies."[43]

A plate depicting *The Priest of Renkoji temple, holding Netaji's portrait and the casket* has a transcription error in its inscription that provokes Anand to insert a bold red line as though pointing to the faulty hieroglyph of language.

Anand's anxiety about the indexical nature of the photographic evidence deployed by the committee is expressed—through his own marginalia—by means of a questioning of anomalies in the transcription of linguistic elements in the image. Anand seeks to derail the indexical narrative of the committee by attending to linguistic glitches deriving from Japanese priests' attempts to Romanize (through a double translation) the natural language of the name Subhas Chandra Bose (in popular prints, in Devanagari this name is endowed with a sacred materiality).

We should also note that Bose's death was *balidan*—sacrifice. In popular images he is sometimes depicted offering his auto-decapitated head to Mother India, recalling the way in which "decapitation became the most potent image of sacrifice in Batailles's thought" and suggesting that we might read the Netaji report images as akin to Eli Lothar's *La Villette Abattoir* photographs, commissioned by Bataille for a Critical Dictionary entry in *Documents* 6 in 1929.

Lothar was "pricked by the sight of a gathering of stray calves feet, still

FIGURE 6.6

"Air crash at Taihoku," *a plate from the* Netaji Inquiry Committee Report, *Government of India, 1956. Annotations by Anand.*

attempting to stand by propping themselves against a wall, or bovine skins crawling across the pavement while weeping trails of blood."[44]

Anand's approach to the photographic images in the Netaji report is venatic. He treats the photographs as entrails to be sifted for divinatory signs. This is one venatic manifestation of the relocation of physiognomy from the face onto new social, historical, and political spaces. Although Carlo Ginzburg would resist my attempt to historicize this historically specific moment and mode of divination, I cannot refrain from citing his observations about ancient Arab physiognomy's grounding in the notion of *firasa*, which Ginzburg interprets as entailing the "capacity to leap from the known to the unknown by inference (on the basis of clues)."[45] And of

FIGURE 6.7

Photomontage depicting Subhas Chandra Bose offering his head to Mother India, ca. 1950.

course, the Bengali practice of "finger-tipping," on which Herschel based his system, was another example of the "low intuition" that Ginzburg eulogizes.

"THERE IS NOTHING NEW EXCEPT WHAT HAS BEEN FORGOTTEN"

That there is "nothing new except what has been forgotten" appears as a chapter epigram in the former viceroy Lord Curzon's memoirs. It might also serve as an appropriate means of drawing our attention to the way in which new modes of divination repeat forms of the earliest photographic practice. Early photography in India was acclaimed for its potential capture of bodies and its ability to act as a new superbody, an infinitely expandable prosthesis. The pioneer medical jurisprudent Norman Chevers in particular, writing in 1856 and 1870, stressed the way in which the camera would extend the forensic eye of the police to remote murder scenes and by recording murder scenes automatically trigger confessions of guilt from those confronted with the enormity of their crimes.

Photography was initially greeted by many as a magical cure for a set of existing representational problems. It seemed to provide perfect chemical traces of the world: the largest spaces could be recorded, the tiniest spaces probed; past events appeared as though they might be recoverable, the retinas of murder victims—if photographed quickly enough—might reveal the identity of their attackers. The camera seemed to be a truly magical prosthesis, and its possibilities seemed limitless.

Many of these possibilities have now been revived, but in largely negative incarnations. Retinal scans are back in fashion, and it is thought that they might still reveal murders, especially if wedded to the alchemy of racial profiling at the border points of humans and images. But such echoes of a familiar history no longer make the camera a liberating prosthesis: they no longer *extend* bodies; rather, they render the body subject to *intrusion*—the cameraman, as Benjamin observed, becomes the *surgeon* in whom, nevertheless, the magician "is still hidden."[46]

Recent Indian experience demonstrates that there are some positive dimensions to this resurgence. Recall William Mazzarella's wonderful discussion of the "rurally imagined transparency machine" produced by the March 2001 *Tehelka* exposé of Defence Ministry corruption in the then BJP government through the use of hidden video cameras; the images these captured were then posted on the Internet. A cameraman reported overhearing villagers saying that a new device had been invented—*"[sab ka] brashtachaar nanga ho jaata hai*[47]...a kind of x-ray machine which exposed naked anyone's corruption the moment they came in front of it"—and that this was the reason the prime minister had not been seen in public for several days.[48]

We might add to this productive incarnation of surveillance the recent use by protestors in Indian-administered Kashmir of camcorders as an alternative to guns. Danish Shervani was viciously beaten by Indian troops in early 2008, a beating filmed by several co-protestors, ready to capture "fleeting and secret images." "Abuses by the security forces were recorded and posted on the Internet"; a press report noted, "The clips speak for themselves."[49]

But machines that reveal all have produced different and much more widespread anxieties in contemporary India. "Voyeur Alert!" and "The Death of Privacy," headlines in the *Times of India* in 2005 describing the placing of spycams in a girls' hostel in Pune, are typical of hundreds of stories that have flooded the Indian press in recent years.[50] This anxiety is so pronounced that it has already been monumentalized in three films: Mahesh Bhatt's 2005 sensationalist and prurient *Kalyug*; Buddhadeb Dasgupta's 2007 *Ami, Iyasin Ar Madhubala*, whose English title is *The Voyeur*,[51] and Anurag Kashyap's huge 2009 hit *Dev. D.*

Kalyug plays innocence against contamination, the interior against the exterior, and the private against the public.[52] Mahesh Bhatt, the director, in whose atelier the film was produced, has related its plot to "real" journalistic narratives. Innocence is established at the beginning in the encounter of an orphaned Kashmiri girl and Kunal Khemu playing a streetwise but honest Mumbaikar. All is idyllic until the honeymoon, when, to cite a popular website review, we are forced to confront "the humiliation and trauma of a young man whose lovemaking during his honeymoon is captured for the multimillion rupee porn market."[53] Renuka, the wife, commits suicide after being told by a policewoman that in every *galli* (backstreet) everyone is watching her on the Internet and on their mobiles. In *Dev. D.* a young women's sexual behavior is captured by her boyfriend on his phone, circulated by a multimedia messaging service (MMS), causing a Delhi-wide scandal. This is understood by all its viewers to directly reference a recent case in the elite Delhi Public School. The shame incurred causes her father to commit suicide and the young woman to become the sex-worker object of Devdas's—the central character's—affection. *Dev D.*, with its unusual explicitness, foul language, celebration of narcotics and alcohol, and eschewal of Kalyug's prurient moralizing, has been an enormous hit with metropolitan youth, for whom it has served as a liberatory watershed in modern commercial cinema.

Other recent films explore photography's prophetic potentiality in remarkably direct ways: *Aa Dekhen Zara* (Come Let's See, 2009) details the central character's—Ray Acharya's—experiences with a Hasselblad camera he inherited from his father that produces images foretelling the future. When he photographs lottery shops, the lists of the future winning numbers appear when he develops the prints. When he photographs racehorses training, the prints reveal their positions at the finishing post. And portraits of certain people, when developed, appear dark and unreadable, prophesizing their death. Another film released in 2009, *Shadow*, was advertised with an image of the blind central character wearing dark glasses above the (English) slogan "He cannot see in real life but he can see in reel life." This further maps the prophetic potential of the lens, which links technics to what is yet to pass.

Dark, unreadable faces are also a feature of the venatic divinatory forms generated by mobile phones technics. Whereas the earliest practices of photography endowed citizens with faces, mobile phone photography seems to provoke a process of defacialization: faces are obscured for reasons of legality and of shame, and mobile phones generate new physiologies in which physiognomy is displaced from the face. There are also technical reasons for this, as mobile phone film director Jnantik Shukla explained. He entered a ninety-second film, *Exist Exit*—shot in just two colors, blue and yellow, "because more colours increase pixellation"—in the 2004 Interfilm Festival in Berlin. Another Indian entry captured mainly lights, which appear clearly on the mobile. "Facial details and quick movements appear blurred, and the phone mike does not record sounds clearly," said the director, Vinod Kuriakose. So his *For Necessary Action*, a film on communal violence, was shot without showing the faces of the characters. "Creativity is about turning limitations into advantages," he concluded.[54]

The scheme I map in this discussion describes three plateaus. First, an early practice characterized, as Benjamin put it, by the "ultimate retrenchment of the face," in which (partly because of photography's technomaterial constraints) the subjects of photography projected themselves into the photograph in a process of temporal elongation and psychological fulfilment. Second, the relocation of the physiognomy of the face onto a more generalized, social physiognomy ("physiognomic aspects of visual worlds") of the street, the crowd, the public. In this plateau individuals had worth inasmuch as they were oriented to a public. Third, and finally, a symmetrical echo, or inversion, of the earliest practices, in which externality is figured as a quality of internality: photography's "de-platonizing" tendency is inverted so that internal forms and practices figure new venatic physiognomies and physiologies.

Tehelka's X-ray immediation and the anxiety driving recent popular films, together with the kind of mobile phone footage involved in recent scandals, are essentially similar: all engage the end point of Benjamin's observation about a smaller and more fleeting photography but also posit a photographic regime of images *without borders*, where the borders are not simply geographic or territorial, but rather are transgressive of the corporeality established by a nineteenth-century photography (the prosthetic superbody) for which the external traces of the face and the body constituted the territory. These new imaging practices and anxieties thus constitute the final movement in trajectory I delineate here. After an initial engagement with the physiognomy of the face and a later moment of social physiognomy, we encounter the transgressed space of a violated individuality, the very individuality (always oriented toward a public) upon which former notions of the public were constructed and that conjures a private oriented *wholly* to the public, an involuted—or inside-out—body, convulsed not by beauty but by surveillance. Internally convulsed, photography thus mediates not the external surfaces of bodies but their entrails—the raw medium of the augurs and haruspices—offering hieroglyphs of possible futures.

Notes

1. "Nachfahr der Augurn und der Haruspexe." Walter Benjamin, "Kleine Geschichte der Photographie," *Das Kunstwerk im Zeitalter seiner technischen Reproduzierbarkeit: Drei Studien zur Kunstsoziologie* (Frankfurt am Main: Suhrkamp Verlag, 1977), 64. English trans., Walter Benjamin, "A Little History of Photography," *Walter Benjamin: Selected Writings*, vol. 2, *1927–1934*, ed. Michael W. Jennings, Howard Eiland, and Gary Smith (Cambridge, MA: Belknap Press of Harvard University Press, 1999), 527.

2. Dan Weikel, "Privacy Concerns Shadow TSA Tool," *Chicago Tribune*, April 18, 2008, http://www.chicagotribune.com/news/chi-body-scannerapr18,0,6843385.story (accessed December 1, 2008).

3. Jacques Attali, *Noise: The Political Economy of Music* (Minneapolis: University of Minnesota Press, 1985), 11.

4. Tom Conley, "Faciality," in *The Deleuze Dictionary*, ed. Adrian Parr (New York: Columbia University Press, 2005), 97.

5. Benjamin, "A Little History," 514.

6. The recent work of Clément Chéroux on the photography of quasi-mesmeric "vital fluids" suggests that the parallelism between the two unconsciouses was far closer than usually thought. He documents the work of individuals such as Hippolyte Baraduc, who worked (as had Freud) closely with Charcot at La Salpêtrière. Louis Darget pursued a similar interest and explicitly invoked divination as a method of reading the resulting photographs: "He deciphered his photographs in the way fortune-tellers interpret the shapes in tealeaves, troubled liquids of all kinds, animals [*sic*] entrails, molten lead, swirling smoke, and cloud formations." Chéroux then suggests that Freudian psychoanalysis repositioned this selfsame divinatory paradigm into an endogenous rather than exogenous field. Clément Chéroux, "Photographs of Fluids: An Alphabet of Invisible Rays," in *The Perfect Medium: Photography and the Occult*, ed. Clément Chéroux et al. (New Haven, CT: Yale University Press, 2005), 121.

7. Benjamin, "A Little History," 512. For a parallel exposition, see also Michael Taussig, "Physiognomic Aspects of Visual Worlds," *Visual Anthropology Review* 8, no. 1 (Spring 1992): 15–28.

8. Benjamin, "A Little History," 518.

9. Walter Benjamin, "The Work of Art in the Age of Mechanical Reproduction," *Illuminations: Essays by Walter Benjamin*, trans. Harry Zohn, ed. Hannah Arendt (New York: Schocken Books, 1968), 226.

10. Benjamin, "A Little History," 520.

11. Dziga Vertov, *Man with a Movie Camera* (Ukraine: Film Studio VUFKU, 1929).

12. "Iconic photographs comprise a gallery that can help one understand liberal-democratic public culture." Robert Hariman and John Louis Lucaites, *No Caption*

Needed: Iconic Photographs, Public Culture and Liberal Democracy (Chicago: University of Chicago Press, 2007), 302.

13. Norman Chevers, *A Manual of Medical Jurisprudence for India*, 3rd ed. (Calcutta: Thacker, Spink and Co., 1870), 74.

14. W. H. Warner, "Photography and Murder," *Journal of the Bengal Photographic Society* 2, no. 5 (July 1863): 39.

15. Partha Chatterjee, "Are Indian Cities Becoming Bourgeois at Last?" In *Body.City: Siting Contemporary Culture in India*, ed. Indira Chandrasekhar and Peter Seel (New Delhi: Tulika Books, 2003), 169.

16. Roland Barthes, *Camera Lucida*, trans. Richard Howard (New York: Hill and Wang, 1982), 95–96.

17. My account of Hooper's activities is entirely indebted for its empirical substance to John Falconer, "Willoughby Wallace Hooper: 'A Craze about Photography,'" *The Photographic Collector* 4 (Winter 1983): 258–285.

18. Cited by Falconer, "Willoughby Wallace Hooper," 263.

19. Ibid., 265.

20. Benjamin "The Work of Art in the Age of Mechanical Reproduction," 236.

21. Cited in Stephen Wheeler, *History of the Delhi Coronation Durbar Held on the First of January 1903 to Celebrate the Coronation of His Majesty King Edward VII Emperor of India* (London: John Murray, 1904), 247.

22. Ariel Varges, "Ace Newsreeler Gives Light on How He Films News of the World," *American Cinematographer* 19, no. 7 (July 1938): 275–276. Varges worked for International News, a Hearst organization, and specialized in filming colonial wars and political struggle: he had previously made films in Macedonia and Mesopotamia and would subsequently film the Italian incursion in Abyssinia (1935) and the Spanish Civil War.

23. Folio 2, ms. Home Political 1922.949, National Archives of India. For a more extensive account of these events, see Christopher Pinney, *The Coming of Photography in India* (London: British Library, 2008), pp. 92–95.

24. Handwritten note dated September 18, 1922, in National Archives of India.

25. I draw here on Kittler's translators' words. Geoffrey Winthrop-Young and Michael Wutz, introduction to *Gramophone, Film, Typewriter*, by Friedrich A. Kittler (Stanford, CA: Stanford University Press, 1999), xxvi.

26. These being photo 125/2(46), *The Murderer of Lord Mayo*; photo 127/(96), *Sher Ali (assassin of Lord Mayo)*; photo 127/(99), *Assassin of Lord Mayo*. See Clare Anderson, *Legible Bodies: Race, Criminality and Colonialism in South Asia* (Oxford, UK: Berg, 2004), 161.

27. Barthes, *Camera Lucida*, 6.

28. Emphasis added. My strangely precise explanation for the transition from photographic cure to poison would, of course, hardly have met with Derrida's approval.

29. Jacques Derrida, *Dissemination*, trans. Barbara Johnson (Chicago: University of Chicago Press, 1981), 71–72.

30. Joseph Mullens, "On the Applications of Photography in India," *Journal of the Bengal Photographic Society* 2, no. 1 (January 1857): 34. Emphasis added.

31. Pierre Bourdieu, *Outline of a Theory of Practice*, trans. Richard Nice (Cambridge, UK: Cambridge University Press, 1977), 86.

32. Anon., "The Strange Case of the Resurrected Prince," *Life*, September 2, 1946, 84.

33. Partha Chatterjee, *A Princely Impostor? The Strange and Universal History of the Kumar of Bhawal* (Princeton, NJ: Princeton University Press, 2003).

34. See Carlo Ginzburg, "Morelli, Freud and Sherlock Holmes: Clues and the Scientific Method," *History Workshop* 9 (Spring 1980): 5–36. Following Ginzburg, I use *venatic*, alluding to hunting, as a synonym for the divinatory and symptomological.

35. Flood, personal communication, 2008.

36. Sachindra Das Gupta, ed., *The Bhowal Case (High Court Judgments)* (Calcutta: S. C. Sarkar, 1941), 412.

37. Ibid., 598.

38. The key adjudication, *Emp v. Sahdeo*, on the veracity of the fingerprint over the facial photograph is cited in Christopher Pinney, *Camera Indica: The Social Life of Indian Photographs* (London: Reaktion, 1997), 71.

39. The conclusions of the 1956 committee that he died in Taiwan and that his ashes are in the Renkoji Temple in Tokyo were overturned by the report of the Mukherjee Commission in 2005.

40. *Netaji Inquiry Committee Report* (New Delhi: Govt. of India, 1956), 1.

41. Ibid., 20.

42. Ibid., 21.

43. Foucault, cited in Tom Gunning, "In Your Face: Physiognomy, Photography, and the Gnostic Mission of Early Film," *Modernism/Modernity* 4, no. 1 (January 1997): 2.

44. Neil Cox, "Sacrifice," in *Undercover Surrealism: Georges Bataille and Documents*, exhibition catalog, ed. Dawn Ades and Simon Baker (Cambridge, MA: MIT Press, 2006), 112–113.

45. Ginzburg, "Morelli, Freud and Sherlock Holmes," 28–29.

46. Benjamin, "The Work of Art in the Age of Mechanical Reproduction," 233.

47. "[All] corruption is made naked…" (author's translation).

48. William Mazzarella, "Internet X-Ray: E-Governance, Transparency, and the Politics of Immediation in India," *Public Culture* 18, no. 3 (Fall 2006): 488.

49. "After the Fast," *Economist*, October 11, 2008: 81.

50. See Abhay Vaidya, "Voyeur Alert: How to Spook the Spooks," *Times of India*, January 13, 2005, http://timesofindia.indiatimes.com/articleshow/989003.cms (accessed December 1, 2008); Jug Suraiya and Vikas Singh, "The Death of Privacy," *Times of India*, January 15, 2005, http://timesofindia.indiatimes.com/articleshow /991395.cms (accessed December 1, 2008).

51. See Kazmi, who describes it as "delv[ing] into the current ogre of spycams and surveillance that leaves no room for individual privacy." Nikhat Kazmi, "Indian Art Film Stalwarts Make a Mark at IFFI," *Times of India*, November 30, 2007, http://timesofindia .indiatimes.com/articleshow/2583375.cms (accessed December 1, 2008).

52. On the kaliyug as cosmological trope, see Christopher Pinney, "Living in the *kal[i]yug:* Notes from Nagda, Madhya Pradesh," *Contributions to Indian Sociology* 33, no. 1–2 (February 1999): 77–106.

53. http://www.nowrunning.com/Movie/Reviews/MovieReview.aspx?movie=2565 (accessed June 30, 2012).

54. Shivangi Ambani, "Cinema's Future: Quickies and Shorties," http:// www.dnaindia.com/lifestyle/salon_cinema-s-future-quickies-and-shorties_9395 (accessed June 30, 2012).

7

Two Masks

*Images of Future History
and the Posthuman in Postapartheid
South Africa*

Rosalind C. Morris

The revolution effected by photography was, for Walter Benjamin, indissociable from the fact that, unlike the work of art that remained linked to its context of production, the photograph could travel.[1] Its capacity to traverse great distances was, in his eyes, the ironic condition of possibility for a new proximity between viewers and objects. And, insofar as proximity enables scrutiny (to the same extent that sacrality prohibits it), the mobility of the photograph could be said to enable (without guaranteeing) a critical possibility. Since the time of Benjamin's writing, a myriad of technological innovations have enhanced, extended, and intensified the flow of images by which the boundaries of social and geopolitical existence may be imaginatively traversed.

It is nonetheless imperative to resist reducing the question of what moves and what moves the viewer in the field of photography to an analysis of the circulation or vectoral trajectories of images.[2] Such issues are not irrelevant, of course. Any anthropology of the mass-mediatized world must continue to probe under what circumstances, by what means, and to what effect images themselves move or are moved. Yet, we cannot presume the selfsameness of the image in motion. In the original conceptual framework of the seminar for which this and the other chapters in this volume were written, "Images without Borders," there was an implicit presumption of an image's stability across space and various conceptual domains. And although we "moved beyond" the rhetorically fortuitous but epistemologically freighted echo of interventionist humanitarianism (the Médecins sans Frontières ghosting our own title), the phrase "images without borders" continued and continues to offer a starting point for questions that exceed those of circulation.

To speak of images *without* borders is, inevitably, to conjure, if only as a hallucinatory memory, the idea of images *with* borders. The borderless image emerges as the negative trace of a prior condition, one defined by its having been bordered. What can it mean, to speak of images with and without borders? Between what domains or elements does the border insert itself in or on the image? between the image and what context? Against what ground does it mark a limit? The truth in painting, as Derrida elaborates,[3] and the truth of the mediatic image, as Samuel Weber argues further,[4] are structured by an act of enframement. This act appears to impose an exterior element and to function as a supplement for an already existent object. In fact, the frame or *parergon*—the border of any image—constitutes it as such, apparently marking off that which is *in* the image from that which is *without*. In the process, it makes the image seem to be the re-presentation of that which is absent; this is the point around which or toward which a subject can orient him or herself. Yet, the frame does not simply divide the figure from its ground. Rather, it produces the effect of a border by being both within and without the picture or image: "The external never remains outside. What's at stake here is a decision about the frame, about what separates the internal from the external, with a border which is itself double in its trait, and joins together what it splits."[5] Samuel Weber remarks that, in photography or rather in the age of technological reproducibility, the frame falls away from the picture to become what he calls a *bright shadow*.[6] If that bright shadow reappears, momentarily but repeatedly in the history of photography, in the technology and the aesthetic of flash, photography's ideology nonetheless claims coterminousness with the world; it continues to repress the frame and the act of enframement. Indeed, this repression of a constitutive enframement in every photograph is achieved in the very moment of that supplementary gesture that adds a border to the image in the form of a white perimeter.

However, Derrida reminds us that the principle of enframement is not merely a property of visual representation. Rather, it defines all efforts at conceptualization, including those associated with humanist aesthetic philosophy. Yet, if the philosophy of the aesthetic has rested on the constitutive effacement of the process of enframement—achieved partly through a displacement of that process into the figure of the border—it is also possible to identify those historical circumstances in which a deconstruction and reconceptualization of the border tend to occur. This is because the process of enframement becomes visible when the structures through which previous focalizations have been organized begin to lose their force. Focalization is more than a way of seeing or a point of view; it is, as I shall discuss below, an ideologically inflected perspective that permits one or another object not only to appear but also to cohere as the object of attention.[7]

The historical questions that emanate from this claim can be posed as follows: When does the work of enframement become visible as a problematic? When are the (or at least some) conceptual categories and hence the distinctions operative in a given milieu made so unstable as to emerge on the horizon of that which can be problematized? When is the object status of the object of vision made questionable? And which objects lose their stability, when, for whom? In this chapter I answer such questions as they assume their force in South Africa, by examining some works of visual and literary art in the period of transition to democracy. I suggest that one can discern an interrogation of the borders of identity as conceived from within the terms of a still culturally, if no longer politically, dominant white imaginary. This interrogation, inscribed on both sides of a cusp of historical transformation, mobilized an old humanist trope—one that counterposes the human and the animal—and simultaneously suggested that the cultural and political transformations attending the end of apartheid would have to entail a radical reproblematization of both humanism and the conceptualization of human/animal relations that undergirds it. The fact of this redrawing manifests itself in figures that confuse or redemarcate the border that previously separated animality and humanity, as the metaphoricity for the social and for the racialized social hierarchy that defined the apartheid era. I am not suggesting that the outcome of this process has been an entirely new figuration of humanity or animality. Rather, I am suggesting that political transition in South Africa was, and perhaps still is, often thought of and addressed in the imaginal idiom of the human/animal relation. I also suggest that this imaginal idiom offers itself as something of a displacement of, if not a solution to, the thinking of racial relation after apartheid. And I claim that, to the extent that it succeeds, new work emanating from a (partially displaced) white cultural elite dramatizes the problem of historical change as one of refocalization. As such, it both reveals the centrality of aesthetico-epistemological transformation to the project of political reform and makes visible the difficulty with and residual resistance to such transformation.

THROUGH A LENS DARKLY: FROM PREHUMANITY TO POSTHUMANITY

Whatever criterion humanism uses to mark the boundary—language or symbolic practice, reason, labor, or a capacity for suffering—it presumes the opposition between a categorically singular humanity and a comparably categorically singular animality. Modernist humanism emphasizes less the capacity for reason or language than that for dissimulation internal to language. It defines the human as the one who "can cheat."[8] And it construes the animal as that sentient being that cannot dissimulate or that, if it can engage in a ruse (as, for example, does the fox), can nevertheless not "cover its tracks" or "pretend to pretend."[9] It is this latter strand within humanism that has emerged so palpably in recent South African discourse about political transformation. The reason for this, I believe, is that the tradition on which both apartheid and its successor rest also presumes, as Arendt so succinctly argued, that the political sphere is where people (historically, white men) appear to each other for the purposes of producing collective action.[10] Accordingly, the racially marked and excluded subject of apartheid was visible (as nonwhite) but denied the capacity to appear in public *as a political subject.*

This is the context within which anxiety about political transformation expresses itself as a concern with dissimulation—in discourses about everything from transparency to corruption. It is also the context in which political change seems to demand a complete rethinking of the animal, the human, and the public. In recent white South African visual art, that concern is not infrequently imagined and figured as a matter of masking, and more specifically as animal masking. In the white literature of this period, it emerges as a reflexive discourse about animality, bestiality, and hybridity.[11] It is not merely incidental that this critique of humanism emerges in South Africa in the very moment that minoritized (though majority) groups acquire the capacity, legally and politically, to claim human rights. Indeed, recent aesthetic production in South Africa forces a consideration of the fact that the interrogation of the human is the troubling and perhaps ironic corollary of the universalization of human rights discourse. One might read it as a symptom of the consciousness attributed to one South African writer, Breyten Breytenbach, by another, J. M. Coetzee: a consciousness that South Africa "has...slid straight from prehumanity to posthumanity."[12] In this chapter I explore this violent convergence, its political implications, and the forms in which it becomes visible. To do so, I examine some works in which the thematization of a failure to sustain the boundary or, in a more positive light, in which the effort to dislodge a categorical boundary between the human and the animal occurs through the specific trope of masking. The image-texts with which I begin come from the oeuvres of Jodi Bieber and Jane Alexander and of the South African writer J. M. Coetzee. They are, however, by no means exceptional in this field. Accordingly, I also invoke the works of other contemporary artists (both visual and literary), drawing on ethnographic materials that have been generated over the last decade and a half, during which time I have been engaged in research in and on life in the gold mining economy of South Africa. I do not intend to read these as representative of a racialized community of artists; such a community does not exist. I nonetheless want to emphasize that their works shall be treated for what they can disclose of a racial unconscious in the moment of its (frequently avowed) displacement from dominance—not because they manifest that unconscious but because of the critical distance they endeavor to take from it. There is, of course, a certain risk in seeking that unconscious in and through figural association. However, while refusing to relegate form to the status of epiphenomenon, I believe that figures can be treated much like Freud treats dream images, as the site of a complex mechanism involving both condensation and displacement, available for reading and revelatory of the historical events in which individuals are singularly caught up.

So, then, let us begin with two images: Jodi Bieber's *Cotlands Baby Sanctuary for HIV/AIDS children, Johannesburg, South Africa* (figure 7.1) and Jane Alexander's *Bom Boy with Workers and Traffic* (figure 7.2). Both of these images were produced by artists self-consciously engaged with the project of reimagining and reimaging South Africa in the aftermath of apartheid. Both seem to make reference to the phenomenon of "gang culture" and the abandonment of children to the street at a time when "human rights" are ostensibly being extended to all persons, whereas previously these rights were unevenly distributed on a racial basis. Jodi Bieber's image appears in a series that she produced while documenting poor white and "colored" life in Johannesburg, especially in Vredepark, Braamfontein, and Westbury. Jane Alexander's image is also one of a series (a series that encompasses several media). It takes its name from graffiti in Cape Town, specifically Long Street, although the referent is less the organized world of gangs than the amorphous universe of displaced and homeless children who inhabit the streets and survive by hustling, more than by violent crime.[13]

There are, of course, formal and thematic similarities that bind these images, beyond their ostensible referent in the pained underworld of South Africa's dispossessed and despite the fact that Bieber's image is a simple photograph and Alexander's is photomontage. In both, a child appears

Figure 7.1
Jodi Bieber, Cotlands Baby Sanctuary for HIV/AIDS children, Johannesburg, South Africa, *from Between Dogs and Wolves, #26 (2004). Courtesy of the artist.*

Figure 7.2
Jane Alexander, Bom Boy with workers and traffic *(1999). Photomontage, pigment on cotton paper, 25 x 35 cm. Art © Jane Alexander/DALRO, Johannesburg/VAGA, New York.*

wearing the mask of a small animal, solitary in a space that bears all the traces of constant movement while nonetheless providing mere backdrop for the child's otherwise alienated presence. There is no apparent source of light in either image (though street lamps appear in Alexander's); there is no sense of the sudden illumination that comes with flash, and, hence, neither conveys the sense of a secret world discovered. Instead, the figures in these images are situated in a plane whose most remarkable characteristic may be the desolation of gray that envelops them. Their near shadowlessness suggests a world that is simultaneously exposed and unilluminated, a world unredeemed by "Enlightenment."[14]

There are also differences. Bieber's child runs, barefooted, in an institutional setting where the open doors seem to signify abandonment more than possibility. But the child is central; his figure organizes the image and solicits our gaze—without at the same time offering us the satisfaction of knowing that our eyes fix him in place. There is, in fact, no sense of the pose, no visible trace of a child's anticipation of being seen—of giving himself to be seen, as Lacan would say. He does not appear to submit to an order in which the Gaze is the locus and form of symbolic power. In contrast, Alexander's child (but is this really a child or some form of eternally immature creature?) occupies the place of the figure in most romantic landscapes, the one that mediates our access to the scene. However, in this case the figure is turned away from the scene. If, when compared with the buoyant mobility of Bieber's child, Alexander's figure appears to be emphatically static and even posed (it is a mannequin, after all, the very form of appearance of the pose), it is nonetheless not turned toward the gaze of the one who views the picture. We might say that the figure of *Bom Boy* orients us without being oriented to us, even when caught in the line of our sight.

Both of these images are suffused with ambiguity, and both of them frustrate any desire on the part of the viewer for power in seeing. This is not merely because there is no reciprocity of gazes; voyeuristic pleasure is easily obtainable, perhaps even intensified when we look upon images of those who are unaware of their status as objects of a gaze. (The stolen glimpse afforded by the snapshot acquires its value here.) Rather, it is because the object of the gaze is, itself, so unstable. We are not sure what we are looking at. And we are unsure of what sees us, or rather, we are unsure of what would see us if the figure turned or if we crossed its path on the side of a road. In Alexander's composition, the road is barely visible; moreover, it does not unify in a directional path any of the movements—that of the helicopter, of the pedestrians on the overpass, or of the automobiles. In the hallway of Bieber's image, the child rushes toward us as though to pass right by. The images leave us with a question: is it the mask or that which is behind it that might see us?

In a way, the mask makes focalization impossible. Typically, focalization inserts us into a point of view such that one or another element comes into focus.[15] However, the mask produces a constant vacillation, interrupts the desire for a single image and with it a single perspective. It materializes, or makes manifest, the dubiousness of the border between face and mask, between what is behind and what covers over that which is behind. The other, in whose field of vision, as Sartre would say,[16] the viewer herself is apprehended as viewing subject-as-object, does not materialize here. There is no cohering horizon made possible by a reciprocation of gazes. These creatures bear the organs of sight but give us no sign that we would be apprehended as bearers of vision, as others in the specular relay. In this way the images stage a truly radical alterity—an otherness with which one cannot fantasize a mirroring relation.[17] At the same time, they make the problem of focalization visible. They thus suggest the possibility that older frameworks for positing and grasping the world are insufficient. It is not merely that one needs a new "perspective," they imply. One needs an entirely new focalization. This refocalization would have as its corollary questions such as, What is childhood in a world where domesticity is also public, where neither the state nor the family function fully as sites of subjectification, where epidemic interrupts the possibilities for generational transmission, or where gangsterism makes the performance of violence on others a mode of initiation, displacing a structure that entailed the violent inscription of law on the body of the initiate? Can humanity (if the category is to be retained) still be thought of in the idiom of animality transformed by labor (as it was for Arendt) or as a taming by law? Or is it better understood as the learning of masquerade? The aesthetic work described here enables such questions, by staging refocalization as one (perhaps the most important) task of political change.

ABNORMALITY AS/AND ANIMALITY: BETWEEN DOGS AND WOLVES?

For South Africans of Bieber's generation and those who came of age before the end of apartheid, perhaps especially those of the working classes in English-speaking white and colored communities, the masked child often evokes the echo of Guy Fawkes Day, that occasion on which people abandon themselves to the carnivalesque pleasure of masquerade. It is this potentially eruptive, potentially destructive, but nonetheless joyous force

of play that Bieber's image conjures. Such play and its ambivalent significations are relatively absent in Alexander's image, whose force derives at least
partly from the uncanny sensation that the one who wears the mask is actually lifeless. The strange quality of this lifelessness might be captured by
the term "inanimacy"—but only because, through an etymological ruse, it
allows us to recognize that the principle of vitality, whether or not human,
must inevitably evoke animality. This is the basis of those philosophies,
most especially that of Heidegger, that identify humanity with a transcendence of mere vitality, and a being toward death.

Bieber is a photojournalist trained initially at the *Star* newspaper, with
long experience as a documentarist of social marginality. This image comes
from a series entitled *Between Dogs and Wolves.*[18] Shot over nearly a decade
beginning in 1995 and published in book form, the series title invokes a
recurrent tropology in that South African discourse that is derivative of
European humanism: the tropology of animality stretched between the
domestic and the wild, in which social abandonment produces the feral
and the feral connotes a potentiality that continually lurks within the
domestic. Here the canine provides a dominant concept-metaphor. The
dog, the most faithful and passive of domestic animals, is counterposed
in Bieber's schema to the wolf, the figure of a rapacity that is simultaneously social and merciless. Bieber is conscious of the stakes in rendering
the postapartheid predicament, especially for those who cannot assume
that democracy means the redistribution of economic resources, in terms
of this canine metaphoricity. She writes, somewhat defensively, "This work
isn't an attempt to show where South Africa is heading, nor does it pretend
to show the full picture of the country. It is a partial view." But, in an effort
to explain her own imagery, she adds, "The legacy of South Africa's past
and poverty created an abnormality in our society."[19]

This abnormality is rarely figured as animality, of course. Animals are
rare in her work, appearing mainly on the periphery of otherwise vacant
landscapes. When they do appear, they seem to convey a banal, rural
domesticity. Thus, for example, a black chicken scratches away in the sand
next to a naked foundation where someone is sleeping, unsheltered, in the
absence of walls or a roof, in the absence of a home whose betrayed promise is the cement slab that now provides only a bed (figure 7.3). It is not an
entirely uncommon sight in South Africa.

Strangely, however, that very figure of betrayed rural domesticity
began to circulate in a monstrous form at the time of Bieber's documentary work, which was also the time of my fieldwork in a community not
far from Johannesburg (in 1999)—an area reputed among social workers,

FIGURE 7.3

Jodi Bieber, Reconstruction and Development—Riemvasmaak, Northern Cape *(1998).*
Courtesy of the artist.

psychologists, and even church workers to have an inordinately high rate of
sexual violence, incest, and other domestic dysfunction. This monstrosity
appeared in (ludicrously improbable) rumors about a white member of the
community who had been reduced to such craven inhumanity as to have
sexually violated a chicken. The story of the chicken both wanted to incite
prurient curiosity and condemned as ridiculous the effort to verify and vali-
date more general claims about the ubiquity of sexual violence in households and more anonymous public spaces—though statistics generated at
both local and national levels provide ample reason for believing that it
is exceedingly widespread, that it takes place mainly within the domestic
sphere, and that it rarely takes the form of anonymous crossracial violence.[20]
I later concluded that the story could best be understood as something like a
decoy, but also a symptom. If a decoy is often enough an inanimate animal,
intended to both lure and distract the attention of animal-as-prey, the symptom is an expression of contradiction. The symptom demands reading, and
reading demands an effort to know what is being condensed and displaced
in the symptom. My conversations in this community were, it always seemed,
inordinately burdened by the compulsion of so many to speak about both
sexual violence and the maltreatment of animals.

Why did talk about these two issues so constantly converge? The link between discourses about animal and minority human rights is not new, of course. Hannah Arendt remarks that in revolutionary Europe, societies for the protection of the Rights of Man were often deemed ridiculous because of their association with and resemblance to societies for the prevention of cruelty to animals.[21] But increasingly, in South Africa (as elsewhere), the extension of human rights is linked to notions of animal rights. The working out of this relationship takes place in the space between efforts to reaffirm a Western humanist legacy by recognizing a failure to actualize its original promise,[22] on the one hand, and a turning to indigenous traditions for alternative concept-metaphors and models of thinking relations between humans and animals, on the other. Of the latter, the archive of /Xam myth, most famously translated and compiled by Lucy Lloyd and Wilhelm Bleek in *Specimens of Bushman Folklore*, has become an especially salient resource. The collection, on which Elias Canetti relied so heavily for his Nobel Prize–winning book, *Crowds and Power*, testifies to a cosmology in which not only the categorical opposition between humanity and animality is absent but also in which the very abstraction, animal, is absent. I have written elsewhere about the forms of mythic thought traced in that book; here I can merely index its significance as the repository of another way of thinking about the phenomenon of "becoming other."[23]

TEXTS AND INTERTEXTS: THE FORKED ANIMAL AND A MAN'S BEST FRIEND

To grasp what is at stake in Bieber's and Alexander's work, it is necessary to move laterally and to consider the discursive context in which their work circulated. Against the backdrop of this renewed interrogation of humanism's axioms, J. M. Coetzee published his experimental work *The Lives of Animals*, commencing an argument that would be pursued in the more formally conventional novel *Elizabeth Costello*, in which the treatment of animals is read as a litmus test of humanism's success or failure.[24] The work of visual artists such as Bieber and Alexander can be fruitfully read in terms of their intertextual relations to the works of writers, Coetzee among them—and, at the same time, writers like Coetzee can be read in terms of the intertextual relations that suture their fiction into a field where Bieber and Alexander do their work. In the complex, mediated conversation between them and in their efforts to exceed the normative discourses that they variously inhabit, the singular achievements of their works can be grasped. A consideration of these intertextualities also makes visible the relationship between the different concept-metaphors of hybridity and of miscegenation and the task of appropriating this sliding chain of signifiers for a politics of transformation rather than a mere diagnostics of racism's failures.

Elizabeth Costello, Coetzee's protagonist in the novel of that name, is pitted against a defender of reason named to signify the Scottish Enlightenment, Thomas O'Hearne, and argues that the industrialization of animal slaughter is testimony to the moral failure of Enlightenment "reason." Her opponent, Mr. O'Hearne, claims that animals do not anticipate their death and hence do not suffer. Accordingly, their treatment ought not to worry humans. In a not incidental moment, given the improbable figure mentioned above of the chicken—as the animal that, so commonly killed, can nonetheless suffer—Elizabeth Costello repudiates her opponent's chilly logic by invoking Albert Camus's childhood trauma at the sight of a chicken's slaughter. She even attributes his adult opposition to the guillotine to this primal scene. Camus, in Elizabeth's analysis, saw immediately the relationship between the cool calculation of his mother's animal slaughter and that of revolutionary faith in humane killing. Animals suffer, she says, echoing Bentham, who, Derrida reminds us, made suffering rather than reason the sine qua non of humanity.[25] Their incapacity to communicate this cannot be read as evidence of their immunity to fear, anxiety, or grief. Their apparent failure to communicate such sentiments is, rather, merely a sign of the impossibility of accessing the interiority of the animal, as most radical other.

Yet, if The Lives of Animals and Elizabeth Costello disclose Coetzee's effort to rethink the question of human rights in light of a vegetarian antimodernism, it is Disgrace that stages the problem of South Africa's future history in terms of the conflict between, on the one hand, the fetish of racial difference that informed apartheid and, on the other, the changing status of animality as the mediator of that difference.[26] In this novel, at least some of the white characters of the fiction (the author's position remains ambivalent) believe that the future of the nation will be haunted by the fact that its history was one in which the black majority was dehumanized by the white minority and subjected to the kind of violence normally reserved for beasts of burden. Some of them even seem to believe, further, that the dehumanized majority may have been reduced to an animality from which neither they nor the country will recover.

At the center of the novel is a scene in which the novel's white protagonist, David Lury, and his daughter, Lucy, are being assaulted by two men and a boy. These men have come, they say, from Erasmuskraal and need to use the telephone. This need turns out to be a ruse, and the men quickly begin the work of both beating and setting alight the aging Lury and raping Lucy. Between the initial striking of David and the subsequent raping of Lucy, the men also shoot the dogs, which are kept by Lucy and her friend in a kennel where they are neutered or occasionally euthanized.[27]

This scene functions as the fulcrum of the novel, the turning point in a relationship that will soon materialize in a discourse on the relationship between the domestic and political worlds. In fact, the moment immediately preceding the assault is filled with an ironically nostalgic conversation about a neighbor in Kenilworth, where David had raised Lucy. Indeed, the transformation in Lury's character precipitated by the assault is marked by a corollary progression in the conceptualization of human/animal relations, and one way to read the novel is to attend to the ways in which forms of social difference are focalized and mediated by animality. One can begin to track the consequences of the changes that result from the reordering and refiguring of these differences by recalling that the men shoot the dogs. One might rephrase this moment of the narrative as follows: the animals had stood between the men and their desire, if only because the animals called attention to it. So they had to be killed. But, of course, the idea of the dog is precisely what had kept the men separate, these people understood as metonyms of racial groups. The men had been treated like dogs. Like the condemned man of Kafka's "In the Penal Colony," who is sentenced to die because he has bitten his master's leg, the oppressed figures here suffer the effect of a performativity inhering in power's speech. In Kafka's tale, not only does the condemned man act like the dog he has been called by his colonial overseer, but also Kafka uses the verb *fessen* to describe his desperate last repast, "fessen" being the word for the ways that animals eat, rather than *essen*, which is used for humans.[28] Afrikaans shares this differentiation, *vreet* being the verb for animal eating, rather than *eet* for human consumption. Although Coetzee writes in English, his texts are saturated by a play upon the differences that become visible only in and through these other languages.

In this world of violent naming, Petrus, the peasant protector of the assailants and future landlord to Lucy, sardonically refers to himself as the "dog-man," a designation that Lury will later assume as the mark of his metamorphosis.[29] And it is the truth effect of this history that the men force the white man and woman not only to recognize but also to inhabit. This is why David Lury can finally and guiltily identify with his assailants in a nightmare of the mirror stage in which his masculinity becomes the basis of crossracial (mis)recognition.[30] (The men, we later learn, had taunted Lucy: "*Go on, call your dogs! No dogs? Then we'll show you dogs!*"[31]) So Coetzee's black men, as seen from within the focalization of the white David Lury, appear to claim to have become what racism made them. In this way Coetzee gives voice to a defensive white minority in the moment it must relinquish its hold on power.

This is what Bieber had called the "abnormality" of apartheid South Africa, an abnormality for which the metaphoric opposition of dogs and wolves seems to her most apt. Interestingly, when Coetzee reviewed the work of Irène Némirovsky for the *New York Review of Books,* he chose the title of one of her novels, *The Dogs and the Wolves,* to describe an overall predicament, one in which assimilationism (dogs) is counterposed to racialized difference (wolves) even as it permits the misrecognition of French barbarism in the form of anti-Semitism.[32] The domestic animal becomes here a figure for the violence internal to the normative order, a violence sustained by the hallucinated outside of something more profoundly wild.

It is here that the question of dissimulation returns, now in the troubling relation between domesticity and wildness figured not only through the canine concept-metaphor but also through its conjunction with the idea of childhood. There is an uncanny resonance between Bieber's and Alexander's strangely masked and immature figures and the most troubling of the three rapists in Coetzee's novel. The "boy" of the trio, who hisses at the dogs and is then terrified by them, is described by the ambiguously focalized narrator as having a "flat, expressionless face and piggish eyes."[33] If the description suggests a mask, it is because the presumptive figure behind appearances here ought to have been innocent yet his expressionlessness, which is the first attribute of the assailants remarked in the text, merely anticipates the later description of the attacking older man, whom Lury depicts as having a face that is "placid, without a trace of anger."[34] The terrifying force of this instability between the appearance and the desired-for interiority of the assailants, an interiority never imagined by the white characters prior to the moment of assault, is made visible, I argue, in the moment that one reads the intertextual relation.

As Coetzee's novel was making headlines in international literary journals, the South African press was taken up by a disturbing videotape showing six white members of the South African Police Department's North East Rand dog unit setting their dogs on three migrant men. The dogs were unrestrained and attacked the men, all from Mozambique, with what would later be described as great savagery. When exposed, not only were the policemen subject to trial, but also the dogs themselves and the entire South African dog-training practice came under international scrutiny. It was suggested that the system, which included confining dogs to cages for long periods of time and denying them affection or even contact with other animals, produced not only "savagery" but also "racism" in the animals. A Swiss dog trainer advised that 90 percent of the dogs be euthanized. He added that the training method had been based not only on white racism but also on white fear of dogs,[35] thus attributing to the process a complex structure of projection and repressed identification. Willie Bester produced what is undoubtedly the best-known artistic response to this awful episode in an enormous metal sculpture composed of found metallic objects, including guns, welded together in the image of police and dogs. *Who Let the Dogs Out?* (2001) appeared at the Grahamstown national arts festival. Although criticized for its heavy-handed literalism, Bester's piece can perhaps be best understood as a visualization of the literal and literalist force of racism's canine metaphors (plate 19). To speak of literalism in this context is to speak of the performativity of the metaphor—of its exceeding the language/action opposition. In this sense we can say that the literalized metaphor is both that which intervenes in the world and that which conserves its normativized form. For the performative, in linguistic terms, achieves its effect only in repetition and only by virtue of an authority that comes from the past.

BETWEEN METAPHOR AND METAMORPHOSIS, OR THE MASK VERSUS HYBRIDITY

The dramaturgy that stages the ensorcelling power of racism's metaphors has been elaborated by a number of South African artists, many of whom have, over the years, attempted to give specific historical form to the persisting tropes of both Western humanism and indigenous South African cosmologies. Toward the end of apartheid, the working through of images about the unstable border between animality and humanity began to appear in a proliferating series of works by artists such as Jane Alexander, David Koloane, and Norman Catherine.

David Koloane's *The Moon and Dog* (1996) presents a ferocious dog standing guard at the perimeter of a nocturnal urban world in which the moon illuminates a landscape that appears bloodied (blue becomes crimson along the vertical axis) and strewn with refuse (plate 20). The dog bares its teeth to the viewer, who is both barred from the city that the animal guards and situated as a viewing subject by this very violent distancing. Very different are the distorted figures of Norman Catherine's imagination (plates 21a and 21b): a many-legged insect is topped by a man's head; a man's arm becomes serpentine; a dog-headed man addresses a human head, severed and propped on an improbably delicate table in a room that is reminiscent of interrogation chambers, with a single light bulb hanging like an albatross. These images are marked by the literal and emphatically delimited divisions within the body of the figure. They suggest a splitting as much as a metamorphosis, though one can discern in them a recognition that the oppositions that previously structured the world are undergoing change. One of the images, in fact, bears the title *Abracadabra*, indicating the transformative effect of a new power.

These works have been elevated to the status of the canonical in recent art history of South Africa. But metamorphosis or, perhaps, more properly speaking, mutancy is most complexly realized in the works of Jane Alexander. *Butcher Boys* (plate 22), her terrifyingly naturalist monsters, though produced at the height of a state of emergency when the prospect of transition seemed remote if not impossible, can be read metonymically as having announced the emergence of a new sensibility while also revealing the violence of a history that the end of apartheid would not fully terminate. The enormity and complexity of that transition may be grasped by considering the unintended (by the artist) readings of the work that have proliferated since the end of apartheid in relation to those that accompanied its making a decade earlier. I offer this reading because it was from within the focalization provided by critics in the postapartheid era that I first encountered *Butcher Boys*, whose inscription as signs of racialized dehumanization served a certain triumphalist narrative and what may well be its ironic structure of racism by reversal. For Alexander, the butcher boys incarnated that extreme violence perpetrated by the apartheid state and its representatives against ordinary men and women, mainly but not always black. The slaughterers, the butcher boys, about whom she heard rumors and whom she saw performing acts of brutality, would later be exposed in the Truth and Reconciliation Commission. When I saw the sculpture a decade after it was unveiled in 1986, I was informed by a well-intentioned museum guide that *Butcher Boys* takes its name from the misnamed men whose job had been to carry slabs of meat on their backs to and from markets and between butchers and the homes of buyers. These men, I was told, were familiar figures in South Africa during the 1950s and 1960s, and in Alexander's sculpture they appear (for the curator) to take the form of the metaphorics within which they had been treated: as men whose bodies have melded with their objects, who have been treated as beasts of burden. Such a reading can be sustained when one looks upon their white-painted bodies, which are open at the back, split as though by a knife. The spines show through these figures, exposing an apparently awful resemblance that the job, one might assume, produces between the men and the meat. I myself remarked that their mouths, like their sexes, are covered over by folds of flesh that have been roughly sutured into place. For Alexander, however, the triangular folds resemble the guards that cricket players wear to protect their genitals.[36]

It is the case, of course, that a work of art signifies in ways its maker can never determine. Art is of the order of trace rather than sign. And there is nothing in the work that prohibits its being read in a manner that associates the white figures with a kind of masking, but as Alexander points out, the drive to read the men as black (albeit painted) cannot entirely be separated from a conception of blackness as violent, whether as a result of historical forces or by natural inclination. For the overwhelming impression exuded by the men of *Butcher Boys* is of violence. It is in the juxtaposition between this signification of butchery and the aura of nonchalance conveyed in the postures of ordinary, almost leisured comfort that the work conveys the violent force that was hiding in civility under apartheid. If, in the aftermath of apartheid, the men in *Butcher Boys* can be read as black, as indeed they have been, and if the crowning of heads by horns can be read as a sign of animality rather than monstrosity, as it has been, this is surely evidence of the failure to refocalize in the sense I have been describing. Indeed, these readings, which are by no means universal, are testimony to a complex history of foreclosure. That foreclosure entails the energetic rejection of both an idea and an affect, both of which would be associated in the transition out of apartheid with the need to become other. We can read the archive of such interpretations of Alexander's work as an archive of transformation's forestalling.[37] And the blockages produced by foreclosure (which, not incidentally, are associated in Lacan's writings with the figure of the hybrid "Wolf-man") may be seen to be traced in her subsequent work.

After the enormous success of *Butcher Boys*, Alexander went on to produce a series of works exploring, among other things, the dehumanizing effects of labor and the often unremarked elements of quotidian life that exceed the reduction of life to labor. Many of these depict black figures in postures of quiet leisure (for example, watching television), but in *Integration Programme*, which first appeared in 1996 at the Fault Lines exhibition, a strange creature of indeterminate age but apparent masculinity sits, ashen in color, next to a hooded black man dressed in the infantilizing uniform of the domestic laborer (which, with its short pants, resembles the school clothes of children). The seated figure seems almost human, though its head is that of a baboon (plates 23a and 23b), and around its neck is a collar with the motto of the Afrikaner Resistance Movement written on it: "*Blaas hoog die vlam vir God, volk en vaderland*" (Raise high the flame for God, people and fatherland). The obviousness of the referent in racist discourse, which likens black men to baboons, is somehow transcended in the sculpture, which mobilizes the naturalism of photography but then draws on the condensational power of the oneiric to pose the figure as a question as much as a description. The improbable tenderness with which the mutant seated figure is treated indexes a transformation that had occurred in Alexander's work in the decade between 1986 and 1996. If, in the years before apartheid's end, she was concerned to make manifest the violence that sustained racial difference but that had been masked with metaphor—by literalizing and visualizing its force—in the years since 1994 the significations of her figures have become more ambiguous.

Alexander's figures have been aptly described by Ivor Powell as zoo-morph manqués,[38] and he rightly attends to the strange combination of innocence and uselessness that characterizes them. Some are child-like, often tiny and vulnerable figures; many are crippled, wounded, or deformed. They still wear the attire of schoolboys and workers, the ubiquitous red rubber gloves of industrial labor in South Africa appearing sometimes as clothing, sometimes as flooring. Now, however, there are also more macabre figures that evoke the apocalyptic nightmares of Hieronymus Bosch or mutations induced by chemical or atomic warfare. Thus, the birds are wingless, unable to fly, their sharp beaks seeming as much like the masks of medieval physicians (which mimicked birds) as natural features of avian anatomy (plate 24).

These figures recur in various tableaux, themselves site-specific. All of the figures in Alexander's uncanny bestiary have names, though these are allegorical. Among the most enigmatic of these is a figure she calls "the harbinger" (plate 25), a creature with a largely human body and a head that appears reminiscent of an antelope (but with misshapen gemsbok horns). This character wears different clothes depending on its installation. In the incarnation that was installed in a courtroom in Singapore, it wore the green uniform of the Pollsmoor prison in South Africa (the installation intending to comment on the status of capital punishment). What makes it so remarkable is its wearing of a mask, one that is, ironically, suggestive of the same animal that we infer lies beneath: a buck of some sort. This mask, affixed with rubber tubing that could easily be a bridle or a device of torture, appears even on the harbinger who goes unclothed. And when the creature is wearing the Pollsmoor prison uniform, it also wears a small photograph of a human being, a woman, which is pinned to its shirt in the manner of a locket. If there is a resonance between these images of absences (the mask and the photograph), the works remain intransigently enigmatic even at the level of their temporality. Are they memorial or anticipatory? Do they portend transformations yet to come or those that have occurred, partially or completely?

Powell captures something of the force (if not the intention) of these figures when he writes of the preverbal that infuses Alexander's new works, but it seems to me that it is less their preverbal quality than their capacity to do what dreams do because of language—displace and condense—that they seem so appropriate to a moment that so many felt was impossible to comprehend but which they nonetheless believed would be haunted by the violence of the past. The Bom boys come from this moment and sometimes appear within the tableaux accompanied by the harbinger. But the harbinger, which often towers above them, is more than an enigmatic presence, doubled and split by a mask that resembles the beast that wears it. Alexander names her figures carefully, and in this title we have the idea of both one who provides hospitality or lodging (a place, even a domestic interior, in which to abide) and one who forewarns. Of what does the harbinger forewarn its visitors? One cannot say for sure. The mask recalls a past in which the creature was a trophy, a detachable fetish of the hunter. The mutant body is nonetheless unequivocal in its manifestation of polyspecies hybridity, whether the result of a past catastrophe or the sign of a future disaster. However, the tiny photograph affixed to the T-shirt suggests something else: a capacity for care, for remembrance, for mourning, and hence for grasping the nature of absence—that capacity whose very absence Coetzee's O'Hearne had made the basis of refusal to attribute rights to the animal. Hybridity is perhaps the dominant signification here, and it is here that Alexander's work converges with Coetzee's and indeed with all those texts organized by the question of what it means to desire differently, against purity. For this is the deeper task of political transformation: to desire differently.

Why, then, animals? What is it that makes the concept-metaphor of the animal move, and what makes it so moving for visual and literary artists alike? How does this concept-metaphor, which is also an image, enable the refocalization that is so necessary to social and political reform? In its displacement of an older architectural metaphorics of class relation and ideological structures (from ground to base and superstructure) and in a context where the state is neither capable nor perhaps desirous of assuming the function of subjectification (through universal education, for example), the animal permits a thinking of race and sociality beyond class. This too is a displacement, though it permits the departure from more functionalist conceptions of the political that once dominated South African political discourse (heavily dominated, in the 1970s and 1980s, by Althusserianism).

MUTANCY AND MISCEGENATION

Coetzee's novel *Disgrace* ends with a submission to a miscegenation, one produced by a violence born precisely of the disavowal of miscegenation. Lucy, the focalizer's (David Lury's) daughter, chooses to bear the child that is a product of her rape. Her decision mystifies her father and has earned Coetzee the perplexity of critics.[39] Coetzee's white male characters enunciate the belief that, having held people apart by rendering them in abstract and impossibly pure racial categories, having instituted that separation through sexualized colonial violence, and having subjected such violence to the additional violence of rationalization and regularization in law, the possibility of crossracial relations born of mutual recognition was rendered impossible by and for whites. And so the miscegenation that could have been utopian, that could have been the willed and amorous transgression of a prohibition on intimacy, appears (in the moment of transition) contained by vengeance and enacted in the very forms that apartheid used to sustain its system of difference. The escape for Coetzee's white male character is to turn toward the animal in order to learn to care for the radical Other. Let us note that the move bypasses a gesture in which mirroring in difference might have permitted love across the racial divide (what South Africans once called the "color bar"). The absolutism of the alterity to which David Lury turns and in the face of which he learns to care (without demanding recognition) appears, in the eyes of many, to mark an ethical gesture of enormous transformative promise. As Lury gradually relinquishes his sense that human beings are created differently than animals to become the chaperone of their deaths, he calls himself "the Dog-Man." When Lucy agrees to accept a new status as his tenant and a member of an extended family that includes both her assailants and their protector, Petrus, she explains it to her father thus:

> "Perhaps that is what I must learn to accept. To start at ground level. With nothing. Not with nothing but. With nothing. No cards, no weapons, no rights, no dignity."
>
> "Like a dog."
>
> "Yes, like a dog."[40]

These are the moments of what Paul Patton terms "becoming animal," and they exhibit for him a "conception of pure life as immanent in the everyday existence of humans and animals alike."[41]

However, this liberatory conception of becoming-animal is available to whites only because it has not been their presumptive status until now.

It is as a relinquishing of dominance and of exclusive claim on the capacity to signify the human in general, that becoming-animal can be a gesture of self-liberation analogous to what Deleuze and Guattari describe as "becoming-minor." Just as silence cannot function as a gesture of refusal for the subaltern, whose illegibility and inaudibility are the presumptive corollaries of her exile from power, so becoming-animal has no capacity to signify the relinquishment of privilege for those who have been relegated to the nonhuman. This does not mean that there are no explorations of becoming-animal in works by black and colored South African artists. They are present in such diverse contexts as /Xam myth about shapeshifting creatures in the first-sitting-there-time and the fantastic skin sculptures of Nandipha Mntambo (plates 26a, b, c, and d).

Nonetheless, these works posit an alternative ontology rather than a technique for escaping humanism's hierarchy. It is not as a relinquishment of dominance that Mntambo summons the hide as mask, in cast figures that evoke both human absence and dense physicality. Here, rather, the elaborations of a particular historical tradition appear as liberations within animality, ones that nonetheless resist abstraction—in the concept of the human and in the commodification of labor. Her works are the product of a laborious process, and each is marked by the shape of her own form. Between the shucked-off hide of the ironically named "Deity" and the elaborate dress of the untranslated "Indlovukati," which alludes to the dresses worn by colonial women in southern Africa in a language they never spoke, there are both ambivalence and an improbable continuity. In both cases the skin of the animal is the medium of potency. The question of the minor lies elsewhere, within the hierarchy already established by humanism between animality and humanity.

Deleuze and Guattari's conception of minor literature—as a transgressive and liberatory literature possible even within the language and space of the dominant—was developed mainly in their reading of Kafka. And *The Trial*'s famous closing lines form the point of most obvious, intertextual reference in *Disgrace*. But less than the last lines, those preceding them ought to be recalled here. For, as he is about to be killed following the relentlessly opaque trial to which he has been subject for reasons he cannot fathom, K sees "a human figure" in a window and wonders whether that person will be a "friend" or "a good person" or "[s]omeone who cares." When K dies "like a dog," Kafka writes, "it seemed as though the shame was to outlive him."[42] If K has been seen by the "human figure," it has offered no humane gesture—neither recognition nor that instinctual care that would be given in the absence of mirroring. This is what it means to be in the place of the dog, if not the animal in general for Kafka. To go unrecognized, even when addressed, and thus uncared for.

The German word translated into English as "shame" is *scham*. It is much closer, in sound and meaning, to the German *schande* than are the English words *shame* and *disgrace*, though as many commentators have noted, *disgrace* in English is an antonym of honor and not of grace and hence is semantically closer to *shame* than to anything else. Coetzee is, of course, a scholar of Germanic languages and has written widely on the translation of Kafka and other German-language writers into English.[43]

When Gayatri Spivak argues against those critics who have conflated Coetzee's and Lury's points of view, accusing Coetzee of the racism that he has ascribed to his characters, by vigorously attending to the focalization through Lury, she remarks on this moment in particular. The intertextuality with Kafka is a function of Lury's focalization, she says. He reads Lucy's accommodation of the rape "not as a beginning in disgraceful equality but the end of civil society...where only shame is guaranteed continuity."[44] Indeed, Spivak suggests that Lucy's gesture constitutes a "refusal to be raped, by instrumentalizing reproduction."[45] This refusal arises from her "generalizing it into all heteronormative sexual practice."[46] Lucy is, after all, a lesbian. The intertextuality relevant to Lucy's predicament, says Spivak, is *King Lear*. It is Cordelia who repeatedly speaks the word *nothing* and who thereby refuses to give her love a convertible value, but it is Lear's description of Edward as "a poor, bare, forked animal" that Spivak calls up as the sign of a feminine disfigurement and which she recognizes as an image of subalternity—the place from which South African postcoloniality must be thought.[47] We might ask whether the female can in fact be disfigured through feminization. Coetzee seems to suggest that this is not possible, and hence it is by submitting to the dog-man and by invoking the figure of the man reduced to the canine (through the citation of Kafka) that Lucy "becomes minor."

In any case there are other visual and literary intertextualities at play in *Disgrace*, the reading of which is necessary if we are to grasp it not only as a literary text but also as part of the social text that is/was transitional South Africa. One of the figures with whom Lury identifies and whose surpassing is crucial to his assumption of the role of "dog-man" is the English Romantic poet Byron. Lury is writing an opera about Byron—into which, he finally concedes, the dog's yelp will find its way as voice. There are reasons beyond Lury's own obsession with Byron to believe that he exercises some significant allure for Coetzee. Byron's long, satirical (and disturbingly anti-Semitic) poem on Napoleon and the evils of a new economy dominated by finance capital, "Age of Bronze," is echoed in the title of the early novel *Age of Iron*,[48] just as the subtitle of Byron's work, *Carmen Seculare et Annus Haud Mirabilis*, is ironically echoed in the recent *Diary of a Very Bad Year* (a work that, like Byron's, combines political and economic philosophy with a more character-centered narrative).[49]

One of Byron's last plays, *Werner; or, The Inheritance*, is a gothic tragedy set at the end of the Thirty Years' War, at a time of political instability when bandits roam the hinterlands and peace is as lawless as war.[50] It is a scenario that many South Africans would recognize. The long, melodramatic narrative includes a count (Siegendorf), disowned by his father for an interracial relation, his brigand son, and a host of coincidental events—a pretender to the count's office is first rescued, then murdered by the son and robbed by the exiled father. It is when they discover each other's misdeeds that father and son are unhappily united. And it is then that their true and shared inheritance is revealed. It is not merely the castle and the power that the rank of count entails; it is also the "disgrace" that befalls the father in the moment that he steals and the son in the moment that he murders.

Many have remarked on the parallels between the characters of Byron's play and those who peopled his own life, but one can also discern many parallels between Werner and David Lury, not the least being the dark women whom they desire and whose possession (more forced in Lury's case) leads to their downfall. Far more interesting, however, is the discourse on passion—which runs so parallel between *Werner* and *Disgrace*. Thus, caught in his criminal act, Ulric answers his father, "If *you* condemn me, yet / Remember *who* hath taught me once too often / To listen to him! *Who* proclaim'd to me / That *there were crimes* made venial by the occasion? / That passion was our nature?... *Who* deprived me of / All the power to vindicate myself and race / In open day, by his disgrace which stamp'd / (It might be) bastardy on me, and on / Himself?" (V.i.439–449). And when laying claim to his own past deeds, the young brigand acknowledges that he had saved Stralehaim's life: "From impulse, as, *unknown*, I would have saved a peasant's or a dog's I slew / *Known* as our foe—but not from vengeance" (V.ii.456–458). The discourse of legitimate crime (the state), the discourse of the passions (violent heteronormativity as romanticism), the discourse of status and separation (purity), these incarcerating discourses against which the young Ulric rails are refocalized in *Disgrace* as the sources of that predicament from which a turn to animality, as the zero point of political reform, appears as an alternative.

Embedded here is the recognition of an indifference—typically offered to animals and peasants—that has been the mode of historical violence and may yet be the form of a survival, if Coetzee as read by Patton is correct. In Byron's text the economizing that comes to supplant indifference—namely, the economizing that called in a debt from a stranger who owed the life that had been saved—results in catastrophe for the entire lineage and even for its race. The closing lines are ones of tragically melodramatic termination: "The race of Siegendorf is passed." It seems improbable that Coetzee was not actively citing this text, which his character as a Byron scholar would surely have known. Moreover, Siegendorf is not just a Germanic name; as the locus of a famous Nazi labor camp in Austrian Burdenland, it was infamously run by Hungarian guards who force-marched their Jewish prisoners in front of the approaching Soviets at war's end and killed most of them.[51] In a novel in which the main character atones by liberating animals from the fate of being beaten with shovels in order to be processed,[52] in the oeuvre of a writer who has explicitly linked the treatment of animals to the treatment of Jews by the Nazis, this resonance seems more than fortuitous.[53]

THE "DOG-MAN": THE END OF (A) RACE, OR BASTARDY VERSUS ANIMALITY

The line "The race of Siegendorf is passed" haunts Coetzee's novel—and Bieber's and Alexander's art—as a kind of cryptic epitaph: a sign over the apartheid era's grave. One temptation is to read the race of Siegendorf as a code for Aryanism and, by extension, Afrikaner nationalism and to read the end of apartheid via the intertext of Siegendorf as the end of racial purity. This too would be to focalize the text through David Lury. But if I am correct and Coetzee is summoning *Werner* as an active intertext, then we must recall that what Ulric believes his inheritance to be is bastardy. For Ulric this is a burden, and for Byron it means the end of the line. For Coetzee the situation is more ambiguous.

That ambiguity can be grasped fully only if we read the fiction in terms of the intertextuality that places his writing and the visual texts of Bieber and Alexander into a relation of exemplarity vis-à-vis the social field. Now, the aporia of exemplarity is not so easily overcome. I am not saying that these texts are representative, nor do these texts provide an adequate basis on which to make the conclusions that I am drawing here. To do so, one would have to survey a much broader field. Yet, my hope is that this trio can indeed be made to disclose something about that field and the signifieds of its ideological signifiers. The nature of those signifieds is not to be found in a one-to-one set of relations, nor in a straightforwardly allegorical reading that lets us map one set of figures onto the other. To the contrary, the very slippage between them is instructive. Thus, we must grasp what is at stake in the movement between the problem of masking, the question of hybridity, and the fear of miscegenation (the latter fear stereotypically narrated in popular and literary narratives of interracial rape).

The fact that so many popular and literary narratives in South Africa focus on interracial rape (focalized by white patriarchy as loss) is crucial for understanding what is at stake. Such rape represents a small proportion of the actual sexual violence in South Africa. Its recurrence in literary and other works thus reveals something else. It makes visible the anxiety about how to transform desire in the service of political change. Insofar as apartheid entailed a prohibition on interracial desire, its transcendence appears to require interracial desire—desire being that which appears to be foreclosed by necessity, to be the very other of necessity. From within a voluntarist conception of the subject (that conception so essential to liberal humanism), desire that does not testify to the autonomy of the subject by virtue of its spontaneity appears to be coerced. It is this understanding of desire that can figure interracial relation only as rape. Within the terms of that presumption, desire across racial difference is deemed a *necessary* token of postracial existence, and it cannot therefore be a desired desire. Rather, it is conceived only as a social need. (It should nonetheless be noted that desire, in a strictly psychoanalytic reading, is that which exceeds the subject and is always already social.)

The resulting "unthinkability" of interracial relationality as a form of mutual desire marks the limits not only of the characters in many contemporary figures and fictions but also of the many authors whose collective text is a reracialized South Africa—one in which pedagogy, as the noncoercive rearrangement of desires, has not yet become the institutional locus for significant epistemological transformation. Now, it may be that Coetzee has given his most troubling character—the boy whose face appears to be a mask—the last word, or at least the most potent means of escaping the incipient evolutionism that undergirds any opposition between necessity and desire. For, as already noted, in the awful prelude to Lucy's rape, the boy feigns an excuse to ask for the telephone. His sister, he says, has had an accident. What accident? She is having a baby. We read this and know what Lucy knows, that the explanation is a lie. But this lie is in a sense true, insofar as reproductivity is rendered here as a mere by-product of other actions and not the telos of intentional action. Now, reading intertextually, we can only greet this troubling statement from the boy whose interiority remains so enigmatic, and who in this indecipherability resembles the masked child of Bieber's image, as a question. That question also mobilizes the mutant forms of Alexander's bestiary. If the accident is the name of the singular, the arrival of what truly surprises us, then this conjoining of accident and reproduction must give us pause. We must pry it loose from the context of its appearance and in a way that does not lead us to assume that what is unfamiliar is also monstrous, in the manner of the mutant creatures whom Alexander lets us see as the progeny of a sterile purism. As Coetzee says in his review of Breytenbach's conflicted memoir and homage to bastardy, *Dog Heart*,[54] it (the accident, including bastardy as an accident of reproductivity) may also intimate the possibility of desiring differently, against racism's categorical boundaries. One must extract such possibilities from the most difficult scenarios, not the easiest. Lury, alas, can care for a dog before he can embrace a racially other man. But in learning to grasp this incapacity as a function of Lury's focalization, we can perhaps grasp that a radical refocalization would also entail a willingness to become other without knowing, in advance, what that would look like.

POSTHUMOUS REFLECTIONS ON BODIES OF WORK IN PROCESS

Moments of political transition in which the distribution of human rights is expanded or contracted are, inevitably, moments in which the imagination of what constitutes humanity, of who counts as human, has to be reengaged. Often enough these moments are marked by efforts to refigure a human/animal opposition through the invocation of animal metaphors linked to different chains of signification and hence are capable of soliciting different sets of associative linkages and metaphoricities. In this chapter I have been interested in a certain transformation and proliferation of the discourse on animality in postapartheid South Africa, in the ways in which that transformation has appeared within the field of vision, and in the implications of that transformation for thinking about the questions of social and political justice that lay at the center of the struggle against apartheid and that continue to define efforts to reform the state in an increasingly neoliberal order. I want to reaffirm my earlier claim that these images are not to be understood as representative, either of the field of artwork in South Africa (which, though emphatically figurative when compared to the art traditions of many other places, is diverse and broad) or of anything like a typical, let alone collective, consciousness. I have spoken of a historical imaginary, one that is afflicted by contradictions that periodically manifest in symptoms that artists variously materialize. This imaginary is now confronted by the need to reorganize conceptual categories that no longer function. It is these conceptual categories, whose borders had been sustained by particular figures of the animal, that are now being reconceived even as they are made the basis of a new social machinery that, however different, continues to interpellate subjects at least partly by specularizing a particular image of the Other.

It must be acknowledged, in concluding, that if the foregoing meditations have any capacity to shed light on some dimensions of South African contemporaneity, it is not simply because of the resonance or even reiteration of the figures of animality within their works. Rather, it is the trope of masking as deployed by visual artists that allows us to open up the problematic of focalization more generally and thereby to ask the question of how worlds are organized, their visibilities structured, and their power distributed. By tracing the complex associations between masking and metamorphosis, mutancy and miscegenation in South Africa, I do not imply their identity but rather hope to enable a reading of the particular forms and concept-metaphors by which social life has been structured and is being rethought today. That reading is a task yet to be accomplished.

Acknowledgments

I would like to thank the Stellenbosch Institute for Advanced Study for affording me a place to read and write, and thus to revisit this paper in preparation for publication. I thank Jane Alexander for her patient clarifications and conversations about her work, as well as all the artists whose images appear in this chapter. My gratitude also goes out to Antjie Krog for a spirited debate about the representation of rape in South African life and literature. Finally, I want to thank Mary Steedly and Patricia Spyer for bringing me and the other contributors together for exchange at the School for Advanced Research, and for the excellent and challenging readings that the other scholars of the group gave my essay in that delightful milieu of discovery and intellectual development.

Notes

1. Walter Benjamin, "The Work of Art in the Age of Its Technological Reproducibility," *Walter Benjamin: Selected Writings*, vol. 4, *1938–1940*, ed. Howard Eiland and Michael W. Jennings (Cambridge, MA: Belknap Press of Harvard University Press, 2003), 251–283.

2. The anthropological question of circulation takes off from Arjun Appadurai's synthetic notion of the social life of things. Recognizing that objects assume different values (both semantic and economic) in different social contexts, Appadurai's concept nonetheless presumes continuity in a thing's status across various interpretive and evaluative domains. By contrast, McKenzie Wark's concept of vectors is intended to recognize the different intensities and often nonreciprocal nature of the flows that carry images between poles of relative power in the age of global media. Arjun Appadurai,

"Introduction: Commodities and the Politics of Value," in *The Social Life of Things: Commodities in Cultural Perspective*, ed. Arjun Appadurai (Cambridge, UK: Cambridge University Press, 1988), 3–63; McKenzie Wark, *Virtual Geography: Living with Global Media Events* (Bloomington: Indiana University Press, 1994).

3. Jacques Derrida, *The Truth in Painting*, trans. Geoff Bennington and Ian McLeod (Chicago: University of Chicago Press, 1987).

4. Samuel Weber, "Art, Aura and Media in the Work of Walter Benjamin," in *Mass Mediauras: Form, Technics, Media*, ed. Samuel Weber (Stanford, CA: Stanford University Press, 1996), 76–107.

5. Derrida, *Truth in Painting*, 331.

6. Weber, "Art, Aura and Media," 88.

7. I draw my understanding of focalization from Mieke Bal, who elaborates a linguistic (narratological) concept to supplement Gombrich's famous reading of an image that might be either a duck or a rabbit but which he claims can be apprehended as one or the other only at any given moment. Mieke Bal, *Murder and Difference: Gender, Genre, and Scholarship on Sisera's Death* (Bloomington: Indiana University Press, 1988); E. H. Gombrich, *Art and Illusion: A Study in the Psychology of Pictorial Representation* (London: Phaidon, 1962). Gombrich himself was drawing upon the discussion of this image in Ludwig Wittgenstein, *Philosophical Investigations* (London: Blackwell, 1958).

8. Hannah Arendt, *On Violence* (New York: Harcourt Brace, 1970), 60.

9. Jacques Lacan, *Écrits: A Selection*, trans. Alan Sheridan (New York: Norton, 1977), 305.

10. Hannah Arendt, *The Human Condition* (Chicago: University of Chicago Press, 1958), 198–199.

11. The category of "white literature" is neither a substantial one reducible to the racial classification of authors nor a description of its subject matter. Admittedly problematic, I use the term here to describe literature focalized from within the epistemology that allows whiteness to signify universality and hence that makes blackness visible as the limit case of what can be generalized.

12. J. M. Coetzee, "The Memoirs of Breyten Breytenbach," *Stranger Shores: Literary Essays, 1986–1999* (New York: Viking, 2001), 250.

13. Jane Alexander, personal communication March 4, 2012.

14. For a discussion of the aesthetic of flash and its relationship to the critical photography of tradition and modernity, see Marilyn Ivy, "Dark Enlightenment: Naitō Masatoshi's Flash," in *Photographies East: The Camera and Its Histories in East and Southeast Asia*, ed. Rosalind C. Morris (Durham, NC: Duke University Press, 2009), 229–258.

15. Bal, *Murder*, 86–87.

16. Jean-Paul Sartre, *Being and Nothingness: A Phenomenological Essay on Ontology*, trans. Hazel E. Barnes (New York: Washington Square Books, 1966), 340–400.

17. It is on precisely this issue that Derrida questions Lacan's concept of the Other, so central to the idea of the mirror stage. He notes that Lacan secretly identifies the animal, the divinity, and law itself; all occupy the same place, analytically, the place of truth, whence speech comes. These are "figures," says Derrida, of the transcendental referent, foundational figures of an Other that is, quite simply, a function of dogma, one rooted in the definition of the human as the one who is capable of pretending to pretend. See Jacques Derrida, *The Animal That Therefore I Am*, trans. David Wills, ed. Marie-Louise Mallet (New York: Fordham University Press, 2008), esp. 130–136.

18. Jodi Bieber, *Between Dogs and Wolves: Growing Up in South Africa* (Stockport, UK: Dewi Lewis Publishing, 2007).

19. Jodi Bieber, *Between Dogs and Wolves*, text for photographic catalog, http://www .jodibieber.com/index.php?pageID=6&navLay=6 (accessed April 30, 2008).

20. For an effort to understand the phenomenon and the discourse about sexual violence in this area, see Rosalind C. Morris, "The Mute and the Unspeakable: Political Subjectivity, Violent Crime, and 'the Sexual Thing' in a South African Mining Community," in *Law and Disorder in the Postcolony*, ed. Jean and John Comaroff (Chicago: University of Chicago Press, 2006), 57–101.

21. Arendt, *Human Condition*, 291. Leela Gandhi offers a counternarrative in which the linkage between figures of the antivivisectionist, anticolonial, and vegetarian movements actively worked to conceptualize an alternative politics in the age of masculinist imperialism. She attributes more force to this convergence than does Arendt. Leela Gandhi, *Affective Communities: Anticolonial Thought, Fin de Siècle Radicalism, and the Politics of Friendship* (Durham, NC: Duke University Press, 2006).

22. This structure of critique has a long tradition, the most exemplary instance perhaps being Max Horkheimer and Theodor Adorno, *Dialectic of the Enlightenment*, ed. Gunzelin Schmid Noerr, trans. Edmund Jephcott (Stanford, CA: Stanford University Press, 2002).

23. Rosalind C. Morris, "Crowds and Powerlessness: Reading //kabbo and Canetti with Derrida in (South) Africa," in *Demenageries: Thinking (of) Animals after Derrida*, Critical Series 35, ed. Anne Berger and Marta Segarra (Amsterdam: Rodopi, 2011), 167–212.

24. J. M. Coetzee, *The Lives of Animals* (Princeton, NJ: Princeton University Press, 2001); and *Elizabeth Costello* (New York: Penguin, 2004).

25. Jacques Derrida, *The Animal That Therefore I Am*.

26. J. M. Coetzee, *Disgrace* (London: Secker and Warburg, 1999).

27. Ibid., 97.

28. Franz Kafka, *The Trial*, trans. Breon Mitchell (1925; New York: Schocken, 1998).

29. Derek Attridge, "Age of Bronze, State of Grace: Music and Dogs in Coetzee's *Disgrace*," *Novel: A Forum on Fiction* 34, no. 1 (Autumn 2000): 98–121; Paul Patton, "Becoming-Animal and Pure Life in Coetzee's *Disgrace*," *ARIEL: A Review of International English Literature* 35, no. 1–2 (Spring 2006): 101–119, special issue, *Law, Literature, Postcoloniality*.

30. David Atwell, "Race in *Disgrace*," *Interventions* 4, no. 3 (2002): 331–341.

31. Coetzee, *Disgrace*, 160.

32. J. M. Coetzee, "Irène Némirovsky: *The Dogs and the Wolves*," *New York Review of Books* 55, no. 18 (November 20, 2008).

33. Coetzee, *Disgrace*, 92.

34. Ibid., 4.

35. Ranjana Khanna, "Indignity," *Positions* 6, no. 1 (2006): 42, special issue, *War, Capital, Trauma*, ed. Tani Barlow.

36. I am grateful to Jane Alexander for her patient explanation of the works and her willingness to listen to and engage the histories of her works' reception.

37. I am influenced in my reading of foreclosure by Gayatri Chakravorty Spivak's account of the foreclosure in *A Critique of Postcolonial Reason* (Cambridge, MA: Harvard University Press, 1999), 4.

38. Ivor Powell, "Inside and Outside of History," *Art South Africa* 5, no. 4 (2007): 34–38.

39. Elleke Boehmer, "Not Saying Sorry, Not Speaking Pain: Gender Implications in *Disgrace*," *Interventions* 4, no. 3 (2002): 344. In an article in the same special issue of *Interventions* devoted to *Disgrace*, Peter McDonald notes the ambivalence of the author's relation to his narrator's consciousness. For McDonald, it is unclear who focalizes our vision in *Disgrace*: Coetzee or David Lurie? He writes, "By giving privileged space to the idea of the white as victim, and by using the colonial nightmare *topos*—the violation of white women—it can also be seen to play up to 'white fears.'" Peter McDonald, "*Disgrace* Effects," *Interventions* 4, no. 3 (2002): 326.

40. Coetzee, *Disgrace*, 205.

41. Patton, "Becoming-Animal," 103.

42. Kafka, *Trial*, 231.

43. J. M. Coetzee, "Translating Kafka," *Stranger Shores: Literary Essays, 1986–1999* (New York: Viking, 2001), 74–87.

44. Gayatri Chakravorty Spivak, "Ethics and Politics in Tagore, Coetzee, and Certain Scenes of Teaching," *Diacritics* 32, no. 3–4 (Fall–Winter 2002): 22. Spivak is strongly allied here with David Atwell when he laments, "How tragic it is that Lucy's emergence into the public sphere in South Africa has been restricted to such crude

readings as the 'Lucy-syndrome'…the notion that one must pay up in order to live as a white South African; or the reverse of this, which is articulated by the ANC—the idea that if whites can think of their adjustment to post-apartheid South Africa only on Lucy's terms, it would be better for them to emigrate." Atwell, "Race in *Disgrace*," 340.

45. Spivak, "Ethics and Politics," 21.

46. Ibid., 24.

47. Ibid., 20–21.

48. Derek Attridge, who titles his review of *Disgrace* by the name of Byron's poem "Age of Bronze," nonetheless makes no reference to the Byronic text and limits his consideration of the title to a reference in Coetzee's novel *Age of Iron*, in which the cancer-ridden patient, Mrs. Curren, fantasizes a gentler age. Attridge, "Age of Bronze, State of Grace," 98.

49. The negotiations between the banned African National Congress (ANC) and the National Party preceding South Africa's transition are widely discussed as ones in which a more Socialist option was relinquished in favor of a neoliberal alternative. Many on the Left in South Africa feel that the decision had as its effect and corollary a failure to redistribute national wealth and to mitigate racialized poverty.

50. Lord George Gordon Byron, *Werner; or, The Inheritance*, in *The Poetical Works of Byron*, ed. F. Gleckner (Boston: Houghton Mifflin, 1975), 671–721.

51. Among the most powerful literary testaments to this experience—shared by so many German-speaking Jews on the periphery of the Austro-Hungarian Empire—are those by the poets Paul Celan and Niklos Radnotti. Coetzee himself reviewed a series of new translations of Celan with this context foregrounded, in J. M. Coetzee, "In the Midst of Losses," *New York Review of Books* 48, no. 11 (July 5, 2001).

52. Coetzee, *Disgrace*, 146.

53. Coetzee's extended review of new Paul Celan translations begins by situating him in his birthplace in Czernowitz, on the edge of the Austro-Hungarian Empire.

54. Breyten Breytenbach, *Dog Heart* (New York: Harcourt, 1999).

8

Explosions of Information, Implosions of Meaning, and the Release of Affects

Ernst van Alphen

Talking about changes in the art world in the early 1990s, Cuban-American artist Felix Gonzalez-Torres noticed that there has been a shift away from the "sloganeering" art that appropriated the media, exemplified by the work of Barbara Kruger, toward a more personal voice. According to Gonzales-Torres a more personal voice is necessary because the recent historical situation requires new modes of contestation. His description of an artwork by American artist Roni Horn is exemplary for this new kind of art and for the way it relates to the viewer:

> The *Gold Field*. How can I deal with the *Gold Field*? I don't quite know. But the *Gold Field* was there. Ross and I entered the Museum of Contemporary Art, and without knowing the work of Roni Horn we were blown away by the heroic, gentle and horizontal presence of this gift. There it was, in a white room, all by itself, it didn't need company, it didn't need anything. Sitting on the floor, ever so lightly. A new landscape, a possible horizon, a place of rest and absolute beauty. Waiting for the right viewer willing and needing to be moved to a place of the imagination. This piece is nothing more than a thin layer of gold. It is everything a good poem by Wallace Stevens is: precise with no

baggage, nothing extra. A poem that feels secure and dares to unravel itself, to become naked, to be enjoyed in a tactile manner, but beyond that, in an intellectual way too. Ross and I were lifted. That gesture was all we needed to rest, to think about the possibility of change. This showed the innate ability of an artist proposing to make this place a better place. How truly revolutionary.... A place to dream, to regain energy, to dare. Ross and I always talked about this work, how much it affected us.[1]

Gonzalez-Torres's description of the *Gold Field* (which dates from 1980–1981) neither deals with signification, the meaning of the work, nor articulates the work within a discursive framework. What it describes, instead, is how this artwork affects him, the viewer. He and his partner enjoyed it initially in a tactile manner. It lifted them. Next, it made them think about the possibility of change, which is why they call it "truly revolutionary." "Change" and "revolution," however, were not the only thoughts they were stimulated to have. Change and revolution also characterize their response to the artwork. They are affected by it in such a way that they are "shocked to thought."[2]

In another text Gonzalez-Torres dwells on the sociohistorical situation, which necessitated a "more personal voice" for works of art. Characterizing this situation tersely, he writes, "Right now we have an *explosion* of information, but an *implosion* of meaning."[3] Here he refers to the situation in which people are bombarded by information that concerns them personally but, strangely, this information does not transform into meaning in their daily lives. One of his examples is the lack of health care in the United States. People are informed about this, they know it, but, according to Gonzalez-Torres, it does not mean much. For example, it does not lead to political positioning, nor does it lead to a specific voting behavior.

In the 1970s and 1980s increasing the accessibility of information and, by doing so, intensifying the production of meaning were important cultural pursuits and political goals. Information was seen as a precondition for meaning production.[4] But if we agree with Felix Gonzalez-Torres's assessment of the 1990s, this cultural and political project has failed because it has turned against itself. The explosion of information has not led to more meaning and better understanding, but rather to an implosion of meaning as such. He suggests that this implosion of meaning has heightened the sensitivity for affect and its transmission. Later in this chapter I elaborate on why the mentioned explosions and implosions have this kind of consequence.

Cultural analyst and psychoanalyst Teresa Brennan also notices an increase of affects at the end of the twentieth century. Her explanation and historical understanding of this increase is, however, rather different from that of Gonzalez-Torres. She argues that, whereas the idea of the transmission of affect was well accepted until the seventeenth century, it faded away after that century because of the rise of individualism since the Enlightenment. Without making a clear distinction between affects and emotions, she assesses that when the notion of the individual gained strength, "it was assumed more and more that emotions and energies are naturally contained, going no further than the skin."[5] Individualism has made it unthinkable that our emotions are not altogether our own, that some of our emotions have been transmitted to us and come from an external source. In an essay on "fear" Brian Massumi also argues that any mode of cultural, political, or social analysis has a problem with understanding affective mechanisms to the extent that it continues to treat the self as a bounded space, even if that boundary is conceived as porous.[6] The belief that emotions are our own and come from within can be sustained because unwanted affects can always be projected onto somebody else. Brennan distinguishes two different ways of processing transmitted affects.

The first is to resist the affect and to project it outward without consciously acknowledging that we are doing so. The second one she calls "discernment," and it consists of consciously examining the affect. What has changed in the course of the 1990s is that the unconscious projection of unwanted affects on others is not as easy as it was in the past: Have boundaries come to matter because self-definition by projection is less available than it was during the past few sexist and colonial centuries—there are now too few willing receptacles—or because of an accumulation of environmentally inflicted affects? Either way, boundaries may matter now because there is too much affective stuff to dispose of, too much that is directed away from the self and with no place to go.[7]

This concern with boundaries and with the increasing failure to maintain these boundaries by means of projection led in the 1990s to the fact, for example, that depression was the most rapidly growing disorder in Europe and the United States. According to Brennan this increase is not coincidental but is instead historically produced, or what she calls "environmentally inflicted." Boundaries, like identities, were not an issue when the transmission of affect had more currency historically. Boundaries especially become an issue in periods when the transmission of affect is denied. In the 1990s, boundaries and identities became contested issues, not only as the result of political and intellectual debates but also because boundaries and identities in themselves were, more and more, experienced as uncertain and porous. This contested status brought with it the results that transmissions of affects increased and that those affects had to be dealt with in one way or another, productively or unproductively (depression). Brennan's assessment of the 1990s and of the increasing role of affects in that decade focuses on contested identities and the difficulty of drawing boundaries and constructing or maintaining identities. Identity politics as a result of feminism and of global, postcolonial changes are seen as the defining historical actors. Gonzalez-Torres's assessment of the same decade differs in the sense that for him both the growing role of media and the explosive growth of the distribution of information were responsible for fundamental changes in the 1990s.[8]

More than forty years ago Susan Sontag, in her programmatic essay "Against Interpretation," pleaded passionately for more serious attention to what I will call the affective operations of art and literature. She declared that the prevalent idea that a work of art is its content, or that a work of art says something, was "mainly a hindrance, a nuisance, a subtle or not so subtle philistinism."[9] According to Sontag the transformation of texts or works of art into meanings is a revenge of the intellect upon the world. "To interpret is to impoverish, to deplete the world—in order to set up a shadow world of 'meanings.'"[10] To counter this tendency she pleads for a more immediate experience of the object or text itself. What is important now is to recover our senses. We must learn to see more, to hear more, to feel more. And she ends her essay with the famous words that "in place of a hermeneutics of art we need an erotics of art."[11]

What is remarkable about her essay is that she too motivates her plea for an erotics of art with a historical urgency. Like Gonzalez-Torres and Brennan, Sontag claims that a fundamental historical change necessitates other artistic practices and processing of them. Although she is talking about the 1960s and not about the 1990s, her assessment of those years necessitates this eroticism. Hermeneutics is not bad in itself, but it has become a harmful or, better yet, powerless mode of reading at this particular historical moment:

> Interpretation takes the sensory experience of the work of art for granted, and proceeds from there. This cannot be taken for granted, now. Think of the sheer multiplication of works of art available to every one of us, superadded to the conflicting tastes and odors and sights of the urban environment that bombard our sense. Ours is a culture based on excess, on overproduction; [the] result is a steady loss of sharpness in our sensory experience.

> All the conditions of modern life—its material plenitude, its
> sheer crowdedness—conjoin to dull our sensory faculties.[12]

Sontag's proposal for more serious attention to the affective operations of art and literature was motivated by a historical condition other than the one discussed so far. The 1960s were not the same as the 1990s. But what these decades have in common is radical change in how subjects relate to their social environment. Whereas an explosion of commodity culture can define the 1960s, an increasing explosion of information culture can characterize the 1990s. In both periods the subject is exposed to an abundance, an abundance that is ultimately sensorial and that brings with it the need for an increased sensitivity for affects.

Another difference is that in Sontag's account the diagnosis does not consist of an implosion of meaning but of a loss of sharpness in our sensory experience. The need for an increased sensitivity of affects is motivated by the fact that our sensory faculties are dulled by the explosion of commodity culture. In her argument against interpretation, an implosion of meaning can, one could argue, even be a solution for realizing this increased sensitivity. Whereas in the 1960s Sontag contests meaning and interpretation, in the 1990s meaning is no longer contested because, according to Gonzalez-Torres, an implosion of it has taken place.

Sontag thinks that the development of another mode of reading and looking will be able to bring our sensory faculties to life again. What is needed is another critical attitude. But as already pointed out at the beginning of my chapter, according to Felix Gonzalez-Torres it is not only a different engagement with texts and art objects that the changing historical conditions ask for but also different modes of artistic and cultural contestation. I would argue that both are needed and that a more sensorial or affective response to artworks is also, at least partly, conditioned by characteristics of artworks and texts.

UNDERSTANDING AFFECT: WHY?

The diagnoses of culture since the 1990s by Felix Gonzalez-Torres and Teresa Brennan, different as they are, imply the urgency to understand better what affect is and how it works. It is clear that several disciplines in the humanities are trying to do precisely that. But what often happens is that when a concept or term becomes fashionable, it loses its meaning. The term is used more and more without any critical ramifications. It is often used in such a way that it means something general, like "personal" or "subjective." But, I argue, affect is the opposite of personal: it is social.

The cultural and social effect of these emerging forms is, itself, often a function of their capacity to generate and transmit affect or to engage a viewer in a particular, transformative way. Thus, the politics of art and literature since the 1990s can no longer be understood simply in terms of its programmatic meaning or message. The new modes of contestation require an "affective approach" in order to reveal how recent culturally and politically engaged work "works." The implosion of meaning, which Gonzalez-Torres notices in the larger sociopolitical domain, is, I contend, also at stake in the artistic and literary domain. But this does not imply that recent art and literature have lost cultural and political impact. Their impact is, instead, established by means of powerful transactions of affect.

But in general, one may claim that much could be gained by thinking through the affective operations of art in cultural theory. As Massumi has claimed, our cultural-theoretical-political vocabulary offers few possibilities to deal with affect. Our entire vocabulary has derived from theories of signification. These theories and approaches "are incomplete if they operate only on the semantic or semiotic level, however that level is defined (linguistically, logically, narratologically, ideologically, or all of these in combination) as a symbolic. What they lose, precisely, is the expression *event*—in favor of structure."[13] In a book on trauma and art, Jill Bennett argues something similar. Not all art is representational, and even if art is representational, many aspects of that art are not and operate instead on the basis of nonrepresentational strategies. Ultimately, art is ill served by a theoretical framework "that privileges *meaning* (i.e., the object of representation, outside art) over *form* (the inherent qualities or modus operandi of art)."[14]

This plea for more attention to the affective operations of art does not at all imply, however, a privileging of a more formalistic approach to art. On the contrary, as already pointed out in the example of Gonzalez-Torres responding to the *Gold Field*, the transmission of affect "shocks" him "to thought." This expression, "shocked to thought," is Deleuzian, and Deleuze has another expression that indicates this intimate relationship between affect and thought, namely "the encountered sign." He introduced the term in his book *Proust and Signs*. The encountered sign is a sign that is felt rather than recognized, or perceived through cognition or through familiarity with the "code." But the sensation of the encountered sign is not an end in itself. For Deleuze this sensation is a catalyst for critical inquiry or thought. For him an affect is a more effective trigger for profound thought than rational inquiry because of the way in which the former grasps us, forcing us to engage involuntarily: "More important than thought there is 'what leads to thought'...impressions which force us to look, encounters which force us to interpret, expressions which force us to think."[15]

Deleuze quotes Proust himself to illustrate the nature of the encountered sign: "The truths which intelligence grasps directly in the open light of day have something less profound, less *necessary* about them than those which life has communicated to us *in spite of ourselves* in an impression, a material impression because it has reached us through our senses."[16] As Bennett explains, in this Proustian and Deleuzian view, art and literature are seen as the embodiment of sensation that stimulates thought.[17] Art does not illustrate or embody a proposition, but it produces sensations or affects that stimulate thought. It is the affective encounter through which thought proceeds and moves toward deeper truth. By means of this affective view of art and literature, Deleuze deconstructs the conventional opposition between philosophy and art, or between thought and sensation. For him both are modes of thinking. But whereas philosophers think in concepts, artists think by means of sensation. "Sensation is generated through the artist's engagement with the medium, through color and line in the case of the painter, so that it is not the residue of self-expression, or a property of some prior self, but emerges in the present, as it attaches to figures in the image."[18]

As modes of thinking, art and literature vie with philosophy. Deleuze seems to agree with Proust's critique of philosophy. The truths formulated by or within a philosophical discourse remain arbitrary and abstract as long as they are based on the goodwill of thinking. Philosophy is based on the conventional. It is "ignorant of the dark regions in which are elaborated the effective forces which act on thought, the determinations which *force* us to think.... Minds communicate to each other only the conventional; the mind engenders only the possible. The truths of philosophy are lacking in necessity, and the mark of necessity."[19] Deleuze quotes Proust again to explain the shortcomings of philosophy: "The ideas formed by pure intelligence have only a logical truth, a possible truth, their choice is arbitrary."[20]

In his book on the painter Francis Bacon, Deleuze explains how sensations are the means of the artist's way of thinking: "Sensation is what is being painted; what is being painted on the canvas is the body. Not insofar as it is represented as an object, but insofar as it is experienced as sustaining *this* sensation."[21]

It is this sustaining of sensation that thrusts viewers into thinking and into an encountered or embodied mode of critical inquiry. The thought activated by the encountered, sensuous sign is truly critical and creative (instead of conventional or arbitrary), for, Deleuze argues, "it does us violence:

it mobilizes the memory, it sets the soul in motion; but the soul in its turn excites thought, transmits to it the constraint of the sensibility, forces it to conceive essence, as the only thing which must be conceived."[22]

WHAT IS AFFECT AND HOW DOES IT OPERATE?

In order to understand better the affective operations of art and literature, I will first take a momentary step backward and try to assess more thoroughly what affect is, how it works, and how it relates to notions with which it is so often confused, like feeling and emotion. And where do affects originate, just in human beings or also in objects, like artworks or texts?[23]

The term "affect" comes from the Latin *affectus*, which means "passion" or "emotion." Affects have an energetic dimension; they are, in Deleuze's words, "intensities." According to Deleuze affect is an intensity embodied in autonomic reactions on the surface of the body as it interacts with other entities. Affect precedes its expression in words and operates independently. According to psychologist Silvan Tomkins, one of the most important theoreticians of affect, affect extends beyond individuals, and it does not pursue the same goals as either drives or cognitive systems. Yet, affect is the essential amplifier of other drives "because without its amplification nothing else matters and with its amplification anything else can matter."[24]

The transmission of such "intensities" has a physiological impact. Affects can arise within a person, but they also come from without. They can be transmitted by the presence of another person but also by an artwork or a (literary) text. They come from an interaction with objects, an environment, or other people. Because of its origin in interaction, one can say that the transmission of affect is social in origin but biological and physical in effect.[25] The experience of affect is usually seen as a kind of judgment. The person who receives the affect has to do something with it. It will be projected outward, or it will be introjected. The projection or introjection of a judgment is the moment when the transmission takes place. As argued before, the notion of affect has had an uncomfortable place in Western, seventeenth-century Enlightenment culture because the Enlightenment's individualism is peculiarly resistant to the idea that our affects are not altogether our own. Affects are not necessarily our own because they may have been transmitted by somebody else or by an object or environment. We are then "possessed" by emotions that have their origin elsewhere or in somebody else.

Affects are judgments or evaluations in the sense that they are the physiological shifts accompanying a judgment (or an evaluation). The physiological shift takes place as a result of the evaluative, positive or negative, orientation toward an object or other person.[26] This notion of affect as physiological shift implies that affects are not the same as feelings. Feelings include something more than a physiological shift or sensory stimulation. They suppose a unified interpretation of that shift or stimulation. For that reason Brennan defines feelings as "sensations that have found the right match in words."[27] Similarly, Jill Bennett defines feeling as "the moment of awareness of affect through which the self is experienced—experienced as deformation of itself."[28] This distinction between affects and feelings implies that affects as such have no particular content or meaning. In themselves they are just energetic intensities.

There are other psychological notions that are often conflated with affect, for instance, emotion. Yet, affects and emotions follow a different logic and pertain to different orders. Emotions are more or less synonymous with feeling, although in some theories emotions consist of a more complex organization of affect than feeling. In the words of Massumi (who, in the wake of Deleuze, uses "intensity" as exchangeable with "affect"), "an emotion is a subjective content, the socio-linguistic fixing of the quality of an experience which is from that point onward defined as personal. Emotion is qualified intensity, the conventional, consensual point of insertion of intensity into semantically and semiotically formed progressions, into narrativizable action-reaction circuits, into function and meaning. It is intensity owned and recognized."[29]

In the affect theory of Silvan Tomkins, the crucial notion is not "intensity" but the more scientific sounding notion of "density of neural firing." He distinguishes a diverse range of basic affects on the basis of three variants of density of neural firing:

> I would account for the difference in affect activation by three variants of a single principle—the density of neural firing. By density I mean the frequency of neural firing per unit of time. My theory posits three discrete classes of activators of affect, each of which further amplifies the sources which activate them. These are stimulation increase, stimulation level, and stimulation decrease.
>
> Thus any stimulus with a relatively sudden onset and a steep increase in the rate of neural firing will innately activate a startle response.... If the rate of neural firing increases less rapidly, fear is activated, and if still less rapidly, then interest is innately activated. In contrast, any sustained increase in the level of neural firing, as with a continued loud noise, would innately activate

the anger response. Finally, any sudden decrease in stimulation
that reduced the rate of neural firing, as in the sudden redaction
of excessive noise, would innately activate the rewarding smile of
enjoyment.[30]

What the Deleuzian affect theorists have in common with Tomkins is
a notion of affect in terms of an energetic "stream," although they call it
"intensity" and Tomkins calls it "neural firing." A difference is, however,
that in the Deleuzian notion affect as such has no content or meaning,
although it produces feelings, emotions, thoughts. Tomkins, in contrast,
develops a taxonomy of affects. Depending on density and temporal length
of the neural firing, it results in, for example, startle, fear, interest, anger,
distress, and shame.

This brings us back to the issue of meaning in relation to affect. When
the person to whom the affect is transmitted does not "project" the affect
outward but "discerns" it, at that moment the affect is given content. The
affect then feels like depression, anger, or anxiety. But the way a transmitted affect is signified differs from person to person. The same affect can be
given a completely different content by another person. Although affects
are social, that is, the result of an interactive process from without, the
linguistic or visual contents or thoughts attached to an affect belong to the
person to whom the affect is transmitted.

Since the same affect can evoke very different feelings or thoughts in
different people, the thoughts, feelings, or images evoked by affects are
not necessarily tied to the affects they appear to evoke. A transmission of
affect between two persons can result in the two people becoming alike;
for example, someone's depression is transmitted to someone else, who
will then feel depressed as a result. This form of transmission is usually
called *entrainment*,[31] or "affective resonance" in Tomkins's work. But it can
also happen that as a result of such a transmission people take up oppos-
ing or different positions in relation to a common affective thread. This is
the case when, for example, somebody's depression gives rise to feelings
of anger in the person to whom the affect was transmitted or when somebody's hyperactivity makes another person feel depressed.

These examples of transmitted affects all concern transmissions
between human subjects. Although these transmissions also imply that our
emotions are not necessarily our own, this is even more difficult to acknowledge when the transmitting agent is not a human subject but a text, a film,
or a painting. I am not referring now to media that especially function as
an intermediary in the transmission of affect that migrates from body to

body. It is obvious that especially film and television have this intermediary role of bodily transmission. For the moment I am now more interested in objects that are not limited to the role of intermediary but that are, for instance, abstract, like Roni Horn's *Gold Field*, which affected Gonzalez-Torrez in such a significant way. In our current time it has become difficult to see such objects as active agents because humanism has led to the idea that everything outside human subjectivity is passive, unconscious, and material.

> Subjective activity takes the definition of itself as the center of all definition and defines all "activity" as having its own character. It labels "passive" everything that is not active in its own way and which it is able to *bend* [*to*] *its will*, passive if it does not assert itself against the subject. The objects making up the environment are seen as passive because they do not carry out intentions of their own. To be active is to carry out an individual intention.... The passive/active dichotomy, as consciousness understands it, is thus a product of the sense of self that divides itself from the rest of the world on the grounds of its difference. Its understanding of activity is synonymous with the idea of individual intentionality.[32]

Yet, the so-called passivity of objects and of matter does not lie in a lack of action but in a lack of free will or intentional agency. Active matter is passive in that it is not individual. But if we reject individual intentionality as the criterion for activity (that is, if we recognize the ideological nature of that criterion), then there is no reason not to acknowledge matter and objects as possibly active.[33] The transmission of affects by texts, films, or paintings is, then, no longer an imprecise, metaphorical way of speaking of our admiration for, or dislike of, these cultural objects. On the contrary, it is an adequate way of describing what cultural objects can do to us and how they are active agents in the cultural and social worlds. It is precisely because of the activity of matter and objects that literature and art can be affective and that we can speak of the affective operations of art.

AFFECT AND THE IMAGE

The explosion of information, the implosion of meaning, and the release of affectivity happen most of all through the dissemination of images. Although modern media such as film and television and new media such as the Internet and cell phones are not exclusively visual, it is their visuality that usually dominates our senses most. In the remainder of this chapter, I address the affectivity of the image and the increase of that affectivity since the 1990s. The visual medium that is my example is that of the webcam, the small camera that sends images to a computer connected to the Internet. After this new medium was introduced in the mid-1990s, it became a standard apparatus in many studios, households, and bedrooms.

When I take the webcam as exemplary for fundamental changes in the role of affectivity of the image, I do not suggest that this medium has any essential function or specificity. Its medium specificity is only partly defined by its technical features and possibilities. It is also determined by how it is used, that is, by historical and cultural practices.[34] And, I argue, the ways webcams are used are especially responsible for new, intense transmissions of affect. New media uses and practices usually cause changes in the media landscape at large. A new medial practice can cause shifts in the functions and practices of other media. For example, the introduction of photography into the media landscape of the mid nineteenth century has deprived painting of, or perhaps we should say liberated it from, some of its functions. The same can be said of the webcam. The webcam has fulfilled some ideals that were earlier pursued by the video camera and longer ago by the film camera. The dream concerning one medium is realized in another, more recent medium. For many webcam users the ambition of a comprehensive representation of the world, spatially and temporally, is finally fulfilled: "The webcam makes possible the endless, unedited film, the eternal film."[35]

The ways and contexts in which webcams are being used are diverse. Its first use is extremely simple, as well as exemplary for most of its later uses. The very first webcam was used in 1993 in the Department of Computer Science at the University of Cambridge for surveilling a coffeepot.[36] In order not to walk in vain to the room where one could get coffee, the so-called "Trojan room," and find there an empty pot, students installed this new apparatus to the pot and connected it to their computers so that they could check from their desk whether there was any coffee left. Two years later they connected these images to the World Wide Web and shared the information with millions of people. That so many people watched these images was not motivated by what the images showed but by what they promised: a comprehensive representation of the world. Soon after, in 1996 Jennifer Ringley, a student from Pennsylvania, materialized part of the promise by showing on the Web images of her life at home in real time that were taken by a camera connected to her computer. Internet users could see everything she was doing: playing with her animals, sleeping, combing her hair, making love with her boyfriend, and so on. The stream of images was life, was unedited, and it was in real time. The webcam is used as lifecam.[37]

As I stated before, the ideal materialized by Ringley's webcam as such is not new at all. There are films and videos in which a similar practice is demonstrated. Andy Warhol's films *Sleep* (1963) and *Empire* (1964) and more recently Bruce Nauman's video installation *Mapping the Studio—All Action Edit (Fat Chance John Cage)* (2002) are probably the most famous examples. *Sleep* shows the poet John Giorno, Warhol's lover in those days, sleeping. He is filmed from a number of different angles, and some shots are repeated. Although this film is not really or not completely in real time, it creates that impression. In this respect, *Empire* is more radical. It consists of eight hours and six minutes of continuous, real-time, black and white film of the Empire State Building, from early evening until nearly 3 AM the next day. In the video installation *Mapping the Studio*, Bruce Nauman records the nocturnal activity in the artist's studio of his cat and an infestation of mice during the summer of 2000. With seven projections and multiple audio tracks of ambient sounds, Nauman used this traffic as a way of mapping the leftover parts and work areas of the preceding several years of other, completed, unfinished, or discarded projects.

Within their media—film and video—these examples are unique, not representative for a medium's specificity but for its exceptional dreams. Ringley's use of the medium of the webcam is not singular but demonstrates in an exemplary way a fundamental change in the 1990s caused by a new media landscape. It has given rise to a great diversity of practical uses of the webcam. Webcams are now focused on mountains so that you can see whether there is enough snow on the ski run; on young children so that the parents can see whether they are still asleep; on roads so that drivers know whether there are traffic jams; on the people behind a computer so that they know what each other looks like.

The latter example demonstrates a fundamental change in visual technologies. The possibility of showing your interlocutor at the chat box what you look like is first of all used by friends and family members in order to enhance the connection and its intimacy. The speaking or writing of words is completed by showing the faces. This possibility is fully exploited in the sex industry. Thanks to the webcam the client can not just chat with the girl or boy who is supposed to fulfill sexual desires, but the girl or boy also shows herself or himself, face and body, while talking with the client. This use of the webcam is extraordinary because voyeurism, a crucial aspect of more traditional visual technologies, is now overshadowed by its complementary other: exhibitionism. Most webcam images shown on the Internet are utterly boring. The first example on the Internet of the coffeepot in the Trojan room is again exemplary. Showing these images seems to be more important than seeing them. The transformation caused by the webcam is that for the first time people who want to be looked at have a medium at their disposal that enables this.

This change is not only exploited by the sex industry but also seems to cause its demise. More and more, people who watch porn movies prefer to watch amateur porn films shown on websites exclusively devoted to these webcam films. That these films are clumsily made and that they usually do not show particularly attractive bodies appears not to be experienced as negative. The point is not *what* viewers are *seeing* but *that* amateur actors are *showing*. It is the identification with these amateurs showing themselves that makes watching them an erotic experience, an experience that is more exciting than watching voyeuristically attractive bodies performing sexual acts. The boredom caused by so many webcam images shown on the Web, pornographic or not, shows retrospectively also the boring nature of pornographic film as such. It is only in the fulfilment of the dream of pornography in webcam images that we become aware of how dull pornographic images always have been. Excitement is not to be located in what can be seen in these images but in the fact that they are shown.[38]

As already argued, this difference is fundamental because it displaces the nature of our relationship to these images from voyeuristic to exhibitionistic. Something similar seems to be at stake in the visual landscape, discussed by Patricia Spyer in her contribution to this volume (chapter 4). In the wake of murderous conflicts with the Muslim population, the Christian population suddenly fills the public space of Ambon City with images of Christ. These images do not impel the voyeuristic desire to see what can be seen in those images. They are rather motivated by the exhibitionistic desire of the Christian population to become more visible.

The attraction of pornographic and other webcam images is foremost produced by their strong reality effect. Their reality effect is stronger than that produced by film images because, paradoxically, they are unedited and clumsily made. That we are aware of the fact that these images were made, and by whom and where and from which position, makes the reality effect only stronger, for the production of these images stems from real life instead of from professional studios, where the production process can be made invisible.

In pre–new media times, intimacy with people you did not know could be experienced only in art and in literature. In other words, we needed art and literature in order to be intimate with strangers. And when I use the term "intimacy," I am not necessarily referring to sexual intimacy. I am using it to indicate a kind of relationship or contact in which we become aware of the most personal desires and anxieties of other people. By identifying with characters and situations in literature or art, we can share desires or anxieties of people we do not know. But this possibility offered by literature and art is conditioned by its fictionality. The webcam has taken over this possibility so far exclusively realized by art and literature. But the way the webcam enables intimacy with people we do not know differs ontologically from the way art and literature do it. Strong as the reality effects of art and literature can be, they are ultimately framed by their fictionality. The intimacy we can have with strangers via webcams is not with fictional persons. They are real (even if they are role playing); they exist, although we do not know them. This increases the reality effect of the intimate "encounters" with them.[39]

The success of the webcam since its invention in the mid-1990s is in a double sense co-responsible for the explosion of information that defines that decade. First of all, because webcams are now everywhere, built into computers or attached to computers, they distribute filmed information over the World Wide Web. But this quantitative explosion of information also has a qualitative dimension: the kind of information spread by webcams is potentially complete and comprehensive.[40] But comprehensive and complete as the webcam information may be, most of it is irrelevant, boring, and ignored by the viewer. That is why the webcam is exemplary not only for the 1990s explosion of information but also for the implosion of meaning. As I have argued, with the webcam, there are for the first time more people who want to be looked at than people who want to look. It is precisely in this displacement from voyeurism to exhibitionism that the intensities of affective mechanisms are released. This does not imply that voyeurism does not rely on affective mechanisms. But unlike exhibitionism it depends on a fascinating visual object, on its meaning; that is, in the visual relationship of exhibitionism, the visual object is much more irrelevant because it is the act instead of the object of exhibitionism that fascinates. When using now the terms "voyeurism" and "exhibitionism," I am no longer applying them in the more limited, erotic sense, as I do in my example of amateur pornography. Rather, I use them in a more general sense, indicating a distinction between a passive consumerist attitude and a more active attitude of self-positioning. This can be erotic, but not necessarily so.

The viewer of these images is not looking for their meaning but gets access to them by means of identification with the exhibitionistic impulse behind them. Watching them is less a matter of signifying transactions

ERNST VAN ALPHEN

than of an event that one experiences directly or bodily. The affective process of identification leads in the case of webcam images to feelings like excitement or anxiety. This counters the affect of boredom produced on the level of signification. The fact that many people continue to look at webcam images (apart from very practical situations of surveillance) should be understood in terms of the affects they produce and enable, not in the shadows of meaning that they nevertheless offer.

Notes

1. Felix Gonzalez-Torres, "The Gold Field," in *Felix Gonzalez-Torres*, ed. Julie Ault (New York: Steidldangin Publishers, 2006), 150.

2. The expression "shocked to thought" refers to the title of a book on expression and affect in the work of Deleuze and Guattari. Brian Massumi, ed., *A Shock to Thought: Expression after Deleuze and Guattari* (London: Routledge, 2002).

3. Robert Nickas, "Felix Gonzalez-Torres: All the Time in the World," in Ault, *Felix Gonzalez-Torres*, 44.

4. Of course, the dissemination of information as a precondition for meaning production is not just an outdated ambition that is no longer relevant for present concerns. Especially in countries that are in transition to democracy, much funding still goes into increasing the amount of information to its population via media initiatives. This is seen as fostering democracy. But at the same time, the limits of this ambition are also recognized because the production of meaning has not been necessarily the result of the increase of information.

5. Teresa Brennan, *The Transmission of Affect* (Ithaca, NY: Cornell University Press, 2004), 2.

6. Brian Massumi, "Everyone You Want to Be: Introduction to Fear," in *The Politics of Everyday Fear*, ed. Brian Massumi (Minneapolis: University of Minnesota Press, 1993), 3–37.

7. Brennan, *Transmission of Affect*, 15.

8. Also, in the field of economics and political economy, the increasing significance of affect in the 1990s has been argued. The claim is that the process of modernization was over and that the global economy was undergoing a process of postmodernization toward an informational economy. In this informational economy the role of "affective labor" was crucial. It was directly productive of capital but also functioned at the very pinnacle of the hierarchy of laboring forms. In the informational economy, production has become communicative, affective, deinstrumentalized, and elevated to the level of human relations—but at a level of human relations entirely dominated by and internal to capital. Although affective labor is immaterial, it is now directly productive of capital, and it has been generalized through wide sectors of the

234

economy. As a component of immaterial labor, affective labor has achieved a dominant position of the highest value in the contemporary informational economy. See Michael Hardt, "Affective Labor," *Boundary* 2 26, no. 2 (Summer 1999): 89–100.

9. Susan Sontag, "Against Interpretation," *"Against Interpretation" and Other Essays* (London: Eyre and Spottiswoode, 1967), 5.

10. Ibid., 7.

11. Ibid., 15.

12. Ibid., 13.

13. Brian Massumi, "The Autonomy of Affect," in *Deleuze: A Critical Reader*, ed. Paul Patton (Oxford, UK: Blackwell, 1996), 220.

14. Jill Bennett, *Empathic Vision: Affect, Trauma, and Contemporary Art* (Stanford, CA: Stanford University Press, 2005), 4.

15. Gilles Deleuze, *Proust and Signs*, trans. Richard Howard (New York: Braziller, 1964), 161.

16. Deleuze, *Proust*, 161.

17. Bennett, *Empathic Vision*, 8.

18. Ibid., 37.

19. Deleuze, *Proust*, 160.

20. Ibid., 162.

21. Deleuze, quoted in Bennett, *Empathic Vision*, 37.

22. Deleuze, *Proust*, 166.

23. For this discussion I rely on the work of Silvan S. Tomkins, Teresa Brennan's *Transmission of Affect*, and Jill Bennett's *Empathic Vision*.

24. Silvan S. Tomkins and Elaine Virginia Demos, eds., *Exploring Affect: The Selected Writings of Silvan S. Tomkins* (Cambridge, UK: Cambridge University Press, 1995), 355–356.

25. Brennan, *Transmission of Affect*, 3.

26. Ibid., 5.

27. Ibid.

28. Jill Bennett, "A Feeling of Insincerity: Politics, Ventriloquy and the Dialectics of Gesture," in *The Rhetoric of Sincerity*, ed. Ernst van Alphen et al. (Stanford, CA: Stanford University Press, 2009), 195–213.

29. Massumi, "The Autonomy of Affect," 221.

30. Tomkins and Demos, *Exploring Affect*, 317.

31. Brennan, *Transmission*, 9.

32. Ibid., 93.

33. To acknowledge matter and objects as possibly active does not, however, imply an animist worldview. The agency that is assigned to matter and objects as a result of

affective transmissions is ultimately relational. The intensity of affect arises between an object—let's say, an art work—and a viewer. Animism, however, is not relational: it attributes the existence of souls or spiritual beings to natural objects.

34. For a discussion of medium specificity, see Rosalind Krauss, *A Voyage on the North Sea: Art in the Age of the Post-Medium Condition* (London: Thames and Hudson, 1999).

35. Bianca Stigter, "Staren naar een stuk kaas," *NRC Handelsblad*, May 2, 2008, 4.

36. This history of the webcam is based on Stigter, "Staren."

37. The fact that the webcam is used as lifecam is even proven by fictional examples. The example of "lonely girl15," who kept a video diary on YouTube, is telling in this respect. It turned out that lonelygirl15 was an actress who was playing this girl. She was, in fact, fictionalizing the real and authentic. This was possible because dominant use of webcams constitutes the webcam as lifecam.

38. For a critical reading of pornography, see Linda Williams, *Hard Core: Power, Pleasure and the Frenzy of the Visible* (Berkeley: University of California Press, 1989).

39. For an analysis of how webcams affect the relationship between private and public, self and Other, see Jose van Dijck, *Mediated Memories: Personal Cultural Memory in the Digital Age* (Stanford, CA: Stanford University Press, 2007).

40. The information provided by webcams is, of course, not really complete and comprehensive. Usually, it is so only in a temporal sense, when it visually controls a specific space twenty-four hours a day. But the view of a space is usually limited, showing solely what comes inside the frame of the camera's lens. Only when several cameras are used from different perspectives can webcams provide complete and comprehensive information in a spatial sense.

9

Making Equivalence Happen

Commensuration and the Architecture
of Circulation

Brian Larkin

In October 2008 the Abuja-based newspaper the *Daily Trust* published a report:

> The Kannywood star and popular comedian Rabilu Musa,[1] alias Dan Ibro, has been sentenced to four months imprisonment for allegedly operating an illegal film company and shooting a film that exposes nudity and immoral acts in contravention of the Kano State censorship laws. The censorship board argued that the film [*Ibro Aluko*], released without authorization, depicts corrupt acts especially during a singing scene in which a song called Mar-Mar was organized with half-naked women dancing in mesmerising steps that attack the sensibilities of the people of Kano State.[2]

The arrest and imprisonment of Dan Ibro, one of Hausa film's most famous stars, marked a public intensification of the struggle that is occurring over the Kano State Censors Board's attempt to "sanitize" the Hausa-language film industry. The previous February the Censors Board imposed a series of draconian laws intended to ensure that films do not "jeopardize the sensibilities of the public" and to protect Hausa society from foreign influences, particularly, "alien/adulterated Singing and Dancing."[3] Public burnings of books and films have been staged by both government and clerics, and the arrests of actors, directors, and singers have sent the film industry into a state of panic and insecurity. Film production in Kano State,[4] the heartland of Hausa film production, has collapsed, and uncensored videos smuggled in from other states are referred to as *koken* (cocaine).[5]

Precisely because Hausa films are hugely popular in northern Nigeria, they have also provoked widespread anxiety over their influence on the morals of young people and women (the two audiences central to the industry). The legions of people who deeply resent them are matched by the huge audiences and devoted followings that films and stars command, and the result is that film has emerged as a very visible site of public debate, outrage, and affection. Critics' anger revolves around several things—the immorality of filmmakers, the rampant consumerism of the films, their perceived threat to Islamic values—but the prime focus has centered on the accusation that Hausa films are "'spoiling" society by bringing in "alien" cultural values. From the beginning, Hausa filmmakers have used themes and formal styles associated with Hindi cinema (the most popular film genre in the north) as a structuring base for their own work, and there is a clear reliance of one upon the other.[6] Song and dance sequences—such as the one that caused so much trouble for Dan Ibro—are the most visible formal example of this borrowing and have become highly charged. The movement of Indian images to Nigeria and the awkward relations that result tell us about the problematics of cultural circulation and the uncertainty generated by copying and repetition.

MOBILE IMAGES

The transnational movement of images has occupied a simply enormous amount of attention in recent years as scholars try to come to terms with the speed and intensity of image economies brought about by new technologies and central to major economic and social transformations. This work takes diverse trajectories. The important influence of Arjun Appadurai in the 1990s came through his insistence on the motility of a series of phenomena—finance, media, migrants—that he combined to define a shift in what we now term globalization. The importance of media for him was not so much in the technologies themselves but in the transformations of community they enabled. Groups such as diasporas and religious movements were enlarged through economic migration and political displacement, and these collectivities, once separated across space, could now live in intimate connection through the speed and ubiquity of new media. Yet, although Appadurai's interest focused more on community than on technology, to make this argument entailed developing a distinctive theory of media. My interest is in two aspects of this. First, Appadurai insisted on the disjunctive nature of circulation, in which media emerge from a variety of centers and move into arenas wholly dislodged from the communities that create them.[7] Second, this disjuncture, which involves the circulation of media out of the publics for which they were formed and into a range of differing arenas, was not propelled simply by the dissemination of objects from a source of origin but was provoked by the intensities of desire mobilized by the groups consuming those cultural forms.[8] Appadurai builds a theory of circulation in which the objects being exchanged are not quite the same thing everywhere but mutable, reconstituted each time through the particular interests of each public through which they move.

One could argue that intensities of desire are also crucial to Michael Warner's related yet very different conceptualization of circulation in his work *Publics and Counterpublics*.[9] For Warner a public is not a preexisting collectivity that then consumes or uses media; it is constituted through the circulation of those media. Whereas kinship, tribal membership, hereditary status, or nationality are things that one "has" regardless of how one participates in these collectivities, one becomes part of a public only through voluntary participation. Texts—written, visual, aural—contain forms of address to a group of strangers whose linking into a public of like-minded individuals can come about only through the consumption of those texts. What realizes a public for Warner is uptake, individuals electing to take part in the public through the active consumption of media.[10] Warner refers to this sometimes as "mere attention," but it is analytically key to his argument, for without the closing of communicative exchange through uptake, publics cannot exist. What Warner pays less attention to, and what Appadurai opens (but does not fully analyze) as part of his theoretical schema, is that uptake is marked by intensities of desire that range from mere attention to full immersion. For Warner the quality of attention is less important than the form of its coming into being,[11] whereas for Appadurai desire is constitutive to the nature of circulation and the communities that result.

Appadurai's and Warner's interest in circulation, however, stands in contrast to the powerful tradition in media theory that views the mobility of images as a technical effect of the working of technologies. In a luminous line of thinkers from Walter Benjamin to Marshall McLuhan to Paul Virilio, the technical ability of media to store data and transmit it across space and time constitutes their dominating feature. McLuhan famously argued that media were important not because they transmitted messages but because they recalibrated the scale and nature of human association. Benjamin before him argued that the revolutionary power of film lay in its technical ability to copy objects and circulate those copies endlessly—the "dynamite of a tenth of a second."[12] More recently, Samuel Weber captures this argument in his analysis of the specificity of television as a medium. For Weber, *tele*-vision is fundamentally about transmission and thus separation. Although the body is fixed in space and time, tele technologies promise to overcome this limitation. Television "*transports* vision as such and *sets* it immediately *before* the viewer."[13] Television is, first and foremost, a method of transmission that overcomes limitations of space. It comprises emplacement, the practice of "setting before."

In placing focus on the technical ability of media to transport and disseminate, Weber looks back to Benjamin, McLuhan, and media theorists such as Paul Virilio. Each of these thinkers emphasizes transmission over distance—the revolutionary power of electronic media to duplicate and circulate information in ever-greater intensities of speed and movement—and the cognitive consequences that result. When Weber writes, "Far and near are no longer mutually exclusive but rather converge and overlap" in a world saturated with television,[14] one can see the umbilical connection to McLuhan and Virilio, who made the most powerful arguments on the power of media to collapse space and time. For Paul Virilio it is almost as if images, words, and sounds are not mobile, because they are already there, the speed of dissemination is so fast.[15] The emergence of real-time telematics has produced for Virilio an instant present, the obliteration of space by speed, where time is not experienced as duration but exposed.[16] Infinite dissemination and repetition, contagion and viral media, speed and transformation, are the figures whereby the movement of images and information are depicted, and together they compose almost a common sense for the ways we think of the movement of images in a globalized world.

This literature goes far in laying out the material processes and philosophical logic that undergird flows of media, but whereas it can tell us about the presence of image A in culture B, it is less successful at examining other social consequences. What sorts of interpretive communities media create, what types of viewing practices and sociabilities result, and what desires call certain texts to move while leaving others stationary cannot be understood through the means of dissemination alone. Material infrastructures create the channels by which media move, and these are crucial to processes of circulation. But so also are semiotic, interpretive processes through which individuals and societies engage through the movements of cultural forms. The power of global flows lies not merely in movement but also in uptake, in their power as a source of imaginative investment in people's lives and their remediation in other cultural forms. This remediation is a form of deep engagement, an intimacy with the Other that is transgressive and both thrilling and threatening.

Like the authors above, I am interested in the conditions of possibility that undergird practices of circulation. I have written elsewhere that circulation can take place only via material infrastructures that shape and delimit the nature of the media they transmit.[17] For objects to circulate, they must be encoded into a specific media platform—a disk, cassette, or filmstrip—in order for them to travel at all. As they do so, the technical operations of the particular storage medium and the infrastructures that support it regulate how movement will occur: where it will go and through which routes, in which situations it will be seen, and so on. There is no understanding of the movement of ideas without taking into account this materiality, which, as Webb Keane has argued, "is a precondition for their social existence. It is also the condition for their historical mutability, their openness to an unspecified range of future possibilities."[18]

Yet, technicist theories of media, though crucial, often privilege the act of encoding and disseminating, placing focus on the procedures whereby copies are produced and circulated in huge numbers in ever-shortening periods of time. The emphasis on technology also leads to a view of dissemination as a form of serial replication in which the same objects move from one place to appear in another. But repetition, as Deleuze argued, always involves forms of difference, and in the dialectic between sameness and difference, acts of radical translation are made possible.[19] My interest is in this difference, especially in the acts of radical translation—or what I call here the production of commensuration and incommensuration—that are as constitutive to the act of circulation as the technological media that disseminate images and sounds. Appadurai created a conceptual space, through his insistence on the disjunctive nature of cultural flows, for the fact that images and ideas cross borders of cultural difference. I want to push this idea further, to look at how practices of uptake (or rejection) are central to the movement (or not) of images and cultural forms. Circulation, in this analysis, should be seen not simply as the unfettered movement of objects disseminated instantaneously and globally by new digital technologies, but as involving complex acts of identification and translation, dependent on the fragile, uncertain nature of uptake.

We can see this process at work by returning to the example of the movement of Indian films to Nigeria cited above. Here two sorts of circulation are at play. Most obvious is the literal presence of Hindi films, which have moved from India to Nigeria encoded in specific media platforms—film reels, VCDs, videocassettes, DVDs. But a quite different sort of movement occurs when Hindi films are promiscuously appropriated in Hausa music, film, and literature. Images travel as objects (VCDs, DVDs) but also as aesthetic forms (Hindi film melodies in Hausa music, song and dance sequences in Hausa film, plotlines in Hausa literature and film) comprising two modalities, each with its own prerequisites. The migration of Hindi cinema into Hausa film is a more radical act of uptake that indicates the fierce desire of people to consume images, to watch them again and again, to remediate them in other forms. This uptake of Indian cinema requires of its consumers a dwelling within its emotions, sounds, and images, and it is this dwelling within that causes so much anxiety for critics. Indian films remain widely available and hugely popular all over northern Nigeria, but this circulation of the second degree—the ability to intercept, copy, adapt, and create—can no longer take place as it once did. With the banning of song and dance sequences from Hausa film, with the purging of "alien" elements that pollute Hausa culture, the flow has ebbed, movement has been retarded, and circulation has slowed. The act of circulation here is not just an effect of technology but a consequence of cultural debates about the nature—the appropriateness or not—of uptake.

The appropriation of Hindi cinema in Hausa cultural forms involves practices that can variably be described as copying, or as borrowing, or as translation. All of these terms refer to the fact that the remediation of one form in another is transformative of both and stimulates reflexive commentary.[20] In the case of Hausa film, for instance, this metacommentary attempts to parse the nature of a sign vehicle, deciding which elements are "indigenous" and authentically Hausa, which derive from elsewhere, and what the proper values to be accorded these elements are to be. The circulation of cultural forms, particularly across different cultural contexts, often provokes an incessant process of valuing and revaluing the forms being trafficked.

INCOMMENSURATE INDIANS

The mobility of images was central to my earlier work, written in the late 1990s, that examined how Indian films saturate popular culture in Muslim northern Nigeria, creating a landscape of nostalgia and spectacle, longing and morality. That project addressed the disjunctive circulation of cultural forms, and in a series of articles I traced the powerful imaginative investment of Muslim northern Nigerians with the themes, styles, and sensibilities of Hindi cinema.[21] Because of this close connection, I was struck at the time by how often people emphasized that Indian films portrayed a world that was "just like" Hausa society and that Indian society and Hausa society were "just the same." A comment by a young Hausa novelist was typical: "Our tradition...and the Indian tradition are just the same. They have capitalists and we have them. There are smugglers and we also have them. There are evil people and we also have evil people. But the only difference is that they used to follow their lovers singing a song and we don't...do this. So our tradition and that of India is almost the same, the difference is only small."[22] This echoes comments I heard frequently that Indian films are based on "real problems" that confront people about love and family and hierarchy and the injustice of the world. Reversing the assumption prevalent in the West that Hindi cinema is escapist fantasy and Hollywood cinema more "realistic," Hausa viewers stressed that Indian films were about everyday issues of constant relevance. As one person put it to me, "Indian films...base their films on their problems and on the problems of the masses," so the films are "educative" for Hausa viewers.[23] The closeness of values seen in the gender relations depicted in the films, the respected place religion occupied in society, the respect shown to parents and seniors, and the overall importance shown toward the family as an organizing principle of society cumulatively gave Hausa the sense that Indians "have culture." "Culture" here referred to something separable from (and often opposed to) Westernization, and that accounted for the oft quoted argument that Indian films showed a world "just like" Hausa society.

In the early 1990s, however, the rise of a Hausa-language film industry began to challenge this prominent place for Hindi cinema by developing popular melodramas whose narrative themes and formal styles were taken from Hindi cinema.[24] This is most clearly evident in the plot focus on issues of romance and sexual interaction and formally vivified by the use of song and dance sequences. Song sequences, wholly absent from Nollywood films, the English-language Nigerian cinema dominant in the south, have come to define Hausa cinema and are seen by filmmakers, censors, and fans alike as central to their popularity. It is hard to overstate just how controversial this feature of film has been in Kano, where it has breathed new life into the music industry, as well as into filmmaking, and where it is both widely popular and bitterly resented as the clearest example of the corruption of Hausa film.

In the press release accompanying his appointment, Abubakar Rabo Abdulkarim, director-general of the Kano State Censors Board, announced that his job was to "sanitize" and professionalize the film industry and that "religion, culture and public dignity cannot be compromised."[25] He focused on the problem of the "pollution" of culture by foreign elements. In an interview with the scholar Carmen McCain, Rabo elaborated on this problem, arguing that the "definition of culture" should be "in the hands of the original people, not the adulterators." Dance sequences in Hausa films, he argued, gave viewers the impression that such sexual intermixing is part of Hausa society, when really "it is the influence of the Indian film [on]...Hausa society [over] 70 years."[26] This "alien culture" thus had to be banned for the protection of Hausa society and Islamic morality. In articulating this critique Rabo amplified widely held anger toward Hausa filmmakers. Previously, royal authorities together with state officials had publicly burned videos; Islamic organizations held a public conference on the negative effects of films on Hausa youth; and a joint meeting of Qur'anic and Islamic schools held a prayer session against "erring filmmakers." Detractors accuse the filmmakers of simply copying whole plots from Hindi films,[27] and an opinion piece in the *Daily Trust* by Muhammad Mahmud summarizes much of the prevailing sentiment. The root of the problem "between society and the filmmakers," he argues, is that they are "planting negative or poisonous cultures in our midst." He continues, "these copycats mostly reproduce and translate alien films," and "their trash is loathed by all moral adults." "The major point of contention between the society and the filmmakers is the issue of singing and dancing," he argues, continuing, "The society abhors [these practices that]...totally differ from our mores."[28]

The result of reaction against Hausa film is that the place of Indian film in Hausa society has shifted, as it is precisely the "Indianness" of the film that has been identified as the "alien" element responsible for corruption. Indian films are being marked as a stranger presence within Hausa film, identifiably foreign and incommensurable with Hausa culture and Islamic values. Hausa filmmakers are accused of being "copycats" who "mostly reproduce and translate alien films" for Hausa audiences.[29] Against this attack filmmakers have lobbied various arguments. On the one hand, they recognize (and welcome) the influence of Hindi film. In an interview Ali Nuhu, the foremost star (and producer) of Hausa film, told me that he grew up reading the Indian film magazine *Stardust* regularly, that he follows the biographies of the Indian stars Amitabh Bachchan and Shahrukh Khan and models his work on the producer Yash Chopra.[30] As Nuhu is credited with starting the turn toward song and dance sequences and is the star most associated with them, this influence is clear. But Hausa filmmakers argue that nothing is inherently wrong with this and that the reason many plotlines in Hindi and Hausa cinema converge is the similarity of cultures between the two societies. This generates a similarity with Islamic culture rather than a variance to it. The use of song and dance, while clearly not part of Hausa society, is not necessarily un-Islamic. As the late pioneering director Tijani Ibraheem pointed out to me,[31] Egyptian films have song and dance. "Are they not Muslim?" he asked. "Islam goes with modernity," he continued, arguing that censorship laws want to ossify Islam and "send it back to the seventh century." What is at stake in this confrontation is that films are being semiotically decoded so that particular elements can be labeled as Indian and thus unassimilable, over and against those who argue for an equivalence between Indian film and Hausa Islamic values. It is a debate produced by the symbolic uncertainty over circulation and the revaluing of values it sets in motion. This all involves an immense reorientation from my earlier research because the position of Indian films has shifted from being "just like" Hausa culture to being completely unlike and foreign. What brings this about, and what does it tell us about the nature of circulation?

COMMENSURATION AND EQUIVALENCE

For cultural circulation to occur, especially across boundaries of difference, modes of equivalence and commensuration have to be identified that allow an element to move from one tradition to another without being identified as illicit. Representations circulate as public material forms that are semiotically complex, offering elements that range from the similar to the unassimilable. When individuals or societies take up images, particularly in the elaborate resignification of Indian films in Nigeria, commensuration has to be achieved by drawing on those elements within the communicative form that denote equivalence and are imposed on those who might deny its possibility, insisting on incommensuration, distinction, and difference. Those aspects of the sign vehicle do not disappear, however, but remain historically present, available to be reenergized should conditions change.

Mikhail Bakhtin made this point in his discussion of the novel as a system of languages. Literary theorists look at the novel as the unmediated expression of the author—what Bakhtin described as the tendency toward monologism and centralization of meaning—when in fact the novel is an assemblage of differing registers: first-person narration; legal, religious, and bureaucratic languages; and so on. The novelist seeks to subsume these languages into his own stylistic unity but can never quite do so, because each professional or subcultural language has its own discursive autonomy, which resists centralization. The autonomy of discourse means that language is never fully under the control of the speaker or writer. At the heart of Bakhtin's argument is the instability produced by the fact that a text can serve two speakers at the same time, expressing other intentions just as the author seeks to control it and use it for her own.[32] This is what happens when critics recognize the double-voicedness of Hausa films that filmmakers argue are set in northern Nigeria, express Hausa realities, and invoke Hausa values and Islamic norms. But those very same images retain the historical residue of their stylistic origin in Indian films and resist incorporation. They seem to serve another master, encoding different values, other religious systems.

In earlier times in Nigeria, when Indian films and Indian culture were seen as similar to Hausa society, audiences focused in on those cultural aspects of Hindi cinema that emphasized equivalence and connection. Other features were also present but seen at the time as differences that were not socially meaningful.[33] What is fascinating about the current censorship controversy in Nigeria is that it mobilizes a critique that could always have been made about Indian cinema yet one that had no compelling social support and thus no social purchase. As conditions have changed, so too has the interpretive struggle over the relation between India and Nigeria and between Hausa culture and Indian culture.

Circulation is not an automatic reflex but something that must be made to happen. This is necessary at the material level of the creation of infrastructures—the fiber-optic cables, shipping lines, and telephone networks that act as the conduits that make movement possible and are, themselves, subject to their own material realities, which mediate the goods they transport. It also happens on the semiotic level. As texts such as Indian films are remediated in other media, this circulation places them within the practical techniques of everyday life, where they become subject to local contests of value. When northern Nigerians claim that Hindi films show a world "just like" Hausa society, it is because people identify similarities in clothing, in modes of affect, in the public performance of rituals, in the relations between the sexes and within families. Each of these acts of identification is an attempt to define a situation in normative terms that place the stress on continuity; they are often acts that do not mark themselves as such—they appear to happen automatically. But these must be recognized as attempts to define an authoritative narrative stressing equivalence between Indian film and Hausa culture and to impose that narrative over competing definitions.

One theoretical conception of circulation that resonates with this idea can be found in the work of the fin-de-siècle writing of French sociologist Gabriel Tarde and his influence on the very different writings of thinkers such as Gilles Deleuze,[34] Michel Serres,[35] Bruno Latour,[36] and Michel

Callon.[37] In *The Laws of Imitation* Tarde argues that practices of imitation and repetition are at the root of all social relations. Ideas and innovations appear in the world—a new technology, a religious act, a mode of ordering political hierarchy—either by conscious design or by accident. Tarde's interest was in the fact that to become more than an isolated incident, to take on social force, these ideas and inventions must propagate through society and the way this occurs is through imitation. Laws, customs, morals, rites, acts of talking and listening, of commanding and obeying, have their roots in moments of innovation that are then passed along by direct instruction, creating complex chains of innovation and repetition. "In the beginning of societies the art of chipping flint, of domesticating dogs, of making bows, and, later, of leavening bread...etc. must have spread like a contagion since every arrow, every flake, every morsel of bread...served as both copy and model."[38] The moment of repetition, of imitation, is what establishes social relations between individuals, and society itself can be seen as an accumulation of mutually imitative actions.

Imitation is about spreading and propagating. Tarde refers to the "contagions" of imitation, whereby religions spread and political ideas disseminate, and it is, at heart, a theory of circulation. It is no accident that contemporary thinkers influenced by aspects of Tarde—Latour and Callon on networks, Deleuze on repetition, Serres on circuits of exchange and their deviations—hone in on differing aspects of this part of Tarde's work. Imitation generates a flux that binds different elements together across separations of space and even time.[39] My interest in this work is that by placing emphasis on the act of imitation, Tarde dislodges the concept of circulation from its focus on dissemination—emanating from something or someone—and toward the other end of the communicative chain, the forms of desire that motivate someone else to imitate. The act of imitation (which is an act comprising bodily techniques, practice, and intention) is born out of the desire of a person (or society) to imitate, to take on board a new practice or new idea. Without this conscious imitation, ideas and inventions cannot move from one place to another, one person to another. "The *thing* which is invented, the *thing* which is imitated is always an idea or a volition, a judgment or a purpose, which embodies a certain amount of *belief* and *desire*."[40] It may be that as an idea disseminates, it moves from being self-consciously copied and debated to becoming "mechanical habit" but that the origin of repetition rests in the form of desire mobilized by the imitator. This is enormously significant for thinking about ideas of circulation.

Another element aspect of Tarde's work that builds on this is his concept of the logical duel. Ideas and practices spread when an individual "prefers a given innovation to others because he thinks it is more useful or more true than others"[41] and decides to imitate. Each new invention or idea must satisfy someone else's desire in order for it to spread, but as it does, it enters into contest with existing ideas it must join with (the logical union) or supplant (the logical duel). There are several problems with Tarde's concepts in that, despite insisting that imitation can be conscious or unconscious, deliberate or spontaneous, voluntary or involuntary, he tends toward conceiving circulation as defined by intellectualist and rationalist decisions reached by individuals and then spread to influence all society. There is a quasi-Habermasian assumption that the victorious idea is one that emerges from the "public clash of reason" to win victory on rational merits. Tarde also perceives the resolution of logical duels as the replacement of one by another. A new idea can unite with an older one (his concept of the logical union), but Tarde largely sees this as occurring when they mutually reinforce each other. He does not take into account the ways in which individuals and groups hold quite contradictory beliefs in their minds at the same time. A new idea might logically refute an older one but not displace it, so both—say, belief in the miraculous operation of Christ's presence in everyday life, combined with a scientific understanding of nature operating according to finite physical laws—form part of a repertoire of mechanisms of explanation and comprehension that people draw upon depending on the particularities of different situations.

For anthropologists, though, the great value of Tarde is his insistence on the forms of desire and belief that go into the practice of imitating and on the contested social and political effects this can have. This is a starkly different idea of circulation from the one of frictionless, ubiquitous flow that undergirds many ideas of globalization. For circulation to occur, a person has to desire it, and should that desire happen, the idea or object that circulates immediately enters into an overdetermined and contested space. While Tarde does not deal with this, it is precisely this contest and struggle, so Bakhtinian in its lineaments, that demands a practice of establishing equivalence in order that circulation can effectively occur. "Every act of imitation is preceded by hesitation on the part of the individual [or society]," Tarde writes, "for every discovery or invention that seeks to spread abroad always finds some obstacle to overcome."[42] While this contest is in place as to which idea is superior, of whether it is truly necessary to imitate something else, there is a hesitation, and "as long as a man hesitates... he refrains from imitation." Flow cannot occur, movement stalls, because circulation for Tarde is not a technical process but a social one. "When he finally imitates it means he has come to a decision."[43]

One can see Tarde's ideas play out in Michel Callon's and Bruno Latour's work on translation and networks, which pushes Tarde further. In *The Pasteurization of France*, for instance, Latour traces how the experimental discovery of microbes' role as a vector in transmitting disease gives rise to new practices of hygiene in French society. He then further charts how these ideas about germs, hygiene, and health become materialized in the routinized practice of serving French schoolchildren pasteurized milk every day at lunch. Latour's interest is in how an idea (about germs, about the effect of heat on germs) formed in a laboratory spreads across society, infiltrating radically different realms such as the social activism of the hygienist movement and the bureaucratic procedures of the French education system. In Tardean terms it is the intensity of desire of hygienists who take up Pasteur's germ theory and begin the "contagion of imitation" through which it spreads through society. But their ideas must in turn be taken up by school administrators and then accepted by parents as the idea extends further and further through society. The link between these radically different, discursive domains, Latour argues, must not be taken for granted as the naturally unfolding outcome of a new piece of knowledge but seen as something that has to be created. This is the work of "translators," people who define what is socially relevant in a situation, who interpret phenomena and impose links between various elements while closing off other ones. They are the actors who impose commensuration over forms of difference. "An idea or a practice cannot move from A to B solely by the force that A gives it," Latour tells us. "B must seize it and *move* it.... An idea, even an idea of genius never moves by its own accord. It requires a force to fetch it, seize upon it for its own motives, move it and often transform it."[44] For Latour and Callon, translation is the act of making connections where none existed between radically differing domains. Commensuration is revealed to be a process of classifying, of defining the context for events, and of asserting the links between them. It is semiotic work.

CONCLUSION

One can see this production of equivalence in a vignette about a trip I made to the cinema in Kano in the mid-1990s. I went with a friend who was a huge Indian film fan. I cannot now remember the name of the film, but it follows the fortunes of a man who erroneously believes that his wife is cheating on him. Wracked by grief and anger, he begins to drink heavily, abusing her verbally and acting out his despair in bold and violent fashion. His virtuous wife, distraught at her husband's erratic behavior, eventually comes to a climatic decision. Visibly upset, she bursts from her family home, and as she does so, the film jumps to a shot of a cow pulling itself from its tether. A series of parallel edits ensues, cutting between the wife running, the cow running, and an image of the well to which both are heading. Just as the wife arrives at the well and tries to throw herself down, the cow runs in front of her, frustrating her actions and saving her life. "You see!" my friend immediately said, turning to me, "They worship cows! Ha!"

My friend's response is indicative of the continual hermeneutics that members of a society engage in as they assess, rank, and judge the import of social phenomena. His instantaneous reaction to the scene draws upon the deep tradition in Islam that emphasizes a divide between people of the book and those of polytheistic religions. That divide is central to the history and theology of Islam. It makes permissible modes of accommodation between Islam, Christianity, and Judaism while insisting on a sharp and irreconcilable alterity between Islam and "paganism." My friend assimilated the active agency of the cow to the stereotype, common in Nigeria, that Indians "worship cows." As he made this connection, he assembled an interpretive grid for the scene he was watching, drawing on Islamic tradition and common (if not accurate) knowledge in which there was no possible connection between him and Indian society. At the same time, he conjured a social persona for me that bypassed alterities of race, religion, and nationality to zero in on a key equivalence. "You see!" he said, using a phatic phrase to establish the commonality between us, "They worship cows!" At that moment and unlike nearly every other moment of my research, I was much more like him than any (Hindu) Indian, and in that moment Hindi films were deeply and fundamentally different. But after the scene passed, things reverted to how they had been, and the measuring of commensuration and incommensuration shifted. Indian films became just like Hausa society once more. I became marked by difference as much as similarity.

The ephemeral nature of this example illustrates of how everyday life is made up of instances in which practices of equivalence and distinction are achieved through pragmatic interactions. Specific elements within a communicative form are assimilated to a range of possible discursive traditions that can be mobilized to make sense of what those elements mean. This can be situational and instantaneous, as in the example here, equivalence dying away almost as soon as it has been achieved, or they can be symbolically marked and attempts to change their meaning more fraught with tension and difficulty, as in the case of the public conflict over censoring Hausa film. Indian films always have contained elements that are irreconcilable with Islamic values. But up until the late 1990s in Nigeria, these represented a difference that did not make a difference. When my friend commented on the alterity of "cow-worshipping" Indians, he did so at a time when powerful forces in society were not working hard to fix the relations between Indian cinema and Nigeria as incommensurable. The encoding of formal elements from Hindi cinema into Hausa film and the massive growth in popularity of that industry began to change that balance. In the 1980s and 1990s Sufi clerics would sponsor bandiri musicians—singers who take Hindi films tunes and sing praises to the Prophet Muhammed—during Maulud celebrations. Now, this remediation has become more conflicted and the desire to stop it heightened. The same films, the same songs, contain elements that allow for powerful emotive forms of identification and other elements that are less assimilable, that maintain their own styles, history, and syntactic makeup and refuse the production of equivalence.

Ideas of circulation that are premised on dissemination often presume that images or ideas that circulate are essentially repetitions of the same thing as it passes from place to place. But as Deleuze reminds us,[45] repetition is inherently about difference and the singularity of each repetition (what he terms the "repeating particular"). Deleuze moves toward contemplating the fact that if we conceive of circulation as a form of repetition, then we are forced to consider the eventness of reappearance rather than assume its technological inevitability. This echoes Tarde's focus on practices of imitation as the mechanisms that facilitate circulation. And these practices themselves are generated by the intensity of desire to take hold of something by way of its copy.

Images that move are polyvocal. Refusing what Bakhtin contemptuously refers to as "the virginal fullness of the object itself,"[46] we need to see these images as dynamic assemblages. To understand which elements of that sign vehicle will be emphasized means focusing on the social actors promoting commensurability (or its obverse), the sets of criteria they draw on to make their claims legitimate, and their hermeneutic parsing of cultural forms, which creates an interpretive grid that has authority. This cannot be decided from within the form itself but through the way the form is made to mean socially—the tacking between the historical nature of the sign vehicle, which sets limits on the sorts of historical claims that can be made, and the skillful work of those interpreting it.[47] Commensuration is a process of establishing classifications, categorizing and making sense of the world.

The language of flows that marks many analyses of cultural globalization tends to privilege the seamless, frictionless movement of images in the world. Provoked by the rise of new technologies of reproduction, what seems most compelling is the capacity of media to reproduce and disseminate images. Digital technologies in particular seem to generate infinite recursion, perfect copies of the original, in unlimited numbers, which spread like wildfire through the viral architecture of the Internet and which, in both the academic and the popular worlds, seem to highlight the borderless, unimpeded, free-flowing nature of global images. Theories of globalization in this tradition emphasize the duplication and dissemination of media rather than the intensities of desire that motivate movement in the first place and the social work that circulation involves. In this chapter I am interested in how commensuration creates the conditions of possibility for the circulation of images. When images circulate across cultural difference, they enter into an inchoate, epistemologically unstable field that calls into being the process of defining equivalence to cope with this instability. For the uptake of images by individuals and communities to occur, equivalence has to be generated. Michael Warner is correct to argue that the uptake of circulating texts is the mechanism by which publics are brought into being. But he is incorrect to suggest that the quality of uptake is not relevant to the style and nature of the public at hand, for it is precisely the intensity of this engagement that differentiates the noncontentious circulation of Hindi cinema from its highly contentious remediation in Hausa film. It is this contest over commensuration that we see at work in the redefinition of Indian films, from revealing a world "just like" Hausa society to showing one that is alien and unassimilable.

Notes

1. "Kannywood" is the term sometimes used to refer to the Hausa-language film industry in the north of Nigeria. It emerged at the same time as the term "Nollywood" used to refer to Nigerian (or English-language) films made in the south of Nigeria.

2. *Daily Trust*, posted to the Internet on October 7, 2008, http://dailytrust.com .ng/ (accessed June 1, 2009).

3. All production companies are now required to register with the Censors Board and be issued with a license; actors, directors, and musicians are also licensed; and no shooting can begin until the script has been submitted and approved in advance of production. See the press releases issued by the Kano State Censors Board, one version of which can be found at http://kanocensorsboard.com (accessed July 7, 2009). See also Carmen McCain, Nazir Hausawa, and Ahmad Alkanaway, "On the Current Censorship Crisis in Kano," http://carmenmccain.wordpress.com/2009/01/13/on-the -current-censorship-crisis-in-kano-nigeria/ (accessed May 28, 2009).

4. Nigeria is a federation. Although filmmaking is banned in Kano State, it

remains legal in the states surrounding Kano, all of which, like Kano, are regulated by Islamic law. Kano, however, is the biggest and most populous state and the dominant center of the film industry. There the issue of filmmaking took on a symbolic importance unmatched elsewhere.

5. Amina Koki Gizo, "Writers, Film-Makers Defy Censors," *Interpress Service* (Nigeria), September 12, 2009.

6. See Brian Larkin, "Itineraries of Indian Cinema: African Videos, Bollywood and Global Media," in *Multiculturalism, Transnationalism and Film*, ed. Ella Shohat and Robert Stam (New Brunswick, NJ: Rutgers University Press, 2003), 170–192. Abdalla Uba Adamu has provided the most detailed analysis of the relation between Hindi cinema and Hausa film. He coined the Hausa term "Bollywoodanci" to describe the language of Hausa cinema and its dependence (in plot, song sequence, or choreography) on mainstream Hindi film. The suffix *anci* in Hausa commonly refers to a language—such as "Turanci" for English, "Farasanci" for French, and so on. Adamu provides a list of Hausa films that draw heavily from Hindi film and the Indian original in *Transglobal Media Flows and African Popular Culture: Revolution and Reaction in Muslim Hausa Popular Culture* (Kano, Nigeria: Visually Ethnographic Productions, 2007); and in "Currying Favour: Eastern Media Influences and the Hausa Video Film," *Film International* 28 (2007): 76–89. In a fascinating discussion he breaks down the degrees of copying engaged in by the industry. Film producers use the term *wankiya* (from "to wash") for washing away someone's ideas and substituting them with your own. This refers to a literal scene-by-scene copy of an Indian original. *Dauraya* (clean up) refers to remembered scenes from previously watched films that are incorporated into a Hausa storyline (see Adamu, "Currying," 84). The majority of films do not explicitly copy in this way but draw heavily on the genres and idioms of popular Hindi *masala* films.

7. "The United States is no longer the puppeteer of a world system of images but is only one node of a complex transnational construction of imaginary landscapes." Arjun Appadurai, *Modernity at Large: Cultural Dimensions of Globalization* (Minneapolis: University of Minnesota Press, 1996), 31.

8. Here Appadurai reveals his reliance on Georg Simmel. Simmel's famous critique of Marx argued that value derives not from relations of production or use value but through the practice of exchange itself; objects move in and out of communities and are subject to differing intensities of desire as they do so. Value, for Simmel, came from this intensity of desire and the ability of objects to resist that intensity (through scarcity) rather than from classic Marxist theories of production.

9. Michael Warner, *Publics and Counterpublics* (New York: Zone Books, 2005).

10. "Most social classes and groups are understood to encompass their members all the time, no matter what. A nation, for example, includes its members whether

they are awake or asleep, sober or drunk, sane or deranged, alert or comatose. Publics are different. Because a public exists only by virtue of address, it must predicate some degree of attention, however notional, from its members." Warner, *Publics*, 87.

11. "The cognitive quality of...attention is less important than the mere fact of active uptake." Warner, *Publics*, 87.

12. Walter Benjamin, "The Work of Art in the Age of Mechanical Reproduction," *Illuminations: Essays by Walter Benjamin*, ed. Hannah Arendt, trans. Harry Zohn (New York: Schocken Books, 1968), 236; Marshall McLuhan, *Understanding Media: The Extensions of Man*, critical ed. (1964; Corte Madera, CA: Gingko Books, 1994).

13. Samuel Weber, "Television: Set and Screen," in *Mass Mediauras: Form, Technics, Media*, ed. Samuel Weber (Stanford, CA: Stanford University Press, 1996), 116.

14. Weber, "Television," 125.

15. Paul Virilio, *Speed and Politics: An Essay in Dromology*, trans. Mark Polizotti (New York: Semiotext(e), 1986); Paul Virilio, *Open Sky*, trans. Julie Rose (New York: Verso, 1997).

16. Virilio, *Open Sky*, 5: Telecommunications are "eliminating all duration and extension of time in the transmission of messages." As a consequence speed is now absolute and duration no longer available. Space is obliterated. "Time no longer passes, it is exposed." The human subject under these conditions becomes a "body-terminal" receiving messages deranging the integrity of our emplacement in space and time and giving us the illusion that the whole world is telepresent.

17. Brian Larkin, *Signal and Noise: Media, Infrastructure and Urban Culture in Nigeria* (Durham, NC: Duke University Press, 2008).

18. Webb Keane, *Christian Moderns. Freedom and Fetish in the Mission Encounter* (Berkeley: University of California Press, 2007), 21–22.

19. Gilles Deleuze, *Difference and Repetition*, trans. Paul Patton (London: Continuum Press, 2004).

20. For the classic statement on remediation, see Jay David Bolter and Richard Grusin, *Remediation: Understanding New Media* (Cambridge, MA: MIT Press, 2000).

21. Brian Larkin, "Indian Films, Nigerian Lovers: Media and the Creation of Parallel Modernities," *Africa* 67, no. 3 (1997): 406–440; Larkin, "Itineraries of Indian Cinema," 170–192; Brian Larkin, "Bandiri Music, Globalization and Urban Experience in Nigeria," *Social Text* 22, no. 4 (2004): 91–112.

22. Cited in Larkin, *Signal*, 165.

23. Cited in Larkin, "Bandiri Music," 101.

24. See Adamu, *Transglobal Media Flows* and "Currying"; Abdalla Uba Adamu, Yusuf M. Adamu, and Umar Faruk Jibril, *Hausa Home Videos: Technology, Economy, Society* (Kano, Nigeria: Center of Hausa Cultural Studies, 2004); Jonathan Haynes, *Nigerian Video Films* (Athens: Ohio University Center for International Studies, 2000); Larkin, *Signal.*

25. Backed by both secular government and religious elites, Malam Rabo, as he is known, formerly head of the Hisbah, the religious police enforcing Islamic law, has embarked on an intense publicity campaign using the radio and other media to berate the film industry for spoiling Hausa youth. He has personally attacked filmmakers, accusing them of licentiousness and homosexuality, warning parents against letting their children join the industry, even recommending they forbid their children from marrying anyone involved in the film industry. As with many things in Nigeria, the reasons for this censorship are complex. While drawing on the norms of Islamic law, Malam Rabo also justifies his actions within a secular language inherited from the fight against cultural imperialism and the need to protect Nigerian values from foreign cultural influences. Some allege that the arrests are politically motivated, pointing out that many of the most high-profile cases involve those seen to have been critical of the Kano state governor. Others have seen it as a way for the governor to adopt a populist issue for his own ends. But even if these accusations are true, it does not explain the ability of the Kano government to tap into widely held anger toward filmmakers. The details of this unfolding campaign, including interviews with filmmakers and musicians who have been attacked, along with an extensive interview with Rabo himself, can be found on the remarkable blog *A Tunaina*, run by the scholar Carmen McCain (http://carmenmccain .wordpress.com/ [accessed June 2010]). As well as her own analysis, McCain includes press releases by the Censors Board and those by various filmmakers' organizations, providing what is an indispensable archive on these matters. Important coverage can also be found (in English and Hausa) on the blog *Bahaushe Mai Ban Haushi* by the respected journalist Ibrahim Sheme (http://ibrahim-sheme.blogspot.com/).

26. http://carmenmccain.wordpress.com/2009/02/13/interview-with-alhaji -abubakar-rabo-abdulkarim-director-general-of-the-kano-state-censorship-board/ (accessed February 13, 2009).

27. Larkin, "Indian Films, Nigerian Lovers"; Adamu, *Transglobal Media Flows*; Adamu, "Currying."

28. *Daily Trust*, April 29, 2008.

29. Ibid.

30. Interview of Ali Nuhu by author, Kano City, January 19, 2002.

31. Interview of Tijani Ibraheem by author, January 21, 2002.

32. Mikhail Bakhtin, *The Dialogic Imagination* (Austin: University of Texas Press, 1981).

33. As noted in my earlier article (Larkin, "Indian Films"), a wariness of Indian films had developed along with the rise of Hausa-language market literature, but this was a minority position rather than the huge public controversy it now is and attitudes toward Indian film and Indian society were markedly positive.

34. Deleuze, *Difference and Repetition*.

35. Michel Serres, *The Parasite*, trans. Lawrence R. Schehr (Baltimore, MD: Johns Hopkins University Press, 1982).

36. Bruno Latour, *The Pasteurization of France*, trans. Alan Sheridan and John Law (Cambridge, MA: Harvard University Press, 1988); Bruno Latour, *We Have Never Been Modern*, trans. Catherine Porter (Cambridge, MA: Harvard University Press, 1993); Bruno Latour, *Reassembling the Social: An Introduction to Actor-Network Theory* (Oxford, UK: Oxford University Press, 2007).

37. Michel Callon, "Society in the Making: The Study of Technology as a Tool for Sociological Analysis," in *The Social Construction of Technological Systems: New Directions in the Sociology and History of Technology*, ed. Wiebe E. Bijker, Thomas P. Hughes, and Trevor J. Pinch (Cambridge MA: MIT Press, 2008), 83–103.

38. Gabriel Tarde, *The Laws of Imitation*, trans. Elsie Clews Parsons (New York: Henry Holt and Co., 1903), 17.

39. Tarde offers the example of a contemporary designer influenced by the work of a Pompeian fresco, thus establishing an imitative relation even though separated by thousands of years.

40. Tarde, *Laws*, 145.

41. Ibid., 141.

42. Ibid., 165.

43. Ibid.

44. Latour, *Pasteurization*, 15–16.

45. Deleuze, *Difference and Repetition*.

46. Bakhtin, *Dialogic Imagination*, 278.

47. For more work on commensuration, see Wendy Nelson Espeland and Mitchell L. Stevens, "Commensuration as a Social Process," *Annual Review of Sociology* 24 (1998): 313–343; Elizabeth A. Povinelli, "Radical Worlds: The Anthropology of Incommensurability and Inconceivability," *Annual Review of Anthropology* 30 (2001): 319–334. For an ethnographically rich account of this process, see Fred Myers's analysis of the movement of Aboriginal art from a ritual form located primarily in the western desert of Australia through circuits of urban political activists, gallery owners, and the international art market. Although not using Latour's conception of "translation," this provides a powerful example of this process at work. Fred R. Myers, *Painting Culture: The Making of an Aboriginal High Art* (Durham, NC: Duke University Press, 2002).

10

Transparency and Apparition

Media Ghosts of Post–New Order Indonesia

Mary Margaret Steedly

> In the genres of mass-imaginary transitivism, we might say, a public is
> thinking about itself and its media. This is true even in the most vulgar
> of the discourses of mass publicity.
>
> —*Michael Warner, "The Mass Public and the Mass Subject"*

On January 28, 2008, Indonesia's former president Suharto died at the
age of eighty-six. His had been an extraordinarily long and eventful life,
marked by what his supporters liked to depict either as a series of fortunate
coincidences or as signs of supernatural blessing. He was a low-level general
in the army when the assassination of six of his superior officers, allegedly
in a Communist Party conspiracy, opened the way to power in 1965. He
bludgeoned his way into the presidency with a retaliatory bloodbath, then
arrested and forced the resignation of the nation's first president, Sukarno.
The self-named "smiling general" Suharto held power for more than thirty
years through military force, rigid control of information, and the demoni-
zation of any form of popular dissent. During that time he amassed enormous wealth for himself and his family, siphoning off billions of dollars
in state funds, according to the anticorruption organization Transparency
International—in addition to the bribes, under-the-table payoffs, and protection money that were the price of doing business in Indonesia under his
"New Order" regime.[1] He resigned from office in 1998 in the aftermath of
deadly riots in Jakarta and other cities. After that, his health reportedly
declined. A series of small strokes left him unable to appear in court to
answer charges of corruption that had been brought against him by the
state, and he was rarely seen outside the family compound in Jakarta.

Suharto was admitted to Pertamina Hospital in Jakarta on January 4, 2008, with anemia and a low heart rate. He developed pneumonia and sepsis and was placed on a ventilator and dialysis machine. His heart stopped briefly, and his doctors thought that death was imminent. He rallied, however, and made an "amazing recovery" before taking another turn for the worse. In the last weeks of his life, Suharto suffered multiple catastrophic organ failures, and his impending death and miraculous recovery were reported in the press repeatedly. After several such unexpected rallies following predictions of his death, doctors said that they were "amazed and baffled" by his stubborn clinging to life.[2] Rumors began to circulate that his life was being extended not by medical but rather by occult means.

Suharto's devotion to Javanese mysticism was common knowledge. He visited numerous shrines and sacred sites; collected magical artifacts, charms, and talismans; and engaged in a range of meditative practices. But these sources of power and protection were now preventing his natural passage from this life. According to some accounts, his death was forestalled by invulnerability spells or by magical implants that had gone bad. In an article in the *Jakarta Post*—ironically published on the day of Suharto's death—the celebrity "paranormal" and member of parliament Permadi had this to say: "There are many strange objects in his body. They are making it difficult for Suharto to die.... The doctors know about this. They can see them in the X-rays. Inside the body of Suharto there are many strange objects."[3] Psychics appeared on television to predict the time of his death, with estimates ranging from several months to four years. Political leaders came to his bedside to offer forgiveness, which, according to Javanese belief, would aid his soul's passage to death. According to Permadi, Suharto's soul could not be released until he and his six children had been forgiven by the victims of his regime: "But [his children] are too arrogant to ask for an apology [*sic*] and say they have done nothing wrong."[4] In these circumstances, a cell phone text message began to circulate, purportedly from Suharto's daughter, who was familiarly known as Mbak Tutut:

> PERMOHONAN IBU SITI HARDIANTI RUKMANA (MBAK TUTUT).
> ATAS NAMA SEMUA ANAK CUCU MANTAN PRESIDEN SUHARTO,
> MOHON PENGAMPUNAN BLIAU PD MASA2 YG LALU. SEBARKAN
> KE 10 TMN DAN PULSA ANDA BERTMBH 500.000 SCR OTOMATIS.
> SUDAH TERBUKTI!! CEPAT, HANYA BERLAKU HR INI (S/D PKL
> 23) HARAP HUBUNGI HARAP HUBUNGI HARAP HUBUNGI.

(Request from Mrs. Siti Hardianti Rukmana [Mbak Tutut]. In

FIGURE 10.1

The smiling general: "Suharto's mystical crimes," Misteri *225 (January 1999).*

the name of all the children and grandchildren of former president Suharto, beg pardon for him for times past. Send [this message] to 10 frnds [*sic*] and 500,000 units wl b [*sic*] added automatically [to your cell phone account]. Already proved!! Hurry, [this offer is] only good today (until 11 pm) Please contact Please contact Please contact).[5]

I assumed that this was a joke, though what made it seem so funny to me was that you could not really be sure. I liked the way it brought together media technology, supernatural belief, and popular political culture in a moment of (literal) graveyard humor. Playing on the popularity of the cell phone and text-messaging and the arrogance of the idea that forgiveness for such heinous crimes could be bought so cheaply (about US$50 per person), the joke's humor was located at the intersection of spiritual and electronic forms of mediation, at the crossroads of mystical and political power. It also pointed to the ubiquity of supernatural belief as interpretive practice in contemporary Indonesia.

This chapter is a reflection on some aspects of the conjuncture of popular supernaturalism and mass media in post–New Order Indonesia. Mass media depictions of ghosts, monsters, magicians, and mummies, which had been frowned on and heavily regulated during much of the Suharto era, when they were regarded as antipathetic to national goals of development and social discipline, have returned to public view, with a vengeance, over the past decade. These spectral images move through a variety of popular media forms, from the anonymous ephemerality of text-messaging to the highly capitalized celebrity film vehicle. In 2003 both *Tempo* and *Gatra* magazines—the Indonesian equivalents of *Time* and *Newsweek*—offered cover stories on the dramatic rise in popularity of supernatural entertainment genres. At the beginning of that year, well before interest in such "demonic programming" (*tayangan setan*) peaked, there were at least eleven prime-time television shows produced and shown in Indonesia with supernatural themes and as many as sixteen national magazines primarily devoted to *jurnalisme klenik* (superstition journalism),[6] and contemporary youth-oriented horror movies were being credited with reviving the moribund Indonesian film industry.

To be sure, these new mystical entertainment forms were not conjured out of thin air. They partook of a range of widely held supernatural beliefs, practices, and techniques, some of them of considerable depth and durability, others more novel and transient, and they imitated or incorporated a range of communicative possibilities and representational modes, from séances and curing rites to oracular poetry and urban legends. They were also influenced by an array of media sources inside and outside Indonesia, including local exploitation films of B-grade horror from the 1970s and 1980s; sensationalist newspaper reporting of witchcraft panics and uncanny objects; popular American movies and television programs like *The Sixth Sense* and *The X-Files*, respectively; Hong Kong martial arts films; and ghost movies from Japan, Thailand, and Korea.

What made the new supernatural genres different from these predecessors was their persistent combination of three key elements: locality, publicity, and visuality. First, they were set in a familiar, recognizable social milieu, one that shared significant features with that of their target audience(s); spectators found themselves addressed by these entertainments in direct and powerful ways. Second, however demographically circumscribed the primary audience of young urban moviegoers may have been, the actual audience was virtually unlimited, given the prevalence of secondary formats (legal and pirated VCDs), informal networks of circulation and distribution (borrowing, resale, reformatting, and a range of Web viewing sites, not to mention ordinary conversational retelling), and circuits of international spectatorship shaped by assumptions about Indonesian filmmakers' "natural" affinity for supernatural and horror-themed entertainment forms.[7] They were readily available, neither esoteric nor restricted, and they claimed to reveal a secret zone of formerly inaccessible or privileged knowledge. Taken together, they generated a multimediated discursive field, a "concatenation of texts through time" that echoed, criticized, plagiarized, and supported one another. In brief, they generated a public—a self-organized discursive community based on communicative openness and stranger-sociality and arrayed around a range of mutually referential and highly reiterative technocultural forms. Finally, this public was shaped by a process of "poetic world-making" to which the problematic visual status of the occult media image was crucial both technically and thematically.[8]

Central to this media aesthetic are notions of concealment, visualization, and revelation, represented in the anecdote of Suharto's deferred death by the X-ray "confirmation" of the presence of "many strange objects" in the ex-president's body. Also, my chapter's title juxtaposes two of the period's discursive keywords, that is, *transparansi* (transparency) in the domain of politics and *penampakan* (apparition) in the realm of the supernatural.[9] What links these two terms is the wish expressed in each for something obscure or unseen to *make an appearance*. This aesthetic of appearance is less concerned with the form or pictorial content of what appears than with anticipation for the moment of (potential) revelation or recognition. All of the new media forms are structured by this aesthetic of appearance, but it is most explicitly addressed in horror films, in which the problem of visualization or penampakan is central not only to the cinematic form but also to the narrative itself.

This chapter has three parts. First, I raise the question of belief as the foundation for any analysis of supernatural image-production. Second, I explore the way that various technologies of image production and dissemination, in conjunction with a particular turn in the political economy of entertainment, fed and reinforced the "occult public sphere" of Indonesian national culture in the post–New Order period.[10] In the final part of the chapter, I turn to films to illustrate and examine the poetic world-making of penampakan in which these new supernatural entertainment forms are engaged. Taken together, I argue, transparency and apparition constitute two variations within a particular post–New Order regime of visuality, in which the compulsion to see and be seen is continually brought to crisis by the terror of seeing and being seen.

"BELIEVE IT OR NOT..."

Western academic studies of supernatural entertainment forms—ghost stories, magical performances, and the like—frequently start from the presumption of disbelief, as if the entertainment value of the supernatural increases in inverse proportion to the decline of its cult value. This is not the case in Indonesia, where the cult and entertainment values of popular supernaturalism coincide and where both persist in fraught relation to official religion(s) and secular rationality. The new media forms of supernatural entertainment tap into a deep vein of interest in, and talk about, magical practices, spirit beliefs, ghost stories, urban legends, and the like. "In this country, everything is mystical," says one character in Joko Anwar's 2007 fantasy-noir film *Kala*, set in an unnamed police state very like late New Order Indonesia. Joko's film, in which a hardboiled police investigation takes an unexpected turn into prophetic time and magical realism, is as much an homage to earlier genres of supernatural entertainment—in particular, comic books and exploitation films—as it is a political thriller, but it makes an important point nevertheless. For most Indonesians, the problem of spirits is not an ontological one but rather a moral one: not whether spirits exist, but what to do with them. People see them in shadows, blame them in adversity, avoid them if possible, and use them in desperation. Supernatural belief is a transitive concept in Indonesia: it is not a matter of whether one believes *in* spirits but rather whether one *believes* (trusts) them.

When I first went to Indonesia in the early 1980s, I was struck by the extent to which middle-class urban Indonesians persisted in finding supernatural presences in their daily surroundings. My colleagues, neighbors, and friends in the Sumatran city of Medan seemed embedded in a spirit-saturated cityscape inhabited by bald-headed ghosts and invisible thieves, sorcerers and sacred shrines, demonic protectors, spirits of those who

FIGURE 10.2

Alfuah, the kuntilanak *(evil female spirit) of the Tanah Abang train station, in "Lairs of the Kuntilanak in Central Jakarta,"* Kismis *8 (July 2003).*

died badly, and leprechaun-like givers of unexpected windfalls. Success at any endeavor generally involved some kind of payoff to influential others, whether bureaucrats, policemen, or spirits, and luck, good or bad, was quickly and commonly read as the result of supernatural intervention. There was an intense and lively traffic in the services of a range of supernatural and alternative practitioners. Urban spirit mediums and curers were frequently called upon to magically enhance a market stall's popularity, improve a college student's test scores, enact or counteract love magic, cure an intractable illness, "clean" a haunted hotel, or correct any of the myriad uncertainties and misfortunes that ran through the everyday life of city dwellers. As Jean and John Comaroff point out for postcolonial South Africa, this is not a case of the persistence of tradition but rather of "retooling culturally familiar technologies as new means for new ends." Like witchcraft, the realm of the supernatural is "expansive and protean," readily adaptable to new concerns and circumstances.[11]

The New Order period, as journalist Dewi Anggraeni put it recently, was characterized by a general "mindset...where behind any façade lurked a bigger, usually quite opaque picture that was the source of hushed, yet lively speculation."[12] State violence was both ubiquitous and obscure, its presence marked by unspoken threat and careful reminders of its past exercise. Secrecy was the source of unending rumors about corruption and the supernatural, in which each revelation led only to deeper, more labyrinthine mysteries. Conspiracy and magic, often intertwined, were the usual explanations for any unexpected outcome. Indonesians voraciously invented and consumed stories of scandal and conspiracy that touched the government, the military, and above all the Suharto circle. As the story of the "many magic objects" secreted in the body of the ex-president suggests, the supernatural was not just another symbolic register for talking about these things; it was an integral part of them.

The end of the New Order had the effect of dispersing ("decentralizing") violence and its images widely. Violence could no longer be understood primarily in relation to the state, which was imagined either as a safeguard against it or as its ultimate source. It could emerge anywhere, unpredictably, in the everyday world, without reason, without warning, and seemingly without recourse. Beyond the visible events of disaster spectatorship,[13] beyond the looming but less visualizable crises of environmental degradation, toxic financial speculation, and the corruption of everything from parking to political office, middle-class city-dwellers encountered—or at least imagined—an array of random dangers: carjackers and criminal taxi drivers, unregulated traffic, Islamic vigilantes, scam artists, pickpockets and drug dealers, youth gangs for hire, toxic haze, tainted food, police brutality, "sin tourism," STDs, and sexual harassment. To be sure, none of the anxieties of post–New Order Indonesia are exactly new, but without a powerful center, both violence and its secrets seem to have taken particularly virulent, unstable forms.

FROM TRANSPARANSI TO APPARITION

It is in this murky and violent context that the two keywords of my title come to the fore. The first, *transparansi*, was adopted by the Indonesian student movement for political reform (Reformasi) that emerged around the time of the Asian financial crisis and was central to the demand for regime change. At heart, "transparency" is an aspiration to the rational ordering of things, a response to corruption, terror, and the mystifying opacity of public events, and one can certainly see why such a dream would appeal to young Indonesians at the turn of the twenty-first century.

Although the term's most immediate referent was the International Monetary Fund's language of fiscal accountability, its conceptual framework derived from a broader international discourse of democratization and anticorruption, exemplified by the nongovernmental organization Transparency International. Within the Reformasi movement, it broadened to incorporate demands for democratization and an end to corruption. By extension it represented a call for universal participation in the institutions of government, an equitable allocation of public and natural resources, an end to censorship, and freedom of access to information by the mass media and the public. Transparansi was not a one-way process: it meant not only being able to "see through" the processes of power but also being able to "see out" of them. Thus, another aspect of transparency was the effort to make visible the experiences of people whose lives had been obscured and distorted by the politics of national development and ethnic favoritism: political outcasts, the poor, religious minorities, marginal social and ethnic communities, women and children. The wish to be recognized by, as much as to see into, the machineries of power was at the heart of what Karen Strassler has called the "reformasi dream of transparency."[14]

In this spirit of transparansi, Indonesia's visual public culture flourished in the decade following Suharto's fall in ways that would have been unimaginable during the repressive years of the New Order. The display of flamboyantly political artworks, engaged documentary filmmaking, "underground" comics, theater and performance, sexually explicit literature and "amateur pornography," graffiti and public murals, and much more were part of a revitalized public sphere nourished by press openness, new media technologies, market demand, and international sponsorship. As Strassler convincingly argues, Reformasi photo exhibitions allowed spectators to vicariously witness through images the momentous events of 1998. It also gave former activists the opportunity to see themselves in action: "The pleasure in visiting [Reformasi photo exhibitions] seemed, for many, to lie in confirming their own place in history."[15]

At the same time, transparency's revelations could also be a source of danger, both in the threat of panoptical surveillance and in the possibility of retribution that they might provoke. In the Indonesian reform movement, these considerations generated a rapid recoil from transparency's full potential, in the form of journalistic discretion, self-censorship, and a turn to less controversial subject matter that could nonetheless convey the same possibility of revelation, the same thrill of exposure, that is, to the fantastic genres of supernatural entertainment.[16]

One of the most surprising, and perhaps least inspiring, aspects of this newly lush mediascape—at least for those of a Habermasian inclination, who understand a vibrant public sphere of rational debate as central to processes of democratization—was the rampant proliferation of media genres devoted to the supernatural. This brings me to my second term, *penampakan*, "apparition." It derives from the root word *tampak*, "to see, notice; be visible or evident," and might be literally translated as "vision," "appearance," or "the condition of visibility." Its popular meaning, however, refers to the manifestation of ghosts or spirits in visible or apprehensible form, which is what I want to indicate with the translation "apparition." This sense of the term was popularized by Leo Lumanto, the celebrity psychic featured on the television program *Percaya Nggak Percaya* (Believe it or not). His biographer, Widi Yarmanto, wrote "Ghost stories are commonplace around us. And their presence is increasingly familiar [*akrab*, intimate, comfortable] on account of the word 'penampakan.' A word that connotes the world of mystery or the supernatural realm. A pale shadow takes a human form, leaves rustle even though there is no breeze, the fragrant odor of incense or the sting of a rotten stench, for instance, can easily be interpreted: there is an apparition! *Penampakan* is identical to 'there is a spirit/demon here' [*di sini ada setan*]."[17] Like the political idiom of transparency, penampakan expresses a wish to make visible something—some force, some mysterious operation of power—that is ordinarily imperceptible. All the genres of popular supernaturalism depend on this moment of recognition or appearance, which may be mediated by an individual with psychic powers or by the technological (or magical) enhancement of the ordinary senses.

For anyone who has attended to Indonesian mass culture, the expanded public interest in what one critic calls "ghosts 'n' gore"[18] during this period was striking. Tabloid magazines reported on "supernatural investigations" and "philosophical news and alternative medicine." The occult economy, once largely underground, was in full public force: psychics set up offices in shopping malls and advertised services ranging from magical money laundering and guaranteed business success to cancer cures and nonsurgical penis enlargement, from spiritual consultations to love charms.[19] On television, supernatural reality shows, known locally as *infotainment horor*, featured psychic explorations and exorcisms of haunted sites; a supernatural game show challenged contestants to spend the night in spooky settings like haunted houses or graveyards. The Indonesian film industry was dominated by horror films, to the extent that one film critic complained, in an annual review of movie releases, that in theaters, "the presence of ghosts and other creatures" was "unavoidable."[20] On Indonesian websites like rileks.com and primbon.com, amateur ghost hunters posted accounts of supernatural encounters and digital images of spectral "orbs" or ghostly presences.[21] These highly interreferential genres reached out to different audiences—horror films and websites to relatively sophisticated urban youth, tabloid magazines to a broader adult readership, and television to multigenerational family viewers—and tapped into a truly national popular discourse of black magic and ghostly presences.

There are, to be sure, important differences—of style, format, and audience, for instance—among these various mediations of the supernatural. Levels of capital investment, apparatuses of production and marketing, modes of consumption, technological opportunities and limitations, generate a range of stylistic conventions and improvisations. Television, the medium most dependent on state regulation and support, reaches its primary audience at home, where families watch together, and is most subject to censorship and calls for reform. The main audience for films is the fifteen- to twenty-five-year-old age group, mainly urban, middle-class students who hang out in air-conditioned shopping malls and go to the movies in groups or on dates—roughly speaking, the younger siblings of the Reformasi generation. Thus, for filmmakers, more important than the restrictions of government or religious censorship are the monopolistic distribution practices of the largest multiplex theater chains, which can determine the success or failure of a film by controlling where and when it will be screened.[22] Tabloid magazines are mostly low-tech, low-art productions supported by ads for a wide range of alternative and mystical healers. Catering to a somewhat older audience, these often lean in the direction of soft porn, as figure 10.2 illustrates. Readers engage with their content in less intense and contained ways; magazines can be read sporadically in fits and starts, in moments of boredom or relaxation, privately and selectively; they can be borrowed and shared or browsed in bookstores and newsstands.

These various supernatural media forms compose what Jodi Dean calls a system of "multiply-integrated communication technologies," which cross-reference, cite, imitate, borrow from, support, utilize, and reinforce one another.[23] They expand their reach further by taking up and reconfiguring circulating elements of local and foreign entertainment media. Their themes and concerns travel rhizomatically through fan chat rooms and reviewers' blogs, in YouTube videos and viewers' comments, and on "ghost recorded by camera" websites, feeding back into everyday talk and in the process thickening and deepening the occult cosmologies of the public sphere.

Unlike supernatural tabloids and infotainment horor TV programming, which represent, at best, minor segments of the national print and telecommunications media, respectively, youth-oriented horror movies have been central to the development and viability of the Indonesian film industry as a whole. A guaranteed audience for locally produced, scary movies, which draw repeat business from young fans with pocket money and free time, can be counted on for strong box-office showings in the important first week of release.[24]

In a recent assessment of the state of Indonesian cinema, filmmaker Nan Achnas commented, "The popularity of Indonesian films also stems from the need to see and identify our faces projected in the big screen. To hear our language, to laugh at the inside jokes, to relate to the image as being ours and to share similar world-view and mental landscapes. In short, it is to experience the common thread of identity of what it takes to be Indonesian. Be it the numerous horror and teenage flicks, or the occasional art-cinema Indonesian film, Indonesian audiences see the commonality in the images being present[ed] on the big screen."[25] More than adult melodrama or teen comedy-romance, contemporary horror films do just that. They echo with the disturbances as much as the desires of modern life, embedding these in local particulars of place and style and setting them in a historical-cultural frame that is frequently sensed more than known by its youthful audience. A decade after Suharto's fall, today's youth endeavor to come to terms with a suppressed national past that can no longer remain buried nor entirely come to light; with consumerism an end in itself and religion a source of violence and social fragmentation; and with the absence of a powerful central figure—the nation's "father"—who personified both terror and security. Horror films offend in so many

FIGURE 10.3

Poetic world-making: horror as a political idiom. "The shrouded corpse accuses." Protest over deaths of Indonesian migrant workers, Malaysian Embassy, Jakarta, June 3, 2009. Reproduced with permission of MigrantCare.

ways the virtues of bourgeois respectability, religious morality, and secular rationalism; the artistic and technical standards of quality filmmaking and cinematic good taste; the ideology of state paternalism and family values; and the progressive spirit of postcolonial developmentalism. At the same time, they confirm repugnant stereotypes of Indonesian primitivism, superstition, and violence and allow young people to "relate to the image" as being theirs in an arena of carnivalesque excess not (altogether) beholden to official values of state, societal, or religious authorities. Without wishing to overstate either the acuity and intellectual freedom of today's young commercial filmmakers or the artistic merits of what are, in truth, market-driven excursions in low taste, I would argue that Indonesian horror films, in which the dream of transparent visibility intersects with the nightmare of apparition, are among the key sites of political *and* poetic world-making for this post-Reformasi generation.

"AUDS SCREAM FOR HORROR HIT"

On October 5, 2001, the low-budget horror film *Jelangkung* premiered in Jakarta. Shot in digital format for less than US$40,000, *Jelangkung* was at first shown in only one small theater in the 21 Multiplex at upscale Pondok Indah shopping mall, because the film's production company, Rexinema, had only one digital projector for screening and could not afford to transfer the movie to the 16-mm format used by mainstream films. Intended to be shown for only four days, at the end of the year *Jelangkung* was still playing in two larger venues in Jakarta, the producers having by then invested in a second digital projector. News reports describe "full houses" and audiences of teens and college students "clamor[ing] to see it." "Auds scream for horror hit," ran the headline in *Variety Asia* magazine, which described the film as a "surprise hit in Indonesia and a tonic for the country's languishing film industry." "I must get a ticket today," one teen girl reported to the *Jakarta Post* nearly two months after the film opened. "Otherwise I'll die from curiosity."[26]

Jelangkung was directed by first-time filmmakers Rizal Mantovani and Jose Poernomo, whose previous media experience had consisted mainly of shooting music videos. Its box office success was buoyed by good word-of-mouth from viewers and some enthusiastic—if patronizing—print reviews. Joko Anwar, who was then the film critic for the *Jakarta Post*, described it as a "guilty pleasure" in spite of "hilariously bad" acting and "cheesy digital effects." "We made a movie that the audiences want to see so we had pop culture in mind while making it," Rizal explained. "We always hear young people talking about scary urban legends, so why not make a movie about it?" And indeed Joko acknowledged, in a slightly backhanded compliment, that "one of the keys to the success of *Jelangkung* is that the movie is at least smart enough for its target audience" of teenage moviegoers.[27] Ticket sales for *Jelangkung* across Indonesia reached one million, even though a pirated VCD version appeared in hawkers' stalls while the film was still being shown

FIGURE 10.4
"Come without welcome, leave without escort." VCD cover, Jelangkung *(Rexinema Productions, Jakarta, Indonesia, 2001).*

in theaters. Its popularity was credited with "resurrecting the Indonesian film industry," which had during the previous decade been effectively killed off by draconian government restrictions on production and distribution, heavy taxes, capricious decisions by the national censorship board, competition

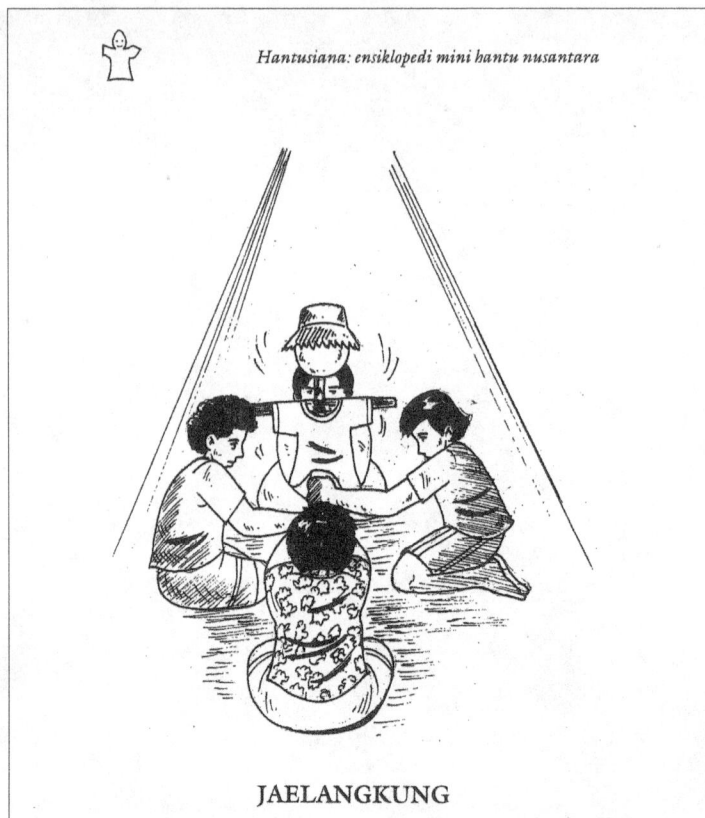

Hantusiana: ensiklopedi mini hantu nusantara

JAELANGKUNG

FIGURE 10.5

Children playing with a jelangkung *puppet. Illustration from Rudi Utomo,*
Hantusiana: A Mini-Encyclopedia of Archipelagic Spooks *(Kalam:*
Kalam Indonesia, 2007).

from television, pirated VCDs and foreign films, and, finally, the Asian
financial crisis.[28]

Filmed in jittery MTV style, *Jelangkung* tells the story of a group of
ghost-hunting teens pursued by a vindictive spirit they have called up by
means of a straw figure known as a *jelangkung*. It was inspired by the low-
tech, digital, chic international success film *The Blair Witch Project* (1999)
and borrowed liberally not only from that film but also from such cult horror flicks as Sam Raimi's *Evil Dead* trilogy; Hideo Nakata's international hit
Ringu (1998) and its sequels; and the American cartoon series *Scooby Doo*.
Originality is not a requirement for horror films—in fact quite the contrary—and *Jelangkung* quickly conjured up a fleet of imitations of its own,

starting with the self-mimetic *Jelangkung 2* (directed by another veteran of the music video scene, Dimas Djayadiningrat). Rizal went on to create a new horror franchise, the equally popular *Kuntilanak* trilogy, which follows the struggles of Samantha, a university student whose spontaneous ability to call up the bloodthirsty *kuntilanak* spirit (a vengeful female demon; see figure 10.2 for one imaginative rendering) brings her to the attention of a satanic Javanese sect (Sekte Mangkoejiwoe) attempting to revive a once prosperous batik business.

In 2006 prolific filmmaker Rudy Soedjarwo turned from frothy teen romance and music films to horror. His first effort in the genre, *Dendam Pocong* (Revenge of the shrouded corpse), (which refers to the Islamic practice of wrapping a corpse and the belief that if the shroud's cord is not untied before burial, the body will not remain in the grave), is set during the anti-Chinese riots of 1998 and deals with the continuing cycles of revenge set off by the violence. The film was banned before its release, presumably for its unsuitable evocations of ethnic conflict. Undeterred, the filmmaker quickly put together a "sequel," *Pocong 2*, and cleverly advertised it as "even scarier than the banned *Pocong!*"[29] The second *Pocong* film downplays the theme of ethnic conflict but keeps the central concept of cyclical violence and supernatural retribution. An instant success, *Pocong 2* generated a flood of shrouded-corpse films—the inevitable sequels *Pocong 3* and *40 Hari Bangkitnya Pocong* (In 40 days the shrouded corpse arises), as well as *Tali Pocong Perawan* (Cord of the virgin's shroud), *Sumpah Pocong di Sekolah* (Curse of the shrouded corpse in school), *Pocong Kamar Sebelah* (The pocong next door), *Pocong Jalan Blora* (The pocong on Blora Street), *Pocong Setan Jompo* (Evil old pocong), set in a demonic nursing home, *Susuk Pocong* (Magical implants of the shrouded corpse), *The Real Pocong*, and, perhaps inevitably, *Pocong vs. Kuntilanak*.[30]

Jelangkung was one of only eight films produced in Indonesia in 2001; in 2007 there were fifty, of which twenty-one were horror movies. Perhaps a better measure of the strength of horror films in the market is the category of "Lebaran" films, which are considered ideal fare for the end of the Muslim fasting month, when moviegoing is at its peak. Of the four films released for Lebaran 2007, three were horror films: the long-awaited *Jelangkung 3*, *Kuntilanak 2*, and *Pocong 3*.[31]

"EVERY ERA HAS ITS OWN HORROR"

From its early years Indonesian cinema has been identified with the horror/supernatural genre. The first supernatural horror film, *Doea Siloeman Oelar Poeti en Item* (Two phantom snakes black and white), appeared

FIGURE 10.6

"Even scarier than the banned Pocong*!" DVD cover,* Pocong 2 *(Sinemart Pictures, 2006).*

in 1934.[32] The heyday of the *film klenik* (superstition film) came in the late 1970s and 1980s, when government policies facilitated and subsidized the production of cheap "exploitation" films for downscale urban "goat-class" theaters and mobile cinemas serving rural villages. Their audience was

Figure 10.7

Suzzanna, the Queen of Indonesian Horror, in The Wedding of Nyai Blorong *(Cancer Mas Pictures, 1983; rereleased on VCD, PT Soraya Intercine Film, 2005).*

understood as rural, uneducated men and the quasi-criminal urban under-class. Often based on folktales and featuring legendary figures, the films of this period are set mostly in the mythic past or in some generic village set-ting.[33] These often feature sexually voracious goddesses, slapstick humor, martial arts duels, cheap special effects, and campy but sadistic violence. In the 1980s such films, which were the only (modestly) sexually explicit genre produced in Indonesia, flourished alongside a relatively vibrant, seri-ous film scene, but by the mid-1990s, horror was about the only film genre being produced in the country.[34]

A further characteristic of the "superstition films" of the 1970s and 1980s is the use of religious symbols (usually but not always Islamic) and the appear-ance of a religious figure such as a *kyai* (Muslim cleric), who resolves the action, often in a deus ex machina manner, and delivers a moral conclusion.

According to Katinka van Heeren, this was an effect of regulation by the Film Censor Board. The board's Subcommittee on Film in Its Relation to Devotion towards the One and Only God declared, "Dialogue, scenes, visualization and conflicts between the protagonist and antagonist in the story have to come around to devoutness and glorification of the One and Only God" and that "the storyline ought to be composed in such a way that it gives the audience the impression that what is bad will definitely receive the consequence and suffer and that what is good will surely receive a reward and happiness." Finding a balance between "erotic elements to the level of smut and kitsch" on the one hand and religious devotion on the other required considerable ingenuity. Sex scenes might be followed by the message "This is not right according to the Qur'an," or the kyai might appear simply to deliver a pious homily at the end of the film. Thus, "there evolved a bizarre situation under the New Order wherein the horror film genre was at once equated with sex and with religious mission (*dakwah*)."[35]

As Hikmat Darmawan, an editor of the Indonesian cinema website Rumahfilm.org, points out, "every era has its own horror," shaped to the contours of its own particular terrors and desires.[36] What makes *Jelangkung* and its successors so different from the New Order exploitation films is that they were aimed at an urban, middle-class youth audience. These viewers had little knowledge of the history or conventions of Indonesian cinema, having been brought up on Hollywood and Asian cinemas rather than local melodrama and slapstick comedy. With this audience in mind, the new horror films played in upscale multiplex theaters, which had previously screened mostly foreign (Hollywood, Japanese, Korean) films. The higher ticket prices for these theaters meant that a film could recoup its investment much more quickly than in the cheaper movie houses. Because the shopping mall and multiplex venues these films played in attracted female viewers as well, sexually explicit elements are downplayed (though erotic elements of the "wet T-shirt" variety are not). This made them appealing for mixed groups or as "date movies"—unlike foreign films, in which embarrassing or provocatively adult sex scenes might unexpectedly appear.

Most of these films were shot with digital cameras on shoestring budgets and tight schedules. Rather than expensive special effects, the films relied on atmospherics, sound effects, eerie music, and clever editing—as well as "amateurish" camera work and bad lighting—to produce suspense.[37] They featured (lower-paid) young actors whose background was in television dramas, music, and fashion. Performances aspired to be naturalistic; characters speak in the pseudo-vernacular of (watered-down) Jakarta dialect and (modified) youth slang rather than in the somewhat stilted, formal

Indonesian typical of earlier melodramas. Characterization is often under-developed, acting is inconsistent, and action is subordinated to mood and anticipation. Plot lines are formulaic: a group of young people unwittingly come in contact with an evil spirit or a ghost, which tracks and kills them one by one in increasingly gruesome fashion.

"Compared to the horror trend of the 80s," an Indonesian blogger writes, "the storyline of horror films now can be said to be more plausible. A different pattern of thinking [about horror] started with the release of *Jelangkung*."[38] Stylistically, these films were a radical departure in that they are driven by a cinematographic rather than narrative sensibility. Character, dialogue, and plot are "neglected" in favor of a "visual aesthetic" of sensory impression and disorienting camerawork. Derived from the world of advertising and music videos, this visual aesthetic of short takes and quick cuts, tight close-ups, hand-held rather than fixed cameras, and impressionistic editing was familiar to the films' young viewers. Set pieces and grand battles were replaced by moody attention to the visual details of the "almost seen," the portentous and the shocking: shadows and mist, flickering lights, the clinging tentacles of aerial roots, a slimy unidentifiable object floating in a bacterial bath, lurid oversaturated colors or wan sepia tones, what one online reviewer referred to as the "semiotics of rain and the metaphorics of grilled duck" (plate 27).[39]

Main characters reflect the target demographic: middle-class high school and college students and young professionals living in Jakarta or another (usually unnamed) city. Settings are familiar as well. Much of the shooting was done on location, in the city streets, apartments, office buildings, schools, train terminals, dance clubs, and cafés that film characters shared with their audience. Sometimes, well-known public locales are specified, as in *The Ghost of Ancol Bridge, Casablanca Tunnel, Ghost Train to Manggarai, The Haunted House in Pondok Indah,* and *The Pocong of Blora Street.* Although Indonesian melodramas were frequently built around concerns over class and social mobility, these were rarely mentioned in horror films.[40] Characters are generally identified with the homogeneous urban super-culture of contemporary Indonesia rather than with any particular ethnic group or region. There were a few notable exceptions to this rule—obviously the banned *Dendam Pocong,* which is set amid the anti-Chinese riots of May 1998, but also the *Kuntilanak* trilogy, with its Javanese ghost and satanic cult, and the 2008 release *Karma,* which concerns a wealthy but cursed Chinese family in Jakarta. Even in these, ethnicity tends to be presented impressionistically, through allusive nuances of setting, rather than addressed directly or through physical stereotyping in the films.[41]

One striking feature of these films is the lack of adult authority figures. Parents are notably absent, and parental figures (teachers, landladies) rarely figure significantly in the action, except as villains, victims, or misguided skeptics. Post–New Order Indonesia may be, as Carla Jones argues, a place "teeming with expertise,"[42] but this is not evident in the world of horror films. Quite the contrary, "experts" are usually either dangerous traffickers in dark arts or misguided rationalists and frequently serve as the first victims of the supernatural forces at work in the film. The young protagonists are on their own.

Unlike the horror films of the New Order era, the new films are also religiously neutral. Although the main characters tend to be responsible, chaste, and dutiful, religious faith is rarely mentioned, even in the vaguest of terms.[43] The religious affiliation of characters are usually not marked, except by implication as non-Muslim: typically, they are given nonidentifying nicknames (Iwank, Andin, Agung, Putri, Maya) or Western names (Samantha, Darwin, Herman, Stella, Sandra).[44] There is no question of the "return of the kyai" or any other religious authority here. Nor is there much chance of a happy or moral ending, deus ex machina or otherwise. At best, supernatural dangers are kept at bay for the moment, with the possibility of a return engagement always kept in final view. Part of this has to do with the obvious commercial value of sequelization, but it also reflects a view of life in which danger is both profound and ubiquitous, everywhere and invisible, and authorities offer little in the way of protection.

While there is often a backstory hinted at in a prologue before the opening credits and usually explained at the end of the film, the main action is, in most cases, set in the present. Everyday matters—finding an affordable apartment, dealing with a devoted but feckless boyfriend, balancing obligations of work and family, conflicts between love and friendship, college initiations, sibling rivalry, and the like—are woven through the story, generating a contextual verisimilitude that is striking when compared with the typical Indonesian teen comedy-romance, in which farfetched plot and ultrarich lifestyles are the norm. In *Pocong 2*, for example, the plot is set in motion when the protagonist, Maya, a university instructor hunting for inexpensive housing, moves into a modern apartment building that turns out to be haunted by a vengeful ghost. Characters are often computer savvy, always carry cell phones, and frequently use digital still or video cameras to try to document the presence of ghosts, but there is none of the "haunted technology" common in pan-Asian horror cinemas, which seems to function as a means of "universalizing" or rather delocalizing these movies to broaden their appeal to an international audience

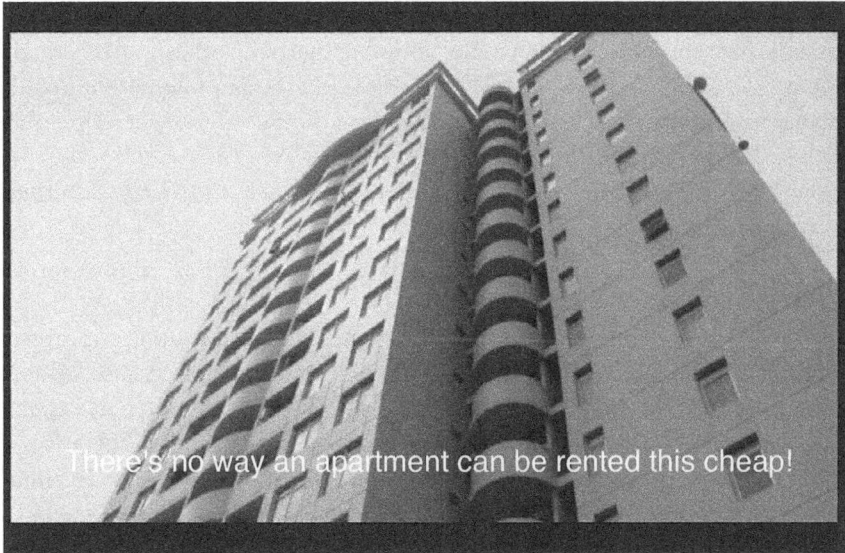

FIGURE 10.8

The haunted high-rise: "There's no way an apartment can be rented this cheap!" Advertisement for Pocong 2 *(Sinemart Pictures, 2006).*

fascinated by the possibility of a generic, haunted modernity.[45] Instead, the presence of personal electronics is more a means of vernacularizing the global modern, highlighting what Kajri Jain describes as a specifically post-colonial condition in which subjects "function across *epistemically disjunct yet performatively networked* worlds: the worlds of bourgeois-liberal and neoliberal modernism on the one hand and those of 'vernacular' discourses and practices on the other."[46]

Indonesians go to horror films to see their own ghosts, which are frightening in very particular—one might say, familiar—ways. The ghosts in these films are resolutely local. Most derive from contemporary urban legends or scary nursery tales and juxtapose up-to-date youth lifestyles with supernatural elements drawn from a broad cultural repertoire that includes vengeful longhaired female ghosts, were-pigs, baby spirit familiars, magicians both black and white, grotesque witches, sexually voracious goddesses, colonial-era revenants, and the shrouded corpses of Islamic burial practice. Vampires, wolfmen, mystical computer viruses, or (at least so far) space aliens seem to have little appeal here.[47] And while American psycho-paths and zombies may still pack the multiplexes, Indonesian spectators seem to mostly prefer their own, homegrown horrors. One fan commented (on an English-language Internet site), "[For] western ghost, you would see the 'human shape' like in zombie, dracula. they are all still human shape. i am not that scare to see western movies too actually. Good in special effect, but still the ghost not so scary.... But then, indonesian movie, like tusuk jelangkung, does made me had goosebumps while watching it. Also thai movie. they were scary too. i think because its involving in myth, lagend and sometimes child bedtime story and added with 'true story' things (whether its true or not)."[48]

THE EDGE OF THE VISIBLE

If Indonesian engagement with the genres of popular supernaturalism is predicated on belief rather than disbelief, then what is it that makes them enjoyable? Clearly, new forms of contextual verisimilitude have made them comfortably plausible for a youth audience wishing "to relate to the image" as being theirs, but familiarity alone is surely insufficient to explain their entertainment value. And why now? One Indonesian journalist argued that in a period of crisis, supernatural stories might seem more credible than news reporting: "Indeed, as has become a natural formula, when a multidimensional crisis becomes increasingly complicated, tales with a whiff of horror become entertaining fare. Superstitious reading matter even shoves aside political news that tends to be evaluated as 'only' lying to the people. They are fed up, frustrated, and feel that they can't find a cure to resolve it."[49] Joko Anwar put it a little differently: "It is probably because there are so many unexplained deaths in this country over such a long period of time that makes our local audiences interested in stories about ghosts who seek revenge from those who have wronged them."[50]

Joko Anwar's association of the revenge theme with the unexplained and unmourned dead—and, it might be added, the tentative efforts that are now being made to disinter, both literally and figuratively, some of the New Order's numerous victims—suggests how ghost stories can, in some cases, create a space for muted political commentary, as well as an idiom of political protest (see figure 10.3, in which demonstrators protesting the abuse of Indonesian overseas workers dress as pocong).[51] They express the predictable concerns and fears of a generation of modern urban youth with little connection to its national past. In these films the dangers that saturate their no longer disenchanted lifeworld emerge from the strange, half-understood powers of traditional culture, fantasies of rural brutality and atavism, the primordial landscape, the imagined residue of colonial oppression, the terrors of national history, and the urge to violence embedded in the human psyche.

Although it is clear that fantasies of magical fortune and ghostly revenge are potent ingredients in this supernatural stew, it would be wrong to suppose that exposure to media violence, either real or imaginary, was its cause. Many of the current Indonesian horror films do begin with an obscure act of past violence—this being, generally speaking, the nature of ghosts. But the depiction of violent acts is not a significant part of these films' appeal. By Hollywood (or Bangkok) standards, very little physical damage is shown in any of the Indonesian genres of supernatural entertainment. What there is tends to appear only in discreet, half-glimpsed flashes, often obscured by rain, shadows, or darkness.[52] This is no doubt partly because of the cost of producing gruesome special effects but more because spectators' interest is in the sight of ghosts rather than gore, as even a cursory reading of fan comments on the Internet will demonstrate. Rather than violence itself, these films deal with its spectral afterlife and with those powerful affective states—terror, anger, desire, hatred, rage, jealousy, envy—that can endure beyond the life of the body. The audience that carries its fear home acknowledges the existence of the ghost as a trace of that affective excess.

As Jean and John Comaroff point out, "the more literally we believe in the axiom 'to see is to know,' the more haunted we are by what hovers beyond the edge of the visible."[53] The play of the seen and the unseen, the fascination of "what hovers beyond the edges of the visible," is of course a standard trope in horror movies everywhere. Indonesian filmmakers take full advantage of it, not just as a scare technique but also as a narrative proposition. What is the relation between seeing and knowing, these films repeatedly ask, or between seeing and being seen, between looking and touching? Does "making an appearance" connote distance or intimacy? How might one imagine an aesthetic of half-seeing, or the visual imaging of something that cannot be seen?

Indonesians go to horror films to see ghosts, but, as most filmgoers know, the apparition is always a disappointment.[54] This is not just a matter of the technical limits of image-production or the prohibitive cost of high-quality special effects. The fundamental affective vector of the horror movie is dread, which is the anticipation of the worst thing that could happen. It is the feeling that builds as the audience waits for the ghost to make an appearance. Once the ghost appears, dread gives way to other emotions—shock, disgust, revulsion, fear, compassion, loathing, relief, sometimes amusement. That is why effective horror films defer the moment of ghostly apparition as long as possible, giving the audience only fragmentary glimpses, hints of spectral presence: a distant song, a wisp of long white hair, a strange hoof-like foot, a clawlike tree branch or a tangle of roots, a pale shadow scuttling at the edge of the visual field.

In an essay on popular horror movies in Ghana, Birgit Meyer points out the ironic modernity of supernatural cinema, in which the technological mediation of the camera reveals a hitherto invisible world of demonic forces and magical powers. "Through the medium of film, the revelation of magic through the eye of the camera becomes a common practice," she writes.

> Providing an extension of the human eye and showing occult forces at work, the camera claims the ultimate power of revelation. In popular cinema it certainly does not act as the "mechanical eye of reason" engrained in a positivist worldview that rules out occult phenomena as "superstitions" but as a mediator of a form of truth-knowledge that successfully transcends the boundary between the visible and the invisible, the physical and the spiritual, and enables people to share its perspective. Asserting that the visible world is dominated by invisible forces, video films paradoxically affirm that transparency is neither given nor achievable in the visible realm but always depends on the revelation of what lies beneath.[55]

Perhaps. Certainly, Indonesia's supernatural tabloids and television reality shows strive to authenticate their visualizations of ghosts and demons, by appealing to religious and secular experts for confirmation, by streaming the message *bukan rekayasa* (not staged/fake) beneath apparition images, and through the presentation of eyewitness testimony and other forms of evidence. Katinka van Heeren links this evidentiary turn in supernatural television programming to the spirit of Reformasi, in which the search for "what lies beneath" the New Order's web of secrecy and historical revisionism led to a general suspicion of official versions of events and a "widespread call for 'facts,' 'truth' and 'authenticity.'" Thus, she argues that the "return of the kyai" in supernatural television programming is not a repetition of New Order expressions of piety but rather one of a number of mechanisms of supernatural authentication and expertise, confirmations of the reality of the camera's revelations.[56]

Indonesian filmmakers too wrap their productions in an aura of authenticity—through the contextual verisimilitude of character, setting, and dialogue, by claiming that the film is "based on a true story," by recounting eerie happenings on the set, or even by internally citing the authority of other supernatural genres. But however much their audiences may believe in the existence of secret powers at work beneath the surface of the visible world, they do not confuse the occult images displayed in cinema with real ghosts. Everyone knows that these are imaginative re-creations, illusions produced by camera tricks and special effects. Much of the fun of these movies is in the "Gotcha!" moment, when illusion and reality momentarily fuse, when the audience is suspended between belief and disbelief, between the desire to see and the urge to look away.

Unlike other genres of popular supernaturalism, which hew much closer to the line of evidentiary visualization of the "ghost recorded by camera" variety, these films (and their audiences) are playing games with the evidence. The figure of the ghost, for all its plausible unreality, is the secret at the heart of the film. All these forms of authentication—captions and verbal labels, expert analysis, eyewitness testimony, contextual verisimilitude, supernatural traces that adhere to the scene of shooting—situate the occult media image within a field of truthfulness that is itself a fiction. What might be called the "truth-knowledge effect" that envelops the film and its apparitional center is not an attempt to reveal its mystery or to contain it within the safe precincts of a higher authority—whether of science, religion, law, or the ocularcentrism of a technologically enhanced visuality. All of these incitements of the real create, via a kind of osmotic shock, leakages in the borders of the film; they allow it to spill over into the world outside the theater in ways that have little to do with either fact or fiction but rather with feeling. The tension between the imaginative creation of the film and the truth claims of its frame establish a fundamental instability in its relation with the audience. Seeing and knowing are decoupled. In this context, what does it mean to see?

Even if, as Meyer suggests, the message of the cinematic medium were that modern technologies of seeing might paradoxically reveal an invisible, mystical ("unmodern") world, that message would be undercut by the inner logic of these films. Protagonists are consistently driven by an evidentiary desire to know—and to know by seeing. The wish to see the ghost—to discern its secret—is the primary impetus behind their actions. Yet, they frequently fail to recognize its presence. Such "nonrecognition scenes" can be comic, as in *Pocong 2* when the shrouded corpse appears in the bathroom with Adam, the designated comic relief character. Adam fails to notice it because he mistakes the smell of the corpse for his own (extended) flatulence. Other scenes are terrifying. In *Kuntilanak* the eponymous demon emerges from an antique mirror while the protagonists sleep, leaving behind only strands of her eerily twisted, white hair. In the violent denouement of *Kuntilanak 2*, the villains of the Sekte Mangkoejiwo are caressed and taunted, then devoured, by a swarm of ghostly figures they cannot see. In *Hantu* (Spectre), five young hikers searching for a mysterious lake "that has never been seen" become lost in the surrounding forest. As they move deeper into the woods, time becomes unstuck—day and night expand and contract unpredictably, and the haunted vegetation begins to play tricks with them. In the unsteady beams of their flashlights or just outside their line of vision, the trees morph into momentarily anthropomorphic forms—a twisted face appears in a weathered trunk, a reaching hand in the branches, or a grasping root—all of which the characters repeatedly fail to see...until it is too late.

In fact, characters in Indonesian horror films spend most of their time *not* seeing, because they are asleep, literally in the dark, or otherwise blind to the presence of the spirits around them. Technology inevitably fails them: camera batteries run down, cell phones encounter "dead zones." Much of the action takes place under conditions of limited visibility—at night, in the rain, in the forest—so the characters' dialogue frequently underscores their (and the spectator's) inability to see what is going on around them. In the final installment (so far) of the *Kuntilanak* saga, Samantha is escorted by a well-equipped search and rescue team to the village of Ujung Sedo, which is said to hold the heart of the mystery of the kuntilanak. "This is the edge of hell," Samantha tells them, "the place where you can truly see ghosts and demons right before your eyes." But once they reach the village, where Samantha's companions run around in the dark and predictably fall victim, one by one, to the kuntilanak, the film is filled with dialogue about not seeing: "I can't see!" "Where are you?" "What's that?" "Can you see anything?"

This ambivalent play of visibility and invisibility is as central to the affective and expressive world-making project of the horror film as it is to the public project of transparency. Both hail the spectator literally as "one who looks" and demand that the viewer look, again and again—look more deeply, in shadowy corners, beyond closed doors, behind the screen, under the skin—for the dreadful secrets of power. At the same time, this act of (repeated) looking brings the spectator-subject into view—to himself or herself, to a public composed of like subjects, and to the powers they are called upon to expose.

Public discourse, says Michael Warner, "lies under the necessity of addressing its public as already existing real persons" at the same time that it calls that public into being. It does this through a mutually constituting interlocution through which its audience comes to recognize itself and to seek recognition (plate 28). Beyond the cinematic intimacy of spectators viewing faces and hearing voices like theirs, the multi- and intermediated genres of supernatural realism allow spectators to imagine themselves as "celebrity subjects," or in this case perhaps as occult celebrity subjects. As Jodi Dean argues, "the drive to be known, and the presumption that what matters is what is known, provides a different economy of subjectivization, one in which the technocultural subject is configured as a celebrity.... The continued configuring of publicity as the ideology of technoculture operates through the production of publicized subjects: in recognizing themselves as known, celebrity subjects posit a public that knows them.... Much ink has been spilled lamenting the effects of the surveillance society but relatively little on the enjoyments that may accompany the sense *that one is known, that people know who we are, that we are somebody.*"[57] Here, as much as in the invisible apparition that makes an appearance through the mediation of the camera or the spiritual eye of the paranormal, is the point of contact with the dream of transparency, with its dual aspirations to see and be seen by the apparatus of state power. But in Indonesian horror films, not only is to see *not* to know, the wish to see/know also can be deadly, precisely because it enables you to be seen as well. Ghosts and demons enter the everyday world mainly because someone is looking for them; they are drawn, it seems, by the seeking gaze. By looking for them, you allow them to see you. Once you do see them, it is too late to escape. Seeing may be a way of knowing, but if the desire for knowledge is the basis of the urge to see, then these films tell us how dangerous such a quest can be.

Dreams of transparency and apparition are always necessarily incomplete, for both are predicated on a darkness to be illuminated, a secret to be exposed, a ghost to materialize. They depend on the suspicion of secret workings, whether of political conspiracy or of occult forces. And once the possibility of the secret—whether provocateur or ghost—has been broached, there is never any end to the possibility of other layers of mystery as yet unrevealed. As Patricia Spyer points out, the "attempt to see through everything...can only emerge when people in fact see nothing at all."[58] Like crime and corruption, like the numbers of the "unexplained dead," ghosts are a kind of public secret. Everyone assumes that they exist, but no one can fully plumb their depths. You can never get to the bottom of "publicity's secrets," as Jodi Dean warns us. "How do we know when we have enough information, when the ultimate secret has been revealed? We don't. We can't—the secret is a matter of form, not content, so it can never fully or finally be revealed."[59] Ghosts too are a matter of form and can never be fully revealed. There is always the possibility of a return, a sequel. Here, in the reciprocal embrace of transparansi/apparition, seeing is not enough, nor is knowing. There is no source of credible authority, no expert to call.

FIGURE 10.9

"You know the secret—Now you die." DVD cover, Kala *(MD Pictures, 2007).*

And there is no escape. This predicament is perhaps most vividly realized in Joko Anwar's *Kala,* in which a gay policeman and a narcoleptic journalist separately follow a trail of grisly murders in search of the secret of the "first president's hidden treasure." Guarded by the white ape-god Hanuman, the treasure carries a dangerous secret: only one person may know about it at a time. As soon as a second person finds out, one of them must die. Thus, the policeman can follow the clues to the treasure only when the journalist remains asleep. You could say that publicity, the sharing of secrets, is itself the treasure's secret. Both deadly and alluring, it draws the seeker into a world of unseen, irresistible forces, in which—as the film's tagline runs—"you know the secret, now you die."

Acknowledgments

Many people have contributed (some perhaps unwittingly) to this exploration of the dark side of Indonesian popular supernaturalism. First, I want to thank Philip and Tinuk Yampolsky, whose friendship and hospitality are unparalleled and who have long been my guides in all matters Indonesian. Jesse Grayman deserves special credit for drawing my attention to Indonesia's "true crime" and supernatural tabloids, back in 1997. Over the years other students, colleagues, and friends have kept me supplied with DVDs, magazines, books, newspaper articles, rumors, and other materials and kept me alerted to a wonderful range of Internet sources on ghostly happenings and on Indonesian movies and popular media in general. I would like to acknowledge them here: Aryo Danusiri, Dadi Darmadi, Veronika Kusumaryati, Doreen Lee, and Karen Strassler. Like everyone who works on popular supernaturalism in contemporary Indonesia, I owe an intellectual debt to James Siegel's work, from his description of the Sri Mulat Theater's "Mrs. Draculla" in early 1980s Solo to his account of Javanese "ninja" witch-hunters of the late 1990s. I also thank Goenawan Mohamed, Dr. A. Budi Susanto, and S. J. and Garin Nugroho for conversations that illuminated larger matters for me. Julia Yezbick helped prepare some of the illustrations. Finally, I owe a special debt of gratitude to Aryo Danusiri, who intrepidly tracked down many of the illustrations in this article, including the "moviegoers" mural and the wonderful 1999 issue of *Misteri* magazine, "Soeharto's Mystical Crimes," which he found in good condition in a used-book stall in Jakarta.

Notes

1. Seth Mydans, "Suharto, from Verge of Death, Is Making a Recovery," *New York Times* [hereafter, *NYT*], January 21, 2008, http://www.nytimes.com/2008/01/21/world/asia/21suharto.html?scp=3&sq=Suharto,%20from%20edge%200f%20death&st=cse (accessed December 8, 2011).

2. Associated Press, "Javanese Believe Ancient Mysticism Shielding Ex-dictator Suharto from Death," *Jakarta Post* [hereafter, *JP*], January 27, 2008, http://www.seasite.niu.edu/flin/suharto_dead.htm (accessed December 8, 2011).

3. Seth Mydans, "As Suharto Clings to Life, Mystics See Spirits' Power," *NYT*,

January 27, 2008, http://www.nytimes.com/2008/01/27/world/asia/27indo. html?scp=1&sq=Suharto,%20from%20edge%200f%20death&st=cse; and "Indonesians Draw Mystical Connections to Suharto," *NYT,* January 25, 2008, http://www.nytimes .com/2008/01/25/world/asia/25iht-ind0.2.9500455.html?scp=2&sq=Suharto,%20 from%20edge%200f%20death&st=cse (accessed December 8, 2011).

4. Associated Press, "Javanese Believe."

5. Thanks to Byron Good and Jesse Grayman for bringing this message to my attention.

6. Heru Pamuji et al., "Tayangan setan: Mengubah duit, mengumbar takut" [Demonic programming: Moving money, spreading fear], *Gatra,* March 15, 2003, 24–31.

7. The Rotterdam International Film Festival 2009, for instance, presented a program of Asian "ghost" films, pointing out that "the specific quality of East Asian horror movies is that the people who make them and the people who watch them actually believe in ghosts." Gertan Zuilhof, "Hungry Ghosts in a Haunted House," introduction to "Hungry Ghosts" program, RIFF 2009, http://www .filmfestivalrotterdam.com/professionals/programme/sections_events_iffr_2009 /signals/signals—hungry-ghosts/hungry-ghosts-introduction.apsx. (accessed December 8, 2011).

8. This paragraph draws on Michael Warner, "Publics and Counterpublics," in *Publics and Counterpublics,* 90 and 114.

9. On the significance of transparency and concealment in New Order and post–New Order Indonesia, see Nils Bubandt, "Rumors, Pamphlets, and the Politics of Paranoia in Indonesia," *Journal of Asian Studies* 67, no. 3 (2008): 789–817; James T. Siegel, *A New Criminal Type in Jakarta* (Durham, NC: Duke University Press, 1998), and *Naming the Witch* (Stanford, CA: Stanford University Press, 2005); Karen Strassler, "Gendered Visibilities and the Dream of Transparency: The Chinese-Indonesian Rape Debate in Post-Suharto Indonesia," *Gender and History* 16, no. 3 (2004): 689–725.

10. The term "occult public sphere" comes from Russ Castronovo, *Necro Citizenship* (Durham, NC: Duke University Press, 2001).

11. Jean Comaroff and John Comaroff, "Occult Economies and the Violence of Abstraction: Notes from the South African Postcolony," *American Ethnologist* 26, no. 2 (1999): 284–286.

12. Dewi Anggraeni, "Book Delves into Intrigues, Surprises in a Slice of Chinese-Javanese History," *JP,* January 25, 2009, http://www.thejakartapost.com/news /2009/01/25/book-delves-intrigues-surprises-a-slice-chinesejavanese-history.html (accessed December 8, 2011).

13. On the concept of disaster spectatorship, see Warner, "Mass Public," 179.

14. Strassler, "Gendered Visibilities."

15. Karen Strassler, *Refracted Visions: Popular Photography and National Modernity in Java* (Durham, NC: Duke University Press, 2010), 231–235. On other expressions of this Reformasi spirit in public art, see Jennifer Lindsay, "A New Artistic Order?" *Inside Indonesia* 93 (July–September 2008), http://www.insideindonesia.org/weekly-articles -93-j-ul-sep-2008/a-new-artistic-order-07091681 (accessed December 8, 2011); Mary-Jo DelVecchio Good and Byron J. Good, "*Indonesia Sakit*: Indonesian Disorder and the Subjective Experience and Interpretive Politics of Contemporary Indonesian Artists," in *Postcolonial Disorders*, ed. Mary-Jo DelVecchio Good and Byron J. Good (Berkeley: University of California Press, 2008), 62–108; Thomas Barker, "VCD Pornography in Indonesia" (paper presented at Asian Studies Association of Australia 16th Biennial Conference, June 26–29, 2006), http://primalscenes.wordpress.com/essays/ (accessed December 8, 2011).

16. On the strategy of journalistic discretion, see Patricia Spyer, "One Slip of the Pen: Some Notes on Writing Violence in Maluku," in *Indonesia in Transition*, ed. Henk Schulte Nordholt and Gusti Asnan (Yogyakarta, Java: Pustaka Pelajar, 2003), 181–200; Sebastian Dettman, "Blaming the Messenger," *Inside Indonesia* 93 (July–September 2008), http://www.insideindonesia.org/edition-93/blaming-the-messenger (accessed January 2, 2011).

17. Widi Yarmanto, *Penampakan Leo Lumanto* (Jakarta, Indonesia: Akoer, 2005), ix.

18. Rizal Iwan, "Resurrecting Fear," *JP*, January 23, 2008, http://www .thejakartapost.com/news/2008/01/23/resurrecting-fear.html (accessed December 8, 2011).

19. Comaroff and Comaroff, "Occult Economies."

20. Nauval Yazid, "Movie Merry-go-round Spinds [*sic*] Faster," *JP*, March 16, 2008, http://old/thejakartapost.com/review2007/fea01.asp (accessed January 23, 2009).

21. Technically termed "backscatter," an orb is an unexpected, typically circular, white or semi-transparent artifact that appears in digital photographs, especially with ultra-compact cameras. While these have been commonly interpreted as signs of ghostly presence, they appear to be caused by the reflection of light off of particles like dust or water droplets.

22. Ary Hermawan, "Distribution Seen as Main Obstacle to Film Industry Growth," *JP*, March 29, 2008, http://www.thejakartapost.com/news/2008/03/28/distribution -seen-main-obstacle-film-industry-growth.html (accessed December 8, 2011); Kim Balmanno, "Box Office: The Secret Numbers Tell the Story," *JP*, March 23, 2008, http:// www.thejakartapost.com/news/2008/03/23/box-office-the-secret-numbers-tell-story. html (accessed December 8, 2011).

23. Jodi Dean, *Publicity's Secret: How Technoculture Capitalizes on Democracy* (Ithaca, NY: Cornell University Press, 2002), 13.

24. According to the Indonesian government's Badan Pusat Statistik, in 2000 more than 50 percent of the population was under twenty-five; about 20 percent was between fifteen and twenty-four. Forty-two percent of the population was urban; urban population has been increasing at more than 10 percent per decade. The next national census was conducted in 2010. See Badan Pusat Statistik Indonesia, http://www.bps .go.id/index.php?news=36 (accessed December 8, 2011).

25. Nan Achnas, "Rebirth of Indonesian Film Industry, and the Glaring Lack of Creativity," *JP*, June 9, 2007, http://www.thejakartapost.com/news/2007/06/09/rebirth -indonesian-film-industry-and-glaring-lack-creativity.html (accessed December 8, 2011).

26. Joko Anwar, "'Jelangkung' a Guilty Pleasure," *JP*, November 25, 2001, http:// www.thejakartapost.com/news/2001/11/25/039jelangkung039-a-guilty-pleasure.html (accessed December 8, 2011); Tony Ryanto, "Auds Scream for Horror Hit," *Variety Asia*, November 26–December 2, 2001, http://www.variety.com/article/VR1117856243?refcat id=19&printerfriendly=true (accessed December 8, 2011).

27. Joko Anwar, "2001 Hints at Signs of Film Industry Recovery," *JP*, December 28, 2001, http://www.thejakartapost.com/news/2001/12/28/2001-hints-signs-film-industry -recovery.html (accessed December 8, 2011).

28. Iwan, "Resurrecting Fear."

29. Evieta P. Fadjar, "Pocong terkubur sensor" [Shrouded corpse buried by censors], *Tempointeraktif*, October 17, 2006, http://www.tempo.co/read/news /2006/10/17/07186217/Pocong-Terkubur-Sensor (accessed December 8, 2011); Eko Hendrawan Sofyan, "LSF hadang 'Dendam Pocong'" [Film Censorship Bureau blocks *Revenge of the Shrouded Corpse*], *Kompas Cybermedia*, October 6, 2006, http://www.kompas .com/ver1/Hiburan/0610/06/133217.htm (accessed April 15, 2009).

30. For a recent "pocong sighting" in Jakarta, see http://www.thejakartaglobe.com /home/ghost-sightings-spark-scenes-of-hysteria-in-indonesian-capital/482256 (accessed December 9, 2011). Thanks to Jesse Grayman and Karen Strassler for bringing this to my attention.

31. The fourth was a romantic comedy, "Get Married." "Like Hollywood *summer movies*, K2 was designed to become a *Lebaran movie* that is filled with a high level of tension and horror without trivializing the need for a storyline that is solid and strong," remarked director Rizal Mantovani (quoted in a press release: Barry Setyawan, "Kuntilanak lepas! Tiket bioskop terjual habis di hari pertama" [*Kuntilanak* is out! Theater tickets sold out on the first day], October 11, 2007, http://movies.groups .yahoo.com/group/cinemagsforum/message/22855 (accessed December 8, 2011).

32. Karl Heider, *Indonesian Cinema: National Culture on Screen* (Honolulu: University of Hawaii Press, 1991); Seno Joko Suyono et al., "Menjenguk film-film horor Indonesia" [Taking a look at Indonesian horror films], *Tempo*, February 17, 2003, http://majalah

.tempointeraktif.com/id/arsip/2003/02/17/LYR/mbm.20030217.LYR85172.id.html (accessed December 8, 2011). Writers who distinguish between "legend films" and true horror films argue that the first Indonesian horror film was either *Tengkorak Idoep* [Living skull] in 1941 or the psychological thriller *Lisa* in 1971. See Nuruddin Asyhadi, "Paramarupa film horor kita" [Visual grammar of our horror films], *"F"* 3 (February–March 2006), http://www.mail-archive.com/filsafat@yahoogroups.com/msg01445 .html (accessed December 8, 2011); Hikmat Darmawan, "Mengapa Film Horor?" [Why horror film?], parts 1 and 2, *Rumah Film,* July 24, 2008, and August 1, 2008, http:// old.rumahfilm.org/artikel/artikel_horor.htm and http://old.rumahfilm.org/artikel /artikel_horor_2.htm (both accessed January 2, 2011).

33. Heider, *Indonesian Cinema*, 44; Katinka van Heeren, "Return of the Kyai: Representations of Horror, Commerce, and Censorship in Post-Suharto Indonesian Film and Television," *Inter-Asian Cultural Studies* 8, no. 2 (2007): 213.

34. One of the ubiquitous and beloved figures of these films was the Eurasian actress Suzzanna, the "Queen of Indonesian Horror." She starred in at least forty-two films, between the 1971 film *Beranak dalam Kubur* [Birth in the grave] and her final appearance, in 2008's *Hantu Ambulans* [Haunted ambulance]. Many of these are still available on cheap VCDs in Indonesian markets. For a tribute to her as an icon of Indonesian horror, see Veronica Kusuma, "Suzzanna dan ideologi film horor" [Suzzanna and the ideology of horror film], *Tempointeraktif,* October 20, 2008, http://www.tempo.co /hg/film/2008/10/20/111141060/Suzanna-dan-Ideologi-Film-Horor (accessed December 8, 2011).

35. Heeren, "Return of the Kyai."

36. Darmawan, "Mengapa film horor?" part 1.

37. For instance, an online reviewer describes the film *Pocong 2* as "possibly the scariest film ever made in Indonesia" and comments that the "amateurish" handheld camera work (by director Rudy Sudjarwo) "only adds to the gripping atmosphere of the film." Ferrysiregar, review of *Pocong 2*, http://www.sinema-indonesia.com/neo /2007/04/02/pocong-22007 (accessed April 2, 2007).

38. Adhitiyaswara Nuswandana, "Kelar cinta remaja, dikejar hantu jadi pilihan" [Teen love is finished, being chased by ghosts is the choice], *Kompas Cybermedia,* December 18, 2006, http://keepmesick.multiply.com/journal/item/1?&show_interstiti al=1&u=%2Fjournal%2Fitem (accessed February 24, 2012).

39. Darmawan, "Mengapa film horor?" part 2. Hikmat traces this particular aesthetic to the influence of surrealist/ethnographic film director Garin Nugroho, one of the few remaining serious filmmakers from the 1980s. Notable for his impressionistic style, attention to local cultures, poetic cinematography, and tendency to emphasize the visual over the narrative aspects of filmmaking, Garin revolutionized television

advertising and has had a hand in training many young filmmakers. The quote is from mumu [Is. Mujiarso], "Semiotika hujan dan metafora bebek panggang" [Grown up digital] (blog), October 23, 2007, http://rumputeki.multiply.com/reviews/item/18 (accessed January 2, 2011).

40. Two interesting exceptions to this are Hanung Bramantyo's period remake of the classic Suzzanna vehicle *Legenda Sundel Bolong* [Legend of the pierced whore] (referring to a seductive, vengeful ghost that can be identified by the gaping hole in her back), set in the turbulent days before the 1965 massacre of alleged Communists and fellow travelers, and the tacky ripped-from-the-headlines *Skandal Cinta Babi Ngepet* [Love scandal of the were-pig], in which a poor village youth married to a girl from a wealthy family turns to black magic to support her in the style to which she is accustomed.

41. On representations of the Chinese in Indonesian films more generally, see Ariel Heryanto, "Citizenship and Indonesian Ethnic Chinese in Post-1998 Films," in *Popular Culture in Indonesia*, ed. Ariel Heryanto (London: Routledge, 2008), 70–92.

42. Carla Jones, "Better Women: The Cultural Politics of Gendered Expertise in Indonesia," *American Anthropologist* 112, no. 2 (2010): 270–282.

43. In the past several years Muslim-themed films have become increasingly popular in Indonesia, from the romantic hit *Ayat-ayat Cinta* [Verses of love] in 2008 to the sentimental 2010 release *Emak Ingin Naik Haji* [Mom wants to go on the haj]. The horror genre still seems to be mostly unaffected by this turn. See Veronica Kusuma, "When Religion Sells: How Cinema Is Used to Create Muslim Identities," *JP*, September 27, 2008, http://www.thejakartapost.com/news/2008/09/27/when-religion-sells-how -cinema-used-create-muslim-identities.html (accessed December 8, 2011).

44. This follows a long-standing convention in Indonesian melodrama or serious film: avoidance of religious censorship by identifying all morally dubious characters as either explicitly or implicitly Christian.

45. See Nauval Yazid, "Asian Horror Cinema: Not Enough to Stand 'Alone,'" *JP*, July 30, 2007, http://www.thejakartapost.com/news/2007/07/30/asian-horror -cinema-not-enough-stand-039alone039.html-0 (accessed December 8, 2011); Tony Ryanto, "Lee, King of Remakes, Translates East into West," *JP*, June 23, 2007, http:// images.thejakartapost.com/news/2007/06/23/lee-king-remakes-translates-east-west. html (accessed December 8, 2011); Bliss Cua Lim, "Generic Ghosts: Remaking the New 'Asian Horror Film,'" in *Hong Kong Film, Hollywood and the New Global Cinema: No Film Is an Island*, ed. Gina Marchetti and Tan See Kam (London: Routledge, 2007), 109–125.

46. Kajri Jain, *Gods in the Bazaar: The Economies of Indian Calendar Art* (Durham, NC: Duke University Press, 2007), 14.

47. This has not always been the case. See, for example, James T. Siegel, *Solo in the New Order* (Princeton, NJ: Princeton University Press, 1986), on the stock characters of

"Draculla" and "Mrs. Draculla" in the Javanese Sri Mulat theater troupe in 1970s Solo. Siegel (p. 321) also reports several alleged "Dracula sightings" in Java and Bali in 1981.

48. "Farah," comment in thread "Pocong horror" on *Indonesia matters* website, July 6, 2008, http://www.indonesiamatters.com/1866/pocong-horror/ (accessed December 8, 2011).

49. Pamuji et al., "Tayangan setan."

50. Joko Anwar, "Mystery Keep Audience Glued to Television Screen," *JP*, July 27, 2002, http://www.thejakartapost.com/news/2002/07/27/mystery-keep-audience-glued -television-screen.html (accessed December 8, 2011).

51. Alex Ong, "Token Gestures," *Inside Indonesia* 100 (April–June 2010), http:// www.insideindonesia.org/edition-100/token-gestures-24041293 (accessed April 16, 2011). A similar "pocong protest," from a demonstration against the post-tsunami Agency for the Rehabilitation and Reconstruction of Aceh and Nias, can be seen at http://www.youtube.com/watch?v=uMkmSLyHWFU. Thanks to Dennis McGilvray for bringing this to my attention. See also Nils Bubandt, "The Spirit Army," *Inside Indonesia* 108 (April–June 2012), http://www.insideindonesia.org/feature/the-spirit -army-02042903 (accessed June 20, 2012).

52. Although American-style slasher films such as the *Saw* series are popular in Indonesia, it is only in the last several years that similar "torture-porn" films have begun to appear there. The first, to my knowledge, was a short film, *Dara*, which was later included in the horror anthology *Takut* [Fear]. Following this trend are psychological thrillers, *Pintu Terlarang* [Forbidden door] by Joko Anwar and the direct-to-video *Kado Hari Jadi* [Anniversary gift], as well as the self-identified "slasher" film *Air Terjun Pengantin* [Newlywed's waterfall] by Rizal Mantovani. For a review of *Kado Hari Jadi*, see Iva, "'Kado Hari Jadi' Crosses the Voyeuristic Boundary," *JP*, June 29, 2008, http:// www.thejakartapost.com/news/2009/06/29/039kado-hari-jadi039-crosses-voyeuristic- boundary.html (accessed December 9, 2011).

53. Jean and John Comaroff, "Transparent Fictions; or the Conspiracies of a Liberal Imagination: An Afterword," in *Transparency and Conspiracy: Ethnographies of Suspicion in the New World Order*, ed. Harry G. West and Todd Sanders (Durham, NC: Duke University Press, 2003), 288.

54. Online film reviewer Dodi Mahendra made the point in reverse, as it were, by ridiculing *Hantu Jeruk Purut* [The ghost of Jeruk Purut (cemetery)]: "This genius producer believes a horror film won't succeed if the ghost appears less than 44 times.... Taking off from that belief, *Hantu Jeruk Purut* has 47 ghostly apparitions." As a result, Dodi concludes, the figure of the film's eponymous headless priest is "only good for giggles." Dodi Mahendra, review of "Hantu Jeruk Purut," Sinema-Indonesia, http:// www.sinema-indonesia.com/neo/2007/04/02/hantu-jeruk-purut-2007/ (accessed

April 2, 2007). Joko Anwar makes a similar point in a critique of *Jelangkung 2*: "Dimas seems to think the success of a horror film depends on how often ghosts appear in a film: Anyone who has watched *The Blair Witch Project* or *Rosemary's Baby* will certainly disagree.... The frequent ghost sightings in Dimas's horror movie generate almost no sense of fear. We see the ghosts show up while a character is taking a shower, while another is sleeping, or while yet another is picking his nose. So what? It's not as though the movie hints that the ghosts are putting the characters' lives in danger. Too bad, as the makeup department has done a good job in giving the ghosts an appearance that could have been disturbing." Joko Anwar, "'Tusuk': Plenty of Ghosts but Few Thrills," *JP*, March 22, 2003, http://www.thejakartapost.com/news/2003/03/22/tusuk039-plenty -ghosts-few-thrills.html (accessed December 8, 2011).

55. Birgit Meyer, "Ghanaian Popular Cinema and the Magic in and of Film," in *Magic and Modernity: Interfaces of Revelation and Concealment*, ed. Birgit Meyer and Peter Pels (Stanford, CA: Stanford University Press, 2003), 200–222.

56. Heeren, "Return of the Kyai," 221.

57. Dean, *Publicity's Secret*, 13.

58. Patricia Spyer, "Fire without Smoke and Other Phantoms of Ambon's Violence: Media Effects, Agency, and the Work of Imagination," *Indonesia* 74 (2002): 36.

59. Dean, *Publicity's Secret*, 42.

11

From Lawrence of Arabia to Special Operations Forces

The "White Sheik" as a Modular Image in Twentieth-Century Popular Culture

Steven C. Caton

This chapter is about an image I call the white sheik, a man racially marked as white who passes (or tries to pass) for an Arab. I argue that he is a "modular" image, in the sense that certain of his features or characteristics (physical and psychological) are malleable and can be detached and recombined to form new images over time, though these images are nevertheless recognizable as belonging to the "white sheik." He has a long history in Anglo-American popular culture, but I am concerned with his genealogy in the twentieth century only. I use the term "genealogy" in a playfully metaphorical sense, for in many ways one can see how historical iterations of this figure are "descended" from or laterally related to other iterations of his image. This chapter traces this image's modularity and genealogy, examining what it appears to be "doing," ideologically and psychologically, in far-flung and diverse historical and cultural contexts. The question remains of what propels this modular image in the first place, such that it can do its ideological and psychological work. To answer that question, I consider the production of the image by apparatuses of colonialist rhetoric, the culture industry and its public spheres, and military strategies of the late twentieth-century US Army. In the conclusion, I return to the analytical problem of this image's modularity and genealogy, arguing that these features are centrally related to how images travel through space and time, the theme of this book.

Five iterations of the white sheik emerged at different times in twentieth-century Anglo-American culture. I examine these using both text and image from popular literature and film, journalism, military biography, and military manuals for purposes of illustration to trace his transformations.[1] Four iterations were huge media events (a popular slide-lecture show, a best-selling novel, and two blockbuster films), a significant reason for the image's widespread dissemination. The white sheik manages to pop up in each historical period's most popular cultural forms and to reach millions of people. The diversity of these media—illuminated slide lecture, romance novel, feature film, war memoir, journalism, and counterinsurgency field manual—attests to how fungible and bankable a figure the white sheik is, moving like currency from one mass-circulating medium to the next and from one historical moment to another.

What interests me is the way in which certain discourses of power (for example, colonialist rhetoric) harness themselves to such powerful media (widely circulating and influential) and propel ideologically laden images like the white sheik into the public sphere. (This is not to say that the image always works as its ideologues had hoped or intended; in fact, the contrary may be the case because of what I call below the dialectics of the image.) Also, the particular works—be they literary or filmic—in which the white sheik appears are, themselves, referenced in subsequent texts of popular culture. This citation makes genealogical relations among the images possible. We shall see, for example, how Norman Schwarzkopf, the general who led US forces in the First Gulf War, evokes in his memoir the figure of T. E. Lawrence, not as one might predict—that is, as a figure constructed by a historian or a literary biographer—but as he appears *specifically* in David Lean's film. Thus, a genealogical connection is made between an immensely popular film and a general's image of himself. Why would a particular work of popular culture like the film *Lawrence of Arabia* become the master trope for the autobiography of one of the nation's most famous generals? The obvious answer is that he knows, or his ghostwriter and publisher know, that many more people who read his book are familiar with the film than with a specific biography of the historical figure, so the epic movie is used to frame a contemporary event, the First Gulf War, and narrate its general's career. In other words, a work of popular culture becomes the lens through which a public is invited to understand a world-historical event.

Perhaps the reason that the white sheik can function symbolically in this way has to do with the fact that he is a dialectical image.[2] Unlike the oil sheik, a figure who emerged in the 1970s in US popular culture in response to the then oil crisis and its political consequences (or going even further back in time to the Barbary coast pirates, the last of whom, Sidi Moulay Ahmed Muhammed ar-Rassouli, emerged as a figure in the US popular imagination when Teddy Roosevelt needed a war in Morocco for internal political reasons), the sheik I am talking about is both Arab and non-Arab; that is, he seems to expertly *masquerade* as an Arab sheik. The masquerade is so skillful, it is presumed that he can pass for an Arab leader better than an Arab could. His whiteness is shifting as well. At times portrayed as white, at other times as white ethnic, and at other times as nonwhite, his racial identity is protean, depending on the historical context in which he emerges. He is a chameleon of gender and sexuality as well: at times hypermasculine, at other times effeminate or at least androgynous; at times heterosexual, at other times bisexual or gay. That this figure has endured so long in popular culture is due in no small measure to these racial, gender, and sexual ambiguities. Different facets of his character can be manipulated for varying ideological projects and publics. But because of this ambiguity, he is also an *unstable* ideological construct, leading, often in the same text, to contradictory readings, ones that can even be subversive of dominant ideological conceptions of the world. This instability is important to capture. It means that his ideological potency is a two-edged sword, at once representing certain dominant ideologies but doing so in ways that have the potential of imminently undermining them.

LOWELL THOMAS AND THE CONSTRUCTION OF "LAWRENCE OF ARABIA": THE WHITE SHEIK IN COLONIALIST DISCOURSE

Lowell Thomas (1892–1981) was one of radio and television's longest running and highest paid news broadcasters and commentators. He readily acknowledged that what launched his fabled career was his lucky "discovery" of T. E. Lawrence (1888–1935) and the chance to tell of Lawrence's legendary exploits in a travelogue-lecture-slide exhibition that toured the eastern United States, Great Britain, and parts of the British Empire from 1919 until about 1926. It is estimated that about four million people saw the show during its run. "I realized that Lawrence was one of the most romantic figures of the war," Thomas confessed toward the end of his memoir, *With Lawrence in Arabia*; "I knew that we had a great scoop" (plate 29).[3]

The origins of the show lay in US involvement in World War One. The twenty-five-year-old Thomas was contacted by, or he himself approached, the US secretary of the interior in 1917 with the idea of propagandizing the European war in the United States, and this because of the isolationist stance many Americans were taking at the time. With financial backing

FIGURE 11.1

Lowell Thomas (from Thomas, With Lawrence in Arabia, *1926).*

from several Chicago businessmen, Thomas headed off to Europe with his wife, Fran, and a Hollywood cameraman by the name of Harry Chase, who shot film of T. E. Lawrence and his raiders and took photographs of the war hero that would later become the illustrations in the show. At first Thomas thought that he would focus on the western front and an appealing, photogenic "doughboy" who would become the hero of his narrative, but all the likely candidates had the unfortunate tendency of getting themselves killed in the trenches or shot out of the air. Nor did the stalemate in the fighting between the Allies and the German forces lend itself to a dramatic story. Nearly at wit's end, Thomas came across General Allenby, who was having some success in leading Allied forces to victory against the Turks in the Near East, and when Jerusalem fell to the Allies in 1918, he decided to visit Allenby's field of operations. Since the great general wanted as little as possible to do with this brash young American, he fobbed him off on a colorful young officer attached to the Arab "irregular" forces under the leadership of Hussein, the emir of Mecca and Medina, and his sons Abdullah and Feisal. This officer was T. E. Lawrence. The war was already winding down by the time Thomas got his footage of Lawrence and returned to America, so he had to reconsider his propaganda goal. No longer a matter of persuading an isolationist American public to join the war effort, it became a way for the public to remember and memorialize it.

The "romance" of Lawrence of Arabia was so appealing to 1920s audiences largely because it helped mythologize World War One. Paul Fussell has, of course, brilliantly analyzed this more general process in his book *The Great War and Modern Memory*,[4] but his theme is for the most part "high" rather than "popular" culture and the western rather than the eastern front, the former of which in both cases were Thomas's concerns. Yet, I would argue that the extraordinary popularity of Thomas's show is attributable to the rhetorical difficulties inherent in justifying and glorifying the war as it was propagated on the western front. Thomas, after all, had personally experienced these difficulties when he failed to find his doughboy or a narrative in which to insert a hero into the European theater of war, which is why Thomas turned to the "Orient" in the first place. A "romantic" representation of the eastern front could help displace the horrible images of the western one. The public saw what a dashing figure Lawrence cut in his Arab robes; the fighting in which he engaged was pictured as no less antique than and almost quaint by comparison with the routine slaughter of men in Europe. Orientalism was essential to creating a place of fantasy and romance, and whereas the British might have searched their souls as to why they slaughtered fellow Europeans, they would have lost little sleep over the Turks, against whom, Thomas said, the Allies had fought a "crusade" to liberate the "Holy Land."

Thomas observed that Lawrence was an insignificant-looking chap dressed in the garb of a British officer but cut a much more dashing figure in the gorgeous raiment of an "Oriental potentate."

One of the pictures from the show is of Lawrence on Thomas's hotel balcony in Jerusalem dressed in Arab costume.

FIGURE 11.2

T. E. Lawrence on the balcony of a hotel room in Jerusalem (from Thomas, With Lawrence in Arabia, *1926).*

FIGURE 11.3

T. E. Lawrence dressed in British uniform and as an Arab sheik (from Thomas, With Lawrence in Arabia, *1926).*

FIGURE 11.4

Two photographs of T. E. Lawrence dressed in the white robes of a Bedouin sheik (from Thomas, With Lawrence in Arabia, *1926).*

Although each individual item of the costume—the dagger, the robe, the headdress—is authentic, the ensemble seems fabricated to appear fantastic but also grand to a Western audience. Most of the pictures of him in the show and the memoir very obviously constructed a figure of the "white sheik," as can be seen from this pair of remarkable photographic portraits.

These images clearly mark Lawrence as "white." The genuineness of the robes notwithstanding, their symbolic function seems to accentuate Lawrence's whiteness, along with his fair hair, blue eyes, and pale skin, which the text never fails to mention. "This young man was as blond as a Scandinavian [p. 4]...Emir Feisal and his fair-haired 'grand vizier' [p. 87] ...the blond shereef [p. 137]...the young shereef, incongruously picturesque with his Anglo-Saxon face [p.183]." It is Lawrence's cultural identity that is ambiguous, sometimes appearing British, at other times Arab. For example, we are told that he was fluent in Arabic and wholly conversant with Arab customs. One of the photographs in the memoir portrays Lawrence squatting on his haunches rather than sitting in a chair, as if to show that he had become inured to life among the Bedouin.

In brief, the audience was supposed to suspend its disbelief when it came to Lawrence's passing for an Arab. The sight of a British officer in Arab clothes, especially when told that he apparently *liked* to dress in this

FIGURE 11.5

T. E. Lawrence and Lowell Thomas outside a tent (from Thomas, With Lawrence in Arabia, *1926).*

fashion, could on occasion alarm, if not panic, an audience of that day, who could easily see this as a betrayal of white civilization. "Going native," as the text hints that Lawrence had done, was no simple or innocent affair in colonial society. To distance the audience from this disquiet, Thomas provided this explanation: "To gain his ends it was necessary for Lawrence to be a consummate actor. He was obliged completely to submerge his European mode of living, even at the risk of winning criticism and ridicule [by] his own countrymen, by appearing in cities like Cairo, where East and West meet, garbed as an Oriental" (p. 366). In other words, Lawrence's "going native" is a disguise, like the mask of an actor onstage, and is related to his deeper political strategies, which seem almost fascistic. Numerous passages such as the following are sprinkled throughout the text: "The magnificent Bedouin clothes that Lawrence wore…were part of his carefully worked-out plan to gain complete mastery over the Arabs" (p. 243). "He brought the disunited nomadic tribes of Holy and Forbidden Arabia into a united campaign against their Turkish oppressors, a difficult and splendid stroke of policy, which caliphs, statesmen, and sultans had been unable to accomplish in centuries of effort!" (p. 7). Colonial rhetoric implies that Arabs

FIGURE 11.6

T. E. Lawrence, the white sheik (from Thomas, With Lawrence in Arabia, *1926).*

are unable to rule themselves because they are "tribal" and tribes by their very nature are "feud addicted," so the intervention of an outside state or a charismatic leader is required. Hence, the colonial deus ex machina of the "white sheik."

Another rhetorical principle is that this sheik had to appear culturally Arab so as to win the respect of his Arab followers, though he had to be racially white in order to overcome the weakness of the Arab race, in particular its violence and unruliness, while keeping the respect of his colonial admirers. The text stresses that Lawrence acquired a deep cultural familiarity with the Arab tribes and that this knowledge was indispensable for his military and political success: "His trips alone among the villages in search of rare rugs and antiquities, that gave opportunity for cultivating that close touch and sympathy with them that subsequently was the basis of his great service in the time of his country's need [p.18]…Lawrence knew that he was being watched constantly by shereefs, sheikhs, and tribesmen, and he knew that they would regard it as a very great compliment to them if he went about, even among his own people, dressed in the costume of the desert [p. 366]…Colonel Lawrence believed in the Arabs, and the Arabs believed in him, but they would never have trusted him so implicitly had he not been such a complete master of their customs and all the superficial external features of Arabian life [p. 374]." These are old Orientalist tropes, of course, but they were recycled at a precise moment in the 1920s when Great Britain successfully (though not without some resistance, particularly in Iraq) established its foothold over oil-rich lands of the Near East. A mandate system was set up, according to which, local rulers, such as Hussein and Feisal would become kings of Iraq, Syria, and Transjordan, but their armies and administrations were staffed by the British, such as Gertrude Bell, or by British-trained local elites—and they were the ones who held the real power, not the Arabs. One of the enduring epithets of the show, in fact, was of Lawrence as the "Uncrowned King of Arabia" (p. 6). The connection between cultural knowledge and military success in insurgency warfare was thus forged and would come up again in the late twentieth-century wars in Iraq and Afghanistan.

Let us turn now to the question of the white sheik's gender. Thomas remarks that when Lawrence stood beside the Arabs, he appeared as a "beardless blond." The emphasis on Lawrence's beardlessness (which is supposed to contrast with Arabs' masculine preference for facial hair) makes him seem adolescent, even effeminate, an impression that is accentuated by his diminutive stature (Lawrence was about five feet seven inches tall). The sartorial excess of his Arab robes, one might add, makes him appear androgynous to a Western audience unused to Arab clothing. Gender ambiguities are heightened when we learn in Thomas's memoir that Lawrence was supposed to have dressed as a veiled native woman in order to go behind enemy lines, ostensibly for purposes of espionage.

"Accompanied by a lone Bedouin of the Anazah tribe named Dahmi, [Lawrence] passed through Turkish lines in his customary female disguise and made his way toward Palmyra [p. 246]…At Amman, in the hills of

FIGURE 11.7

"Gypsy Woman," one of T. E. Lawrence's alleged disguises (from Thomas, With Lawrence in Arabia, *1926).*

Moab, east of Jordan, Lawrence went through the Turkish lines disguised as a Bedouin Gipsy. He spent the afternoon prowling about the defenses surrounding the railway station, and, after deciding that it would be futile for his Arabs to attempt to capture it, on account of the size of the garrison and the strength of the artillery, he started toward the desert" (p. 251). Men dressing as women in order, paradoxically, to "penetrate" army lines is not unheard of in military annals of the Middle East. Ehud Barak, the former prime minister of Israel, is supposed to have led a raid on Lebanon, dressed as a woman, and participated in the assassination of three PLO leaders.[5] But then Thomas makes a curious observation: "For even though [Lawrence] did wear the robes and accoutrements of a shereef of Mecca, *he only actually posed as an Oriental when he slipped through Turkish lines wearing the veil of a native woman*" (p. 371, emphasis added). In other words, Lawrence's gorgeous shareefean robes never fooled anybody, least of all, of course, the Turks; the text claims that it was only when he was cross-dressing that he could finally pass for an Arab—albeit a female one. What is the purpose of this revelation about Lawrence as a white man masquerading as a woman in order to pass for an Arab? Is it a way of hinting at his homosexual identity? Perhaps. Yet, there is no evidence that Thomas had any inklings of it. If it is a male fantasy of total mastery, it is an ironic one, to say the least, and, as it turns out, not even that is assured, for we learn that dressed as a Bedouin woman, Lawrence was occasionally harassed by Turkish soldiers (p. 251). On the one hand, of course, this could be pure cross-dressing hijinks, but it betrays a homophobic anxiety that undercuts the trope of male (and by extension, colonial) mastery that the text is constantly trying to assert. For that reason, the image of the white sheik as a veiled woman is a dialectical one, at once projecting a fantasy of total control but implicitly or unconsciously calling it into question.

In many ways Thomas's construction of "Lawrence of Arabia" is remarkable for exhibiting all the modular elements of the white sheik—his racial, gender, and sexual ambiguity; his cultural passing; and his cultural knowledge of the Other combined with military expertise—that would be repeated and reshuffled in subsequent iterations extending over a century. The show gave birth to a protean figure, to say the least.

THE SHEIK, ROMANCE NOVEL (1919) AND FILM (1921): AN IMAGE FOR FEMALE READERSHIP AND SPECTATORSHIP

In the postwar period an antifeminist reaction set in against more than just the overabundance of women in a formerly male-dominated workforce. It also set in against a new concept of female beauty, the flapper, who had a boyish figure and flaunted her independent ways, especially in what was perceived as her flagrantly open sexuality. The conservative press of the day explained her as only the latest symptom of a dangerous decline in morality, even a degeneracy in the white race, that seemed to be evident everywhere. At the same time in the twenties when the term "flapper" entered into public parlance, the word "sheik" came to be used to signify a virile, priapic male, a violent lover who masters females by sexual prowess and physical force. It is against this background of changing notions of gender, sexuality, and ethnicity as captured in the terms "flapper" and "sheik" that we have to read Edith M. Hull's romance novel *The Sheik* (1919).[6] If the war created a relatively powerful and affluent female workforce, the latter also became the basis of a new reading public and, we might add, a new film spectatorship. *The Sheik* tapped into that female public in contradictory yet powerful ways.[7]

The novel's protagonist, Lady Diana Mayo, had grown up an orphan but was raised in the lap of British aristocratic luxury and has come to Algeria to have an adventure. She possesses many of the cultural attributes of the flapper of the period. Both the novel and the film stress her strongly independent will, as when she insists on undertaking an excursion into the desert accompanied only by her Arab guides and porters against the wishes of her brother. Diana's androgynous appearance is remarked upon several times, and she is apparently uninterested in sex. "'I have never been kissed in my life,'" she warns a suitor in the garden of the Biskra Hotel in Algeria where she and her brother are staying.

It bears remembering that the period during and after World War One was one of unprecedented discussion and expression of female sexuality. Freud was not the only important figure to insist that women had powerful erotic urges. But what outrages the guardians of gender and sexuality in the novel and the film more than anything else is that Diana's behavior threatens the patriarchal order, as evinced in the blunt criticism she receives from her brother, to which she responds, "My life is my own to deal with, and I will deal with it exactly as I wish and not as any one else wishes… I will never obey any will but my own." Her brother then throws back at her what in hindsight of the events to come seems like a curse: "Then I hope to Heaven that one day you will fall into the hands of a man who will make you obey."[8]

His name is Sheik Ahmed, and we are made to assume that he is a full-blooded Arab. He has already seen Lady Diana in the garden of the Biskra Hotel and has hatched a plot to abduct her. She tries to flee and, because of her superb horsemanship, gives Ahmed a gallant chase, but he eventually catches up with her and lifts her out of her saddle. His brute strength proves too much for her. He takes her back to camp and that evening ravishes her. Orientalism has everything to do with the depiction of this rapist.

"He was pitiless in his arrogance, pitiless in his Oriental disregard of the woman subjugated. He was an Arab, to whom the feelings of a woman were non-existent. He had taken her to please himself, to amuse him in the moments of his relaxation" (p. 92). Hull's text is not the least apologetic or equivocal in its ideological explanation for the rape: "She had paid heavily for the determination to ignore the restrictions of her sex laid upon her."[9]

To readers of the day, the rape might not have even been the most scandalous part of the tale, for in the very heart of the text lurks the horror of miscegenation. "Only rage filled her—blind passionate rage against the man who dared to touch her, who had dared to lay his hands on her, and those hands the hands of a native. A shiver of revulsion ran through her."[10] By the end of their encounter, however, she ignores the racial divide between her lover and herself, for in spite of (or perhaps because of) the sheik's brutality, she has fallen in love with him, and he with her. By then, too, the flapper has given way to a different kind of woman. "The alert, vigorous boyishness that had been so characteristic was gone. Her slim figure drooping listlessly in the big chair, her white face with the new marks of suffering on it, and her wide eyes burning with dumb misery, were all purely womanly."[11]

Yet, the novel holds out a surprise ending in which we learn that Ahmed is not Arab after all but, as I would dub him, a white sheik; more exactly, he is the son of a Spanish mother and an English lord, which leaves open the ambiguity of his racial identity and thus makes him a socially acceptable mate for Diana. With this revelation, a dialectic is set in motion between self and Other, Western patriarchy and Oriental one. If Diana's brother was unable to discipline her, it is because Western patriarchy had faltered. One had to travel to the Orient to find a stronger, redemptive one.

The movie is adapted from the novel, but there are significant changes. The most important of these is that Sheik Ahmed, not Diana, is at the center of the narrative (showcasing Valentino's stardom), thus foregrounding the problematic nature not so much of her gender and sexuality as of his. In keeping with this change of focus, the film is concerned with the transformation of his character and supposed redemption. In fact, it is she who redeems him, not the other way around. The second important change is that the rape never occurs. The threat of it is constant, but the act is always deferred, until in fact it never happens because Ahmed is spiritually transformed and his urge is dissipated. This may have had to do with Hollywood censorship, but I doubt it. I argue that it is more likely to do with a narrative about race and ethnicity in the United States in the 1920s.

Let us consider a scene from the film to see how the sheik is redeemed.

Diana is in the sheik's camp against her will. In the novel the sheik gives her a beautiful jade necklace to wear as a present, but in the film this is replaced by a crucifix. Indeed, it throws back the reflection of the studio lights like a beacon gleaming in the darkness. Diana tries to escape, but the sheik has no trouble subduing her. He holds her in his arms and kisses her, and the viewer is taken aback by the contrast between the powdery white face and arms of Diana and the darker face and hands of the sheik. Just then, one of the sheik's henchmen tells him that the horses have stampeded in a sandstorm and that he is needed to help recapture them. Given a temporary reprieve, Diana retreats into the tent's interior, where she flings herself in despair on the edge of the bed. We see her now from the front, her tearful eyes raised heavenward, the crucifix gleaming ever more brightly at her neck, and her hands clasped in prayer. Upon returning, the sheik stands behind and above her prostrate figure and grins lasciviously as he is about to grab his prize, but then he stops in his tracks, presumably because of the power of Christian prayer. Lust gives way to guilt and remorse, and he turns from his victim, shuffling toward the tent's entrance, his body as limp as a deflated phallus. Cut to the next morning. The sheik has a breakfast tray prepared on which he delicately places a red rose. Rapacious desire has given way to chivalrous love, white slavery to Christian marriage.

What does this story about such an ambiguously white sheik, who becomes civilized and thus a suitable mate for a bourgeois white woman, have to do with the United States in the 1920s? It is well known that from the late nineteenth century until roughly 1920, the United States saw an unprecedented number of immigrants coming into the country from parts of the world that were classified as nonwhite according to prevailing scientific and popular cultural categories of the day. Great Britain had experienced some migration from its African, Asian, and Middle Eastern colonies, but very little by comparison with the United States. Various minority groups were beginning to lobby for civil rights and argue their cases in the courts on the grounds that they were "white." Mathew Jacobson in his book *Whiteness of a Different Color* explains how the courts wrestled with racial and cultural categories of the day when the claimants seemed, to all intents and purposes, assimilated to bourgeois American culture yet were still "nonwhite" in terms of their skin color and other phenotypic traits.[12] Along racial binaries of black and white there emerged in the courts and other public discourses the more ambiguous category of white ethnicity. I suggest, therefore, that the love story of Diana and Ahmed is a parable, not of a white man who would be sheik, as in Thomas's story of Lawrence, but of the sheik who would be white. He had to learn to act white, learn to tame his savagery, in order to become a fit mate for the white Christian female in the American polity.

THE FILM *LAWRENCE OF ARABIA* (1962): A POSTCOLONIAL DISCOURSE

Let us now jump four decades to 1962 and the movie *Lawrence of Arabia*. Insofar as the figure of the white sheik continues to play a vital part in the history of American popular culture, it is owing in no small measure to director David Lean's complex and visually powerful film, originally released in 1962 but then restored and reedited for rerelease in 1989.

There is a genealogical link between Thomas's construction and the movie's. Indeed, the link is quite self-conscious: Lowell Thomas appears in the movie as newspaper reporter Jackson Bentley, who explains in an interview with Prince Feisal that he is looking for a "romantic figure" to draw the Americans into war; later, we see him photograph and interview Lawrence in his white robes, very much as the historical Thomas had done. However, the Lawrence legend, as Thomas created it, had by this time in the mid to late 1950s come under critical scrutiny and revision, whether by British biographers such as Richard Aldington or Arab ones such as Salman Mousa, and the movie's figuration of the white sheik incorporates these complications.[13] For example, it emphasizes the fascistic sides of the white sheik that Thomas had lauded naïvely (perhaps because fascism was not yet on the rise when he did his show), and rather than the saintly figure Thomas evokes, the movie makes him out to be demonic and in the end half mad. He is thus fundamentally transformed.

The film's theater brochure, sold in cinema houses at the time of its initial release, depicts the white sheik Lawrence and an Arab boy running across the sand dunes (plate 30). This still is taken from a scene in the movie in which the two are rushing to save another Arab boy, who has fallen into quicksand. Taken out of context, the image is highly suggestive: the white sheik would appear to be the Arab's double, and the Arab is desperately trying to elude his grasp. The political and psychological message of the film is condensed into a single frame.

But the movie owes something as well to the white sheik as constructed in Valentino's film. From the point of view of filmic technique, we are a far cry, of course, from its naïve art. An international picture of its kind could make a decent profit only if it sold well to educated, middle-class audiences *outside* the United States, and this meant that it more often than not engaged cultural and political questions (such as cultural hegemony and colonialism) in more complex, self-critical, and progressive ways than has usually been argued for Orientalist films.[14] The white sheik's power is undermined by the irony of his situation and by the sardonic, often critical commentary he receives from other characters, including Arab ones, with the result that by the end of the movie he has little moral authority left. In that precise sense Adorno had in mind, he becomes a negative dialectical image, never being able to resolve the contradictions within himself.

When does the white sheik make his appearance in the film? It is after the desert raiders led by Sharif Ali (the black sheik) but inspired by the British officer, Lawrence, successfully cross the Nefud Desert.[15] Exhausted, he prepares to go to sleep as his erstwhile friend Sharif Ali decides to throw his army uniform into the fire. In the transition into the next scene, we see Lawrence rise phoenixlike from the fire to become a quite different kind of being, an Arab, presumably, though an Arab who is all white and diaphanous, the white sheik. Lawrence is encouraged by Sharif Ali and the Bedouin to go off into the desert to get used to his new outfit. On a white salt pan that looks like a theatrical stage, he enacts a playful pantomime in which he bares his dagger in order to look at himself in the blade's reflection, greets in a deeply reverential bow his own shadow on the dunes, and holds up the sides of his white robe as though they were wings and scampers across the salt pan like a mythical, winged creature. He comes to a careening halt when he realizes that he is not alone but is being watched by an Arab, the redoubtable Sheik Auda Abu Tayyi (played by Anthony Quinn), who asks in astonishment, "What are you doing, British?" Unlike the Turks in Lowell Thomas's show, the Arabs are not fooled by his attempts at cultural passing, the trope of colonial mastery thereby undermined.

Peter O'Toole's performance, which is at once playful, exuberant, funny, charming, and campy, is as audacious in its day as Valentino's was in his. Let us consider the contradictory nature of the white sheik's masculinity. But rather than examine it in the scene above, let me try to illustrate its contradictions by looking at two posters that advertised the movie, one in 1962 and the other in 1989, both meant to frame the problem for audiences.

In the 1962 Argentinean poster, we see an image that Columbia Pictures was distributing worldwide (plate 31). It is a face in the shape of a comic theater mask (masquerade being a crucial motif in this movie), a face that is obscured presumably by the shadow of the headdress, which is white and merges into the desert background around it. The overall impression is that of a sphinx. What is asserted of masculinity in the poster is perhaps apparent from the square jaw and the strong but fine nose, and these, in combination with the political image of militant Arabs, suggest the "rebel male" that was very much a construct in both British and US films at the time. We have only to think of the torturously introspective and edgy performances of Montgomery Clift, Marlon Brando, and James Dean. On the other side of the Atlantic, there were Dirk Bogarde and others representing marginal and socially problematical males, the most unnerving portrait of whom is perhaps Jimmy Porter in Osbourne's play *Look Back in Anger* (1957). O'Toole's performance plays on the fraught distinction between male and female in ways that I think were unprecedented for the time and hints at sexual ambiguities in the character in a complex and even sympathetic way.

Now contrast the 1962 poster with the one advertising the 1989 restoration (plate 32). The face is recognizably O'Toole's because he had by then become an international film star. He stands on a sand dune, his robe blown by the wind. The image looks like a composite. One half is a man's body—the robes outlining a slim but strong physique, the arm hanging down at the side, and the foot struck confidently outward—while the other half looks like a woman's, with the headdress streaming in the wind like long hair, the robes billowing out like a skirt, the arm crooked and held at the waist as though clutching a purse, and the foot demurely in front. This advertising art was clearly pushing a reading of the movie that might pique the gender-blurring interests of moviegoing audiences of the 1980s and 1990s, but it was also possible because much had happened in gender and sexual politics between 1962 and 1989, in particular, feminism and gay liberation. These had changed the ways in which masculinity might be received and even destabilized.

But we cannot leave the movie's image of the white sheik without pointing out one fundamental difference between Valentino's character and O'Toole's. Valentino's "white sheik" is redeemed by the powers of the virtuous Christian female, whereas there is no such moral uplift for O'Toole's Lawrence. That "fall" is conveyed by Lawrence's white robes growing ever more sullied and blood-stained the deeper he is mired in violence and cruelty. And the dagger he draws in the scene in which he dons his white robes for the first time, whose blade he uses narcissistically as a mirror, is later shown dripping with blood. Downfall, not redemption, is this white sheik's fate.

SCHWARZKOPF OF ARABIA

During and immediately after the First Gulf War, images of T. E. Lawrence circulated everywhere in the press. One of the inadvertently humorous images was a photograph of General Norman Schwarzkopf in Arab robes next to the emir of Kuwait, which appeared in the general's autobiography, *It Doesn't Take a Hero*.[16] The general reports that he had tried on the robes in his private quarters, gazing at himself in the mirror, which occasioned this confession in his memoir: "Turning self-consciously this way and that, I couldn't help but think of the film *Lawrence of Arabia*, in which Peter O'Toole, dressed in Arab garb for the first time, twirls slowly around on the sand dunes admiring himself."[17]

It was remarked by Lowell Thomas that Lawrence's success as a guerilla leader was owing in no small measure to his willingness to "go native" and indeed his flare for it. Schwarzkopf intimates that his success as a field operator (possibly even a Special Forces officer) and later as a general depended on exactly the same thing. At a bridge-blessing ceremony in South Vietnam, which he relates in his memoir, he was given a glass of pig blood with scotch to drink, and while the US advisor would not drink his, Schwarzkopf downed the mixture unflinchingly. One is reminded of the scene in *Lawrence of Arabia* in which O'Toole is given Bedouin food to eat for the first time, which he does with a barely perceptible look of dread on his face. Schwarzkopf remarks, "My Vietnamese counterparts were surprised and pleased," and then adds significantly, "Simply by drinking that toast of scotch and blood, I'd begun building ties that would prove vital in battle."[18] The importance of cultural knowledge to military tactics in late twentieth-century warfare will become even more starkly evident in our consideration of the Special Operations Forces.

ANTHROPOLOGY AND SPECIAL OPERATIONS FORCES

Anthropology, arguably the discipline most concerned with understanding the Other, became a significant academic subject roughly around the period of World War One. An interesting historical coincidence is that at the same time Lawrence was living and campaigning with the Bedouin, the Polish-born, British-trained anthropologist Bronislaw Malinowski (1886–1942) was living among the Trobriand Islanders in Melanesia, creating the role model of the field anthropologist for generations of anthropologists to come. In the entry to *A Diary in the Strict Sense of the Term* dated January 9, 1918, he wrote, "I know that if I had to go to war, I would have gone calmly and without much inner fuss. Now: place my everyday life in that heroic frame...."[19]

In other words Malinowski was describing fieldwork as a heroic military exploit, the anthropologist as the soldier hero and the foreign culture as the field of conquest or battle. And the reverse occurred in the postwar representations of the military war hero Lawrence as illustrated in Thomas's show and memoir. Lawrence had turned himself into the anthropological fieldworker, becoming proficient in Arabic, living among the Bedouin and adopting their customs, wandering with them in the desert—all for the aims of military victory and colonial rule. The idea that military success depends on cultural knowledge of the enemy would be repeated by other white sheiks involved in Middle East wars, such as we have just seen in the case of General Schwarzkopf and as we will see in the case of Special Operations Forces officers fighting in Afghanistan and Iraq. But it is in the immediate aftermath of World War One that the fateful convergence of two conceits, the war hero and the anthropologist, was forged.

In the *U.S. Army Marine Corps Counterinsurgency Manual*, T. E. Lawrence is prominently mentioned as one of the precursors of US Army Special Operations Forces officers (SOFs), soldiers especially trained in counterinsurgency.[20] During the Vietnam War they were known as the "Green Berets," made famous in US popular culture of that era through films and toys. One of the things the manual stresses is the importance of cultural knowledge and linguistic competence for counterinsurgency work. US anthropology has clearly informed its discussion of culture. "Culture is a 'web of meaning' shared by members of a particular society or group within a society" and is further defined as

> A system of shared beliefs, values, customs, behaviors and artifacts that members of a society use to cope with their world and with one another.
>
> Learned, through a process called enculturation.
>
> Shared by members of a society; there is no "culture of one."
>
> Patterned, meaning that people in a society live and think in ways forming definite, repeating patterns.
>
> Arbitrary, meaning that Soldiers and Marines should make no assumptions regarding what a society considers right and wrong, good or bad.[21]

Language is defined as a part of culture, and the manual states that it comprises both "grammatical knowledge" and appropriate social-situational use and verbal and nonverbal signs.[22] Even if an SOF has to use a translator or an interpreter, he is advised to have at least a basic understanding of the "social environment," especially status differences and how to index them, if he is to be effective in his field of operations. Appendix C of the manual gives detailed instructions on how to evaluate linguistic needs and obtain support for them.

The US Army has defined the Special Forces' function as one of providing the "glue" that keeps warring factions together in a military campaign and relaying information about the enemy back to the air force so that it can do its "pinpoint" bombing. In the US-led war in Afghanistan, the SOF was a US soldier who worked behind enemy lines (the Taliban) with native insurgent forces (the Northern Alliance). If he was not fluent in one of the languages indigenous to Afghanistan, such as Pashto, he hired a local bilingual translator to work with him. He understood tribal social organization and political leadership and would appear partially dressed in "native" garb, be it nothing more than a headdress perhaps or a shawl draped over his shoulder, to show solidarity with local cultural actors.

A portrait of such an SOF, Captain Dan Kearney, can be found in the February 24, 2008, *New York Times Sunday Magazine*. He was stationed in Afghanistan's Korengal Valley, where he conducted counterinsurgency military operations. The valley was beset by tribal factions, some of whom had allied themselves to foreign jihadists, and part of Kearney's job was to figure out local tribal organization to see whether the US military could intervene on the side of the anti-jihadists. "Kearney tried...sending e-mail messages to anthropologists and Afghan experts to get their guidance."[23] He even did genealogies of local families to understand their relationships to one another. In short, he resembles almost exactly the figure that Lawrence of Arabia made famous almost a hundred years ago—the "white sheik" who is part of a colonialist narrative of Western military intervention to "liberate" the Middle East.

Captain Kearney may have had to improvise his learning of local social structure and cultural systems, but it is clear to the US Army that, as it will be conducting more and more of its operations in non-Western settings—operations requiring sophisticated linguistic and cultural knowledge—soldiers will either have to be given new training or rely upon surrogates, such as embedded translators and cultural anthropologists, to help them with the "cultural" work entailed in counterinsurgency operations. For some time now, special camps have been set up in California's Mojave Desert to simulate Iraqi villages (complete with Iraqi men and women brought over from Iraq to play the part of the locals), exposing soldiers to the difficulties of interethnic conflicts and training them to react in culturally and strategically appropriate ways.[24] Cutting-edge techniques of "intercultural communication" are applied, with the aim of making soldiers "anthropologically sensitive." They learn, for example, that saying "Salaam Aleykum" is not a perfunctory greeting in Arabo-Muslim culture but a sign of respect that, if not uttered, will prevent a transaction from taking place. This is not the first time such camps have been in existence; to my knowledge, they were first set up during the 1990s Balkan wars, when the United States had a peacekeeping mission in Kosovo, except that they were located in the Rockies to simulate high-altitude conditions, with Serbo-Croatians living in stone villages. One suspects that such camps will continue to exist, the scenery, the set, and the actors shifting depending on the world conflict in which the US military becomes involved.

Short of (or perhaps in addition to) going to cultural and counterinsurgency boot camp, will soldiers continue to rely on embedded linguists/translators/anthropologists to do the work of "field anthropologists"? Professional anthropologists have collaborated with the US military in counterinsurgency tactics (providing local cultural knowledge, using network analysis to penetrate jihadist systems, and doing what amounts to ethnographic analysis of cultural data brought back from military field operations). This is dismaying but ought not come as a surprise. It was, after all, anthropology that invented fieldwork and ethnography as methods of knowledge that long ago were turned into techniques of power. That fateful convergence was set in the origins of World War One, between the figures of T. E. Lawrence and the anthropologist Bronislaw Malinowksi, though not even I could have imagined that this convergence would lead to the "embedding" of anthropologists in the front lines of Iraq, helping soldiers understand the social, political, and cultural contexts in which they exercise their force. And what has happened to the figure of the sheik? Does he still soldier on in someone like Captain Kearney, or has he now bifurcated into two figures that historically were one, because of the specializations required to fight the US counterinsurgency wars? The US Department of Defense has apparently reevaluated its HTS (Human Terrain System) and the embedding of anthropologists in the field of battle, no doubt because of the risk and controversy such tactics have raised. Instead of embedding anthropologists, it is now sending US army officers to school to learn about the Middle East, its languages, cultures, and politics, so that they will be better informed than Captain Kearney was in waging war against an enemy Other. In other words, the figures of the soldier and the scholar have combined once again, and we have returned full circle to Lawrence of Arabia.

CONCLUSION

In this chapter I examine the image of the "white sheik" as it circulated in Anglo-American popular culture in the twentieth century. That image, as we have seen, is not self-identical in the various media texts in which he appears. To analyze this representational complexity, I have developed the concept of the sheik as a modular figure. Whereas Lowell Thomas's representation of T. E. Lawrence combined the sheik, the soldier, and the scholar qua Arabist in one figure, these qualities were detached from one another in contemporary warfare and relocated in two different persons who were nonetheless coexistential, the soldier and the embedded anthropologist. For various reasons mentioned above, these two figures have combined again into the single figure of the white sheik. Race is one module of this figure, as are gender and sexuality, and from *The Sheik* (both movie and book) to *Lawrence of Arabia*, they have been reshuffled to serve different ideological ends. The concept of the modular figure captures the sheik's representational complexity.

But there is a problem with such modularity. What ensures the continuity or discontinuity of such figural representation in history? Or, to put the question somewhat differently, if he has a genealogy, how does one trace its links? Take, for example, the poster art advertising the film *Lawrence of Arabia*. The same figure is rerepresented, creating two differently gendered images of the sheik appealing to different audiences, circa 1961 and 1989. *Continuity* of the two images separated in time by more than a quarter-century is assured, of course, by the fact that they reference the same film, and its history of reception adds a layering or depth to the sheik's identity that makes him more interesting, not less, and potentially also more circulatable. Horizontal *juxtaposition* is no less important for securing a "family of resemblances" of the sheik's images, as in the 1920s, when Lowell Thomas's depiction of Lawrence on the one hand and Edith Hull's romance "hero" and the film's adaptation of him on the other were circulating in slide-lecture show, romance novel, and Hollywood film. It may have been coincidental that these three media events occurred at more or less the same time, but it is likely that their audiences overlapped and that their respective representations of the sheik would have invited comparisons and resemblances in the public imagination. The latter-day continuity of the Special Operations Forces officer with T. E. Lawrence is secured by *citation*, as in the "quoting" of the film *Lawrence of Arabia* in a military autobiography or the reference to the historical figure and his memoir, *Seven Pillars of Wisdom*, in the *U.S. Army Marine Corps Counterinsurgency Manual*. Whereas in the beginning of the First Gulf War through the 2003 invasion and occupation of Afghanistan and Iraq, this quoting of Lawrence's sheik was used more or less self-consciously to frame the US involvement in the Middle East, that citation seems now to have abated somewhat, though for reasons that are not entirely clear. Is it felt by propagandists to have become something of a cliché and therefore a rhetorical liability (though clichés are useful precisely because they are banal)? Or is it because the negative dialectical features of the "Lawrence as sheik" figure make him unstable for an ideological support of the war and the propagandists sense this? And if that is the case, has the image of the white sheik not so much been politically as psychologically repressed, leading to his uncanny reoccurrence in someone like Captain Kearney? Obviously, a genealogy of an image like the white sheik can become difficult when his traces seem to be invisible.

Finally, let me say something about what I loosely call a media *industry* connected with an image's mobility, or capitalist production and consumption and the public sphere tied to both (originally through print media but increasingly also through film, television, and now the Internet). Images like the sheik, as I said earlier, have to sell movies. To sell commodities on a global scale, such bankable images have to cross borders in cultural space, requiring consideration of commodity fetishization and standardization as Horkheimer and Adorno formulated them in "The Culture Industry." Economically successful products of popular culture breed imitations and formulaicness (though with slight variation, hence the usefulness of the sheik's modularity). Indeed, their success also breeds product lines such as toys and fashions (both of which are particularly lucrative film industry spin-offs).

Does the "white sheik" have a future in Anglo-American popular culture in the sense that new iterations of him based on his modularity and his genealogy are in the offing? It is hard to imagine that he would not have, given his significance as an ideological and psychological figure, especially for the US Army lately. One of the things the history of the white sheik demonstrates is that world events like World War One, which needed a "romance" in order for it to be remembered at all, or the Second Gulf War, which needed a popular explanatory frame through which it could be understood, if it could be at all, "make use" of such a figure. As long as Anglo-American power remains tragically entangled with wars in foreign cultures, the sheik and his masquerade will remain on the stage for some time to come.

Notes

1. Some of this material has been treated elsewhere; see Steven C. Caton, *Lawrence of Arabia: A Film's Anthropology* (Berkeley: University of California Press, 1999); and "The Sheik: Instabilities of Race and Gender in Transatlantic Popular Culture of the Early 1920s," in *Noble Dreams, Wicked Pleasures: Orientalism in America, 1870–1930*, ed. Holly Edwards (Princeton, NJ: Princeton University Press, 2000), 99–117. My discussion of the

Special Operations Forces officer and my analysis of him as a latter-day iteration of the white sheik are wholly new to this chapter. The argument that there is a genealogical line of descent from T. E. Lawrence as the first popular cultural production of the white sheik to the Special Operations Forces officer of today is something I suggested in a lecture at Harvard University in April 2000 and have developed more fully here.

2. I borrow this notion from the following works: Theodor W. Adorno, *Negative Dialectics* (New York: Continuum Publications, 1994); Max Horkheimer and Theodor W. Adorno, "The Culture Industry," *Dialectic of the Enlightenment*, trans. John Cumming (New York: Continuum Publications, 1989), 120–167; Walter Benjamin, "The Work of Art in the Age of Mechanical Reproduction," *Illuminations: Essays by Walter Benjamin*, ed. Hannah Arendt, trans. Harry Zohn (New York: Schocken Books, 1969), 217–251, and "A Small History of Photography," *One-Way Street and Other Writings*, trans. Edmund Jephcott and Kingsley Shorter (London: Verso, 1979), 240–257. I do a dialectical analysis of the film *Lawrence of Arabia* in Caton, *Lawrence*, 1999, closely following the thinking on "negative dialectics" of Adorno. This is not a Hegelian dialectic of thesis, antithesis, and synthesis, rather, it is an *unresolved* dialectic. For Adorno, this nonresolution meant that a discourse of power was always subject to an imminent critique and because of dialectical images was unstable or insecure. What Benjamin insisted on was a negative dialectic located in *concrete or surface* forms such as the tracery of images. Accordingly, the figure of the sheik has antithetical features that have to do with race, gender, and sexuality, and these antitheses are never completely resolved, nor are they always the same from period to period. Indeed, one might argue that for that very reason they are endlessly recombined in the modular way that I describe in this chapter, at once a resource of power and its potential undoing.

3. Lowell Thomas, *With Lawrence in Arabia* (New York: Century Co., 1924), 370. Except where noted, all quotes in this section are from this text.

4. Paul Fussell, *The Great War and Modern Memory* (New York: Oxford University Press, 1975).

5. See Connie Bruck, "The Commando: Ehud Barak Took Huge Risks and Trusted No One. Now He Is Alone," *New Yorker*, April 17, 2000: 82.

6. Almost nothing is known of the writer Edith Maude Hull, a nom de plume taken to preserve anonymity. Though she had her predecessors, the most important having been Robert Hutchins and his 1909 blockbuster *The Garden of Allah*, she was dubbed "the queen of desert romance" and was to secure a lasting place in the history of the romance genre.

7. See Miriam Hansen, *Babel and Babylon: Spectatorship in American Silent Film* (Cambridge, MA: Harvard University Press, 1991), especially chapters 3 and 11.

8. E. M. Hull, *The Sheik* (New York: Small, A. L. Burt, 1919), 28.

9. Ibid., 88.

10. Ibid., 53.

11. Ibid., 243.

12. Matthew Jacobson, *Whiteness of a Different Color: European Immigrants and the Alchemy of Race* (Cambridge, MA: Harvard University Press, 1999).

13. Richard Aldington, *Lawrence of Arabia: A Biographical Enquiry* (London: Collins, 1955); Suleiman Mousa, *T. E. Lawrence: An Arab View*, trans. Albert Butros (London: Oxford University Press, 1966).

14. See Caton, *Lawrence.*

15. The contrast between a "dark" sheik and a "white" one, to be found in all the texts we have examined so far, is obviously important. In both the novel and the film *The Sheik*, the white sheik, Ahmed, is contrasted with the much darker and more evil Sheik Obeid. See Caton, "The Sheik." The problem of the "dark" sheik comes up again in the first movie poster for the movie, discussed later in this chapter.

16. H. Norman Schwarzkopf (with Peter Petre), *It Doesn't Take a Hero* (New York: Bantam, 1992).

17. Ibid., 284.

18. Ibid., 110.

19. Bronislaw Malinowski, *A Diary in the Strict Sense of the Term* (Stanford, CA: Stanford University Press, 1967), 180.

20. See *The U.S. Army Marine Corps Counterinsurgency Manual* (Chicago: University of Chicago Press, 2007).

21. Ibid., 89.

22. Ibid., 93–94.

23. Elizabeth Rubin, "Captain Kearney's Quagmire," *New York Times*, February 24, 2008, sec. 11, 42.

24. See the documentary film *Full Battle Rattle* by Tony Gerber and Jesse Moss (New York: First Run Features, 2008).

References

Achnas, Nan. "Rebirth of Indonesian Film Industry, and the Glaring Lack of Creativity." *Jakarta Post,* June 9, 2007. http://www.thejakartapost.com /news/2007/06/09/rebirth-indonesian-film-industry-and-glaring-lack -creativity.html. Accessed December 8, 2011.

Adamu, Abdalla Uba. "Currying Favour: Eastern Media Influences and the Hausa Video Film." *Film International* 28 (2007): 76–89.

———. *Transglobal Media Flows and African Popular Culture: Revolution and Reaction in Muslim Hausa Popular Culture.* Kano, Nigeria: Visually Ethnographic Productions, 2007.

Adamu, Abdalla Uba, Yusuf M. Adamu, and Umar Faruk Jibril. *Hausa Home Videos: Technology, Economy, Society.* Kano, Nigeria: Center of Hausa Cultural Studies, 2004.

Ades, Dawn, and Simon Baker, eds. *Undercover Surrealism: Georges Bataille and Documents.* Exhibition catalog. Cambridge, MA: MIT Press, 2006.

Adorno, Theodor W. *Negative Dialectics.* New York: Continuum Publications, 1994.

"After the Fast." *Economist,* October 11, 2008, 81.

Aitken, Stuart C., and Deborah P. Dixon. "Imagining Geographies of Film." *Erdkunde: Archiv für Wissenschaftliche Geographie* 60 (2006): 326–336.

Akbari, Suzanne C. "Imagining Islam: The Role of Images in Medieval Depictions of Muslims." *Scripta Mediterranea* 19–20 (1998–1999): 9–27.

Aldington, Richard. *Lawrence of Arabia: A Biographical Enquiry.* London: Collins, 1955.

Althusser, Louis. "Ideology and Ideological State Apparatuses." *Lenin and Philosophy and Other Essays,* 127–186. New York: Monthly Review Press, 1971.

al-Alwani, Taha Jaber. "*Fatwa* Concerning the United States Supreme Courtroom Frieze." *Journal of Law and Religion* 15, no. 1/2 (2000–2001): 1–28.

REFERENCES

al-Funaysan, Sa'ud. "Drawing Pictures and Producing Animated Cartoons." http://www.islamtoday.com/showme2.cfm?cat_id=2&sub_cat_id=811. Accessed November 28, 2008.

Ambani, Shivangi. "Cinema's Future: Quickies and Shorties." http://www.dnaindia .com/lifestyle/salon_cinema-s-future-quickies-and-shorties_9395. Accessed June 30, 2012.

Amis, Martin. "The Age of Horrorism." Parts 1 and 3. *Observer*, September 10, 2006.

Anderson, Clare. *Legible Bodies: Race, Criminality and Colonialism in South Asia*. Oxford, UK: Berg, 2004.

Anggraeni, Dewi. "Book Delves into Intrigues, Surprises in a Slice of Chinese-Javanese History." *Jakarta Post*, January 25, 2009. http://www.thejakartapost.com /news/2009/01/25/book-delves-intrigues-surprises-a-slice-chinesejavanese -history.html. Accessed December 8, 2011.

Anidjar, Gil. *Semites: Race, Religion, Literature*. Stanford, CA: Stanford University Press, 2007.

Anon. "The Strange Case of the Resurrected Prince." *Life*, September 2, 1946.

Anwar, Joko. "2001 Hints at Signs of Film Industry Recovery." *Jakarta Post*, December 28, 2001. http://www.thejakartapost.com/news/2001/12/28/2001-hints- signs-film-industry-recovery.html. Accessed December 8, 2011.

———. "'Jelangkung' a Guilty Pleasure." *Jakarta Post*, November 25, 2001. http://www .thejakartapost.com/news/2001/11/25/039jelangkung039-a-guilty-pleasure .html. Accessed December 8, 2011.

———. "Mystery Keep Audience Glued to Television Screen," *Jakarta Post*, July 27, 2002. http://www.thejakartapost.com/news/2002/07/27/mystery-keep -audience-glued-television-screen.html. Accessed December 8, 2011.

———. "'Tusuk': Plenty of Ghosts but Few Thrills." *Jakarta Post*, March 22, 2003. http://www.thejakartapost.com/news/2003/03/22/tusuk039-plenty-ghosts -few-thrills.html. Accessed December 8, 2011.

Appadurai, Arjun. "The Colonial Backdrop—Photography." *Afterimage* 24, no. 5 (March–April 1997): 1–7.

———. "Disjuncture and Difference in the Global Cultural Economy." *Public Culture* 2, no. 2 (1990): 1–24.

———. "Introduction: Commodities and the Politics of Value." In *The Social Life of Things: Commodities in Cultural Perspective*, edited by Arjun Appadurai, 3–63. Cambridge, UK: Cambridge University Press, 1988.

———. *Modernity at Large: Cultural Dimensions of Globalization*. Minneapolis: University of Minnesota Press, 1996; New Delhi: Oxford University Press, 1997.

———, ed. *The Social Life of Things: Commodities in Cultural Perspective*. Cambridge, UK: Cambridge University Press, 1988.

Arendt, Hannah. *The Human Condition*. Chicago: University of Chicago Press, 1958.

———. *On Violence*. New York: Harcourt Brace, 1970.

Arthur, Charles. "Censor Lifts UK Wikipedia Ban." *Guardian*, December 9, 2008.

Asad, Talal. *Formations of the Secular: Christianity, Islam, Modernity.* Stanford, CA: Stanford University Press, 2003.

———. *Genealogies of Religion: Discipline and Reasons of Power in Christianity and Islam.* Baltimore, MD: Johns Hopkins University Press, 1993.

———. "Modern Power and the Reconfiguration of Religious Traditions." *Stanford Electronic Humanities Review* 5, no. 1 (1996). Special issue, *Contested Polities: Religious Disciplines and Structures of Modernity.*

Associated Press. "Javanese Believe Ancient Mysticism Shielding Ex-dictator Suharto from Death." *Jakarta Post,* January 27, 2008. http://www.seasite.niu.edu/flin /suharto_dead.htm. Accessed December 8, 2011.

Asyhadi, Nuruddin. "Paramarupa film horor kita" [Visual grammar of our horror films]. *"F"* 3 (February–March 2006). http://www.mail-archive.com /filsafat@yahoogroups.com/msg01445.html. Accessed December 8, 2011.

Attali, Jacques. *Noise: The Political Economy of Music.* Minneapolis: University of Minnesota Press, 1985.

Attridge, Derek. "Age of Bronze, State of Grace: Music and Dogs in Coetzee's *Disgrace.*" *Novel: A Forum on Fiction* 34, no. 1 (Autumn 2000): 98–121.

Atwell, David. "Race in *Disgrace.*" *Interventions* 4, no. 3 (2002): 331–341.

Badan Pusat Statistik Indonesia. http://www.bps.go.id/index.php?news=36. Accessed December 8, 2011.

Bajac, Quentin. *L'image Révélée: L'invention de la Photographie.* Paris: Gallimard / Réunion des Musées, 2001.

Bakhtin, Mikhail. *The Dialogic Imagination.* Austin: University of Texas Press, 1981.

Bakker, Freek L. "The Image of Muhammad in *The Message,* the First and Only Feature Film about the Prophet of Islam." *Islam and Christian-Muslim Encounter* 17, no. 1 (2006): 77–92.

Bal, Mieke. "Invisible Art, Hypervisibility, and the Aesthetics of Everyday Life." In *Nichts/Nothing,* edited by Martina Weinhart and Max Hollein, 81–104. Frankfurt: Schirn Kunsthalle, 2006.

———. *Murder and Difference: Gender, Genre, and Scholarship on Sisera's Death.* Bloomington: Indiana University Press, 1988.

Balmanno, Kim. "Box Office: The Secret Numbers Tell the Story." *Jakarta Post,* March 23, 2008. http://www.thejakartapost.com/news/2008/03/23/box-office-the -secret-numbers-tell-story.html. Accessed December 8, 2011.

Barendregt, Bart A. "Mobile Religiosity in Indonesia: Mobilized Islam, Islamized Mobility and the Potential of Islamic Techno Nationalism." In *Living the Information Society in Asia,* edited by Erwin Alampay, 73–92. Singapore: Institute of Southeast Asian Studies, 2009.

Barker, Thomas. "VCD Pornography in Indonesia." Paper presented at Asian Studies Association of Australia 16th Biennial Conference, June 26–29, 2006. http://primalscenes.wordpress.com/essays/. Accessed December 8, 2011.

Barthes, Roland. *Camera Lucida.* Translated by Richard Howard. New York: Hill and Wang, 1982.

REFERENCES

————. *Mythologies*. Translated by Annette Lavers. New York: Hill and Wang, 1972.

————. "Rhetoric of the Image." In *Image, Music, Text*. Edited and translated by Stephen Heath, 32–51. 1964; New York: Hill and Wang, 1977.

Batra, Lalit. "Out of Sight, Out of Mind: Slum-Dwellers in 'World-Class' Delhi." In *Finding Delhi: Loss and Renewal in the Megacity*, edited by Bharati Chaturvedi, 16–36. New Delhi: Penguin Books Delhi, 2010.

Batra, Lalit, and Diya Mehra. "Das neoliberale Delhi: Der Blick vom Trümmerfeld eines planierten Slums." In *Mumbai Delhi Kolkata: Annäherungen an die Megastädte Indiens*, edited by Ravi Ahuja and Christiane Brosius, 157–172. Heidelberg: Draupadi, 2006. Revised and reprinted as "Slum Demolitions and Production of Neo-liberal Space: Delhi." In *Inside the Transforming Urban Asia: Processes, Policies and Public Actions*, edited by Darshini Mahadevia. New Delhi: Concept Publications, 2008.

Baviskar, Amita. "Between Violence and Desire: Space, Power and Identity in the Making of Metropolitan Delhi." *International Social Science Journal* 55 (2003): 89–98.

Beck, Ulrich. *World at Risk*. Cambridge, UK: Polity Press, 2008.

Becker, Adam H. "The Ancient Near East in the Late Antique Near East: Syriac Christian Appropriation of the Biblical East." In *Antiquity in Antiquity: Jewish and Christian Pasts in the Greco-Roman World*, edited by Gregg Gardner and Kevin Osterloh, 394–415. Tübingen: Mohr Siebeck, 2008.

Beisi, Liu, and Xu Qixian, eds. *Gugong zhencang renwu zhaopian huicui*. Beijing: Zijincheng chubanshe, 1994.

Belting, Hans. *An Anthropology of Images: Picture, Medium, Body*. Translated by Thomas Dunlap. Princeton, NJ: Princeton University Press, 2011.

Benjamin, Walter. "Kleine Geschichte der Photographie." In *Das Kunstwerk im Zeitalter seiner technischen Reproduzierbarkeit: Drei Studien zur Kunstsoziologie*. Frankfurt am Main: Suhrkamp Verlag, 1977.

————. "A Little History of Photography." *Walter Benjamin: Selected Writings*. Vol. 2, *1927–1934*. Edited by Michael W. Jennings, Howard Eiland, and Gary Smith, 507–530. Cambridge, MA: Belknap Press of Harvard University Press, 1999.

————. "Paris, Capital of the Nineteenth Century." *The Arcades Project*. Edited by Howard Eiland and Kevin McLaughlin. Translated from German by R. Tiedemann. 1939; Cambridge, MA: Belknap Press of Harvard University Press, 1999.

————. "A Small History of Photography." *One-Way Street and Other Writings*. Translated by Edmund Jephcott and Kingsley Shorter, 240–257. London: Verso, 1979.

————. "The Work of Art in the Age of Its Technological Reproducibility." 3rd version. *Walter Benjamin: Selected Writings*. Vol. 4, *1938–1940*. Edited by Howard Eiland and Michael W. Jennings, 251–283. Cambridge, MA: Belknap Press of Harvard University Press, 2003.

————. "The Work of Art in the Age of Mechanical Reproduction." *Illuminations: Essays by Walter Benjamin*. Edited by Hannah Arendt. Translated by Harry Zohn, 217–251. New York: Schocken Books, 1968 [hardcover], 1969 [paperback].

Bennett, Jill. *Empathic Vision: Affect, Trauma, and Contemporary Art*. Stanford, CA: Stanford University Press, 2005.

———. "A Feeling of Insincerity: Politics, Ventriloquy and the Dialectics of Gesture." In *The Rhetoric of Sincerity*, edited by Ernst van Alphen et al., 195–213. Stanford, CA: Stanford University Press, 2009.

Bharucha, Ruzbeh. *Yamuna Gently Weeps: A Journey into the Yamuna Pushta Slum Demolitions*. New Delhi: Sainathann Communications, 2006.

Bickers, Robert, Jamie Carstairs, Yee Wah Foo, and Catherine Ladds. *Picturing China, 1870–1950: Photographs from British Collections*. Chinese Maritime Customs Project Occasional Papers no. 1. Bristol, UK: University of Bristol, 2007.

Bieber, Jodi. *Between Dogs and Wolves: Growing Up in South Africa*. Stockport, UK: Dewi Lewis Publishing, 2007.

Bland, Kalman P. *The Artless Jew: Medieval and Modern Affirmations and Denials of the Visual*. Princeton, NJ: Princeton University Press, 2002.

Boehmer, Elleke. "Not Saying Sorry, Not Speaking Pain: Gender Implications in *Disgrace*." *Interventions* 4, no. 3 (2002): 342–351.

Boespflug, François. *Caricaturer Dieu: Pouvoirs et dangers de l'image*. Paris: Bayard, 2006.

Bogue, Ronald. *Deleuze on Music, Painting, and the Arts*. London: Routledge, 2003.

Bolter, Jay David, and Richard Grusin. *Remediation: Understanding New Media*. Cambridge, MA: MIT Press, 1999 [hardcover]; 2000 [paperback].

Bomsdorf, Clemens. "Danish Museum to Buy Muhammad Cartoons Which Sparked Global Riots." *Art Newspaper*, January 31, 2008.

Bourdieu, Pierre. *Outline of a Theory of Practice*. Translated by Richard Nice. Cambridge, UK: Cambridge University Press, 1977.

Bourdieu, Pierre, L. Boltanski, R. Castel, and J. C. Chamboredon. *Un Art Moyen: Essai sur les Usages Sociaux de la Photographie*. 2nd ed. 1965; Paris: Les Éditions de Minuit, 2007.

Bourgois, Philippe, and Jeffrey Schonberg. *Righteous Dopefiend*. Berkeley: University of California Press, 2009.

Brah, Avtar. *Cartographies of Diaspora: Contesting Identities*. London: Routledge, 1996.

Bray, Jennifer. "The Mohammetan and Idolatry." *Studies in Church History* 21 (1984): 89–98.

Brennan, Teresa. *The Transmission of Affect*. Ithaca, NY: Cornell University Press, 2004.

Breytenbach, Breyten. *Dog Heart*. New York: Harcourt, 1999.

Brooks, David, and Gail Collins. "The Power in a Photo." *New York Times*, May 4, 2011. http://opionator.blogs.nytmes.com/2011/05/04/the-power-in-a-photo/?ref=politics. Accessed December 7, 2011.

Brosius, Christiane. *India's Middle Class: New Forms of Urban Leisure, Consumption and Prosperity*. New Delhi: Routledge, 2010.

Brown, Percy. *Indian Architecture (Buddhist and Hindu)*. 2nd ed., revised and enlarged. Bombay: D. B. Taraporevala Sons and Co., n.d.

REFERENCES

Brown, Wendy. *Regulating Aversion: Tolerance in the Age of Identity and Empire*. Princeton, NJ: Princeton University Press, 2006.

Bruck, Connie. "The Commando: Ehud Barak Took Huge Risks and Trusted No One. Now He Is Alone." *New Yorker*, April 17, 2000.

Bubandt, Nils. "Rumors, Pamphlets, and the Politics of Paranoia in Indonesia." *Journal of Asian Studies* 67, no. 3 (2008): 789–817.

———. "The Spirit Army." *Inside Indonesia* 108 (April–June 2012). http://www .insideindonesia.org/feature/the-spirit-army-02042903. Accessed June 20, 2012.

Bumiller, Elizabeth. "We Have Met the Enemy and He Is Powerpoint." *New York Times*, April 26, 2010. http://www.nytimes.com/2010/04/27/world/27powerpoint .html?hp&_r=0. Accessed December 6, 2011.

Bunzl, Matti. *Anti-Semitism and Islamophobia: Hatreds Old and New in Europe*. Chicago: Prickly Paradigm Press, 2007.

Butler, Judith. *Frames of War: When Is Life Grievable?* London: Verso, 2009.

———. "Torture, Photography, and the Limits of the Secular." Distinguished Lecture, presented at The Center for Religion and Media, New York University, October 26, 2006.

Byron, George Gordon, Lord. *Werner; or, The Inheritance*. In *The Poetical Works of Byron*, edited by F. Gleckner, 671–721. Boston: Houghton Mifflin, 1975.

Cahn, Walter B. "The 'Portrait' of Muhammad in the Toledan Collection." In *Reading Medieval Images: The Art Historian and the Object*, edited by Elizabeth Sears and Thelma K. Thomas, 51–60. Ann Arbor: University of Michigan Press, 2002.

Caldeira, Teresa. *City of Walls: Crime, Segregation, and Citizenship in São Paulo*. Berkeley: University of California Press, 2001.

Callon, Michel. "Society in the Making: The Study of Technology as a Tool for Sociological Analysis." In *The Social Construction of Technological Systems: New Directions in the Sociology and History of Technology*, edited by Wieber E. Bijker, Thomas P. Hughes, and Trevor J. Pinch, 83–103. Cambridge, MA: MIT Press. 2008.

Cameron, Nigel, and L. Carrington Goodrich. *The Face of China as Seen by Photographers and Travelers, 1860–1912*. Millertown, NY: Aperture, 1978. Catalog of an exhibition first shown at the Philadelphia Museum of Art, April 15–June 25, 1978.

Camille, Michael. *The Gothic Idol: Ideology and Image-Making in Medieval Art*. Cambridge, UK: Cambridge University Press, 1989.

Cartwright, Lisa, and Stephen Mandiberg. "Obama and Shepherd Fairey: The Copy and Political Iconography in the Age of the Demake." *Journal of Visual Culture* 8 (August 2009): 172–176.

Casey, Michael. *Che's Afterlife: The Legacy of an Image*. New York: Vintage Books, 2009.

Castronovo, Russ. *Necro Citizenship*. Durham, NC: Duke University Press, 2001.

Caton, Steven C. *Lawrence of Arabia: A Film's Anthropology.* Berkeley: University of California Press, 1999.

———. "The Sheik: Instabilities of Race and Gender in Transatlantic Popular Culture of the Early 1920s." In *Noble Dreams, Wicked Pleasures: Orientalism in America, 1870–1930*, edited by Holly Edwards, 99–117. Princeton, NJ: Princeton University Press, 2000.

Causey, Andrew. *Hard Bargaining in Sumatra: Western Travelers and Toba Bataks in the Marketplace of Souvenirs.* Honolulu: University of Hawaii Press, 2003.

Cavanaugh, William T. "Sins of Omission: What 'Religion and Violence' Arguments Ignore." *Hedgehog Review: Critical Reflections on Contemporary Culture* 6, no. 1 (2004): 35–50.

Centlivres, Pierre, and Micheline Centlivres-Demont. "Une étrange rencontre: La photographie orientaliste de Lehnert et Landrock et l'image iranienne du prophète Mahomet." *Études photographiques* 17 (2005): 5–15.

———. "The Story of a Picture: Shiite Depictions of Muhammad." *ISIM Review* 17 (Spring 2006): 18–19.

Certeau, Michel de. *The Possession at Loudun.* Translated by Michael B. Smith. Chicago: University of Chicago Press, 2000.

Chatterjee, Partha. "Are Indian Cities Becoming Bourgeois at Last?" In *Body.City: Siting Contemporary Culture in India*, edited by Indira Chandrasekhar and Peter Seel, 170–185. New Delhi: Tulika Books, 2003.

———. *A Princely Imposter? The Strange and Universal History of the Kumar of Bhawal.* Princeton, NJ: Princeton University Press, 2003.

Chauvel, Richard. "Ambon's Other Half: Some Preliminary Observations on Ambonese Moslem Society and History." *Review of Indonesian and Malaysian Affairs* 14 (1980): 40–80.

Cheney, Lynne V. *Humanities in America: A Report to the President, the Congress, and the American People.* Washington, DC: National Endowment for the Humanities, 1988.

Chéroux, Clément, et al. *The Perfect Medium.* New Haven, CT: Yale University Press, 2005.

———. "Photographs of Fluids: An Alphabet of Invisible Rays." In *The Perfect Medium: Photography and the Occult*, edited by Clément Chéroux et al., 114–138. New Haven, CT: Yale University Press, 2005.

Chevers, Norman. *A Manual of Medical Jurisprudence for India.* 3rd ed. 1856; Calcutta: Thacker, Spink and Co., 1870.

Chun, Wendy Hui Kyong. *Control and Freedom: Power and Paranoia in the Age of Fiber Optics.* Cambridge, MA: MIT Press, 2006.

Chun, Wendy Hui Kyong, and Thomas Keenan, eds. *New Media, Old Media.* New York: Routledge, 2006.

Coetzee, J. M. *Disgrace.* London: Secker and Warburg, 1999.

References

————. *Elizabeth Costello*. New York: Penguin, 2004.

————. "In the Midst of Losses." *New York Review of Books* 48, no. 11 (July 5, 2001).

————. "Irène Némirovsky: *The Dogs and the Wolves*." *New York Review of Books* 55, no. 18 (November 20, 2008).

————. *The Lives of Animals*. Princeton, NJ: Princeton University Press, 2001.

————. "The Memoirs of Breyten Breytenbach." *Stranger Shores: Literary Essays, 1986–1999*, 249–260. New York: Viking, 2001.

————. "Translating Kafka." *Stranger Shores: Literary Essays, 1986–1999*, 74–87. New York: Viking, 2001.

Comaroff, Jean, and John Comaroff. "Occult Economies and the Violence of Abstraction: Notes from the South African Postcolony." *American Ethnologist* 26, no. 2 (1999): 279–303.

————. "Transparent Fictions; or the Conspiracies of a Liberal Imagination: An Afterword." In *Transparency and Conspiracy: Ethnographies of Suspicion in the New World Order*, edited by Harry G. West and Todd Sanders, 287–300. Durham, NC: Duke University Press, 2003.

Conley, Tom. "Faciality." In *The Deleuze Dictionary*, edited by Adrian Parr, 98–100. New York: Columbia University Press, 2005.

Conlon, Edward. "Paying Attention." *New Yorker*, September 12, 2011. http://www.newyorker.com/talk/2011/09/12/110912ta_talk_conlon. Accessed February 10, 2012.

Cox, Neil. "Sacrifice." In *Undercover Surrealism: Georges Bataille and Documents*, edited by Dawn Ades and Simon Baker, 112–113. Cambridge, MA: MIT Press, 2006.

Crone, Patricia. "Islam, Judeo-Christianity, and Byzantine Iconoclasm." *Jerusalem Studies in Arabic and Islam* 2 (1980): 59–95.

Daniel, Norman. *Islam and the West, the Making of an Image*. Oxford, UK: Oneworld, 1993.

Darmawan, Hikmat. "Mengapa Film Horor?"[Why horror film?]. Part 1. *Rumah Film*, July 24, 2008. http://old.rumahfilm.org/artikel/artikel_horor.htm. Accessed January 2, 2011.

————. "Mengapa Film Horor." Part 2. *Rumah Film*, August 1, 2008. http://old.rumahfilm.org/artikel/artikel_horor_2.htm. Accessed January 2, 2011.

Das, Veena, and Arthur Kleinman. Introduction to *Remaking a World: Violence, Social Suffering, and Recovery*, edited by Veena Das and Arthur Kleinman, 1–30. Berkeley: University of California Press, 2001.

Das Gupta, Sachindra, ed. *The Bhowal Case (High Court Judgments)*. Calcutta: S. C. Sarkar, 1941.

Davies, Caroline. "Wikipedia Defies 180,000 Demands to Remove Images of the Prophet." *Observer*, February 17, 2008.

Davis, Joshua. "The Secret World of lonelygirl15." *Wired Magazine* 14, no. 12 (December 2006): 232–239.

Dean, Jodi. *Publicity's Secret: How Technoculture Capitalizes on Democracy*. Ithaca, NY: Cornell University Press, 2002.

Deleuze, Gilles. *Difference and Repetition*. Translated by Paul Patton. London: Continuum Press, 2004.

———. *Proust and Signs*. Translated by Richard Howard. New York: Braziller, 1964; Minneapolis: University of Minnesota Press, 2004.

Deleuze, Gilles, and Felix Guattari. *A Thousand Plateaus: Capitalism and Schizophrenia*. Translated by Brian Massumi. Minneapolis: University of Minnesota Press, 1987.

Derrida, Jacques. *The Animal That Therefore I Am*. Edited by Marie-Louise Mallet. Translated by David Wills. New York: Fordham University Press, 2008.

———. *Dissemination*. Translated by Barbara Johnson. Chicago: University of Chicago Press, 1981.

———. *The Truth in Painting*. Translated by Geoff Bennington and Ian McLeod. Chicago: University of Chicago Press, 1987.

Dettman, Sebastian. "Blaming the Messenger." *Inside Indonesia* 93 (July–September 2008). http://www.insideindonesia.org/edition-93/blaming-the-messenger. Accessed January 2, 2011.

Devji, Faisal. "Back to the Future: The Cartoons, Liberalism, and Global Islam." http://www.opendemocracy.net/conflict-terrorism/liberalism_3451.jsp. Accessed May 15, 2009.

———. *Landscapes of the Jihad. Militancy, Morality, Modernity*. London: Hurst and Co., 2005.

Dhar-Kamath, Shampa. "Will the Boom Last?" *India Today* 30, no. 5 (February 2005): 40–47.

Dijck, José van. *Mediated Memories: Personal Cultural Memory in the Digital Age*. Stanford, CA: Stanford University Press, 2007.

Donald, Stephanie, Eleonore Kofman, and Catherine Kevin, eds. *Branding the Cities: Cosmopolitanism, Parochialism and Social Change*. London: Routledge, 2008.

Doostdar, Alireza. "Religious Commodities, Magical Circulations, and the (Im)moral Economy of Iran." http://www.doostdar.com/articles/magical_circulations .pdf. Accessed November 15, 2008.

Douglas, Allen, and Fedwa Malti-Douglas. *Arabic Comic Strips, Politics of an Emerging Mass Culture*. Bloomington: Indiana University Press, 1994.

Dumit, Joseph. *Picturing Personhood: Brain Scans and Biomedical Identity*. Princeton, NJ: Princeton University Press, 2003.

Dupont, Veronique. "The Idea of a New Chic Delhi through Publicity Hype." In *The Idea of Delhi*, edited by Romi Khosla, 78–93. Mumbai: Marg Publications, 2005.

Dupont, Veronique, Emma Tarlo, and Denis Vidal, eds. *Delhi: Urban Space and Human Destinies*. Delhi: Manohar, 1996.

REFERENCES

Eco, Umberto. *A Theory of Semiotics.* Bloomington: Indiana University Press, 1979.

Edwards, Elizabeth, and Janice Hart, eds. *Photographs Objects Histories: On the Materiality of Images.* London: Routledge, 2004.

Eickelman, Dale F., and Jon W. Anderson. "Redefining Muslim Publics." In *New Media in the Muslim World: The Emerging Public Sphere,* edited by Dale F. Eickelman and Jon W. Anderson, 1–18. Bloomington: Indiana University Press, 2003.

Elias, Jamal J. "Visual Images and Religious Pedagogy in Islam: *Du'ā* Girl and the Comic Book." Lecture, Hagop Kevorkian Center for Near Eastern Studies, New York University, October 2005.

Emaar MGF Land Limited. *Commonwealth Games Village 2010.* http://emaarmgf.com /CGV/index.html. Accessed December 29, 2008.

Emon, Anver M. "On the Pope, Cartoons, and Apostates: Shari'a 2006." *Journal of Law and Religion* 22 (2006): 303–321.

Espeland, Wendy Nelson, and Mitchell L. Stevens. "Commensuration as a Social Process." *Annual Review of Sociology* 24 (1998): 313–343.

European Convention on Human Rights. http://www.hri.org/docs/ECHR50.html #C.Art10. Accessed December 5, 2008.

Fabian, Johannes. *Time and the Other: How Anthropology Makes Its Object.* New York: Columbia University Press, 1983.

Fadjar, Evieta P. "Pocong terkubur sensor" [Shrouded corpse buried by censors}. *Tempointeraktif,* October 17, 2006. http://www.tempo.co/read/news/2006 /10/17/07186217/Pocong-Terkubur-Sensor. Accessed December 8, 2011.

Falconer, John. "Willoughby Wallace Hooper: 'A Craze about Photography.'" *The Photographic Collector* 4 (Winter 1983): 258–285.

"Farah" [pseud.]. "Pocong horror." July 6, 2008. http://www.indonesiamatters .com/1866/pocong-horror/. Accessed December 8, 2011.

Fassler, Manfred. *Urban Fictions: Die Zukunft des Städtischen.* Munich: Fink, 2006.

Ferrysiregar. Review of *Pocong 2.* http://sinema-indonesia.com/neo/2007/04/02 /pocong-22007/. Accessed April 2, 2007.

"Fifteen People Killed in Northern Nigeria Muslim Cartoon Protests." *USA Today,* February 18, 2006.

Flood, Finbarr Barry. "Between Cult and Culture: Bamiyan, Islamic Iconoclasm and the Museum." *Art Bulletin* 84, no. 4 (2002): 641–659.

———. "From the Prophet to Postmodernism? New World Orders and the End of Islamic Art." In *Making Art History: A Changing Discipline and Its Institutions,* edited by Elizabeth Mansfield, 31–53. New York: Routledge, 2007.

———. *Islam and Image: Polemics, Theology and Modernity.* London: Reaktion, forthcoming.

———. "Light in Stone: The Commemoration of the Prophet in Umayyad Architecture." In *Bayt al-Maqdis.* Part II, *Jerusalem and Early Islam.* Oxford Studies in Islamic Art 9, edited by Jeremy Johns, 311–359. New York: Oxford University Press, 2002.

———. *Objects of Translation: Material Culture and Medieval "Hindu-Muslim" Encounter.* Princeton, NJ: Princeton University Press, 2009.

Flori, Jean. "La caricature de l'Islam dans l'Occident medieval: Origine et significa- tion de quelques stereotypes concernant l'Islam." *Aevum* 66, no. 2 (1992): 245–256.

Foucault, Michel. *The History of Sexuality.* Vol. 1, *An Introduction.* Translated by Robert Hurley. New York: Vintage Books, 1990.

Fouché, Gwladys. "Cartoons Published in Jordan." *Guardian,* February 2, 2006.

———. "Danish Paper Rejected Jesus Cartoons." *Guardian,* February 6, 2006.

Freedberg, David. *The Power of Images: Studies in the History and Theory of Response.* Chicago: University of Chicago Press, 1989.

French, Lindsay. "Exhibiting Terror." In *Truth Claims: Representation and Human Rights,* edited by Mark Philip Bradley and Patrice Petro, 131–156. New Brunswick, NJ: Rutgers University Press, 2002.

"French Magazine Sued over Cartoons." February 7, 2007. http://english.aljazeera .net/news/europe/2007/02/2008525143158419749.html. Accessed November 29, 2008.

"French Muslim War Graves Defaced." http://news.bbc.co.uk/2/hi/europe/7333344 .stm. Accessed December 2, 2008.

al-Funaysan, Sa'ud. "Drawing Pictures and Producing Animated Cartoons." http://www.islamtoday.com/showme2.cfm?cat_id=2&sub_cat_id=811. Accessed November 28, 2008.

Fussell, Paul. *The Great War and Modern Memory.* New York: Oxford University Press, 1975.

Gamboni, Dario. *The Destruction of Art: Iconoclasm and Vandalism since the French Revolution.* London: Reaktion, 2007.

Gandhi, Leela. *Affective Communities: Anticolonial Thought, Fin de Siècle Radicalism, and the Politics of Friendship.* Durham, NC: Duke University Press, 2006.

Gaonkar, Dilip, and Elizabeth A. Povinelli. "Technologies of Public Forms: Circulation, Transfiguration, Recognition." *Public Culture* 15, no. 3 (2003): 385–398.

Ge Tao. *Juxiang di lishi—Zhaoxiang yu Qingmo Minchu Shanghai shehui (1844–1920)* [A material history—Photography in late Qing and early Republican Shanghai society (1844–1920)]. MA thesis, Shanghai Academy of Social Sciences, 2003.

Gell, Alfred. *Art and Agency: An Anthropological Theory.* Oxford, UK: Clarendon Press, 1998.

George, Kenneth M. "Ethics, Iconoclasm and Qu'ranic Art in Indonesia." *Cultural Anthropology* 24, no. 4 (2009): 589–621.

———. *Picturing Islam.* Hoboken, NJ: Wiley-Blackwell, 2010.

———. "Signature Work: Bandung 1994." *Ethnos* 64, no. 2 (1999): 212–231.

Gerber, Tony, and Jesse Moss. *Full Battle Rattle.* New York: First Run Features, 2008. Documentary film.

References

Gerth, Karl. *China Made: Consumer Culture and the Creation of the Nation.* Cambridge, MA: Harvard University Press, 2003.

"Ghost Sightings Spark Scenes of Hysteria in Indonesian Capital." *Jakarta Globe,* December 2, 2011. http://www.thejakartaglobe.com/home/ghost-sightings -spark-scenes-of-hysteria-in-indonesian-capital/482256. Accessed December 9, 2011.

Ginsburg, Faye D., Lila Abu-Lughod, and Brian Larkin. Introduction to *Media Worlds: Anthropology on New Terrain,* edited by Faye D. Ginsburg, Lila Abu-Lughod, and Brian Larkin, 1–38. Berkeley: University of California Press, 2002.

Ginzburg, Carlo. "Morelli, Freud and Sherlock Holmes: Clues and the Scientific Method." *History Workshop* 9 (Spring 1980): 5–36.

Gizo, Amina Koki. "Writers, Film-Makers Defy Censors." *Interpress Service* (Nigeria), September 12, 2009.

Glasze, Georg, Chris Webster, and Klaus Frantz, eds. *Private Cities: Global and Local Perspectives.* London: Routledge, 2006.

Goldstone, Brian. "Violence and the Profane: Islamism, Liberal Democracy, and the Limits of Secular Discipline." *Anthropological Quarterly* 80, no. 1 (2007): 207–235.

Gombrich, E. H. *Art and Illusion: A Study in the Psychology of Pictorial Representation.* London: Phaidon, 1962; Princeton, NJ: Princeton University Press, 1984.

Gonzalez, Valérie. "The Double Ontology of Islamic Calligraphy: A Word-Image on a Folio from the Museum of Raqqada (Tunisia)." *M. Uğur Derman Festschrift,* 313–340. Istanbul: Anabasım A.Ş., 2002.

Gonzalez-Torres, Felix. "The Gold Field." In *Felix Gonzalez-Torres,* edited by Julie Ault. New York: Steidldangin Publishers, 2006.

Good, Mary-Jo DelVecchio, and Byron J. Good. "*Indonesia Sakit:* Indonesian Disorder and the Subjective Experience and Interpretive Politics of Contemporary Indonesian Artists." In *Postcolonial Disorders,* edited by Mary-Jo DelVecchio Good and Byron J. Good, 62–108. Berkeley: University of California Press, 2008.

Gordon, Robert. "Backdrops and Bushmen: An Expeditious Comment." In *The Colonizing Camera: Photographs in the Making of Namibian History,* edited by Wolfram Hartman, Patricia Hayes, and Jeremey Silvester, 111–117. Cape Town: University of Cape Town Press, 1998.

Gottschalk, Peter, and Gabriel Greenberg. *Islamophobia: Making Muslims the Enemy.* New York: Rowman and Littlefield, 2008.

Grabar, Oleg. "Les portraits du prophète Mahomet à Byzance et ailleurs." *Comptes rendus de l'académie des inscriptions et belles-lettres* 146, no. 4 (2002): 1431–1445.

Grabar, Oleg, and Mika Natif. "The Story of Portraits of the Prophet Muhammad." *Studia Islamica* 96 (2003): 19–38.

Gregg, Melissa, and Gregory J. Siegworth. "An Inventory of Shimmers." In *The Affect Reader,* edited by Melissa Gregg and Gregory J. Seigworth, 1–28. Durham, NC: Duke University Press, 2010.

Greider, William, and Richard Harwood. "Hanafi Muslim Bands Seize Hostages at 3 Sites." *Washington Post*, March 10, 1977.

Griffiths, Alison. *Wondrous Difference: Cinema, Anthropology and Turn-of-the-Century Visual Culture.* New York: Columbia University Press, 2001.

Groebner, Valentin. *Who Are You? Identification, Deception, and Surveillance in Early Modern Europe.* Boston: MIT Press, 2007.

Gruber, Christiane Jacqueline. "Between Logos (Kalima) and Light (Nūr): Representations of the Prophet Muhammad in Islamic Painting." *Muqarnas* 26 (2009): 1–34.

———. "The Prophet Muhammad's Ascension (Mi'rāj) in Islamic Painting and Literature: Evidence from Cairo Collections." *Bulletin of the American Research Center in Egypt* 185 (Summer 2004): 24–31.

Guillaume, A. *The Life of Muhammad.* Oxford, UK: Oxford University Press, 2003.

Gunning, Tom. "In Your Face: Physiognomy, Photography, and the Gnostic Mission of Early Film." *Modernism/Modernity* 4, no. 1 (January 1997): 1–29.

———. "Phantom Images and Modern Manifestations." In *Fugitive Images: From Photography to Video,* edited by Patrice Petro. Bloomington: Indiana University Press, 1995.

Habermas, Jürgen. *The Structural Transformation of the Public Sphere: An Inquiry into a Category of Bourgeois Society.* Translated by Thomas Burger. Cambridge, MA: MIT Press, 1991.

Hannerz, Ulf. *Transnational Connections, Culture, People, Places.* New York: Routledge, 2002.

Hansen, Miriam. *Babel and Babylon: Spectatorship in American Silent Film.* Cambridge, MA: Harvard University Press, 1991.

Hardt, Michael. "Affective Labor." *Boundary* 2 26, no. 2 (Summer 1999): 89–100.

Hariman, Robert, and John Louis Lucaites. *No Caption Needed: Iconic Photographs, Public Culture, and Liberal Democracy.* Chicago: University of Chicago Press, 2007.

Hasan, Noorhaidi. "The Making of Public Islam: Piety, Middle Class and Youth in Indonesia's Democratising Politics." Unpublished book manuscript, n.d.

Haynes, Jonathan. *Nigerian Video Films.* Athens: Ohio University Center for International Studies, 2000.

Heeren, Katinka van. "Return of the Kyai: Representations of Horror, Commerce, and Censorship in Post-Suharto Indonesian Film and Television." *Inter-Asian Cultural Studies* 8, no. 2 (2007): 211–226.

Heider, Karl. *Indonesian Cinema: National Culture on Screen.* Honolulu: University of Hawaii Press, 1991.

Hermawan, Ary. "Distribution Seen as Main Obstacle to Film Industry Growth." *Jakarta Post*, March 29, 2008. http://www.thejakartapost.com/news/2008/03/28/distribution-seen-main-obstacle-film-industry-growth.html. Accessed December 8, 2011.

Heryanto, Ariel. "Citizenship and Indonesian Ethnic Chinese in Post-1998 Films." In *Popular Culture in Indonesia,* edited by Ariel Heryanto, 70–92. London: Routledge, 2008.

REFERENCES

Herzfeld, Michael. "Spatial Cleansing: Monumental Vacuity and the Idea of the West." *Journal of Material Culture* 11 (2006): 127–149.

Hevia, James L. "The Photography Complex: Exposing Boxer-Era China (1900–1901), Making Civilization." In *Photographies East: The Camera and Its Histories in East and Southeast Asia*, edited by Rosalind C. Morris, 99–103. Durham, NC: Duke University Press, 2009.

Hillenbrand, Carole. *The Crusades, Islamic Perspectives.* Edinburgh: Edinburgh University Press, 1999.

Hodgson, Marshall. "Islam and Image." *History of Religion* 2 (1964): 220–260.

Hofmann, Werner. "Die Geburt der Moderne aus dem Geist der Religion." In *Luther und die Folgen für die Kunst,* edited by Werner Hofmann, 23–71. Munich: Prestel-Verlag, 1993.

Holland, Patricia. *Picturing Childhood: The Myth of the Child in Popular Imagery.* London: I. B. Tauris, 2004.

Holsinger, Bruce. *Neomedievalism, Neoconservatism, and the War on Terror.* Chicago: Prickly Paradigm Press, 2007.

Horkheimer, Max, and Theodor W. Adorno. "The Culture Industry." *Dialectic of the Enlightenment.* Translated by John Cumming, 120–167. New York: Continuum Publications, 1989.

Horkheimer, Max, and Theodor W. Adorno. *Dialectic of the Enlightenment.* Edited by Gunzelin Schmid Noerr. Translated by Edmund Jephcott. Stanford, CA: Stanford University Press, 2002.

Howarth, Herbert. "Jewish Art and the Fear of the Image." *Commentary* 9 (1950): 148.

Hoyland, Robert. "Writing the Biography of the Prophet Muhammad: Problems and Solutions." *History Compass* 5, no. 2 (2007): 581–602.

Hull, E. M. *The Sheik.* New York: Small, A. L. Burt, 1919.

Huyssen, Andreas. "Geographies of Modernism in a Globalizing World." *New German Critique* 34, no. 1 100 (2007): 189–207.

International Crisis Group. *Indonesia: The Search for Peace in Maluku.* Asia Report no. 31. Jakarta: ICG, February 8, 2002.

Iva. "'Kado Hari Jadi' Crosses the Voyeuristic Boundary." *Jakarta Post,* June 29, 2008. http://www.thejakartapost.com/news/2008/06/29/039kado-hari-jadi039 -crosses-voyeuristic-boundary.html. Accessed December 9, 2011.

Ivy, Marilyn. "Dark Enlightenment: Naitō Masatoshi's Flash." In *Photographies East: The Camera and Its Histories in East and Southeast Asia*, edited by Rosalind C. Morris, 229–258. Durham, NC: Duke University Press, 2009.

Iwan, Rizal. "Resurrecting Fear." *Jakarta Post,* January 23, 2008. http://www .thejakartapost.com/news/2008/01/23/resurrecting-fear.html. Accessed December 8, 2011.

Jacobson, Matthew. *Whiteness of a Different Color: European Immigrants and the Alchemy of Race.* Cambridge, MA: Harvard University Press, 1999.

Jain, Kajri. *Gods in the Bazaar: The Economies of Indian Calendar Art.* Durham, NC: Duke University Press, 2007.

Jing Lin. "E huang Nigula ershi quanjia zhao" [A portrait of the Russian Tsar Nicholas II and his family]. *Zijincheng* [The Forbidden City] 76 (1993): 27.

Johnson, Frank Edward. "Here and There in North Africa." *National Geographic Magazine* 25 (January–June 1914): 1–152.

Johnson, Ken. "Situation: Ambiguous." *New York Times,* May 7, 2011. http://www .nytimes.com/2011/05/08/weekinreview/08johnson.html?scp=4&sq= situation+room+photo&st=nyt. Accessed December 7, 2011.

Jones, Carla. "Better Women: The Cultural Politics of Gendered Expertise in Indonesia." *American Anthropologist* 112, no. 2 (2010): 270–282.

Jonge, Nico de, and Toos van Dijk, eds. *Tanimbar—De Unieke Molukken: Fotos van Petrus Drabbe.* Leiden: Periplus Editions / C. Zwartenkot, 1995.

Kafka, Franz. *The Trial.* Translated by Breon Mitchell. 1925; New York: Schocken, 1998.

Kaur, Raminder, and William Mazzarella, eds. *Censorship in South Asia: Cultural Regulation from Sedition to Seduction.* Bloomington: Indiana University Press, 2009.

Kazmi, Nikhat. "Indian Art Film Stalwarts Make a Mark at IFFI." *Times of India,* November 30, 2007. http://timesofindia.indiatimes.com/articleshow /2583375.cms. Accessed December 1, 2008.

Keane, Webb. *Christian Moderns: Freedom and Fetish in the Mission Encounter.* Berkeley: University of California Press, 2007.

———. "Freedom and Blasphemy: On Indonesian Press Bans and Danish Cartoons." *Public Culture* 21, no. 1 (2009): 47–76.

———. "Sincerity, 'Modernity,' and the Protestants." *Cultural Anthropology* 17, no. 1 (2002): 65–92.

Khan, Naveeda. "Images That Come Unbidden: Some Thoughts on the Danish Cartoon Controversy." *Borderlands e-journal* 9, no. 3 (2010): 1–14.

Khanna, Ranjana. "Indignity." *Positions* 16, no. 1 (2006): 29–77. Special issue, *War, Capital, Trauma,* edited by Tani Barlow.

Khilnani, Sunil. *The Idea of India.* Delhi: Oxford University Press, 1997.

Kimmelman, Michael. "Outrage at Cartoons Still Tests the Danes." *New York Times,* March 20, 2008.

King, G. R. D. "The Paintings of the Pre-Islamic Ka'ba." *Muqarnas* 21 (2004): 219–230.

Klausen, Jytte. *The Cartoons That Shook the World.* New Haven, CT: Yale University Press, 2009.

Klima, Alan. *The Funeral Casino: Mediation, Massacre, and Exchange with the Dead in Thailand.* Princeton, NJ: Princeton University Press, 2002.

Kopytoff, Igor. "The Cultural Biography of Things: Commoditization as Process." In *The Social Life of Things: Commodities in Cultural Perspective,* edited by Arjun Appadurai, 64–91. Cambridge, UK: Cambridge University Press, 1986.

REFERENCES

Krauss, Rosalind. *A Voyage on the North Sea: Art in the Age of the Post-Medium Condition.* London: Thames and Hudson, 1999.

Kroeber, Alfred L. "Ancient *Oikoumenê* as an Historic Culture Aggregate." *Journal of the Royal Anthropological Institute of Great Britain and Ireland* 75 (1945): 9–20.

Kusno, Abidin. "Guardian of Memories: Gardu in Urban Java." *Indonesia* 81 (2006): 95–149.

———. "Whither Nationalist Urbanism? Public Life in Governor Sutiyoso's Jakarta." *The Appearances of Memory: Mnemonic Practices of Architecture and Urban Form in Indonesia* 25–48. Durham, NC: Duke University Press, 2010.

Kusuma, Veronica. "Suzanna dan Ideologi Film Horor" [Suzanna and the ideology of horror film]. *Tempointeraktif,* October 20, 2008. http://www.tempo.co/read /news/2008/10/20/111141060/Suzanna-dan-Ideologi-Film-Horor. Accessed December 8, 2011.

———. "When Religion Sells: How Cinema Is Used to Create Muslim Identities." *Jakarta Post,* September 27, 2008. http://www.thejakartapost.com/news /2008/09/27/when-religion-sells-how-cinema-used-create-muslim -identities.html. Accessed December 8, 2011.

Lacan, Jacques. *Écrits: A Selection.* Translated by Alan Sheridan. New York: Norton, 1977.

Lahiri-Dutt, Kuntala, and David J. Williams. *Moving Pictures: Rickshaw Art of Bangladesh.* Ahmedabad, India: Mapin Publishing, 2010.

"Lairs of the Kuntilanak in Central Jakarta." *Kismis V,* no. 8 (July 2003), 17–23.

Larkin, Brian. "Bandiri Music, Globalization and Urban Experience in Nigeria." *Social Text* 22, no. 4 (2004): 91–112.

———. "Indian Films, Nigerian Lovers: Media and the Creation of Parallel Modernities." *Africa* 67, no. 3 (1997): 406–440.

———. "Itineraries of Indian Cinema: African Videos, Bollywood and Global Media." In *Multiculturalism, Transnationalism and Film,* edited by Ella Shohat and Robert Stam, 170–192. New Brunswick, NJ: Rutgers University Press, 2003.

———. *Signal and Noise: Media, Infrastructure and Urban Culture in Nigeria.* Durham, NC: Duke University Press, 2008.

Latour, Bruno. *The Pasteurization of France.* Translated by Alan Sheridan and John Law. Cambridge, MA: Harvard University Press, 1988.

———. *Reassembling the Social: An Introduction to Actor-Network Theory.* Oxford, UK: Oxford University Press, 2007.

———. *We Have Never Been Modern.* Translated by Catherine Porter. Cambridge, MA: Harvard University Press, 1993.

Latour, Bruno, and Peter Weibel, eds. *Iconoclash: Beyond the Image Wars in Science, Religion and Art.* Cambridge, MA: MIT Press, 2002.

Lawrence of Arabia. Film. Directed by David Lean. Columbia Pictures, 1962; 1989.

Ledgerwood, Judy. "The Cambodian Tuol Sleng Museum of Genocidal Crimes:

National Narrative." In *Genocide, Collective Violence, and Popular Memory: The Politics of Remembrance in the Twentieth Century*, edited by David E. Lorey and William H. Beezley, 103–122. Wilmington, DE: Scholarly Resources, 2002.

Lee, Benjamin, and Edward LiPuma. "Cultures of Circulation: The Imaginations of Modernity." *Public Culture* 14, no. 1 (2002): 191–213.

Lepenies, Wolf. *Entangled Histories and Negotiated Universals: Centers and Peripheries in a Changing World*. Frankfurt: Campus, 2003.

Lim, Bliss Cua. "Generic Ghosts: Remaking the New 'Asian Horror Film.'" In *Hong Kong Film, Hollywood and the New Global Cinema: No Film Is an Island*, edited by Gina Marchetti and Tan See Kam, 109–125. London: Routledge, 2007.

Lindsay, Jennifer. "A New Artistic Order?" *Inside Indonesia* 93 (July–September 2008). http://www.insideindonesia.org/weekly-articles-93-j-ul-sep-2008/a-new-artistic-order-07091681. Accessed December 8, 2011.

Liu, Beisi, and Qixian Xu, eds. *Gugong zhencang renwu zhaopian huicui* [A selection from the palace collection of photographs of human subjects]. Beijing: Zijincheng chubanshe, 1994.

MacDougall, David. *The Corporeal Image: Film, Ethnography and the Senses*. Princeton, NJ: Princeton University Press, 2005.

MacGaffey, Wyatt. "Astonishment and Stickiness in Kongo Art: A Theoretical Advance." *Res: Anthropology and Aesthetics* 39 (2001): 135–150.

Mahendra, Dodi. Review of "Hantu Jeruk Purut." Sinema-Indonesia. http://sinema-indonesia.com/neo/2007/04/02/hantu-jeruk-purut-2007/. Accessed April 2, 2007.

Mahmood, Saba. "Religious Reason and Secular Affect: An Incommensurable Divide?" *Critical Inquiry* 35 (2009): 836–862.

———. "Secularism, Hermeneutics, and Empire: The Politics of Islamic Reformation." *Public Culture* 18, no. 2 (2006): 323–347.

Malinowski, Bronislaw. *A Diary in the Strict Sense of the Term*. Stanford, CA: Stanford University Press, 1967.

Mamdani, Mahmood. *Good Muslim, Bad Muslim: America, the Cold War, and the Roots of Terror*. New York: Three Leaves Press, Doubleday, 2004.

Manovich, Lev. *The Language of New Media*. Cambridge, MA: MIT Press, 2002.

Marcus, George, and Fred Myers, eds. *The Traffic in Culture: Refiguring Art and Anthropology*. Berkeley: University of California Press, 1995.

Marien, Mary Warner. *Photography: A Cultural History*. London: Laurence King Publishing, 2002.

MASS MoCA. *InVisible: Art at the Edge of Perception*. Exhibition, Massachusetts Museum of Contemporary Art, North Adams, MA, February–June 2010.

Massad, Joseph. "Re-Orienting Desire: The Gay International and the Arab World." *Public Culture* 14, no. 2 (2003): 361–385.

Massumi, Brian. "The Autonomy of Affect." In *Deleuze: A Critical Reader*, edited by Paul Patton, 217–239. Oxford, UK: Blackwell, 1996.

REFERENCES

———. "Everyone You Want to Be: Introduction to Fear." In *The Politics of Everyday Fear*, edited by Brian Massumi, 3–37. Minneapolis: University of Minnesota Press, 1993.

———, ed. *A Shock to Thought: Expression after Deleuze and Guattari*. London: Routledge, 2002.

Mazzarella, William. "Internet X-Ray: E-Governance, Transparency, and the Politics of Immediation in India." *Public Culture* 18, no. 3 (Fall 2006): 473–505.

———. *Shoveling Smoke: Advertising and Globalization in Contemporary India*. Durham, NC: Duke University Press, 2003.

McCain, Carmen, Nazir Hausawa, and Ahmad Alkanaway. "On the Current Censorship Crisis in Kano." http://carmenmccain.wordpress.com/2009/01/13/on-the-current-censorship-crisis-in-kano-nigeria/. Accessed May 28, 2009.

McDonald, Peter. "*Disgrace* Effects." *Interventions* 4, no. 3 (2002): 321–330.

McKeown, Adam. *Melancholy Order: Asian Migration and the Globalization of Borders*. New York: Columbia University Press, 2008.

McLuhan, Marshall. *Understanding Media: The Extensions of Man*. Critical edition. 1964; Corte Madera, CA: Gingko Books, 1994.

Meyer, Birgit. "Ghanaian Popular Cinema and the Magic in and of Film." In *Magic and Modernity: Interfaces of Revelation and Concealment*, edited by Birgit Meyer and Peter Pels, 200–222. Stanford, CA: Stanford University Press, 2003.

Michalski, Sergiusz. *The Reformation and the Visual Arts: The Protestant Image Question in Western and Eastern Europe*. London: Taylor and Francis, 1998.

Michelmore, Christina. "Old Pictures in New Frames: Images of Islam and Muslims in Post–World War II American Political Cartoons." *Journal of American and Comparative Cultures* 23, no. 4 (2000): 37–50.

Mirzoeff, Nicholas. *Watching Babylon: The War in Iraq and Global Visual Culture*. New York: Routledge, 2005.

Mitchell, W. J. T. *Cloning Terror: The War of Images, 9/11 to the Present*. Chicago: University of Chicago Press, 2011.

———. *Iconology*. Chicago: University of Chicago Press, 1986.

———. "Migrating Images: Totemism, Fetishism, Idolatry." In *Migrating Images: Producing–Reading–Transporting–Translating*, edited by Petra Stegmann and Peter Seel, 14–24. Berlin: House of World Cultures, 2004.

———. *Picture Theory*. Chicago: University of Chicago Press, 1994.

———. "There Are No Visual Media." *Journal of Visual Culture* 4, no. 2 (2005): 257–266.

———. *What Do Pictures Want? The Lives and Loves of Images*. Chicago: University of Chicago Press, 2005 [hardcover]; 2006 [paperback].

Mookerjee, Debraj. "It's More Than 'Just Hopping.'" *Celebrating Vivaha* 6, no. 3 (2007): 48–49.

Morris, Errol. *Believing Is Seeing: Observations on the Mysteries of Photography*. New York: Penguin, 2011.

Morris, Rosalind C. "Crowds and Powerlessness: Reading //kabbo and Canetti with

Derrida in (South) Africa." In *Demangeries: Thinking (of) Animals after Derrida*. Critical Studies 35, edited by Anne Berger and Marta Segara, 167–212. Amsterdam: Rodopi, 2011.

———. "The Mute and the Unspeakable: Political Subjectivity, Violent Crime, and 'The Sexual Thing' in a South African Mining Community." In *Law and Disorder in the Postcolony*, edited by Jean and John Comaroff, 57–101. Chicago: University of Chicago Press, 2006.

———. "Photography and the Power of Images in the History of Power: Notes from Thailand." In *Photographies East: The Camera and Its Histories in East and Southeast Asia*, edited by Rosalind C. Morris, 121–160. Durham, NC: Duke University Press, 2009.

Moti, Melvin. *No Show*. Leiden: Mostert Leiden Press, 2004.

Mousa, Suleiman. *T. E. Lawrence: An Arab View*. Translated by Albert Butros. London: Oxford University Press, 1966.

Mullens, Joseph. "On the Applications of Photography in India." *Journal of the Bengal Photographic Society* 2, no. 1 (January 1857): 33–34.

Müller, Sabine. "Alexander's India: Terra Incognita as Propaganda." *atopia* 8 (October 2005).

Mullins, Molly. *Culture in the Marketplace*. Durham, NC: Duke University Press, 2001.

mumu [Is Mujiarso]. "Semiotika hujan dan metafora bebek panggang" [Grown up digital] (blog). October 23, 2007. http://rumputeki.multiply.com/reviews /item/18. Accessed January 2, 2011.

Mydans, Seth. "As Suharto Clings to Life, Mystics See Spirits' Power." *New York Times*, January 27, 2008. http://www.nytimes.com/2008/01/27/world/asia/27indo .html?scp=1&sq=Suharto,%20from%20edge%20of%20death&st=cse. Accessed December 8, 2011.

———. "Indonesians Draw Mystical Connections to Suharto." *New York Times*, January 25, 2008. http://www.nytimes.com/2008/01/25/world/asia/25iht-ind0 .2.9500455.html?scp=2&sq=Suharto,%20from%20edge%20of%20 death&st=cse. Accessed December 8, 2011.

———. "Suharto, from Verge of Death, Is Making a Recovery." *New York Times*, January 21, 2008. http://www.nytimes.com/2008/01/21/world/asia/21suharto .html?scp=3&sq=Suharto,%20from%20edge%20of%20death&st=cse. Accessed December 8, 2011.

Myers, Fred R. *Painting Culture: The Making of an Aboriginal High Art*. Durham, NC: Duke University Press, 2002.

Nancy, Jean-Luc. "The Image—The Distinct." *The Ground of the Image*. Translated by Jeff Fort, 1–14. New York: Fordham University Press, 2005.

Netaji Inquiry Committee Report. New Delhi: Government of India, 1956.

Neumeyer, Erwin, and Christine Schelberger. *Popular Indian Art: Raja Ravi Varma and the Printed Gods of India*. New Delhi: Oxford University Press, 2003.

Nickas, Robert. "Felix Gonzalez-Torres: All the Time in the World." In *Felix Gonzalez-Torres*, edited by Julie Ault, 39–51. New York: Steidlangin Publishers, 2006.

REFERENCES

Nordström, Alison. "Making a Journey: The Tupper Scrapbooks and the Travel They Describe." In *Photographs Objects Histories*, edited by Elizabeth Edwards and Janice Hart, 81–95. London: Routledge, 2004.

Nuswandana, Adhitiyaswara. "Kelar cinta remaja, dikejar hantu jadi pilihan" [Teen love is finished, being chased by ghosts is the choice]. *Kompas Cybermedia*, December 18, 2006. http://keepmesick.multiply.com/journal/item /1?&show_interstitial=1&u=%2Fjournal%2Fitem. Accessed February 24, 2012.

Ong, Aihwa. *Flexible Citizenship: The Cultural Logics of Transnationality*. Durham, NC: Duke University Press, 1999.

Ong, Alex. "Token Gestures." *Inside Indonesia* 100 (April–June 2010). http://www .insideindonesia.org/edition-100/token-gestures-24041293. Accessed April 16, 2011.

Pamuji, Heru, Bambang Sulistiyo, Kholis Bahtiar Bakri, and Manan Ghozi. "Tayangan setan: Mengubah duit, mengumbar takut" [Demonic programming: Moving money, spreading fear]. *Gatra*, March 15, 2003, 24–31.

Pancaroğlu, Oya. "Signs in the Horizon: Concepts of Image and Boundary in a Medieval Persian Cosmography." *Res: Anthropology and Aesthetics* 43 (2001): 31–41.

Pang, Laikwan. "Photography, Performance, and the Making of Female Images in Modern China." *Journal of Women's History* 17, no. 4 (2005): 56–85.

Parameshwar, Dilip Gaonkar, and Elizabeth A. Povinelli. "Technologies of Public Forms: Circulation, Transfiguration, Recognition." *Public Culture* 15, no. 3 (2003). 385–397.

"Pastry Targeted as the Cartoon Jihad Continues." February 17, 2006. http://www .spiegel.de/international/0,1518,401509,00.html. Accessed November 30, 2008.

Patton, Paul. "Becoming-Animal and Pure Life in Coetzee's *Disgrace*." *ARIEL: A Review of International English Literature* 35, no. 1–2 (Spring 2006): 101–119. Special issue, *Law, Literature, Postcoloniality*.

PBS, "America Remembers 911." Jay Ruesler 9/11 "Video Quilt" Multimedia Project. http://www.pbs.org/newshour/multimedia/september-11-responses/. Accessed September 12, 2011.

Pinney, Christopher. *Camera Indica: The Social Life of Indian Photographs*. London: Reaktion, 1997.

———. *The Coming of Photography in India*. London: British Library, 2008.

———. "Four Types of Visual Culture." In *Handbook of Material Culture*, edited by Christopher Tilley et al., 131–144. London: Sage Publications, 2006.

———. "Introduction: 'How the Other Half…'" In *Photography's Other Histories*, edited by Christopher Pinney and Nicholas Peterson, 1–14. Durham, NC: Duke University Press, 2003.

———. "Living in the kal[i]yug: Notes from Nagda, Madhya Pradesh." *Contributions to Indian Sociology* 33, no. 1–2 (February 1999): 77–106.

———. "Photographic Portraiture in Central India in the 1980s and 1990s." In *Portraiture: Facing the Subject*, edited by Joanne Woodall, 131–144. Manchester, UK: Manchester University Press, 1997.

———. *Photography and Anthropology*. London: Reaktion, 2011.

———. *"Photos of the Gods": The Printed Image and Political Struggle in India*. London: Reaktion, 2004.

Pinney, Christopher, and Nicolas Peterson, eds. *Photography's Other Histories*. Durham, NC: Duke University Press, 2003.

Pipes, Daniel. *The Rushdie Affair: The Novel, the Ayatollah, and the West*. New York: Carol Publishing Group, 1990.

Poole, Deborah. "An Excess of Description: Ethnography, Race and Visual Technologies." *Annual Review of Anthropology* 34 (2005): 159–170.

———. *Vision, Race, and Modernity: A Visual Economy of the Andean Image World*. Princeton, NJ: Princeton University Press, 1997.

Povinelli, Elizabeth A. "Radical Worlds: The Anthropology of Incommensurability and Inconceivability." *Annual Review of Anthropology* 30 (2001): 319–334.

Powell, Ivor. "Inside and Outside of History." *Art South Africa* 5, no. 4 (2007): 34–38.

Price, Mary. *The Photograph: A Strange, Confined Space*. Stanford, CA: Stanford University Press, 1994.

Rasza, Maple. "'Riot Porn': Protest Video and the Production of Unruly Political Subjects." Unpublished manuscript, n.d.

Reenen, Daan van. "The *Bilderverbot*, a New Survey." *Der Islam* 67 (1990): 27–77.

Ricalton, James. *James Ricalton's Photographs of China during the Boxer Rebellion: His Illustrated Travelogue of 1900*. Edited by Christopher Lucas. Lewiston, NY: Edwin Mellen Press, 1990.

Richard, Paul. "In Art Museums, Portraits Illuminate a Religious Taboo." *Washington Post*, February 14, 2006.

Rodgers, Walter. "Pig Insult Sparks West Bank Violence." http://www.cnn.com /WORLD/9707/01/israel.palestinians/. Accessed December 2, 2008.

Rose, Fleming. "Why I Published the Muhammad Cartoons." *New York Times*, May 31, 2006.

Roth-Ey, Kristin. *Moscow Prime Time*. Ithaca, NY: Cornell University Press, 2011.

Rubin, Elizabeth. "Captain Kearney's Quagmire." *New York Times*, February 24, 2008.

Rugoff, Ralph. *A Brief History of Invisible Art*. San Francisco: California College of the Arts, 2005. Exhibition catalog.

Ryan, Rosalind, and agencies. "Danish Newspapers Reprint Muhammad Cartoon." *Guardian*, February 13, 2008.

Ryanto, Tony. "Auds Scream for Horror Hit." *Variety Asia*, November 26–December 2, 2001. http://www.variety.com/article/VR1117856243?refcatid=19&printerfri endly=true. Accessed December 8, 2011.

REFERENCES

————. "Lee, King of Remakes, Translates East into West." *Jakarta Post*, June 23, 2007. http://images.thejakartapost.com/news/2007/06/23/lee-king-remakes -translates-east-west.html. Accessed December 8, 2011.

Safwat, Nabil F. "The Ḥilyah: The Verbal Image of the Prophet." In *The Art of the Pen: Calligraphy of the 14th to 20th Centuries*, edited by Nabil F. Safwat and Mohammed Zakariya, 46–50. London: Nour Foundation, in association with Azimuth Editions and Oxford University Press, 1996.

Said, Edward W. *Orientalism*. New York: Penguin Books, 1978.

Salvatore, Armando, and Dale F. Eickelman, eds. *Public Islam and the Common Good*. Leiden: Brill, 2004.

Sanabani, Faris. "Tolerance on Trial: Why We Reprinted the Danish Cartoons." March 15, 2006. http://jurist.law.pitt.edu/forumy/2006/03/tolerance-on-trial-why -we-reprinted.php. Accessed November 28, 2008.

Sánchez, Rafael. "Intimate Publicities: Retreating the Politico-Theological in the Chávez Regime in Venezuela." In *Political Theologies: Globalization and Post- Secular Reason*, edited by Lawrence Sullivan and Hent de Vries, 401–426. New York: Fordham University Press, 2006.

Sartre, Jean-Paul. *Being and Nothingness: A Phenomenological Essay on Ontology*. Translated by Hazel E. Barnes. New York: Washington Square Books, 1966.

Sayyid, S. *A Fundamental Fear: Eurocentrism and the Emergence of Islam*. New York: Zed Books, 2003.

Schwarzkopf, H. Norman. *It Doesn't Take a Hero*. With Peter Petre. New York: Bantam, 1992.

Scott, James C. *Seeing like a State: How Certain Schemes to Improve Human Conditions Have Failed*. New Haven, CT: Yale University Press, 1998.

Serres, Michel. *The Parasite*. Translated by Lawrence R. Schehr. Baltimore, MD: Johns Hopkins University Press, 1982.

Setyawan, Barrie, publicist. "Kuntilanak lepas! Tiket bioskop terjual habis di hari pertama" [*Kuntilak* is out! Theater tickets sold out on the first day]. October 11, 2007. http://movies.groups.yahoo.com/group/cinemagsforum/message /22855. Accessed December 8, 2011.

Sharlet, Jeff. "Jesus Killed Mohammed: The Crusade for a Christian Military." *Harper's* 318, no. 1908 (May 2009): 31–43.

The Sheik. Directed by George Melford. Hollywood, CA: Paramount Pictures, 1921. Videocassette.

Shohat, Ella. "Sacred Word, Profane Image: Theologies of Adaptation." In *A Companion to Literature and Film*, edited by Robert Stam and Alessandra Raengo, 23–45. Malden, MA: Blackwell, 2004.

Siegel, James T. *Naming the Witch*. Stanford, CA: Stanford University Press, 2005.

————. *A New Criminal Type in Jakarta*. Durham, NC: Duke University Press, 1998.

————. *Solo in the New Order*. Princeton, NJ: Princeton University Press, 1986.

Silverman, Kaja. *The Threshold of the Visible World*. New York: Routledge, 1996.

Simpson, James. *Under the Hammer.* Oxford, UK: Oxford University Press, 2010.

Slackman, Michael, and Hasan M. Fattah. "Furor over Cartoons Pits Muslim against Muslim." *New York Times,* February 22, 2006.

Soage, Ana Belen. "The Danish Caricatures Seen from the Arab World." *Totalitarian Movements and Political Religions* 7, no. 3 (2006): 363–369.

Sofyan, Eko Hendrawan. "LSF hadang 'Dendam Pocong.'" *Kompas Cybermedia,* October 6, 2006. http://www.kompas.com/ver1/Hiburan/0610/06/133217.htm. Accessed April 15, 2009.

Sontag, Susan. "Against Interpretation." *"Against Interpretation" and Other Essays.* London: Eyre and Spottiswoode, 1967.

———. *On Photography.* 1977; New York: Picador, 2001.

Sorkin, Michael, ed. *Variations on a Theme Park: The New American City and the End of Public Space.* New York: Hill and Wang, 1992.

Soucek, Priscilla P. "The Life of the Prophet: Illustrated Versions." In *Content and Context of Visual Arts in the Islamic World,* edited by Priscilla P. Soucek, 193–218. University Park: Penn State University Press, 1988.

Sperber, Dan. "Anthropology and Psychology: Towards an Epidemiology of Representations." *Man,* n.s., 20, no. 1 (1985): 73–89.

———. "Interpreting and Explaining Cultural Representations." In *Beyond Boundaries: Understanding, Translation, and Anthropological Discourse,* edited by Gísli Pálsson, 162–183. Oxford, UK: Berg, 1994.

Spiegelman, Art. "Drawing Blood: Outrageous Cartoons and the Art of Outrage." *Harper's* 312 (June 2006): 43–52.

Spivak, Gayatri Chakravorty. *A Critique of Postcolonial Reason.* Cambridge, MA: Harvard University Press, 1999.

———. "Ethics and Politics in Tagore, Coetzee, and Certain Scenes of Teaching." *Diacritics* 32, no. 3–4 (Fall–Winter 2002): 17–31.

Spyer, Patricia. "Blind Faith: Painting Christianity in Postconflict Ambon." Special issue, *Social Text* 26, no. 3 96 (2008): 11–37.

———. "Fire without Smoke and Other Phantoms of Ambon's Violence: Media Effects, Agency, and the Work of Imagination." *Indonesia* 74 (2002): 21–36.

———. "One Slip of the Pen: Some Notes on Writing Violence in Maluku." In *Indonesia in Transition,* edited by Henk Schulte Nordholt and Gusti Asnan, 181–200. Yogyakarta, Java: Pustaka Pelajar, 2003.

———. "Orphaned Landscapes: Religion, Violence, and Visuality in Post-Suharto Indonesia." Manuscript in progress.

———, ed. *Border Fetishisms: Material Objects in Unstable Spaces.* London: Routledge, 1998.

Stegmann, Petra, and Peter Seel, eds. *Migrating Images: Producing–Reading–Transporting–Translating.* Berlin: House of World Cultures, 2004.

Stewart, Kathleen. *A Space on the Side of the Road: Cultural Poetics in an "Other" America.* Princeton, NJ: Princeton University Press, 1996.

REFERENCES

Stigter, Bianca. "Staren naar een stuk kaas." *NRC Handelsblad,* May 2, 2008.

Strassler, Karen. "Gendered Visibilities and the Dream of Transparency: The Chinese-Indonesian Rape Debate in Post-Suharto Indonesia." *Gender and History* 16, no. 3 (2004): 689–725.

———. *Refracted Visions: Popular Photography and National Modernity in Java.* Durham, NC: Duke University Press, 2010.

Strickland, Debra Higgs. *Saracens, Demons, and Jews: Making Monsters in Medieval Art.* Princeton, NJ: Princeton University Press, 2003.

"Suharto's Mystical Crimes." *Misteri* 225 (January 1999).

Suraiya, Jug, and Vikas Singh. "The Death of Privacy." *Times of India,* January 15, 2005. http://timesofindia.indiatimes.com/articleshow/991395.cms. Accessed December 1, 2008.

Suyono, Seno Joko, et al. "Menjenguk film-film horor Indonesia" [Taking a look at Indonesian horror films]. *Tempo,* March 23, 2003. http://majalah.tem pointeraktif.com/id/arsip/2003/02/17/LYR/mbm.20030217.LYR85172 .id.html. Accessed December 8, 2011.

Tarde, Gabriel. *The Laws of Imitation.* Translated by Elsie Clews Parsons. New York: Henry Holt and Co., 1903.

Tarlo, Emma. *Clothing Matters: Dress and Identity in India.* Chicago: University of Chicago Press, 1996.

Taussig, Michael. "Physiognomic Aspects of Visual Worlds." *Visual Anthropology Review* 8, no. 1 (Spring 1992): 15–28.

Taylor, Charles. *Modern Social Imaginaries.* Durham, NC: Duke University Press, 2004.

———. *A Secular Age.* Cambridge, MA: Belknap Press of Harvard University Press, 2007.

Taylor, L. G. "Iconophobia: How Anthropology Lost It at the Movies." *Transition* 69 (1996): 64–88.

Theophanis Chronographia. Hildesheim, Germany: G. Olms, 1963.

Thomas, Lowell. *With Lawrence in Arabia.* New York: Century Co., 1924.

Tolan, John. "Un cadavre mutilé: Le déchirement polémique de Mahomet." *Le Moyen Âge* 105 (1998): 62.

———. *Saracens: Islam in the Medieval European Imagination.* New York: Columbia University Press, 2002.

Tomkins, Silvan S., and Elaine Virginia Demos, eds. *Exploring Affect: The Selected Writings of Silvan S. Tomkins.* Cambridge, UK: Cambridge University Press, 1995.

Tremlett, Giles. "Police Raid over Sex Cartoons of Spanish Prince." *Guardian,* July 21, 2007.

Trouillot, Michel-Rolph. "The Otherwise Modern: Caribbean Lessons from the Savage Slot." In *Critically Modern: Alternatives, Alterities, Anthropologies,* edited by Bruce M. Knauft, 220–237. Bloomington: Indiana University Press, 2002.

U.S. Army Marine Corps Counterinsurgency Manual. Chicago: University of Chicago Press, 2007.

Utomo, Rudi. *Hantusiana: A Mini-Encyclopedia of Archipelagic Spooks.* Kalam, Indonesia: Kalam Indonesia, 2007.

Vaidya, Abhay. "Voyeur Alert: How to Spook the Spooks." *Times of India,* January 13, 2005. http://timesofindia.indiatimes.com/articleshow/989003.cms. Accessed December 1, 2008.

Varges, Ariel. "Ace Newsreeler Gives Light on How He Films News of the World." *American Cinematographer* 19, no. 7 (July 1938): 275–276.

Varma, Jayant. "Property Watch." *India Today Buyer's Guide,* July–September 2006, 8–14.

Varma, Pavan. *The Great Indian Middle Class.* Delhi: Penguin, 1998.

Varshavsky, S., and B. Rest. *The Hermitage during the War of 1941–1945.* Translated by Arthur Shkarovsky-Raffe. St. Petersburg: Slavia, 1995.

Vertov, Dziga. *Man with a Movie Camera.* Ukraine: Film Studio VUFKU, 1929.

Virilio, Paul. *Open Sky.* Translated by Julie Rose. New York: Verso, 1997.

———. *Speed and Politics: An Essay in Dromology.* Translated by Mark Polizotti. New York: Semiotext(e), 1986.

Walsh, Declan. "Church Ablaze as Cartoon Protests Continue across Globe." *Guardian,* February 20, 2006. http://www.guardian.co.uk/world/2006/feb/20 /pakistan.muhammadcartoons. Accessed July 15, 2009.

Wark, McKenzie. *Virtual Geography: Living with Global Media Events.* Bloomington: Indiana University Press, 1994.

———. "The Weird Global Media Event and the Tactical Intellectual." In *New Media, Old Media,* edited by Wendy Hui Kyong Chun and Thomas Keenan, 265–276. New York: Routledge, 2006.

Warner, Michael. "The Mass Public and the Mass Subject." *Publics and Counterpublics,* 159–186. New York: Zone Books, 2002.

———. "Publics and Counterpublics." *Publics and Counterpublics,* 65–124. New York: Zone Books, 2002.

———. *Publics and Counterpublics.* New York: Zone Books, 2002 [hardcover]; 2005 [paperback].

Warner, W. H. "Photography and Murder." *Journal of the Bengal Photographic Society* 2, no. 5 (July 1863): 39.

Weber, Samuel. "Art, Aura and Media in the Work of Walter Benjamin." In *Mass Mediauras: Form, Technics, Media,* edited by Samuel Weber, 76–107. Stanford, CA: Stanford University Press, 1996.

———. "Television: Set and Screen." In *Mass Mediauras: Form, Technics, Media,* edited by Samuel Weber, 108–128. Stanford, CA: Stanford University Press, 1996.

Weikel, Dan. "Privacy Concerns Shadow TSA Tool." *Chicago Tribune,* April 18, 2008. http://www.chicagotribune.com/news/chi-body-scannerapr18,0,6843385 .story. Accessed December 1, 2008.

REFERENCES

Wells, Liz, ed. *Photography: A Critical Introduction.* 3rd ed. London: Routledge, 2004.

Wheeler, Stephen. *History of the Delhi Coronation Durbar Held on the First of January 1903 to Celebrate the Coronation of His Majesty King Edward VII Emperor of India.* London: John Murray, 1904.

Williams, Linda. *Hard Core: Power, Pleasure and the Frenzy of the Visible.* Berkeley: University of California Press, 1989.

Williams, Raymond. *Television: Technology and Cultural Form.* 3rd ed. New York: Routledge, 2003.

Winegar, Jessica. "The Humanity Game: Art, Islam, and the War on Terror." *Anthropological Quarterly* 81, no. 2 (2008): 651–681.

Winthrop-Young, Geoffrey, and Michael Wutz. Introduction to *Gramophone, Film, Typewriter,* by Friedrich A. Kittler. Stanford, CA: Stanford University Press, 1999.

Wittgenstein, Ludwig. *Philosophical Investigations.* London: Blackwell, 1958.

Wue, Roberta. "Essentially Chinese—The Chinese Portrait Subject in Nineteenth-Century Photography." In *Body and Face in Chinese Visual Culture,* edited by Katherine R. Tsiang and Wu Hung, 257–280. Cambridge, MA: Harvard University Press, 2005.

Xiao, Yongsheng. *Huayi · jijin · Lang Jingshan* [Painterly intent, assembled silks: Lang Jingshan]. Taibei, Taiwan: Xiongshi, 2004.

Yarmanto, Widi. *Penampakan Leo Lumanto.* Jakarta, Indonesia: Akoer, 2005.

Yazid, Nauval. "Asian Horror Cinema: Not Enough to Stand 'Alone.'" *Jakarta Post,* July 30, 2007. http://www.thejakartapost.com/news/2007/07/30/asian-horror -cinema-not-enough-stand-039alone039.html-0. Accessed December 8, 2011.

———. "Movie Merry-go-round Spinds [*sic*] Faster." *Jakarta Post,* March 16, 2008. http://old/thejakartapost.com/review2007/fea01.asp. Accessed January 23, 2009.

You Mei shounüe riji [Diary of disdainments endured during a journey through America]. Comp. unknown. Reproduced in *Lidai riji congchao* [Diachronic compendium of diaries]. Vol. 155, 609–634. Edited by Delong Li and Bing Yu. Beijing: Xueyuan Chubanshe, 2006.

Zelizer, Barbie. *Remembering to Forget: Holocaust Memory through the Camera's Eye.* Chicago: University of Chicago Press, 2000.

Zuilhof, Gertan. "Hungry Ghosts in a Haunted House." 2009. Rotterdam International Film Festival. Introduction to "Hungry Ghosts" program. http://www .filmfestivalrotterdam.com/professionals/programme/sections_events _iffr_2009/signals/signals—hungry-ghosts/hungry-ghosts-introduction .aspx. Accessed December 8, 2011.

Zukin, Sharon. *The Cultures of Cities.* Boston: Blackwell, 1995.

Index

School for Advanced Research Advanced Seminar Series

PUBLISHED BY SAR PRESS

GRAY AREAS: ETHNOGRAPHIC
ENCOUNTERS WITH NURSING HOME
CULTURE
  Philip B. Stafford, ed.

PLURALIZING ETHNOGRAPHY: COMPARISON
AND REPRESENTATION IN MAYA CULTURES,
HISTORIES, AND IDENTITIES
  John M. Watanabe & Edward F. Fischer, eds.

AMERICAN ARRIVALS: ANTHROPOLOGY
ENGAGES THE NEW IMMIGRATION
  Nancy Foner, ed.

VIOLENCE
  Neil L. Whitehead, ed.

LAW & EMPIRE IN THE PACIFIC:
FIJI AND HAWAI'I
  Sally Engle Merry & Donald Brenneis, eds.

ANTHROPOLOGY IN THE MARGINS
OF THE STATE
  Veena Das & Deborah Poole, eds.

THE ARCHAEOLOGY OF COLONIAL
ENCOUNTERS: COMPARATIVE
PERSPECTIVES
  Gil J. Stein, ed.

GLOBALIZATION, WATER, & HEALTH:
RESOURCE MANAGEMENT IN TIMES OF
SCARCITY
  Linda Whiteford & Scott Whiteford, eds.

A CATALYST FOR IDEAS: ANTHROPOLOGICAL
ARCHAEOLOGY AND THE LEGACY OF
DOUGLAS W. SCHWARTZ
  Vernon L. Scarborough, ed.

THE ARCHAEOLOGY OF CHACO CANYON:
AN ELEVENTH-CENTURY PUEBLO
REGIONAL CENTER
  Stephen H. Lekson, ed.

COMMUNITY BUILDING IN THE TWENTY-
FIRST CENTURY
  Stanley E. Hyland, ed.

AFRO-ATLANTIC DIALOGUES:
ANTHROPOLOGY IN THE DIASPORA
  Kevin A. Yelvington, ed.

COPÁN: THE HISTORY OF AN ANCIENT
MAYA KINGDOM
  E. Wyllys Andrews & William L. Fash, eds.

THE EVOLUTION OF HUMAN LIFE HISTORY
  Kristen Hawkes & Richard R. Paine, eds.

THE SEDUCTIONS OF COMMUNITY:
EMANCIPATIONS, OPPRESSIONS,
QUANDARIES
  Gerald W. Creed, ed.

THE GENDER OF GLOBALIZATION: WOMEN
NAVIGATING CULTURAL AND ECONOMIC
MARGINALITIES
  *Nandini Gunewardena &
  Ann Kingsolver, eds.*

NEW LANDSCAPES OF INEQUALITY:
NEOLIBERALISM AND THE EROSION OF
DEMOCRACY IN AMERICA
  *Jane L. Collins, Micaela di Leonardo,
  & Brett Williams, eds.*

IMPERIAL FORMATIONS
  *Ann Laura Stoler, Carole McGranahan,
  & Peter C. Perdue, eds.*

OPENING ARCHAEOLOGY: REPATRIATION'S
IMPACT ON CONTEMPORARY RESEARCH
AND PRACTICE
  Thomas W. Killion, ed.

SMALL WORLDS: METHOD, MEANING,
& NARRATIVE IN MICROHISTORY
  *James F. Brooks, Christopher R. N. DeCorse,
  & John Walton, eds.*

MEMORY WORK: ARCHAEOLOGIES OF
MATERIAL PRACTICES
  Barbara J. Mills & William H. Walker, eds.

FIGURING THE FUTURE: GLOBALIZATION
AND THE TEMPORALITIES OF CHILDREN
AND YOUTH
  Jennifer Cole & Deborah Durham, eds.

TIMELY ASSETS: THE POLITICS OF
RESOURCES AND THEIR TEMPORALITIES
  *Elizabeth Emma Ferry &
  Mandana E. Limbert, eds.*

DEMOCRACY: ANTHROPOLOGICAL
APPROACHES
  Julia Paley, ed.

CONFRONTING CANCER: METAPHORS,
INEQUALITY, AND ADVOCACY
  Juliet McMullin & Diane Weiner, eds.

DEVELOPMENT & DISPOSSESSION: THE CRISIS OF FORCED DISPLACEMENT AND RESETTLEMENT
Anthony Oliver-Smith, ed.

GLOBAL HEALTH IN TIMES OF VIOLENCE
Barbara Rylko-Bauer, Linda Whiteford, & Paul Farmer, eds.

THE EVOLUTION OF LEADERSHIP: TRANSITIONS IN DECISION MAKING FROM SMALL-SCALE TO MIDDLE-RANGE SOCIETIES
Kevin J. Vaughn, Jelmer W. Eerkins, & John Kantner, eds.

ARCHAEOLOGY & CULTURAL RESOURCE MANAGEMENT: VISIONS FOR THE FUTURE
Lynne Sebastian & William D. Lipe, eds.

ARCHAIC STATE INTERACTION: THE EASTERN MEDITERRANEAN IN THE BRONZE AGE
William A. Parkinson & Michael L. Galaty, eds.

INDIANS & ENERGY: EXPLOITATION AND OPPORTUNITY IN THE AMERICAN SOUTHWEST
Sherry L. Smith & Brian Frehner, eds.

ROOTS OF CONFLICT: SOILS, AGRICULTURE, AND SOCIOPOLITICAL COMPLEXITY IN ANCIENT HAWAI'I
Patrick V. Kirch, ed.

PHARMACEUTICAL SELF: THE GLOBAL SHAPING OF EXPERIENCE IN AN AGE OF PSYCHOPHARMACOLOGY
Janis Jenkins, ed.

FORCES OF COMPASSION: HUMANITARIANISM BETWEEN ETHICS AND POLITICS
Erica Bornstein & Peter Redfield, eds.

ENDURING CONQUESTS: RETHINKING THE ARCHAEOLOGY OF RESISTANCE TO SPANISH COLONIALISM IN THE AMERICAS
Matthew Liebmann & Melissa S. Murphy, eds.

DANGEROUS LIAISONS: ANTHROPOLOGISTS AND THE NATIONAL SECURITY STATE
Laura A. McNamara & Robert A. Rubinstein, eds.

BREATHING NEW LIFE INTO THE EVIDENCE OF DEATH: CONTEMPORARY APPROACHES TO BIOARCHAEOLOGY
Aubrey Baadsgaard, Alexis T. Boutin, & Jane E. Buikstra, eds.

THE SHAPE OF SCRIPT: HOW AND WHY WRITING SYSTEMS CHANGE
Stephen D. Houston, ed.

NATURE, SCIENCE, AND RELIGION: INTERSECTIONS SHAPING SOCIETY AND THE ENVIRONMENT
Catherine M. Tucker, ed.

THE GLOBAL MIDDLE CLASSES: THEORIZING THROUGH ETHNOGRAPHY
Rachel Heiman, Carla Freeman, & Mark Liechty, eds.

KEYSTONE NATIONS: INDIGENOUS PEOPLES AND SALMON ACROSS THE NORTH PACIFIC
Benedict J. Colombi & James F. Brooks, eds.

BIG HISTORIES, HUMAN LIVES: TACKLING PROBLEMS OF SCALE IN ARCHAEOLOGY
John Robb & Timothy R. Pauketat, eds.

REASSEMBLING THE COLLECTION: ETHNOGRAPHIC MUSEUMS AND INDIGENOUS AGENCY
Rodney Harrison, Sarah Byrne, & Anne Clarke, eds.

Participants in the School for Advanced Research advanced seminar "Images without Borders, " co-chaired by Patricia Spyer and Mary M. Steedly, May 4–8, 2008. *Standing, from left*: Ernst van Alphen, Barry Flood, Christopher Pinney, Oliver Moore, Brian Larkin; *seated, from left*: Rosalind Morris, Patricia Spyer, Mary Margaret Steedly, Steve Caton. Photograph by Jason S. Ordaz.